The
Memorial
Cup

The
Memorial Cup

Canada's National Junior Hockey Championship

**Richard Lapp
and
Alec Macaulay**

**Foreword by
Paul Henderson**

HARBOUR PUBLISHING

Harbour Publishing
P.O. Box 219
Madeira Park, BC
V0N 2H0
Canada

Published with the assistance of the Canada Council and the Province of British Columbia through the British Columbia Arts Council

THE CANADA COUNCIL | LE CONSEIL DES ARTS
FOR THE ARTS | DU CANADA
SINCE 1957 | DEPUIS 1957

Cover, page design and composition by Martin Nichols, Lionheart Graphics.

Printed and bound in Canada.

Cover photos: Memorial Cup, Fedorak Photo. Player photos, top to bottom; Eric Lindros (Oshawa Generals), Mario Lemieux (Montreal *Gazette*), Trevor Linden (Richard Lapp collection), Cam Neely (Art Thompson, courtesy WHL). Back cover photo: Calgary Canadians, 1926 cup champions (Manitoba Archives/N2002).

Key to photograph sources: MA, Manitoba Archives; MA/FC, Manitoba Archives/Foote collection; GA/HHF, Graphic Artists, Hockey Hall of Fame; HHF, Hockey Hall of Fame. All photos not credited are courtesy the Richard Lapp collection.

Canadian Cataloguing in Publication Data

Lapp, Richard M., 1956–
   The Memorial Cup

   Includes index.
   ISBN 1-55017-170-4

   1. Memorial Cup (Hockey) 2. Hockey—Canada—History.
3. Hockey—Canada—Statistics. I. Macaulay, Alec. 1963– II. Title.
GV848.4.C3L36 1997   796.962'62'0971   C97-910832-2

CONTENTS

Key to Hockey Organizations

CAHA	Canadian Amateur Hockey Association
CHL	Canadian Hockey League
CMJHL	Canadian Major Junior Hockey League
MAHA	Manitoba Amateur Hockey Association
MJHL	Manitoba Junior Hockey League
NHL	National Hockey League
NOHA	Northern Ontario Hockey Association
OHA	Ontario Hockey Association
OHL	Ontario Hockey League
OMJHL	Ontario Major Junior Hockey League
PCHA	Pacific Coast Hockey Association
QJHL	Quebec Junior Hockey League
QMJHL	Quebec Major Junior Hockey League
SJHL	Saskatchewan Junior Hockey League
WCHL	Western Canada Hockey League
WCJHL	Western Canada Junior Hockey League
WHA	World Hockey Association
WHL	Western Hockey League

FOREWORD

by Paul Henderson

When I was touring Canada on the 25th anniversary of the 1972 Summit Series between Team Canada and Team USSR, people sometimes explained the impact of that tournament by saying it was our system against theirs. The Soviet hockey system was built on military-style discipline and heavy handed control from the top down, like everything else Soviet. But what exactly is the Canadian hockey system? What is it that allows Canada to win more major international hockey tournaments, year in and year out, than countries ten times its size, while Canadian players dominate the game's elite league?

You can find a big part of the answer in this book. Since 1919 Canada has nurtured its young hockey talent through a network of minor leagues that once each year brings the best of the best together in one winner-take-all contest for the most storied junior hockey trophy in the world, the Memorial Cup. The history of the Memorial Cup is the history of the Canadian game in a nutshell: the story of a system built out of passion for the game, from the ground up.

In the early days league organization was a bit wonky and anyone could challenge for the Cup. In 1920 the Toronto Canoe Club even took a run at it. What's more, they won. Early refs didn't have whistles—they skated around the ice clanking big handbells. They were no good for making yourself heard over the crowd but darned handy for defending yourself in a brawl. You don't find criticism of the officials in the newspaper writeups of some of the early Cups because the reporters and the officials were the same guys. In one final the teams took the ice only to find their uniforms looked so much alike you couldn't tell one from the other. Another match was protested because agents for the winning team had sprinkled their opponents' gear with itching powder. Another one between the Quebec Remparts and the St. Catharines Black Hawks was disrupted by brawling between separatists and federalists.

From those bumpy beginnings Canadian junior hockey developed and the Memorial Cup match evolved into a prestigious tournament which not only offers coast-to-coast TV audiences some of the most exciting hockey in the world, it also provides a preview of the talent that will shape the pro game in years to come. From Howie Morenz to Guy Lafleur to Eric Lindros, the Memorial Cup has served to give the world its first glimpse of the game's future superstars. Sometimes, though, the big names fell on their butts. Other times the star of the game was someone who went back to the family farm and never was heard of again. Others were heard of plenty, but in fields other than hockey. It would take several books to tell everything that happened in eight decades of Memorial Cups, but Richard Lapp and Alec Macaulay have recorded the essentials on these pages and filled an important gap in the history of Canada's game.

I played in the 1962 Memorial Cup with the old Hamilton Red Wings of the Ontario League and although it tends to be overshadowed by events that took place in Moscow ten years later, it still ranks up there as one of the highlights of my life. The date is still etched in my memory: May 8th. There was an added thrill in that we were the underdog team that year. We finished fourth in regular season play, and faced the runner-up, St. Catharines, in the league playoff. That was our toughest battle. They had big name players like Phil Esposito and Dennis Hull, and the series went the distance but we finally put them down. After that we rolled over Niagara Falls, St. Mikes and Quebec to the final against Edmonton. I remember Ed Bush, the coach, telling us before we went out on the ice, "The chance to win a championship is something that only a very few ever get, even guys who spend their whole careers in the NHL, so don't hold anything back." We won by playing with the most determination. That's also part of the Canadian system.

The
1920s

A hockey game in the 1920s looked a lot different than it does today. For one thing, the rules were different. Under the influence of rugby, hockey had no forward passing, a rule that was gradually eliminated zone by zone. There were usually only eight or nine players on the team: the goalie, five skaters and a few substitutes. Two referees governed the match, using handbells rather than whistles to signal stoppages in play. In the early years of Memorial Cup competition, a total-goal playoff series was favoured over the best-of-three games or round robin formats introduced later. Cumulative goals, not wins, determined the champion, and if a game went into overtime, it was typically for a full ten-minute session with no sudden death.

Junior hockey in Canada looked different in those days too. Some teams, like the Regina Patricias, were as familiar to the hockey fan of the twenties as they are today. Others, including the Toronto Canoe Club Paddlers, the Fort William War Veterans and the University of Manitoba Varsity—all champions in the Memorial Cup's first decade—reflected an amateur game that was based on grassroots and collegiate foundations. However, some things haven't changed. Just as a spectator at the 1990 Memorial Cup could catch a glimpse of "The Next One," Eric Lindros, fans in the twenties were introduced to future pro stars like Charlie Conacher and Howie Morenz in Memorial Cup competition. Many junior players graduated to the expanding professional ranks.

The 1920s was a decade of upheaval for professional hockey. The first half of the decade saw a rivalry between Frank and Lester Patrick's Pacific Coast Hockey Association and the National Hockey League. By 1926, the PCHA and Western Canada Hockey League had given way to a growing but still unstable NHL, taking a while to settle into the solid foundation of the "original six." During the 1920s and 1930s, the NHL included familiar names like the Toronto Maple Leafs, Montreal Canadiens, Boston Bruins, New York Rangers, Detroit Red Wings and Chicago Blackhawks. But there were also now-forgotten franchises like the Montreal Maroons, Hamilton Tigers, New York Americans, Toronto St. Pats, Pittsburgh Pirates, Detroit Cougars (later Falcons), St. Louis Eagles and Philadelphia Quakers.

Perhaps most familiar to today's junior hockey fan was the intensity of competitors and fans alike. Whether huddling outside a Regina newspaper office to hear patchy play-by-play commentary over a megaphone or raising a ruckus in the old Arena Gardens on Toronto's Mutual Street, Canadian fans in the twenties displayed the same emotions and rivalries that the Memorial Cup tournament continues to stir up today. Then as now, junior hockey teams carried their fans' sentiments onto the ice and into hard-fought games.

Howie Morenz, star of the Stratford Midgets, drew as much attention at the junior level as he would in the NHL.

The **1919** Memorial Cup

It is fitting that the first-ever game of the Memorial Cup was delayed by an hour and fifteen minutes to allow hockey fans to greet one of the Canadian regiments returning from World War One. After all, it was for these veterans, streaming home in the wake of the November 1918 armistice, that the trophy was named. The first tournament—a two-game total-goal contest at Toronto's Arena Gardens—featured many of the hallmarks of future Memorial Cup competition: an east vs. west showdown, a generous sprinkling of up-and-coming stars, and controversy. The 1919 tournament featured the University of Toronto Schools, a reflection of the collegiate nature of Canadian junior hockey in its early days, against the Regina Patricias, whose name would become a junior hockey fixture.

The University of Toronto team advanced to the final after narrowly defeating Woodstock in the Ontario Hockey Association semi-final. That two-game, total-goal series introduced some heated controversy to the first run for the Memorial Cup. Before the final game, the Woodstock Players' jock straps, undershirts and pads were smeared with pepper and itching powder by parties unknown. Woodstock coach William Breen was suspicious that someone had meddled with his players' skates as well. Furthermore, there were allegations of bookies gambling on the series, which were likely related to the equipment-tampering. The Woodstock team, which included future NHLers Bill and Frank Carson, sought a rematch from the OHA executive, but its plea went unheard. The University of Toronto went on to wrap up the Eastern Canadian championship by whipping the Montreal Melvilles 8–2 in a sudden death one-game final.

The Regina Pats, meanwhile, had advanced at the expense of the Young Men's Lutheran Club of Winnipeg, securing the Western Canadian Abbott Cup and a berth in the inaugural Memorial Cup championship. "Toronto fans are greatly worked up over their juniors and they are just a little afraid that their favourites are going to get beaten," reported W. J. Finlay, sports editor for the *Winnipeg Free Press*. "However, it looks like a great game and, in our opinion, should be in doubt right to the finish." The first game, played on March 19, was anything but in doubt, as the University of Toronto steamrolled to a 14–3 victory.

Finlay gushed, "Travelling at a dizzy pace from start to finish and uncorking team play that was a revelation to the Western fans, the University of Toronto Schools' nifty young hockey machine cantered through the Regina Patricias in such a commanding style that they not only swamped the westerners 14–3 but outclassed them from stem to stern." The eastern press, not eager to welcome the western invaders, called the game a ridiculous sham. Some went so far as to suggest that, for the second game, the Patricias should be replaced by OHA runners-up Woodstock. "It was not known tonight whether the Patricias would default the second game on Saturday night," sneered the Canadian Press. "It is a moral certainty that they cannot pull down the lead."

The Pats did show up for the second game, on March 22. This time, Toronto

University of Toronto Schools, Senior Hockey Team. HHF

posted a 15–5 victory to win the series by a combined total of 29–8. Finlay was in a generous mood when he reported the results of the second game. "Though the score was threefold on them the Pats played much better hockey than they did on opening night," he argued, "and the score is no indication of the play." His account ended on a positive note concerning the officiating. "Two sporting scribes, Billy Finlay of the *Winnipeg Free Press* and Lou Marsh of the *Toronto Star*, handled the game, which was very clean." Lou Marsh was a legendary sports writer with the *Star* and the Lou Marsh trophy, awarded annually to Canada's outstanding athlete, was named for him. The Billy Finlay referred to was himself! Two journalists covering the game also officiated it, quite a common event in those days.

Standouts in the series included Toronto forwards Don Jeffrey and captain Jack Aggett, who scored 9 goals each for Toronto, and defenceman Dunc Munro. Munro went on to play seven years with the Montreal Maroons and one with the Montreal Canadiens, winning a Stanley Cup with the Maroons in 1926. Toronto was backstopped by goaltender Joe Sullivan, who would go on to become a well-known physician and Canadian senator. The Schools were managed by Frank Selke Sr. and coached by Frank Carroll, who had previously been a trainer on two Stanley Cup-winning teams, the Toronto Blue Shirts of 1913–14 and the Toronto Arenas of 1917–18. It was the first and last Memorial Cup for the University of Toronto. As for the Pats, it was a tough beginning, but it was only the beginning. They would be back.

The **1920** Memorial Cup

Like the inaugural Memorial Cup and many since, the 1920 tournament was dominated by a team from Toronto, the Canoe Club Paddlers, a powerful squad whose folksy monicker concealed a collection of all-star calibre players. The Paddlers squared off in a two-game, total-goal final against the Selkirk Fishermen, who hailed from a town northeast of Winnipeg on the Red River. The Paddlers were so dominant in Ontario at the time that reporter W. J. Finlay noted they had ironically become disliked in their own province. "They are very unpopular here," he offered, "owing to the fact that they were picked up from different parts of the country and moulded into one strong aggregation, and have such a big advantage over all the Ontario teams."

En route to playing Selkirk, the Paddlers had posted some impressive victories. They lost their first game 6–5 to the Stratford Midgets, a team that featured future NHL superstar Howie Morenz, but then roared back with a 10–2 win to take the two-game, total-goal affair 15–8. The Paddlers then hammered Quebec champions Loyola College of Montreal 16–4. Alfred "Pit" Lepine, a centre with Loyola College, would go on to win Stanley Cups with the Montreal Canadiens in 1930 and 1931. In the west, the Calgary Monarchs went down to Selkirk 11–5 on the round by scores of 8–2 and 3–3. Especially outstanding in the second game was future NHL Hall of Famer Cecil "Tiny" Thompson, who blocked 41 shots for Calgary. Thompson was a goalie in the NHL for twelve seasons, ten for the Boston Bruins and two for the Detroit Red Wings. He was voted to the NHL's first all-star team twice, and to the second team two more times.

On March 23, the 1920 Memorial Cup opened at the Arena Gardens on Mutual Street. The Paddlers led 2–0 and 4–1 at the period breaks. Finlay described the event as follows: "After putting up a game battle for two periods, in which they displayed a lot of class against superior odds, coach Stan Kennedy's Fishermen faded badly in the final session and were forced to submit to a 10–1 beating at the hands of Carroll's hand-picked Canoe Club stars in the first game for the junior hockey championship of Canada. Starting off badly, when they appeared to be affected by stagefright, the Fishtown lads finally caught themselves and were unlucky to be 2 goals down in the first session, and when they came back and outplayed their heavier and older opponents though outscored 2–1 in the second stanza, the three thousand fans began to take notice and cheered them loudly for their plucky work. But they had shot their bolt in their strenuous efforts in the second period, as they were badly outplayed in the final spasm, when the locals ran in 6 goals, mostly by fast combination play, in which the scorer worked in on top of the net."

As for the Canoe Club, Finlay observed that Billy Burch, Toronto's scoring leader with 4 goals and 3 assists, was especially sharp. "Burch, at centre, is a long rangy boy, who is a wonderful backchecker and a wonder in carrying the puck," he rhapsodized.

The Canoe Club Paddlers wrapped up the Memorial Cup on March 25 with a 5–4 victory. "The canoeists showed little interest in the game," according to one report, "and the handful of spectators expressed disappointment in the comparatively small score." For the only time in Memorial Cup history until the 1970–71 season, a team issued a challenge to the Memorial Cup champion. The invitation to spar was accepted, and the Fort William Beavers travelled to Toronto on March 31 for a one-game showdown. The sudden death game resulted in a lopsided rout for Toronto, who soundly thrashed Fort William 11–1. Billy Burch once again led the Toronto scoring attack with 5 goals, Wilfred "Texas" White adding four. Lionel Conacher and Harold Applegath rounded out Toronto's scoring with single markers.

Burch, a native of Yonkers, New York, would go on to play 11 seasons in the NHL with the Hamilton Tigers, New York Americans, Boston Bruins and Chicago Blackhawks. Carroll had previously coached the Toronto Arenas to the 1917–18 Stanley Cup and was a trainer with the 1913–14 Toronto Blueshirts when they captured the Stanley Cup. Also on the Toronto roster were goaltender Roy Worters, who later played twelve years with the Pittsburgh Pirates, New York Americans and Montreal Canadiens, and rightwinger Tex White, a future

Toronto Canoe Club Paddlers. Top row (l to r): Roy Worters, Lionel Conacher, Billy Burch, Wilfred White. Second row: John A. Mollenhauer, Francis McCurry, Frank Moore, Harold Applegath. Third row: Cyril Kelly, Sydney Hueston. Bottom row: W.C. Gowland (timekeeper), Bart Howitt (timekeeper), T.F. Livingstone (secretary-treasurer), R.F. Wilson (president), W.H. Reid (manager), W.C. Baker (goal umpire), Dick Carroll (coach). HHF

Philadelphia Quaker, Pittsburgh Pirate and New York American. Lionel "Big Train" Conacher, a hockey immortal, skated twelve years with the Americans, Pirates, Montreal Maroons and Chicago Blackhawks winning Stanley Cups with Chicago in 1934, and as the player–coach of the Montreal Maroons in 1935.

The **1921** Memorial Cup

The third Memorial Cup was notable for the emergence of a player destined to become one of the NHL's greatest stars: Howie Morenz. Morenz, the centrepiece of the Stratford Midgets' attack, drew as much attention at the junior level as he would in the NHL. One of Stratford's eastern playoff opponents, The Seaforth Highlanders Hockey Club, went so far as to protest Morenz's presence on the Midgets on the grounds that he was over-age—and the wrong gender. It seems that due to a clerical error, Morenz had been registered as a female on his birth certificate. Following an investigation by the OHA, this problem was rectified and the protest rebuffed. Morenz continued to play.

While Morenz and the Midgets were romping to the eastern championship—they lost just one of seventeen regular season and playoff games—the Winnipeg Falcons dominated the west with playoff victories over the Regina Victorias and the Fort William YMCA. Then it was on to Toronto for the Falcons, a team that had been formed from the Young Men's Lutheran Club of the Icelandic Lutheran Church, one of the early cornerstones of Manitoba junior hockey. The final series opened on March 24, with the Falcons posting a stunning 9–2 victory. Centre Wally Fridfinnson fired a hat trick for the Falcons, while rightwinger Harold McMunn sniped a pair of tallies. Art Somers, Harry Neil, Frank Woodall and Sammy McCallum all recorded single markers. Morenz and Lou "Red" Richards had the goals for Stratford. The two-game aggregate series appeared to be in the bag for the Falcons.

It wasn't. Unwilling to roll over, the Stratford Midgets turned out to be sleeping giants, and roared to life in the second game on March 26. "From the commencement of the game, the Midgets under the direction of coach Toad Edmunds forced the pace," read one report. "By close backchecking and heavy bodychecking they stopped the rushes of the speedy westerners and bit by bit backed them into defensive tactics. At the end of the second period they had worn them to a shadow of the team which won in such an outstanding fashion in the first game. In the third period, the Falcons got 4 shots on Harry Rushton, while the Midgets bombarded the Falcons' net minutes at a time."

Howie Morenz tallied a hat trick, and the Midgets got superb performances from Carson, Roth and Richards on the way to a 7–2 win. But the Stratford comeback had fallen two goals short for the series victory. The Falcons won 11–9 on total goals, recording the west's first Memorial Cup triumph. Players like Fridfinnson, Somers and McCallum were much in the limelight for the Falcons, but a large measure of the glory went to Winnipeg goaltender Freddie "Scotty" Comfort. So intense and sustained was the Stratford attack in the second game

Winnipeg Falcons. Top row (l to r): Dave Patrick, Sammy McCallum, Scotty Comfort, Harry Neil, W. McPherson. Middle row: Frank Woodall, Wally Fridfinnson, Harold McMunn, Art Somers. Bottom row: J. Austman (trainer), Connie Neil (manager and coach), F. Thordarson (secretary-treasurer), T. Swainson (trainer). MA/N9111

that Comfort was given immense credit for allowing only 7 goals. The scorers for Stratford in the last game were Morenz with 3, Roth with 2, and Richards and Carson with single goals. Fridfinnson and Somers were the Falcons' marksmen.

Winnipeg defenceman Harry Neil went on to coach the Winnipeg Monarchs to the 1932, 1935 and 1937 Memorial Cup finals, winning the last two times. Art Somers played seven seasons with the Chicago Blackhawks and New York Rangers, winning the Stanley Cup in 1933 with New York. Stratford's Frank Carson would enjoy a seven-year career in the NHL with the Montreal Maroons, New York Americans and Detroit Red Wings, winning the Stanley Cup with the Maroons in 1926. As for Howie Morenz, he became one of hockey's greatest legends, playing fourteen years with the Montreal Canadiens, New York Rangers and Chicago Blackhawks. As a centre, he won three Stanley Cups with the Canadiens in 1924, 1930 and 1931, before dying tragically of complications from a broken leg in 1937. In 1950, a Canadian Press poll voted him the greatest hockey player of the first half of the century.

The **1922** Memorial Cup

1922 marked the first time that the Memorial Cup championship was held outside of Toronto. The games were played at Shea's Amphitheatre in Winnipeg, where neither finalist was on home ice. The Regina Patricias, who had established themselves as the premier franchise in Western Canada, faced off against the Fort William War Veterans, a team that was not picked by many to reach the final.

Coached by Graham Reid, the Pats eliminated the Calgary Hustlers in their first interprovincial series, then continued on to Winnipeg to play the University of Manitoba Junior Hockey Team. The Pats lost the opener of the two-game, total-goal series by 4–1, but closed the gap in the following game, leading 3–0 after three periods. The Pats then struck for 2 overtime goals by leftwinger Harvey Naismith and centre Syl Acaster to win the series 6–4. Naismith and Acaster played on a line centred by captain Howie Milne, one of the best-known sports figures on the prairies. The year after his Memorial Cup experience, the North Dakota native played in the 1923 Grey Cup final with the Canadian Football League's Regina Roughriders. He later coached and managed the Regina Monarchs to the 1928 Memorial Cup, switched back to football to coach the Roughriders, and worked the 1931 Grey Cup final at Montreal as an official.

In eastern Canada, Fort William's Great World War Veterans Association narrowly avoided elimination in their semi-final against the Kenora Thistles. With his team trailing 4–1, Fort William's coach Stan Bliss had benched his star centre John Bates for the first two periods. Bates hit the ice in the third period and came through with two goals, setting up another to force overtime. The Forts scored three times in overtime to win the series. Meanwhile, Toronto Aura Lee defeated Iroquois Falls for the Ontario championship after an exhausted Iroquois Falls team were forced to play two games in one day. The Falls had defeated North Bay to win their region, but had used an ineligible player and were forced to play a hastily scheduled rematch the next morning in Toronto. Iroquois Falls managed to eliminate North Bay again, but the haggard team was no match for Aura Lee, who shut them down 4–0 the same afternoon. Aura Lee eliminated Quebec titleholders McGill University and headed to Shea's Amphitheatre in Winnipeg for the Memorial Cup final, not knowing which team they would face.

At the time, it was common for the Thunder Bay region to be grouped with the west, which meant that Fort William would play the Pats to determine who would meet Aura Lee. To save money, however, the Canadian Amateur Hockey Association ruled that Fort William would stay where they were, and Aura Lee would play them en route to Winnipeg. The Toronto team didn't figure to have too much trouble with Fort William. The story persists that Aura Lee had checked much of their baggage straight through to Winnipeg. But Aura Lee's season ended in Fort William, where the War Vets stunned them 5–3 in a one-game sudden death playoff. It was the team from Fort William, not Toronto, that made the trip west to Winnipeg to face the waiting Pats.

The championship series opened on March 20. The War Vets led 3–1 after

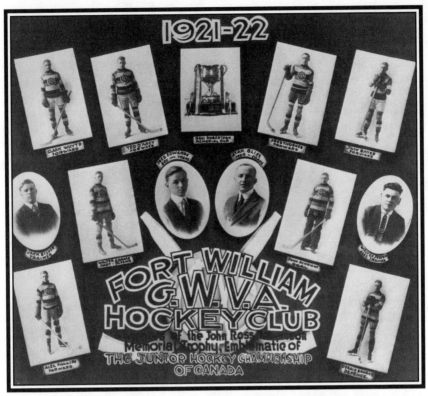

Fort William War Veterans. Top row (l to r): Clark Whyte, Ted D'Arcy, Fred
Thornes, Jack Bates. Middle row: Jack Silver (trainer), Walter Adams, Fred
Edwards (secretary-treasurer), Stan Bliss (manager and coach), John Enright,
Walter Jessop (trainer). Bottom row: Alex Phillips, Gerald Bourke.

the first period, but trailed 4–3 going into the third after Acaster struck for 3 consecutive goals. Clark "Clucker" Whyte, a speedy rightwinger, provided Fort
William with the victory by scoring the tying and winning goals, his second and
third of the game. Captain Walter Adams, a standout defenceman and younger
brother of NHLer Jack Adams, and leftwinger Fred "Shorty" Thornes also scored
for the victors, while Naismith had Regina's first goal. Regina believed it had
scored a tying goal late in the third period when the goal umpire ruled that the
puck had entered the Fort William goal. However, referee Billy Breen overruled
the call, making a decision that would be crucial to the outcome of the series.

Two nights later, the War Veterans played the Patricias to a 3–3 draw. That
was enough to give Fort William a slim 8–7 series victory. The *Regina Leader* called
it "one of the most heartbreaking finishes ever seen in a cup final. Regina went
down to defeat with colours flying." Clucker Whyte again proved to be Regina's
undoing, scoring all three of his club's goals. The champions attributed much of
their success to their mascot, a kitten. The fuzzball, garbed in the team colours,
appears with the Fort William underdogs in the team victory photograph.

The **1923** Memorial Cup

One of the most intriguing aspects of the 1923 Memorial Cup final is that it was refereed by future NHL star Lionel "Big Train" Conacher. During his career, Conacher experienced championship hockey at many levels and from many perspectives. Having won the Memorial Cup in 1920 with the Toronto Canoe Club, he would go on to claim the Stanley Cup as a defenceman with the 1934 Chicago Blackhawks and also in the following year as the player–coach of the Montreal Maroons. In the spring of 1923, Conacher oversaw a tournament in which the University of Manitoba battled the Kitchener Colts in a two-game aggregate series.

The strong University of Manitoba club went through its local league with only one loss—its first match of the season—against another impressive Manitoba junior team, the Winnipeg Tammany Tigers. The latter's roster included Art Chapman and goaltender Charles "Chuck" Gardiner, who had a splendid career at the NHL level. As captain of the Chicago Blackhawks, Gardiner fought a serious tonsil infection while leading his team to the 1934 Stanley Cup. He died two months later and was inducted into the Hall of Fame in 1945. Chapman also made it to the NHL, serving for ten years with the Boston Bruins and New York Americans.

Coached by Hal Moulden and captained by leftwinger Murray Murdoch, the University students scored a total of 67 goals in their league games and allowed only 14. They qualified for the Abbott Cup final with an 8–1 sudden death victory over Brandon, subsequently seizing the prize on March 14 after a 10–7 two-game, total-goal series against the Calgary Canadians. The University of Manitoba then journeyed to Fort William, Ontario to meet the Fort William Cubs, with the winner scheduled to travel to Toronto's Arena Gardens for the Memorial Cup. In a physical game, the two teams skated to a 3–3 tie in game one. Clark "Clucker" Whyte, captain and star rightwinger of the Cubs, was laid out twice by the University players' hard hits. The following night, Manitoba posted a 6–1 victory, winning the series 9–4.

Murray Murdoch scored 9 of the University of Manitoba's 14 goals in the 1923 Memorial Cup finals.

University of Manitoba. Top row (l to r): S.B. Field (secretary-treasurer), R.L. Bruce (manager), Bert Andrews (president), Hal Moulden (coach), Walter Robertson (trainer). Middle row: A.J. Chapman, Blake Watson, Murray Murdoch, Art Puttee, Jackie Mitchell, A. Johnson. Bottom row: J.A. Wise, C.E. Williams, C.S. Doupe, F. Robertson, Bob Moulden. MA/N3912

The same tough intensity was evident in the eastern playoffs, where the Kitchener Colts dumped the University of Toronto Varsity 4–1 to claim the OHA championship. The Colts moved on to edge Iroquois Falls 3–2 in a one-game provincial final. According to a Canadian Press report from Toronto, it was a nasty match. "Near the close of the game, Harold Dewar, an Iroquois Falls defenceman, charged Maurice Schnarr and was given a match foul," the account read. "Later he hit inspector Bond of the Toronto police force and was taken to the police station." Coached by Hen Sturm, Kitchener whipped Montreal 10–4 in a sudden death game in Toronto to advance to the Memorial Cup final.

The tournament opened on March 22, with Manitoba showing "superior speed, and courage, uncanny checking and resourcefulness" according to the Canadian Press. They pounded Kitchener 7–3. The score had been tied 2–2 after one period, but the Varsity boys banged in 5 straight goals in the second—4 by Murray Murdoch—to put the game away. Four nights later, Manitoba earned the Memorial Cup with a second consecutive 7–3 victory, giving them the round by a 14–6 aggregate. Murdoch bettered his 4-goal opening game by scoring five times and setting up 1 goal. All told, he scored 9 of Manitoba's 14 goals over the two games.

Murdoch went on to an eleven-year career with the New York Rangers, winning Stanley Cups in 1928 and 1933. He also was the original NHL ironman, playing 508 consecutive games. Kitchener's Albert "Babe" Siebert, a native of Plattsville, Quebec, would go on to play in the NHL for fourteen seasons with the Montreal Maroons, New York Rangers, Boston Bruins and Montreal Canadiens. He was a teammate of Murdoch on the 1933 Stanley Cup champion New York Rangers. Siebert's life came to an untimely end when he drowned in Lake Huron on August 25, 1939.

The **1924** Memorial Cup

The 1924 Memorial Cup was not a round robin in the formal sense, but it marked the first time that four teams gathered in one town to decide junior hockey supremacy in Canada. This came about partly by necessity. The Winnipeg Amphitheatre, built in 1909, was the only rink between Toronto and Vancouver that had artificial ice. Rather than worry about spring thaws, the CAHA booked the western semi-final and final into the old Amphitheatre, and decided to stage the Memorial Cup final there as well. The Regina Pats, the Calgary Canadians, the Winnipeg Tammany Tigers and the Owen Sound Greys were the participants.

The Pats won the Saskatchewan junior hockey championship for the eighth straight season. They trounced Broadview 15–0 in the first game of the series, with junior sensation Syl Acaster scoring seven times and adding two assists. This display prompted Broadview to default the second game, making the Pats southern champions. Next in line was a team from Outlook, the northern Saskatchewan victors, who also defaulted the second game after losing the first 5–2. Winnipeg's Tammany Tigers won the Captain W. J. "Ollie" Turnbull championship of Manitoba by trouncing Dauphin 13–2 in a sudden death playoff. In fairness to Dauphin, their local rink had collapsed during the winter of 1924 and the team had been hampered by a lack of ice time. In Alberta, the Calgary Canadians advanced with 7–5 and 10–3 victories over the Coleman Canadians.

In eastern Canada, the Owen Sound Greys—disadvantaged by lack of home competition and playing all but three games that season on the road—defeated the Kitchener Colts to win the Ontario regional crown and then eliminated the Kenora Thistles, champions of the Thunder Bay district. They won the OHA championship by defeating the North Bay Trappers 4–2 in a single game, and gained eastern supremacy by disposing of the Montreal Westmounts, Quebec provincial champions.

The four winning teams converged on Winnipeg in March. After some complicated negotiations, the CAHA decided that the Pats would play the Tammany Tigers on March 18 and 20. The winner of that series would play the Calgary Canadians on March 22 and 24, with the survivor taking on the Owen Sound Greys in the Memorial Cup. The two-game, total-goal final was scheduled for March 26 and 28.

The Winnipeg Amphitheatre, home of the 1924 Memorial Cup, was the only rink between Vancouver and Toronto that had artificial ice. MA/FC2122

Regina opened the tourney with a 2–0 victory over the Tigers on third-period goals by Acaster and Ken Doraty. Doraty made history with the Toronto Maple Leafs in 1933 by scoring the winning goal to ice Boston in Stanley Cup hockey's first overtime marathon. Press reports noted the play of Regina defencemen Johnny Gottselig and Jack Gilhooley, along with goaltender Jack Cunning— whose nickname, "the Elongated Custodian," is surely one of the least lyrical in hockey history. Regina wrapped it up two nights later, beating the Tigers 7–2 to win the round 9–2. Gottselig scored a hat trick while Acaster and Eric "Cowboy" Pettinger added two each. Winnipeg's goals came from rightwinger Harvey "Bun" Stephenson and defenceman Dick Davis.

The Pats then faced the Canadians, beating Calgary 4–2 in the opener. But the Alberta team came thundering back in game two. They led 4–2 at the end of regulation time, tying the total-goal series and forcing overtime. At 6:25 into the extra frame, Calgary's Stewart Adams slammed home the tie-breaker. The *Winnipeg Tribune* beamed that "while obviously disappointed, the Regina players were gripped by a superior feeling of sportsmanship and gathered at centre ice at the Winnipeg Amphitheatre to give three cheers for the Canadians."

Calgary went on to meet the Owen Sound Greys for the Memorial Cup. The Greys were led by such future pros as Ralph "Cooney" Weiland, Edward "Teddy" Graham, James "Dutch" Cain and Melville "Butch" Keeling. But the star of the championship was Owen Sound's sixteen-year-old goalkeeper, Headley Smith. In the first tilt, his club defeated Calgary 5–3, Weiland and Keeling scoring 2 goals each and George Elliot getting a single.

When the second game ended in a 2–2 tie, coach E.T. Hicks and his Owen Sound Greys went home with the Memorial Cup and a 7–5 two-game total score. It was not a popular victory. "No team escaped with a championship after being so badly outplayed at the Winnipeg Amphitheatre as the easterners did," read the game report. "For fifty minutes of the sixty they were behind their own centre, battling desperately to stave off attacks of the western lads and they succeeded though outclassed and outplayed." A lot of credit for the Greys' victory went to Smith, their youthful goalkeeper. "This young lad staved off what looked like certain defeat by his marvellous stops." The week ended with what has become a Memorial Cup tradition. After their hard-fought battle, the four teams sat down together for a celebration dinner.

From Owen Sound, "Butch" Keeling played twelve years in the NHL with Toronto and the New York Rangers. He won the Stanley Cup with the Rangers in 1933. James "Dutch" Cain spent two seasons with the Montreal Maroons and

Owen Sound Greys.

The four finalists for the 1924 Memorial Cup were the Owen Sound Greys, the Regina Pats, the Calgary Canadians and the Winnipeg Tammany Tigers. Owen Sound emerged as the champions.

Toronto Maple Leafs. "Cooney" Weiland played eleven years with Boston and was the NHL scoring champion in 1930 with 73 points. He was a player on two Stanley Cup champion teams in 1929 and 1939, and he also coached Boston to the Stanley Cup in 1941. After leaving the pros, Weiland launched a successful coaching career at Harvard University.

Calgary's Stewart Adams went on to be a solid leftwinger with the Chicago Blackhawks and Toronto Maple Leafs. Vic Ripley, also a leftwinger, played seven seasons in the NHL with the Boston Bruins, Chicago Blackhawks, New York Rangers and St. Louis Eagles.

The **1925** Memorial Cup

Memorial Cup finals have always been an opportunity for hockey fans to watch players emerge as stars or leaders, primed to make the jump to the professional ranks. But there have also been great juniors who did not make it at the professional level. The hard-nosed 1925 final featured one such player—the Regina Pats' Syl Acaster—who, though he did not move on to an NHL career, won the lasting respect of fans and players alike as a junior. By the spring of 1925, the CAHA had decided to do away with the two-game, total-goal system. Under the new rules, the champions of eastern and western Canada would meet in a best-of-three series.

The Regina Pats had gathered momentum along the road to the final by defeating the Saskatoon Wesleys and the University of Manitoba Varsity, Memorial Cup champions in 1923. In Tommy Cook and Andy Blair, the Varsity had two future Stanley Cup-winning players on its roster. Blair, a native of Winnipeg, skated with the 1932 Toronto Maple Leafs while Cook played for the 1934 Chicago Blackhawks. But it was Acaster, rather than any future NHLer, who emerged as the hero in this series.

Johnny Gottselig, one of the Pats' stars who went on to an NHL career, remembered the turning point of the series with the University of Manitoba

Varsity. "We were meeting the University of Manitoba in Regina after having lost the first game of the series," he recalled. "Manitoba went ahead with eight seconds to play in the third period and it looked like we were out. Frank Ingram was so disgusted, he chucked his stick into the crowd, and then came the face-off after that Winnipeg goal. Syl Acaster took the draw, skated in, shot and scored to tie it up and we won in overtime." The Pats beat Manitoba in the third and deciding game before brushing past Calgary and then Fort William en route to the Memorial Cup.

In eastern Canada, the Sons of Ireland from Quebec eliminated the Ottawa New Edinburghs, but lost to Toronto Aura Lee, an all-star aggregation selected by the OHA. Aura Lee—an all left-shot team—had defeated Sudbury of the Northern Ontario Hockey Association by 7–5. In the eastern final they removed the Owen Sound Greys, defending 1924 Memorial Cup champions, to enter the Memorial Cup final against Regina. Bill Marsden, Aura Lee manager and coach, said he was looking for a tough series. "They're a clean-cut crowd of athletes, officered by good sportsmen," he allowed after watching the Pats practise. "I look for a strenuous series. Their defence is what impresses me; they seem to have an edge on us in that department." An executive member of the OHA, W. W. Davidson, praised "the solid, chunky build of the Pats. Aura Lee figures the Pats can't use their body, but I have a feeling that every man out there can show the easterners something in that respect." He turned out to be right.

Game one on March 23 attracted about 3,000 fans to Toronto's Arena Gardens. No goals were scored through two periods, and finally Acaster connected at 4:05 of the third. It appeared that Regina had the game wrapped up but Johnny McPherson tied the game by dribbling a rolling shot through Pats goaltender Jack Cunning. Even so, the Pats prevailed in overtime, winning 2–1 on Frank Ingram's goal just 37 seconds in.

The Pats won it all on March 25 when they downed Aura Lee 5–2 in a game marred by a nasty brawl. "I am danged if I know whether I should chronicle what happened at the Arena Gardens last night by rounds or periods," wrote Lou Marsh in the *Toronto Star*. "But whichever is proper, I wouldn't have missed the jamboree for all the greenbacks a greyhound could

Johnny Gottselig of the 1925 Memorial Cup-winning Regina Pats was one of the game's greatest stickhandlers.

Regina Patricias (l to r): Frank Foster (secretary-treasurer), Bert Acaster (vice president), Fred Ueland (president), Ike Morrison, Jack Crapper, Bert Dowie, Jack Cranstoun, Al Acaster, Al Ritchie (manager and coach), Johnny Gottselig, Jack Cunning, Stan Fuller, Ken Doraty, Frank Ingram, Bill Griston (trainer), Percy Ryan (trainer).

hurdle." Aura Lee led 1–0 when Reg McIlwaine was penalized for tripping Acaster. While he was in the penalty box, the Pats scored twice and never looked back. Although the game was later tied 2–2, the Pats continued to dominate. "The game was the fastest and most brilliant junior exhibition played in Toronto this season," Norman B. Albert reported in the *Regina Leader*.

The donnybrook started when Toronto's Alex "Shrimp" McPherson and Ken Doraty began fighting. "Before it was over every player on both teams, including the subs, were out on the ice standing toe to toe and exchanging blows," according to Albert. "The police finally entered the affair and when it was all over Alex 'Shrimp' McPherson and Doraty were in the penalty box, having a good laugh and apologizing to each other." The fight was a handful for the two referees, Harold Farlow and Alex Irvin, the brother of hockey great Dick Irvin Sr.

In 1963, almost forty years after the fact, former Pats coach Al Ritchie recalled the second period fisticuffs to Ron Campbell of the *Regina Leader-Post*. "Everybody dropped their sticks and squared off," he said. "As I recall we were at a distinct disadvantage because the Aura Lee team, coached by Marsden, were joined by their teammates from the players' bench. I grabbed a stick and with the threat of splitting a couple of heads, I managed to keep my spares on the bench. After all we were within ten minutes of winning the championship and I wanted to have some fresh replacements ready for action when play resumed. The fight was pretty much of a draw despite the fact that Acaster whipped about four or five of those eastern guys."

Acaster contributed points as well as his fists to the game, netting one tally for Regina, who also got 2 goals from Doraty and a single from Jack Cranstoun. Perhaps the best tribute to Acaster's skill and toughness is the fact that his junior teammates, some of whom went on to win the Stanley Cup, held his ability in such high regard. "That Acaster was the greatest amateur ever to play," Johnny Gottselig said later. "He didn't get to the National Hockey League, but he did star in the minors with the Minneapolis Millers, Oklahoma City Warriors, St. Louis Fliers (later Flyers), Tulsa Oilers, Duluth Hornets and Wichita Blue Jays of the American Hockey Association. But during his first season in the minors he received a concussion and it seemed no one wanted to take a chance on him in the majors."

In 1986, Danny Gallagher of the *Regina Leader-Post* interviewed Pats' goaltender Jack Cunning. Gallagher asked him if any one player had stood out during the 1925 season. Cunning replied, "We had a fellow by the name of Acaster. He was a centre and he sure opened the eyes of Toronto. In my humble opinion he was the Wayne Gretzky of our day. He could score, he could carry the puck... he was a treat to watch."

The **1926** Memorial Cup

The Memorial Cup spent its first half-decade moving between Ontario and Manitoba but by the mid-twenties the rest of the west was beginning to emerge as a junior hockey hotbed. Taken by Regina in 1925, the young trophy went farther west in 1926. The Calgary Canadians squeaked into the final by edging the hometown Tammany Tigers at Shea's Amphitheatre in Winnipeg. Future NHL star Paul Thompson delivered the overtime goal that won the game 3–2, allowing Calgary to take the two-game, total-goal western championship series 6–5. In the east, the Queen's University Queens of Kingston also scraped by to the final in a controversial best-of-three series victory over Fort William. Spirits ran high in the second game and referee Harold Mitchell had to be escorted by police to the Fort William YMCA while local fans pelted him with ice and snowballs.

But the controversial Mitchell was back on the ice for the Memorial Cup final, which opened on March 23 in the Winnipeg Amphitheatre, once again a best-of-three series. In the first game, Kingston scored a 4–2 victory over Calgary. However, the Canadians' Paul Thompson was described as the best man on the ice and according to a game report, Calgary "passed up numerous opportunities to score and found an almost insurmountable barrier in Bill Taugher in the Kingston nets. Harold Mitchell of Toronto and Fred 'Steamer' Maxwell of Winnipeg handled the game and the former came in for the crowd's disapproval on several occasions for the strict interpretation of the rules. A little less bell ringing would no doubt have speeded up the game considerably."

The Canadians bounced back in game two with a 3–2 victory, forcing the first

Paul Thompson scored the overtime goal that edged the Calgary Canadians past the Winnipeg Tammany Tigers and into the Memorial Cup finals in 1926. Calgary went on to beat the Queen's University Queens of Kingston.

sudden death game for the Memorial Cup. The very next night, on March 26, Calgary took a 3–0 lead into the third period. "Tonight's game was lightning fast," one reporter wrote. "Calgary opened with a burst of speed which netted a goal in the opening session and 2 in the second. The Canadians completely dominated the game until Kingston put up their fighting finish in the last period. Calgary had increased their lead to 3 in the middle spasm and the Kingston rally only fell short of tying the count by the smallest of margins. Thompson of Calgary was again the outstanding player on the ice." The Canadians hung on for another 3–2 victory and Alberta's first Memorial Cup. Thompson scored the game's first and third goals, the latter standing up as the game and championship winner. Ronnie Martin also scored for Calgary, while Buster Hartley and Carl Voss replied for Kingston.

Voss played for the 1938 Stanley Cup champion Chicago Blackhawks at the end of his eight-year, eight-team NHL career. Actually, three players from the 1926 Memorial Cup tournament, Voss, Thompson and Peter Palangio, played together on the 1938 Blackhawks. Palangio also skated for Montreal and Detroit in his five-year NHL career. Paul Thompson celebrated two Stanley Cup victories over his thirteen years in the NHL, one with the New York Rangers in 1928 and another with Chicago in 1934. Thompson was the Blackhawks' leading scorer for six consecutive seasons, from 1933 through 1938. He then coached the NHL team from 1939 until 1945. Other Calgary players to skate in the NHL were Donnie McFadyen, who spent four years in Chicago; Ronnie Martin, who played two seasons with the New York Americans; Irvine Frew, who divided three years between the Montreal Maroons, Canadiens and St. Louis Eagles; and Tony Savage who played one season with the Canadiens and Bruins.

Calgary Canadians. MA/FC1107

The 1927 Memorial Cup

The Arena Gardens on Toronto's Mutual Street was an exciting place to watch hockey games in the 1920s. Before Maple Leaf Gardens opened on November 12, 1931, the Arena Gardens was the main artificial ice surface in southern Ontario, attracting major hockey championships at various levels. The building seated 8,000 spectators, but more were often crammed in. Many fans would sleep overnight to purchase tickets for events; some even pitched tents outside the Gardens. Once the puck was dropped, crowds became raucous and rowdy, punctuating their cheers with musical instruments and cowbells.

The Memorial Cup tournament returned to Mutual Street in 1927, not with the traditional showdown between west and east, but between two teams from Ontario's vast expanse northwest of Toronto. The Port Arthur West Ends' trek to the 1927 Memorial Cup final started to get serious in mid-March, around the time the ice in their home facility turned to slush. The West Ends, or "Westies" as they were known, journeyed to Winnipeg to meet the winner of a series between the Regina Pats and the Winnipeg (Elmwood) Millionaires. The victorious Pats then faced the West Ends, who hailed from Thunder Bay on the western shore of Lake Superior. Regina continued their winning ways by taking the first installment of the two-game, total-goal series 2–1, but they could not hold on. In the second outing, Port Arthur erased the deficit, defeating the Pats 4–1 to take the series 5–3.

In the east, the Owen Sound Greys defeated Northern Ontario champions Iroquois Falls for the right to enter the eastern final. Owen Sound then won the east with a 5–1 victory over the Montreal Amateur Athletic Association.

The Memorial Cup final, a best-of-three series, opened on March 25 in front of 7,000 fans at the Arena Gardens. Lou Marsh again doubled as referee and journalist. "In a thrilling, nerve-wracking game, the Owen Sound Greys defeated Port Arthur 5–4," according to Canadian Press. "The losers gave a rare display of courageous playing by coming from behind, on three occasions, to tie the score and by battling the Greys to a standstill in the closing minutes of the game, when they fought desperately to again even matters up." The game was decided with only four and a half minutes remaining, when Greys captain Martin Lauder scored the third goal of a natural hat trick—the first 2 coming earlier in the third period—to cap an outstanding clutch effort by Owen Sound.

The second match on March 28 picked up where the first left off, driving at a burning pace throughout the entire game. The teams were tied 1–1 after one period, Owen Sound led 2–1 after two, and the score was tied again after three. The game extended into a ten-minute, non-sudden death session, in which the Greys broke loose for 3 goals while the Westies managed only 1. The hero of the night was Harold "Shrimp" McDougall, who tallied 4 goals for the Greys, including 2 in overtime. The 5–3 victory gave coach Father John Spratt and his team the second and last Memorial Cup for Owen Sound.

Defenceman Roger Jenkins was just fifteen years old when he skated for the losing Port Arthur cause. An Appleton, Wisconsin native, Jenkins played in the

Owen Sound Greys. Top row (l to r): F. Campbell (executive), E.S. Pratt (secretary-treasurer), R.A. Vincer (president), Father J. Spratt (coach), R. Wilson (executive). Middle row: N. Whetton (trainer), Alvin Moore, Martin Lauder, Harold McDougall, Jack Markle, Hillis Paddon, A. Bennett (manager). Bottom row: John Grant, H. Smith, Benny Grant, John Beattie.

NHL from 1931 through 1939 with the Montreal Maroons, Montreal Canadiens, Boston Bruins, Toronto Maple Leafs, New York Americans and Chicago Blackhawks. He was a member of the Blackhawks' 1934 and 1938 Stanley Cup championship teams. From the Owen Sound Greys, Johnny "Red" Beattie played nine seasons with the NHL, mostly with the Boston Bruins. Martin Lauder played in Boston as well, starting a handful of games on the Bruins' defence.

The **1928** Memorial Cup

"Kid overconfidence has whipped some of eastern Canada's best amateur hockey clubs. Will the same trick play havoc with the western Monarchs?" So a *Regina Leader* writer ruminated on the eve of the Memorial Cup final between the Regina Monarchs and the Ottawa Gunners. Although Regina was favoured to win, the Gunners had raised some eyebrows in Ontario after upsetting the also-favoured Toronto Marlboros.

"All Toronto is pulling for the boys from the West," noted the same report, ending with a flourish of hometown bravado reminiscent of a World War One news dispatch. The *Leader* lauded the Monarchs as "successors to the Regina Pats, Canadian junior champions of 1925, who ended a sensational conquest by manly ability in the icy arena fighting with Aura Lee in old British fashion with bared hands. The morning *Regina Leader* will megaphone a detailed account from the *Leader* office. It will come direct from Toronto's Arena Gardens, ringside as it were, and fans who wish to nibble the odd peanut and smoke the odd cigarette outside the building will be rewarded with a complete description of the play."

The Regina Monarchs had been formed from the ashes of two Regina junior teams, the Pats—who would return—and the Falcons, and they were coached by Howie Milne, a star player with the Pats in the 1922 Memorial Cup playoffs. The Monarchs defeated the Kenora Thistles to get to the final and were picked by many to sweep the series. Ottawa put up stiff resistance, however, and the Monarchs narrowly edged the Gunners 4–3 in the first game of a best-of-three final.

The hero of the night was Regina leftwinger Harold "Mush" March of Silton, Saskatchewan. He scored all 4 of the Monarchs' goals. "His speedy, brilliant hockey earned him rounds and rounds of applause from the great crowd," enthused the *Leader*. "As the game wore on, Mush's every appearance with the puck was the signal for applause." Ottawa got its first goal from Earl Armstrong and its last two from Syd Howe, a substitute who only played in the final series. They fired

back in the second game, played to a packed house in the smaller Varsity Arena. Ottawa emerged with a 2–1 victory and a deadlocked series on goals by Frank Quinn and Tommy McInenly.

Syd Howe, despite not scoring a goal in that game, was again a standout for Ottawa. Mush March continued his scoring streak, nailing Regina's only goal early in the second period. To this point, he had accounted for all of the Monarchs' championship goals, but did not dominate in the second game the way he did in the first. "A salient factor on the night's play," the *Leader* determined, "was the strict attention that the eastern artillery men paid to March, the right wing speedster from the prairies. March was checked so closely and rigorously that it took everything he had to hold his own."

Speedy leftwinger Harold "Mush" March led the Regina Monarchs to Memorial Cup victory in 1928.

Regina Monarchs. The caption with this archival photograph reads (l to r): "Ross Robson (president), A. Whittleton (secretary-treasurer), Carl Bergl, Harold March, Len Dowie, Harold Shaw, Howie Milne (manager and coach), Jim Langford, K. Williamson, G. Parron, R. Bentley (trainer)."

But March and the Monarchs broke loose with a vengeance in the third and deciding game. It poured rain outside while about 9,000 fans cheered on their favourites inside the Arena Gardens. March scored the game's first goal—the only goal of the first period—giving him Regina's first 6 goals in the series. Harold Shaw made it 2–0 early in the second period, tallying what would prove to be the championship winner. Also scoring for Regina were Len Dowie with a pair of goals, and Swede Williamson and Chuck Farrow with 1 each. Armstrong tallied Ottawa's only marker in a 7–1 loss. Regina goaltender and captain Jim Langford was solid between the pipes throughout the series.

The western press was gleeful over Regina's victory. "The Monarchs livened up the play and when the scrappy Gunners wanted to draw them into a donnybrook in the last stanza, the prairie lads from the Golden West just laughed at them, out-speeded them and outmanoeuvred them and went in to ring an unmerciful whipping on the Capital City artillerymen," wrote Norman Albert in the *Leader*.

The referees of the 1928 Memorial Cup were Clare Devlin and Billy Keane, the great-uncle of future Montreal Canadiens captain Mike Keane. The stars of each team, March and Howe, emerged as blue-chip NHL picks. The 5'5" March played seventeen years with Chicago, winning the Stanley Cup in 1934 and 1938. Syd Howe would play with the original Ottawa Senators, Maple Leafs, Red Wings, Philadelphia Quakers and St. Louis Eagles. He won three Stanley Cups with the Red Wings in 1936, 1937 and 1943.

The **1929** Memorial Cup

The Toronto Marlboros were upset by the Ottawa Gunners in the 1928 eastern final, but they would not be denied the following year. No team has won more Memorial Cups than the Toronto Marlboros. Their first came in the last year of the roaring twenties, when the "Marlies," coached by Frank Selke and powered by future NHL stars Charlie "the Bomber" Conacher and Harvey "Busher" Jackson, defeated the Elmwood Millionaires in a best-of-three series. The Millionaires, a Winnipeg-based team coached by Bert Marples, came awfully close to not making it to the 1929 Memorial Cup.

Elmwood's two-game, total-goal western playoff series against the Kenora Thistles went right down to the wire. The Thistles brought a 1-goal edge to Winnipeg, maintaining it into the third period of the second game. But when defenceman Len Burrage scored late in regulation time, the Millionaires recorded a 2–1 victory to tie the series and force an over-time period. Speedy substitute rightwinger Billy Kendall scored in the extra frame to win it for Elmwood, moving the team into the Abbott Cup final against the Calgary Canadian-Falcons. Game one, played in the Winnipeg Amphitheatre on March 20, ended in a 1–1 tie. In game two, Calgary appeared to be safely on their way to the Memorial Cup as they were

Harvey "Busher" Jackson led the attack for the Toronto Marlboros in their 1929 Memorial Cup victory.

up 3–1 midway through the third period. But three minutes and thirty seconds later, the Millionaires found themselves protecting a 4–3 lead! Thanks to three lightning-fast goals, Elmwood posted a 4–3 victory and advanced to the Memorial Cup final.

In the east, the Ottawa Shamrocks under coach Hans "Hap" Shouldice eliminated the Montreal Victorias 2–1 in a sudden death game, setting up an eastern championship with the Toronto Marlboros. Ottawa managed a 4–3 victory in game one but were subsequently outgunned 3–1—with Charlie Conacher scoring all three goals—to lose the series 6–5 to Toronto.

The Memorial Cup, a best-of-three series, opened on March 29 at the Arena Gardens. The Marlboros won the opener 4–2 in overtime. Toronto's line of centre Eddie Convey between leftwinger Busher Jackson and rightwinger Conacher—known as the Three Musketeers—led the way. Max Hackett put the Marlies on the board in the first period, but Norm McQuade tied the score at 1:20 of the second. Convey put Toronto out in front again late in the period, but Elmwood's Bill Gill scored the only goal of the third period to force overtime.

Toronto scored twice in the extra period, Jackson getting both goals on perfect passes from Conacher.

Two nights later, the teams met once more before 8,000 fans. The score was tied 1–1 after the opening period, Convey scoring for Toronto and Albert "Spunk" Duncanson for the Millionaires. Conacher scored the only goal of the second period to give Toronto a 2–1 edge going into the final frame. Four minutes into the third, he scored his second goal—which would stand up as the Memorial Cup winner—and Hackett followed it up to give Toronto a 4–1 lead. Belfast-born rightwinger Bobby Kirk had Elmwood's other goal in their 4–2 loss.

Kirk later skated briefly in the NHL with the 1938 Rangers and coached the

Alex "Mine Boy" Levinsky, along with 1929 Memorial Cup-winning Toronto Marlboro teammates Red Horner, Charlie Conacher and Harvey "Busher" Jackson, went on to play for the Toronto Maple Leafs' first Stanley Cup championship team in 1932.

Flin Flon Bombers to the 1957 Memorial Cup title. Billy Kendall, an NHLer for five years, won the Stanley Cup with the 1934 Blackhawks. Five players from the triumphant Marlboro team went on to the NHL. Eddie Convey saw action with the New York Americans, while Alex "Mine Boy" Levinsky, Red Horner, Charlie Conacher and Busher Jackson were all members of the Maple Leafs' first Stanley Cup championship team in 1932. Levinsky, who spent most of his nine NHL years in Toronto and Chicago, won another Cup with the Leafs in 1938. Horner joined the Leafs before the 1929 junior season had ended and just missed the Marlboros' first Memorial Cup triumph. He went on to play twelve years with the Leafs and was inducted into the Hockey Hall of Fame in 1965. Conacher played twelve years for the Maple Leafs, Red Wings and New York Americans; he also coached the Blackhawks from 1948 to 1950. Busher Jackson

Toronto Marlboros. Top row (l to r): Ellis Pringle, Harry Montgomery, Bert Cartan (president), Laurie Moore, Charles Coulter (vice president), "Red" Horner, Alex Levinsky. Middle row: Jim Darragh, Max Hackett. Bottom row: Harvey Jackson, Clarence Christie, Conn Smythe (vice president), Frank J. Selke (coach), Eddie Convey, William J. D'Alesandro (manager), William F. Christie (vice president), Bob Gamble, Charlie Conacher.

played fifteen years in the NHL with Toronto, Boston and the Americans. Both Conacher and Jackson, members of the Maple Leafs' famous "Kid Line" of the 1930s (along with Joe Primeau), were inducted into the Hall of Fame.

The
1930s

It must have been a vivid and exhilarating experience for a sixteen-, seventeen- or eighteen-year-old hockey player, used to playing in front of a few hundred spectators, to travel to the new world-class Maple Leaf Gardens in Toronto, compete in games before crowds numbering in the tens of thousands and be covered by national radio and print media. With the advent of the Great Depression, the 1930s marked a rough time for Canadians. In spite of this, or perhaps because of it, there were some signs of prosperity for junior hockey and the sport in general. The best-of-three format for Memorial Cup finals was expanded to best-of-five in 1937. Radio broadcasts of the tournaments began—by the legendary Foster Hewitt no less. Attendance figures for the tournaments were very healthy: the 1938 five-game final drew over 55,000 spectators. All of the final series played in the 1930s took place either in Winnipeg in the venerable Shea's Amphitheatre, named for the adjacent Shea's brewery, or in Toronto, where the old Arena Gardens gave way in 1932 to the Maple Leaf Gardens. Teams from Ontario and Manitoba dominated; the 1930 Regina Pats were the only team outside these two provinces to take home a championship during the decade.

The game was speeding up and taking its present shape, with offside rules at the trend-setting professional level modified in 1929 and 1930, installation of the centre red line and permission of the kind of forward passing fans today are familiar with. But the nature of the game was still notably old-fashioned. The fact that there was no limit to how many players could be sent off at once on penalties gave rise to some humorous moments. Two referees still patrolled the ice, and they still carried handbells, not whistles. Most significant was the level of competition. Toe Blake, Bobby Bauer, Harold Ballard and Hap Day were a few of the names to make an impression on Memorial Cup competition in the 1930s, proving more than ever that the junior leagues were a durable framework for the development of players, coaches and managers.

The "Flying Frenchmen" line, made up of Paul Rheault, team captain Pete Belanger and Romeo Martel, was the core of the 1935 Winnipeg Monarchs roster. MA/N3902

The 1930 Memorial Cup

The Regina Pats rolled into the 1930 Memorial Cup final with a string of four straight playoff shutouts. After blanking the Calgary Canadians twice, coach Al Ritchie's team carried on to Winnipeg, where they trounced the Elmwood Millionaires 8–0 in a two-game series. Ready for the final at Shea's Amphitheatre in Winnipeg, the Pats patiently waited for the West Toronto Nationals to arrive. West Toronto had survived a tough playoff grind and had to ride the train to Winnipeg. The Pats—well rested and on a roll—were favoured to claim the championship.

Although West Toronto featured some impressive talent, the Pats were the speedier of the two teams, boasting a pressing offence and a system of backchecking that foiled the Nationals in game one. West Toronto fought "a plucky but futile battle," according to Dave Dryburgh of the *Regina Leader*. "When the smoke of the combat had cleared away, Al Ritchie's band of speed merchants were found to be on the long end of a 3–1 score." Nonetheless, the Regina shutout streak had been broken. Having made this dent in the Pats' veneer of invincibility, the Nationals came out blasting in game two.

In the unhurried yet dramatic reporting style typical of the era before television—with radio still in its infancy and newspapers the sole purveyors of hockey stories—Dryburgh pondered the significance of a win for each team. "Forty seconds to go and the score tied; to one team a goal would mean the Dominion junior hockey championship; to the other an opportunity to force another contest before the holders of the Memorial Cup for 1930 could be decided. That was the situation that faced the Regina Pats and West Toronto at the Winnipeg Amphitheatre on Saturday night in the second game of the title series."

West Toronto opened up a 2-goal lead only to watch Regina wrestle back a 3–2 victory and claim the championship. Dryburgh's description of the play that led to the winning goal is no less colourful. "Gordon Pettinger slid the disc over to Ken Moore on the right boards—the winger seemed to skate too far into the

Gordon Pettinger of the 1930 Memorial Cup-winning Regina Pats went on to greater glory in the NHL, playing with the Rangers, Red Wings and Bruins.

corner but he eventually took a shot which Ronald Geddes, the Toronto goalie, saved with his pads. Darting in after the rebound, the dusky Regina winger picked it up and slipped it across the goalmouth—it was hardly more than a tap and the puck stopped dead less than three feet from the goalmouth. There was nobody on hand to pick it up and it seemed for a second that the opportunity was lost—but everyone had forgotten about Moore. Skating around the cage at top speed in order to get back in the play again, the winger grabbed the rubber that he himself had slid across the mouth of the citadel and backhanded it over the prostate form of Geddes."

The West Toronto Nationals had some fine players, including future NHLers Bob Gracie, John "Red" Doran and Bill Thoms. Thoms had a thirteen-year pro career, winning the Stanley Cup with the Toronto Maple Leafs in 1932 and the Montreal Maroons in 1935. Gracie played with six different teams during a splendid nine-year NHL career. Doran, a defenceman, played with the New York Americans, Detroit Red Wings and Montreal Canadiens.

From the victorious Pats team, three members went on to greater glory: Frank "Buzz" Boll, Gordon Pettinger and Eddie Wiseman. Boll played eleven years in the NHL with Toronto, Boston and the New York Americans. Wiseman

Regina Patricias (l to r): Pete Egan (president), Brian Peebles (vice president), Gail Egan (mascot), Clarence Acaster, Eddie Wiseman, Ralph Redding, Art Dowie, Ken Campbell, Dave Gilhooley, Al Ritchie (manager and coach), Gordon Pettinger, Thorman Boll, Joe Dutkowski, Len Rae, Ken Moore, Lon McPherson, Bert Acaster (executive), Bob Bentley (trainer).

skated for ten seasons with the Americans, Red Wings and Bruins, while Pettinger spent eight seasons with the Rangers, Red Wings and Bruins. Both Pettinger and Wiseman won Stanley Cups with Boston, Pettinger in 1939 and Wiseman in 1941.

The **1931** Memorial Cup

The 1931 Memorial Cup championship was almost anticlimactic for the Elmwood Millionaires. Picked by many to be fodder for the Regina Pats, the Millionaires, on the strength of a miraculous Hail-Mary goal, overcame Regina in a hard-fought western championship. The defending champion Pats had been favoured to repeat as Abbott Cup victors to represent the west in the national championship. Some said the 1931 Pats were a stronger team than the previous year's powerhouse, which kept the Millionaires off the scoreboard in the 1930 western final. This time, Regina rode a stunning six-game shutout streak into Winnipeg to face Elmwood again in a two-game series.

The 1931 series began with a continuation of the streak, with the Pats blanking the Millionaires 1–0. But Regina's juggernaut was halted in dramatic fashion in the second game. "Fighting Elmwoods Eliminate Pats in Epic Match," blared the headline of the *Regina Leader* the next day. "The fighting Millionaires humbled Regina's famed Pats," the *Leader* continued, "defeating them 4–2 in a dramatic twenty-minute overtime struggle." Elmwood actually came from behind to win. Down by 1 goal early in the game, the Millionaires—who needed to win by 2 goals to prevail in the total-goal series—scored twice in the third period to tie and send the game into overtime.

The Pats scored early in the first extra session and it seemed that the Millionaires were through, but with fifteen seconds left, Millionaires defenceman Kitson Massey lifted a high shot from just over his own blue line. The puck arched up into the Amphitheatre lights and Regina goalkeeper Kenny Campbell lost track of it. Looking around frantically, he turned behind him to find goal

Team captain Bill MacKenzie led the
Elmwood Millionaires to Memorial Cup
victory in 1931.

judge Stewart MacPherson pointing into the net. The puck, lifted
from the other side of centre ice,
had dropped in over Campbell's
shoulder. It was a new series. The
shaken Campbell regained his
composure and kept the
Millionaires at bay until 3:25 in
the second ten-minute overtime
period, when rightwinger Albert
"Spunk" Duncanson, a crafty
stickhandler, wriggled through
the Pats' defence and punched
home the winner for the 1931
Abbott Cup. The Millionaires
were on their way to Toronto.

Waiting for them there were
the Ottawa Primroses, who had
defeated the Montreal Amateur
Athletic Association and Niagara
Falls Cataracts to claim the eastern
championship. Game one of the
best-of-three Memorial Cup final
was played before more than
5,000 fans at Arena Gardens. After
so narrowly snatching victory
from Regina, the Winnipeg club
seemed unable to focus, and
Ottawa posted a 2–0 shutout. However, the second game went to Elmwood by a
2–1 count, forcing a third and deciding match. Elmwood was reported to have
held a wide edge in play in both games, but the Canadian Press observed that
"the close checking of the gallant Ottawa band in their defensive zone prevented
the Millionaires from carrying their flashing thrusts right to the goalmouth. The
contest was not brilliant but the close score and frequent penalties kept the fans
in constant excitement."

Having played the first two games in Toronto, the teams travelled to Ottawa
for the final contest. Nine thousand fans rocked the Auditorium, at the time the
largest assemblage ever to watch a game in Ottawa. But the hometown crowd
went home disappointed. "The Winnipeg Elmwoods, a battling band of sturdy
youths with skating speed galore, are enthroned today as Canada's junior hockey monarchs," proclaimed the papers afterward. "They won the title by handing
the Ottawa Primroses a 3–0 defeat that left no doubt as to their superiority."

Ottawa's Bill Cowley played thirteen years in the NHL, most of them in
Boston. He won the Stanley Cup with the Bruins in 1939 and 1941. Centre J. T.
"Tag" Millar coached the Montreal Royals to a 1949 Memorial Cup victory, the
first by a Quebec-based franchise. Winnipeg's George Brown played three seasons

Elmwood Millionaires (clockwise from bottom left): Archie Creighton, George Brown, Don "Duke" McDonald, Albert "Spunk" Duncanson, Kitson Massey, Art Rice-Jones, Gordie MacKenzie, Norm Yellowlees, Boyd Johnston, Cliff Workman, Bill MacKenzie, Earl Adam (manager).

with the Montreal Canadiens, while team captain Bill MacKenzie spent seven years in the NHL, mostly with Chicago and the Montreal Maroons. MacKenzie, a rushing defenceman who provided a preview of the Doug Harvey style, won the Stanley Cup in 1938 with Chicago, where he occasionally doubled on right wing. Ironically, he also coached the Brandon Wheat Kings in their losing effort against Tag Millar's Montreal Royals in the '49 Memorial Cup.

The 1932 Memorial Cup

The 1932 Memorial Cup championship was a tight contest between two tenacious hockey teams, but it is also significant as the first championship appearance of a hockey legend. When the Sudbury Cub Wolves defeated the Winnipeg Monarchs to take the 1932 championship, it was the first taste of victory for a man whose name would become synonymous with winning, Hector "Toe" Blake. The Cub Wolves began to turn heads when, as Northern Ontario champions, they arrived in Toronto to face the Marlboros. Thirteen thousand fans packed the brand new Maple Leaf Gardens to watch an upstart Sudbury team sting the Marlies 3–0 in the first game of the series. However, Toronto was not finished, and counterattacked fiercely in game two. William Walsh, a reporter for the Toronto Mail and Empire, called the confrontation "a game that must go down as a classic, an epic for hockey history that may never be repeated."

A sensational effort by Toronto's Jack Shill, who fired 3 goals past Sudbury

Bryan Hextall, the patriarch of one of the great
hockey families, played for the Winnipeg
Monarchs, runners-up in the 1932 Memorial Cup.

goaltender Anthony Healey in twenty-six seconds, gave Toronto a 4–1 lead at the end of three. Shill's heroics tied the series at 4 goals and forced overtime, but Sudbury recovered its poise and scored at 7:35 of the extra period, advancing the Cub Wolves along the playoff trail. Sudbury defeated the Ottawa Shamrocks and the Montreal Amateur Athletic Association to advance to the Canadian final. The Winnipeg Monarchs, who had just polished off the Saskatoon Wesleys, were waiting for the Cub Wolves.

The Memorial Cup final opened on March 31 at Shea's Ampitheatre. "Despite being outweighed, the Sudbury youngsters blazoned forth in their speed and passing game to sizzle in and around the blocking defensive style native to all big teams with a margin of goals in their favour," wrote J. P. Fitzgerald in the *Toronto Telegram*. "Sudbury beat the defence often enough to give their supporters and well wishers cause to hope for the best." Even so, the Monarchs prevailed in a 4–3 victory. But the Wolves evened the series in the second game, edging Winnipeg 2–1 after ten minutes of overtime. The game was a close-checking, chippy affair that only settled down after a brawl in the second period. It was also a game in which Toe Blake demonstrated the superlative skating and checking that would bring him to prominence in the NHL.

There was a mad scramble for the 5,500 tickets available for the final game of the series. Even in the midst of the Depression, people were willing to pay the 10 dollars per ticket demanded by scalpers. Those who did were treated to a tough defensive struggle. Dalton Smith, a slight Sudbury centre back in action after being knocked out in the second game, placed a neat shot past Art Rice-Jones in the Winnipeg cage early in the first period. Behind Healey's goaltending, Sudbury proceeded to give the Monarchs a lesson in the defensive style that the

Winnipeg club thought they had perfected. The Cub Wolves held on for a 1–0 victory, taking the Memorial Cup two games to one.

The Wolves' victory sparked an explosion of celebrations all over Northern Ontario. In Sudbury, people poured into the streets for an all-night party of drinking, singing and lighting bonfires. When the team arrived home, they were greeted by 20,000 admirers in a fanfare that included brass bands, the Mayor presenting a key to the city, and a fire truck parading the heroes through the city. "There was a hot time in the home town when word was flashed from Winnipeg that Sudbury had triumphed," enthused one reporter. "Scenes reminiscent of Armistice Day were enacted as the entire folks in the populace thronged into the downtown section to shout acclaim to the courageous little hockey band. Even undertakers' hearses bore emblems of rejoicing."

Toe Blake played on three Stanley Cup-winning teams in Montreal: the 1935 Maroons and the Canadiens in 1944 (when he scored the winning goal) and 1946. As a player, Blake picked up 527 points in 578 NHL games, most of them as a leftwinger on the famous "Punch Line" with Maurice "Rocket" Richard and Elmer Lach. Even more famous for his coaching exploits, Blake directed the Habs to an amazing eight Stanley Cup titles in 1956–1960, 1965, 1966 and 1968. He

Sudbury Cub Wolves. Top row (l to r): Jack McInnes, Peter Fenton, Bob McInnes, Anthony Healey, Red Porter, Don Price. Middle row: Larry LaFrance, Sam Rothschild (coach), Max Silverman (manager), Hector "Toe" Blake. Bottom row: Ivan Fraser, Max Bennett, Dalton "Nakina" Smith, Adelard LaFrance, Gordon Grant.

was inducted into the Hockey Hall of Fame in 1966.

Cub Wolves rightwinger Max Bennett and leftwinger Adelard LaFrance Jr. both saw limited action with the Montreal Canadiens. Centre Dalton J. "Nakina" Smith also played sparingly in the NHL with Detroit and the New York Americans. The Monarchs' roster included defenceman Robert "Pinkie" Davie, who would play with the NHL's Boston Bruins. Bryan Hextall, who played briefly on the 1932 Monarchs, graduated to the pros as a rightwinger with the New York Rangers. Hextall, the patriarch of one of hockey's great families, was a member of the Rangers for eleven seasons, including 1940, when they won their third Stanley Cup.

The **1933** Memorial Cup

The 1933 Memorial Cup final was one of the hottest and closest in the history of the series. The Newmarket Redmen, a smallish but game team, took on the Regina Pats, who were making their fourth tournament appearance in eight years. The Pats moved past the Saskatoon Tigers in their play-offs and then the Brandon Native Sons, anchored by future goaltending great Turk Broda, in a close western final. The Redmen, who had been decimated by injuries in their eastern playoff run, actually made a bid to cancel the second game of the Richardson Cup championship against the Montreal Royals. Their request was denied, the game was played and the battered Redmen prevailed 1–0 on a long shot from centre ice by future Maple Leaf Norman Mann.

Future goaltending great Walter "Turk" Broda was the anchor of the Brandon Native Sons whose hopes for a 1933 Memorial Cup appearance were extinguished by the Regina Pats in a close western final.

Game one of the Memorial Cup series was played on April 4 at Maple Leaf Gardens. Newmarket won 2–1 in a "thrilling struggle," as described by Willis Entwistle in the *Regina Leader-Post.* "Newmarket has the fastest junior hockey team that I have seen for many a year," he wrote. "They skate like the old 1925 Pats—just like lightning." As for the 1933 Pats, Entwistle admitted that "comparisons are odious but, at first glance, the present Pats are hardly as electrical as their predecessors. They are, however, a hardworking smooth combination and should fare much better in the second game."

There were almost 8,000 fans in the Gardens on April 6, when the Redmen repulsed Regina 2–1 in triple overtime. The championship clincher was a match in which the officiating generated considerable controversy. With less than two minutes left in the third overtime period, Redman Don Willson scored with a hard shot from outside the Pats' defence, sending the crowd into joyous excitement. The goal came with two Regina skaters in the penalty box, and prompted an unruly outburst from some of the Pats as they surrounded referee Johnny Mitchell. The official was jostled by Alex Kerr and cut in the face by a stick during the melee.

"I never saw a more partisan official in my life," Regina coach Al Ritchie complained to reporter Lou Marsh after the game. "He gave us penalties we did not deserve and he allowed Newmarket to get away with things for which they should have been penalized." Marsh, an erstwhile official, wrote, "There is no excuse for any player attacking an official and Kerr, as instigator, is about sure to be asked to be paraded on the official carpet: he may get a suspension." In fact, four of the Pats—Kerr, Franks, Cunningham and Bill Cairns—were immediately suspended by the CAHA.

Alex Motter, a member of the losing Pats, played in the NHL for the 1943 Stanley Cup champion Detroit Red Wings. Newmarket's Norman Mann suited

Newmarket Redmen. Back row (l to r): Max Smith, Fred Thompson, Jim Law, Gordon Manning, F. Duncan, Bernard McHale, W.W. Osborne, R.L. Pritchard. Middle row: Bill Mann, L.G. Reilly (secretary), Bill Hancock (coach) Stan Smith (manager), M. Ogilvie, Aubrey Marshall, Jimmie Parr, Andy Davis, Lyman B. Rose (president). Front row: Ran Forder, Regis "Pep" Kelly, Frank "Chief" Huggins, Howard Peterson, "Silver" Doran, Don Willson, Norman Mann, "Red" McArthur, "Gar" Preston, Melville "Sparky" Vail.

up for the Toronto Maple Leafs during the 1939 and 1941 seasons. In addition to Mitchell, the other official in the 1933 tournament was Alex Irvin, brother of hockey immortal Dick Irvin Sr., who became well known during an NHL coaching career with the Maple Leafs, Montreal Canadiens and Chicago Blackhawks. In 1933, the hockey world was still a small place.

The 1934 Memorial Cup

St. Michael's College of Toronto has built some fine junior hockey teams, many of whom contended for Memorial Cup championships in the early decades of the tournament. One of the best was the team of 1934 which defeated the Edmonton Athletic Club Roamers to take home the first of four cups for the college. The 1934 St. Michael's team, referred to as "the greatest aggregation of junior puck chasers gathered together in a decade," was the only club in Memorial Cup history to win by going undefeated through both the regular season and the playoff rounds.

This powerful Toronto team was coached by Dr. W. J. "Jerry" LaFlamme, and featured such players as Bobby Bauer, Reg Hamilton, Arthur Jackson, captain Regis "Pep" Kelly, Nick Metz, Don Willson, Clarence Drouillard and goaltender Harvey Teno, all of whom played in the NHL. Kelly and Willson came over from the Newmarket Redmen, the defending Cup champions. St. Michael's bulldozed the Charlottetown Abegweits for the eastern championship, winning by 12–2 and 7–2 in the two-game series. Edmonton also won decisively—by scores of 7–3 and 4–0—over the Port Arthur West Ends, who had previously defeated the Kenora Thistles.

The Memorial Cup final, a best-of-three affair, was set for April 3 at Shea's Amphitheatre. The St. Michael's squad arrived early and drew considerable attention in practice. "Four hundred curious railbirds watched the Toronto Irish go through their paces for nearly an hour at the Amphitheatre rink," the Canadian

Bobby Bauer, one of the members of the outstanding St. Michael's College of Toronto team, went on to play for ten years with the Bruins in the NHL.

Press reported. "There was scarcely a spectator who was not visibly impressed by the skill and hockey ability of the easterners. Not having a spare goalie along, St. Michael's invited Walter 'Turk' Broda, net custodian for the Winnipeg Monarchs from the Manitoba Junior Hockey League, to guard one cage. After being blazed at from all sides during the practice, 'Turk' seemed inclined to pick St. Michael's for two straight victories."

Broda was as reliable at picking a winner as he would prove to be at stopping pucks. St. Michael's opened with a 5–0 victory over Edmonton. Canadian Press opined that "the smooth-skating, sharpshooting Irish from the Queen City downed the western champions with a torrid attack in the second period but in the first and third periods the Edmontonians put up a better attack." On April 5, more than 4,500 fans showed up for game two. St. Michael's won their first Memorial Cup championship, thanks to a 6–4 victory, but the outcome wasn't decided until twenty minutes of overtime had been played. "The husky lads who wear the double blue of St. Michael's College in Toronto are the kings of junior hockey in Canada," wrote Sam G. Ross for Canadian Press. "The boys from the Alberta capital never quit trying, and they matched the hockey skill of the easterners all through the eighty minutes of hockey that left every player nearly exhausted. It was their ability to finish off attacks that gave the easterners their win."

The powerful St. Michael's club is regarded as one of the finest collections of talent ever to capture the Memorial Cup. Its 1934 alumni went on to collectively win a total of ten Stanley Cups. Bobby Bauer, a Hall of Famer, won in 1939 and 1941 during a ten-year career with the Boston Bruins. Nick Metz won four Cups in twelve years as a Toronto Maple Leaf. Arthur Jackson played twelve years with Toronto, Boston and the New York Americans, winning the Stanley Cup with the Bruins in 1941 and the Maple Leafs in 1945. Reg Hamilton, who played twelve years with Toronto and Chicago, helped the Leafs to championships in 1942 and 1945. Other Toronto players to skate in the

Captain Regis "Pep" Kelly led St. Michael's College of Toronto to Memorial Cup victory in 1934. The St. Michael's squad is regarded as one of the finest collections of talent ever to capture the Cup.

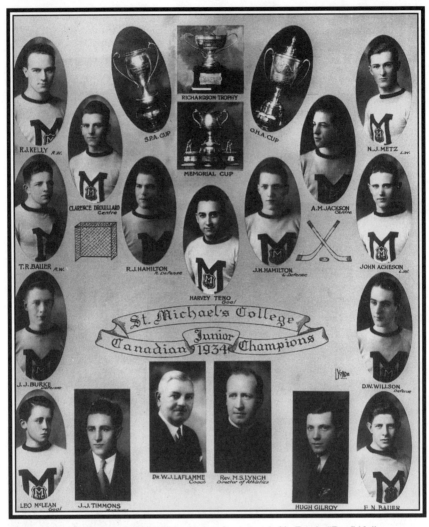

Toronto St. Michael's College (clockwise from top left): Regis "Pep" Kelly, Clarence Drouillard, John Hamilton, Harvey Teno, John Hamilton, Art Jackson, Nick Metz, John Acheson, Don Willson, Frank Bauer, Hugh Gilroy (trainer), Rev. M.S. Lynch (director of athletics), Dr. W.J. LaFlamme (coach), J.J. Timmons (manager), Leo McLean, J.J. Burke, Bobby Bauer. HHF

NHL include Regis Kelly, who spent almost eight years with Toronto and Chicago, and Don Willson, who saw brief ice time with the Canadiens. Edmonton's Colville brothers, Neil and Matthew, played twelve and nine years respectively with the New York Rangers. They won the Stanley Cup together in 1940 with the New York Rangers.

The **1935** Memorial Cup

The 1935 final was a rematch of the 1932 series between the Sudbury Cub Wolves and the Winnipeg Monarchs. This time, the best-of-three final in Shea's Amphitheatre featured some of the strangest moments ever in Memorial Cup competition. Sudbury wasn't favoured to come out of the east, but surprised the pundits by defeating the favoured Ottawa Rideaus. Meanwhile, the Monarchs eked out a victory over the Saskatoon Wesleys to take the west. Winnipeg's roster featured the "Flying Frenchmen" line of Pete Belanger, Romeo Martel and Paul Rheault.

The Memorial Cup final opened on April 9 before more than 4,500 hockey fans. "Thirteen times the red light flashed on as the high-scoring band of youngsters travelled at full clip and sought goals and still more goals," wrote Herbert A. Honey of the Canadian Press. Game one belonged to the Monarchs, who posted a 7–6 victory. But two nights later the Wolves reversed their fortune with a 7–2 victory. The game, however, wasn't as one-sided as it appears in cold print. Winnipeg went on an undisciplined penalty spree in the final two minutes and gave up 3 powerplay goals as a result.

One by one, four Winnipeg players were sent off the ice, there being no limit to the number of players that a team could be shorthanded at one time.

The Winnipeg Monarchs' behind-the-scenes squad included (l-r) Bert Pelletier, trainer; Bill Webber, manager; Harry Neil, coach; Pat Quinn, president and Sid Chulu, secretary. MA/N3900

Incredibly, in the final fifteen seconds, Winnipeg had only two men on the ice, netminder Paul Gauthier and defenceman Ken Barker. Barker had returned from the box just as the Monarchs' mild-mannered captain and centreman Pete Belanger—frustrated by the penalty-killing nightmare left in his hands—was penalized for cracking Don Grosso over the head after the Wolves' player scored. Had Barker not been set to return, the Winnipeg goaltender would have been left on the ice all by himself.

"Monarch fans were dissatisfied with referees Alex Irvin of Winnipeg and Hap Shouldice of Ottawa," the Canadian Press understated. "They showed their displeasure at frequent minor penalties meted out to the Manitobans by showering peanuts and programs onto the ice. Play was halted several times in order to clear the ice." After the game, Monarchs coach Harry Neil wouldn't stand for any criticism of Shouldice in the Winnipeg dressing room. "He's a square referee who calls 'em as he sees 'em," Neil said.

Shouldice, who went on to a career as a Canadian Football League official, and Irvin were still the referees for game three, played on April 13. It was a close-checking contest in which Winnipeg players regained their composure. Another oddity took place during this game. In the midst of a flourish around the Sudbury net, the timekeeper in the Amphitheatre began ringing his bell, signifying the end of the first period. Neither of the officials heard the bell, and play continued, whereupon Monarchs defenceman Ken Barker scored. Though time had elapsed on the Amphitheatre clock, the goal was allowed since a period was technically not over until an official blew the play dead. Hence, the goal was listed as having been scored at 20:01 of the first period. Winnipeg scored three more times to the Wolves' once and took the deciding game 4–1.

"The mantle of Dominion junior hockey supremacy today was draped around the slim shoulders of Winnipeg Monarchs," Honey wrote. "Neil's brigade,

Winnipeg Monarchs. The caption with this archival photograph reads (l to r): "Paul Gauthier, Pete Belanger, Paul Rheault, Johnny Prokaski, Fred White, Burr Keenan, Jack Boyd, Wilf Field, Romeo Martel, Joe Krol, Ken Barker, Pat Quinn (president), Sid Chulu (secretary), Harry Neil (coach), W. Webber (manager), Bert Pelletier (trainer)."

with the artistry of master swordsmen, parried a slower but more rugged eastern offensive with spectacular netminding and lightning raids to bring Canadian supremacy to the west."

Sudbury's lineup featured defenceman Charles "Chuck" Shannon, who would play briefly with the New York Americans in the NHL. Forward Wilbert Carl "Dutch" Hiller played nine years in the NHL, winning Stanley Cups with the New York Rangers in 1940 and the Montreal Canadiens in 1946. Don "The Count" Grosso's eight-year pro career included a Stanley Cup with the 1943 Detroit Red Wings. Winnipeg's roster included Wilf Field, who skated five years with the Montreal Canadiens, Chicago Blackhawks, New York Americans and Brooklyn Americans, and Joseph "Marty" Krol, who enjoyed a short career with the Brooklyn Americans and New York Rangers.

The **1936** Memorial Cup

Harold Ballard made one of the first of his many marks on the Toronto hockey scene in 1936, when he managed the West Toronto Nationals to a Memorial Cup championship against the Saskatoon Wesleys. By the 1936 season, Ballard had brought in Clarence "Hap" Day as his coach. Day, a member of the first Maple Leaf team to win the Stanley Cup in 1932, was an active rearguard on the Maple Leafs' roster while coaching the Nationals. Whenever Day was unavailable to coach, the infamous Ballard ran the bench himself.

The Nationals, who hadn't lost a regular season game since February, defeated the Oshawa Red Devils and the Kitchener-Waterloo Unionjacks to seize the OHA title. Coach Hobb Wilson's Wesleys, meanwhile, defeated the Elmwood Maple Leafs in Winnipeg to emerge as the western standard bearers. The best-of-three Memorial Cup series opened at Maple Leaf Gardens on April 10. "It was one of the greatest junior battles here in Toronto in several years," stated the Canadian Press. "Both clubs backchecked fiercely but the eastern titlists' play showed more finish when they barged past the heavy Wesley rearguards. The Saskatchewan huskies seemed to find difficulty in controlling the puck." The Nationals skated to a 5–1

John "Bucky" Crawford, pictured wearing an early hockey helmet, played defence for the 1936 Memorial Cup champion West Toronto Nationals.

victory over Saskatoon in game one.

The series ended three nights later. Wesleys centre Frank Dotten got his side on the board first with the opening period's lone goal. Defenceman John "Bucky" Crawford tied it for Toronto, and the teams headed for the third tied at 1–1. In the extra frame, Bob Laurent and rightwinger Johnny "Peanuts" O'Flaherty put Toronto out front 3–1 before Dotten narrowed the deficit to 1. It remained for National Roy Conacher to score the final goal of the series. "Fighting fiercely all the way, Wesleys outplayed the Nationals through most of the hard-fought struggle and a crowd of 3,500—disappointingly small for a Dominion final—will not soon forget the western huskies' dazzling attack," the Canadian Press reported. West Toronto posted a 4–2 victory, sweeping the series and winning its first Memorial Cup.

Harold Ballard was not the only notable to be involved in the 1936 tournament. Toronto's lineup included the nineteen-year-old Conacher twins, Roy and Bert, brothers of NHL stars Charlie and Lionel. Roy Conacher played eleven years in the NHL with Boston , Detroit and Chicago, winning the Stanley Cup with the Bruins in 1939 and 1941. His teammate for both victories was Bucky Crawford, who spent thirteen years with Boston. Crawford was the first player in the big league to wear a helmet, when he donned some primitive headgear to protect his bald head. Other Nationals to move on to the NHL include Robert "Red" Heron, who spent four years with the Maple Leafs, Canadiens and New York Americans. Bill Jennings split five seasons between Detroit and Boston, while Johnny "Peanuts" O'Flaherty played a handful of games with the Americans of New York and Brooklyn. Hap Day went on to coach the Maple Leafs to five Stanley Cups in 1942, 1945, and 1947–49. He was inducted into the Hall of Fame in 1961. One of the two referees in the series was Clarence Campbell, who would serve as President of the NHL from 1946 to 1977.

West Toronto Nationals. Back row (l to r): Jack Sinclair, Carl Gamble, Ted Robertson, F. Murray, Johnny Crawford, Reg Langford, Bert Conacher, D. Fritz, H. Newland (trainer), Roy Conacher, Red Heron, Alf Johnson. Front row: Bill Thompson, Bill Jennings, Johnny O'Flaherty, W. Kerr, Dr. H. MacIntyre, Harold Ballard (manager), G. Shill, Bob Laurent, Fred Hall.

The **1937** Memorial Cup

Winnipeg hockey fans never had to wait long for something to cheer about in the early days of the Memorial Cup. Represented at various times by teams such as the Monarchs, Falcons and Elmwood Millionaires, the city contended often for the junior title. Two years after they won the title in 1935, the Winnipeg Monarchs were hoping to claim another as they faced the Copper Cliff Redmen in a best-of-five series at Maple Leaf Gardens.

"I don't know much about the eastern junior teams," said Winnipeg coach Harry Neil, whose club entered the final with an overall record of 25–5–3, "but I believe we have a good chance." Neil's remarks may have been slightly offhand. Although the Copper Cliff Redmen—formerly the Newmarket Redmen—had just been organized late in the summer of 1936, coach Max Silverman was able to obtain some excellent hockey talent, and his team established an authoritative presence as it marched through the 1937 eastern playoffs. The team from Copper Cliff—a mining community near Sudbury—defeated Timmins to become Northern Ontario champions before accomplishing a pair of upset victories against highly regarded St. Michael's College from Toronto. They then made short work of the Montreal Victorias before demolishing the Ottawa Rideaus 12–3 and 12–1 to claim the George Richardson Trophy. In the eastern playoffs, the Redmen had outscored their opponents 67–19.

Team captain Alf Pike scored the Memorial Cup-winning goal for the Winnipeg Monarchs.

Winnipeg coach Neil thought his first line of captain and centre Alf Pike, leftwinger Dick Kowcinak and rightwinger Johnny McCreedy—men who had played together since they were fourteen years old—gave the Monarchs an attack potent enough to counter the speedy Copper Cliff trio of rightwinger Roy Heximer, left-winger Robert "Red" Hamill and centre Pat McReavy. The teams faced off on April 10 for what promised to be an exciting final. Fans were not disappointed. Pike, McCreedy and Kowcinak took the initiative for much of game one,

Winnipeg Monarchs. Back row (l to r): W. Webber (manager), Jack Atcheson, Jack Fox, Bert Pelletier (trainer), Dick Kowcinak, Ted Dent, Remi Vanaele, Harry Neil (coach). Front row: Lucien Martel, Denny Robinson, Ami Clement, Alf Pike, Zenon Ferley, Pete Langelle, John McCreedy, Paul Rheault. On floor in front: Bob Somers (mascot). MA/N3909

with McCreedy scoring twice and Pike once to open a seemingly solid 3–0 lead. Many Copper Cliff fans began heading for the exits.

But the Redmen mounted a late-game comeback that was nothing less than spectacular. It began with Heximer scoring at 17:39 of the third. One minute later, Copper Cliff was awarded a penalty shot by referees Clarence Campbell and Cecil "Babe" Dye, who also sent Pike to the penalty box for tripping Roy Heximer in the goalmouth. Heximer got his revenge by scoring at 18:30 and, with Pike still in the penalty box, completing an astonishing hat trick by putting away the tying goal at 19:16. The game winner came barely five minutes into overtime, when Redman winger Red Hamill stole the puck while his team was shorthanded and led one of the most remarkable comebacks in Memorial Cup history.

The Monarchs evened the series in game two, squeezing out a 6–5 victory before more than 8,000 fans. The seesaw struggle was decided only after two periods of overtime. The third game was another tight affair, with the Monarchs hanging on for a 2–1 victory. Determined to tie the game, the Copper Cliff forwards managed to hit the post four times, but their luck seemed to be spent. The Memorial Cup final was decided on the afternoon of April 17, before 11,455 fans at Maple Leaf Gardens. "Climaxing one of the most spectacular junior series in history," said the Canadian Press, "the Winnipeggers whitewashed Copper Cliff Redmen 7–0." Copper Cliff had a distinct edge in play in the first period, but were unable to score. When the Monarchs erupted for 3 goals in the second, the proverbial writing was on the wall. "We were beaten by a better team," Coach

Silverman admitted afterwards. "I can speak now and I can say that these Monarchs are just about the best junior team I've seen."

Three players from the 1937 Winnipeg club—Alf Pike, Pete Langelle and Johnny McCreedy—joined Stanley Cup-winning teams. Pike played six years with the Rangers, winning the championship in 1940. He also coached the Rangers in 1960 and 1961. Langelle and McCreedy spent four and two years respectively in Toronto. They both won Stanley Cups with the Leafs, Langelle in 1942 and McCreedy in 1942 and 1945. Red Hamill and Pat McReavy of the Redmen played for the Boston Bruins and won the Stanley Cup, Hamill in 1939 and McReavy in 1941. Despite having won his name on the Stanley Cup, McReavy never played a regular season game in the NHL, while Hamill played twelve years for Boston and Chicago.

The 1938 Memorial Cup

The Oshawa Generals and St. Boniface Seals were still young organizations when they met in the 1938 Memorial Cup final. A four-to-one favourite, Oshawa had a lethal weapon in Billy "The Kid" Taylor, a young sniper who would make two consecutive standout showings in the tournament. The Seals, who had not been expected to move out of Manitoba, stole the western title by upsetting the Winnipeg Monarchs. "We were very much the underdogs," the Seals' Wally Stanowski recalled some years later. "The depression was still on and we had holes in our sweaters and socks and poor equipment, and Oshawa was all spic and span."

The Memorial Cup final, a best-of-five series at Maple Leaf Gardens, opened on April 9 in front of 9,500 fans. The beginning of game one was delayed when St. Boniface protested the length of Oshawa's sticks. One to two inches were sawed off half a dozen sticks before the game proceeded. Despite this indignity, the Generals prevailed 3–2. "It was the east's victory but the west drew the hosannas," said the Canadian Press. Even in a losing cause, defenceman Wally Stanowski was drawing

"We were very much the underdogs," said Wally Stanowski of the St. Boniface Seals, 1938 Memorial Cup champions.

comparisons to NHL great Eddie Shore. Canadian Press described the Seals' player as "a demon speedster, whose ghost-like rushing left the fans gasping." Billy Taylor was involved in all of Oshawa's goals, scoring once and setting up his team's other two tallies.

In game two, St. Boniface goaltender Doug Webb, a first-year junior player, blanked the Generals 4–0 before 10,413 fans. The pundits who had picked the Generals as heavy favourites were beginning to doubt themselves. "Those who install the Seals as favourites for teen-age puck honours aren't basing their predictions on the score of last night's tussle," Ed Fitkin wrote in the Toronto *Globe and Mail*, "but by the decisive manner in which the western champion outplayed the Generals over most of the route. They're not a great team. They're not in the same hockey society as the Winnipeg Monarchs because of their lack of smoothness. But they are a great hockey machine."

The Generals evidently didn't read the Toronto papers. They won the third game 4–2. "Main reason for Seals downfall was an eagle-eyed, nimble-footed goalie, Bob Forster," Canadian Press reported. "Forty-three shots were fired at him in the Oshawa net and only twice was he beaten." In game four, the Generals outplayed the Seals for fifty minutes and held a 3–1 lead more than twelve minutes into the third period. But 5 goals in the last half of the third propelled St. Boniface to a 6–4 victory, forcing a fifth game.

"As unpredictable as any cock fight, the series to date had supplied a full quota of thrills to the record crowds attending the games," reported Canadian Press prior to the deciding game on April 19. The Seals put the series away with a flourish, winning 7–1 before 15,617 fans. At the time, it was the largest crowd ever to witness a hockey game—junior or professional—in Canada. Ralph Allen of the

St. Boniface Seals. Back row (l to r): G. Schettler (secretary), J. Crawford (vice president), Ed Haverstock (trainer), Gil Paulley (manager), Peter "Patch" Couture, Bert Janke, Jack Messett, Wally Stanowski, Fred Barker (president), C. Murchison (vice president), M. Kryschuk (coach), Doc Roy, F. Yedon (trainer). Front row: F. Nicol, Hermie Gruhn, Herb Burron, G. Gordon, Billy Reay, Bill McGregor, J. Simpson, Doug Webb. On floor in front: C. Murchison, Jr. (mascot). MA/N9096

Winnipeg Tribune wrote that "you would have to thumb the pages of Webster's dictionary from A to Z to dig up enough adjectives to describe the sensationalism provided as the Seals won the all-Canada final." Hockey fans agreed. The average attendance per game for the series was 11,278, another record. The Seals returned to Winnipeg's CNR Union Railway Station to find a wild festive jamboree awaiting them, as fans with plastic seals paraded around the railway property.

Billy Taylor, who had figured in 11 of Oshawa's 12 goals, and Wally Stanowski would be teammates in the NHL. They played on the Stanley Cup-winning Toronto Maple Leafs in 1942. Stanowski won the Stanley Cup three more times with Toronto in 1945, 1947 and 1948 before being traded to the New York Rangers, where he capped off a ten-year NHL career. The Seals' Billy Reay played most of his eight-year career in Montreal, where he helped the Canadiens win the Cup in 1946 and 1953. He later coached more than one thousand games in the NHL with the Chicago Blackhawks and Toronto Maple Leafs.

The **1939** Memorial Cup

The Oshawa Generals were a new but already dominant franchise in the late 1930s and early 1940s. Over the years, they would prove to be one of Canadian hockey's most enduring junior teams, giving fans their first glimpses at players like Bobby Orr and Eric Lindros. The 1939 best-of-five Memorial Cup final pitted Oshawa, led by Billy "The Kid" Taylor, against the Edmonton Athletic Club Roamers. Taylor entered the series as the OHA regular season scoring champion with 22 goals and 31 assists in only fourteen games.

The Memorial Cup final opened in Maple Leaf Gardens on April 10. More than 7,000 fans watched Taylor score five times in a 9–4 Oshawa victory. Afterwards, the Roamers complained that they were having problems adjusting to the atmospheric conditions inside the Gardens. "I could hardly breathe after I had been on the ice a minute or so," said fatigued Roamer George Agar. "Whew it was hot." The Canadian Press joked that "the Roamers will discard their underwear and change goalies in an effort to even the series. The westerners, used to a dry climate, wilted in the heavy-moist Toronto air."

Game two, played on April 12, also belonged to Taylor. This time, the "Blond Bomber"—Taylor had no shortage of nicknames—scored 4 goals and set up 5 others. The Generals won 12–4. A newspaper called the game "one of the greatest scoring orgies ever witnessed in championship hockey." Responding to a reporter's query, Taylor quipped, "No sir, they weren't any tougher than in the first game. Better tell them to send back to Edmonton for another goalkeeper."

The cocky shooter was drawing enormous attention. Sportswriter Elmer Dulmage profiled Taylor during the tournament for Canadian Press. "Billy the Kid, 19 years old and marked for delivery to the Toronto Maple Leafs has the Edmonton Roamers and the paying clientele by the ears," Dulmage wrote. "The Roamers can't stop him and the fans can't get over him. He's so amazingly good that Dick Irvin, Bill Cowley, Shore, Art Ross, Conn Smythe, Lester Patrick and the likes of these Stanley Cup characters refuse to believe what they see. Billy has the National Hockey League nobility rubbing its eyes." Patrick, the general manager of the New York Rangers, called Taylor "the greatest junior I have seen in twenty years. The way Taylor passes is incredible. I will venture to say that there aren't more than half a dozen centres in the National Hockey League who lay down passes as well as he does. Taylor does everything else well. He should have a great career."

But Edmonton was not ready to throw in the towel. The team stubbornly jumped back into the series with a 4–1 victory in game three, with 11,698 fans in attendance. Centre Elmer

Oshawa's Billy "The Kid" Taylor racked up 9 goals and 4 assists in the four-game Memorial Cup victory over Edmonton.

Kreller was assigned to shadow Billy the Kid. "Outstanding in the victory was Kreller, a chunky speedster who handcuffed Taylor," the press reported. "Taylor, in disgust, sometimes would stay back at his own goal and Kreller would stay right with him as the play surged around the Edmonton goal." The tenacious Roamer offered, "I was never so happy in all my life. I don't think I ever worked so hard before. All I thought of was Taylor. I didn't even think of the puck. I didn't care whether I scored. But I was determined to keep Taylor from scoring. At times he was going to bite off my head but I didn't care." Taylor took the extra attention in stride. He said, "I told Kreller in the first period that I was going out for a drink and I asked him to come along and hold the glass. We'll take them the next game. We'll get that first goal and they'll never catch us."

The Roamers tried the same defensive tactic in the fourth game and got early results. They entered the third period leading 2–1 but, in their efforts to hold Taylor, other Oshawa players managed to break away. The Generals scored three times in the third, and Oshawa claimed the Memorial Cup with a 4–2 victory. Taylor was held to 1 assist. "Who said we were a one-man hockey team?" asked Oshawa goaltender Dinny McManus. Billy "The Kid" Taylor finished the series with 9 goals and 6 assists in 4 games. He praised Elmer Kreller, calling him "a honey of a checker, a darn nice guy and a clean player—you can't take anything away from him." Some 15,000 Generals fans sang, danced and built bonfires in the streets of Oshawa. It was the biggest celebration the city had seen since the end of World War One.

After starring performances in two straight Memorial Cup finals, Taylor embarked on a solid but disappointing NHL career. He played for Toronto,

Oshawa Generals. Back row (l to r): Sam Johnson (trainer), Matt Leyden (manager), Tracy Shaw (coach), C.E. McTavish (vice president), Neil Hezzelwood (secretary), S.E. McTavish (treasurer), W. Pearson (executive). Middle row: Joe Delmonte, Don Daniels, Jim Drummond, George Ritchie, Gerry Kinsella, Nick Knott, Orville Smith, Jud McAtee. Front row: Dinny McManus, Norm McAtee, Billy Taylor, J.B. Highfield (president), Roy Sawyer, Gar Peters, Les Colvin. On ground in front: Harry Tresise (stick boy).

Detroit, Boston and the New York Rangers, accumulating 87 goals and 180 assists in 323 games over seven seasons. He was one of the league's top scorers for a few seasons, but he never lived up to the early expectations. The highlight of Taylor's career was a Stanley Cup with the Maple Leafs in 1942, and the low point was definitely March 9, 1948. NHL President Clarence Campbell suspended the Memorial Cup hero for life, along with Bruins teammate Don Gallinger, for betting on NHL games. Campbell's explanation was terse: the pair were hit with life suspensions "for conduct detrimental to hockey and for associating with a known gambler." Billy Taylor never played again.

He remained a hockey outcast until August 27, 1970, when President Campbell and the NHL's Board of Governors reinstated him and Gallinger. Taylor dabbled in coaching, and did some scouting for the Philadelphia Flyers, Washington Capitals and Pittsburgh Penguins. He died in 1990 at the age of seventy-one.

The Generals' William "Nick" Knott played a year with the Brooklyn Americans, and brothers Norm and Jud McAtee skated briefly with the Boston Bruins and Detroit Red Wings, respectively. From the Edmonton roster, John McGill played four years with the Boston Bruins, and Ken "Beans" Reardon won the Stanley Cup in 1946 with the Montreal Canadiens, where he played seven years.

The
1940s

The Memorial Cup finals of the 1940s clearly reflected the decade to which they belonged. It was a pivotal time for the tournament, and for hockey in general. The junior championships continued to attract record crowds, even during the war years, and teams from Quebec and British Columbia were involved for the first time. In 1943, a best-of-seven-games format was adopted, and some tough and intense playoff series ensued. In a real sense, the best-of-fives that went eight games complemented an unsettled social era.

For the first half of the decade, the Memorial Cup series was held almost exclusively in Maple Leaf Gardens. But fans in towns like Moose Jaw, Brandon and Regina, the centres of regions that supplied many great junior prospects, had glimpses of their boys in championship action as the 1940s wore on.

The NHL meanwhile had settled into the two-decades-long Original Six era. Junior competitors like Ted Lindsay, "Red" Kelly and Dickie Moore were stepping right into hockey's golden era. Many would go on not to the NHL but to war. In the early 1940s, many young players died for their country, their early promise and hopes for the future unfulfilled.

Cal Gardner led the Winnipeg Rangers to Memorial Cup victory in 1943.

The **1940** Memorial Cup

The Oshawa Generals started the 1940s the same way they ended the 1930s, competing for the Memorial Cup. This time, the final was an all-Ontario affair against the Kenora Thistles. If they won, the Generals would become the first team ever to win back-to-back championships.

The feisty Kenorans, picked by few to get anywhere in the junior title chase, won the Manitoba Amateur Hockey Association junior south division title. They advanced to face a succession of powerhouses—the Winnipeg Monarchs, the Brandon Elks, the Elmwood Millionaires and the Port Arthur Juniors—and emerged as surprise Manitoba champions. Because of their proximity to Manitoba, western Ontario teams such as Kenora and Port Arthur played in the MAHA and were therefore considered as "western."

The Thistles played the Edmonton Athletic Club in an oddball best-of-five western final starting in Edmonton and finishing in Winnipeg. Two of the games ended in ties with no decisions reached in the limited overtime periods. Game two, won 7–1 by Edmonton, featured three penalty shots and three separate brawls, the biggest of which drew ten Edmonton policemen onto the ice. Kenora recorded the rare feat of taking a best-of-five series with two wins when they snatched a pair of victories on their adopted "home" ice at the Winnipeg Amphitheatre.

The Thistles stayed in Winnipeg to await the Generals for the Memorial Cup final.

Oshawa returned to the tournament for the third consecutive season, having disposed of the Verdun Maple Leafs in the eastern final.

The 1940 Generals, coached by Tracy "The Fox" Shaw, displayed power and class in every department. They iced a team featuring a solid core of returning players, including goaltender Dinny McManus, Don Daniels, Nick Knott, Gar Peters, Orville Smith, George Ritchie and brothers Norm and Jud McAtee, team captain and winner of the OHA scoring championship that year. Shaw betrayed no lack of confidence in his team. "Kenora seems

Charlie Rayner

As goaltender and team captain, Claude Rayner was the backbone of the 1940 Memorial Cup finalist Kenora Thistles.

to have plenty of speed and a fairly strong defence but our polish and finish around the net will finish them," he predicted. The well-balanced Thistles were coached by Bobby Benson, an Olympic gold medal winner with the Winnipeg Falcons in 1920, and led by netminding captain Claude Rayner and Bill "The Beast" Juzda, a defenceman considered to be one of the toughest bodycheckers in the game.

The championship series opened in the Winnipeg Amphitheatre, with Oshawa posting a hard-fought 1–0 victory behind McManus' goaltending. "Play was rough in the early minutes," reported the *Regina Leader-Post*. "Hard play between the two teams came to a head late in the first session when Juzda, trying to bodycheck Jud McAtee of Oshawa, sent him flying into the boards. The pair rose with their fists flying and a brief free-for-all broke out. Six Winnipeg policemen rushed onto the ice as the trouble started. Only the twelve players on the ice were involved."

R. H. "Shorty" Elliott, Kenora's manager, wasn't concerned with the loss, reminding the press that his team had come back after being hammered 7–1 by Edmonton in game two of the western Abbott Cup final. "If we can come back from a licking like that, we're not worrying about our 1-goal defeat tonight," he said. "We'll go home with the Memorial Trophy yet."

But Oshawa went up 2–0 in the series with a 4–1 victory in the second game. The Thistles matched the Generals in speed and stickhandling ability, but the Generals were smoother on the attack and showed more finish around the goal. In game three, the Thistles showed signs of finally hitting their stride, as they hung on for a 4–3 win. Forty-five hundred fans watched Oshawa's series lead cut to 2–1.

"The boys played their best hockey in years, even if they did seem a little shaky near the end," said Coach Benson, "and if we can take this next one we'll be home free." But the Thistles' dream ended in the fourth meeting, when Oshawa posted a 4–2 victory before fewer than 3,000 fans.

When it was over, the teams mixed and mingled in the Kenora dressing room in a remarkable display of sportsmanship. "The Thistles hardly had time to unlace their skates before the Generals rushed in to laud the fighting spirit of the Kenora boys," reported Hugh C. Chatterton in the *Kenora Daily Miner and News*. "The cry of 'three cheers' rang out for each individual player and when the turn came for Juzda, the hardy Thistles blueliner, the Oshawans, many of them bearing bruises from Bill's jolting bodychecks, discarded words and hoisted the 185-pound defenceman off his feet."

This impressive second straight championship for the Generals ended on a somewhat ignominious note. The newly crowned junior champions journeyed from Winnipeg to Regina a few days later to play an exhibition game against the Regina Abbott-Generals. Some 1,500 spectators gathered in the Queen City Gardens to witness Regina hammer the young Oshawa dynasty 12–6.

Dave Dryburgh of the *Regina Leader-Post* noted the folly of such late-season exhibitions. As he pointed out, Regina had "everything to gain and nothing to lose."

Nonetheless, the Generals' accomplishment of back-to-back championships was a sign of things to come. Over the next half-decade, the Oshawa team would

Oshawa Generals. Back row (l to r): Harry Tresise (stick boy), Sam Johnson (trainer), Matt Leyden (manager), Tracy Shaw (coach), Neil Hezzelwood (secretary), C.E. McTavish (vice-president), S.E. McTavish (treasurer), T.H. Coppin (executive). Middle row: Don Daniels, Ron Wilson, Jack Hewson, Orville Smith, George Ritchie, Nick Knott, Wally Wilson, Gar Peters, Bud Hellyer. Front row: Dinny McManus, Jud McAtee, Roy Sawyer, J.B. Highfield (president), Norm McAtee, Frank Eddolls, Doug Turner. On ground in front: Buddy Taylor (mascot).

figure prominently at the highest levels of junior competition.

The Generals would also go on to send many players to the NHL. From the 1940 team, several players made short-lived appearances in the big league: Nick Knott with Brooklyn, Jud McAtee with Detroit, Norm McAtee with Boston, and Wally Wilson with Boston. Defenceman Frank Eddolls enjoyed the most success, spending eight years with the Canadiens and Rangers. From the Thistles, Bill Juzda played nine years for the New York Rangers and Toronto Maple Leafs, winning the Stanley Cup with the Leafs in 1949 and 1951. Thistles leftwinger Doug Lewis played briefly for the Montreal Canadiens.

The **1941** Memorial Cup

1941 marked the first time in four years that the Oshawa Generals did not figure in the Memorial Cup final. They came close, but a roadblock in the form of the Montreal Royals barred their way. The Royals were the first-ever team from Quebec to play in a national junior championship.

Coached by Lorne White and led by centre Ken Mosdell and netminder Ross Ritchie, the Royals defeated Oshawa 3–1 in a best-of-five eastern final, despite the absence of four players who were writing exams at McGill University. The west was represented by the Winnipeg Rangers, coached by former NHLer Lawrence "Baldy" Northcott.

The Rangers emerged victorious after a tough western final against the powerful Saskatoon Quakers, whose roster was a virtual checklist of future NHL stars.

The Quakers had a standout in Keith Allen, a Stanley Cup winner with the Detroit Red Wings before managing the Philadelphia Flyers to a pair of NHL titles in 1974 and 1975. Also prominent were Tony Leswick, who played on three Stanley Cup-winning Red Wing teams, future Hall of Famer Harry Watson, who won the Stanley Cup five times with Detroit and Toronto, and Hal Laycoe, a defenceman who spent eleven seasons in the NHL before becoming the first coach of the Vancouver Canucks in 1970. The western final in the Winnipeg Amphitheatre went seven games, with the Rangers—led by the line of Sam Fabro, Bill Robinson and Les Hickey—prevailing.

The best-of-five Memorial Cup final opened at Maple Leaf Gardens on April 21. The Royals were without three regulars, still writing exams. A thirty-six-hour train ride brought the Rangers to Toronto just twelve hours before game time. But Winnipeg showed few ill effects from their journey, winning the opener 4–2.

Still, the Rangers knew they were in for a fight. "They're unlike anything we've met so far," Winnipeg centre Bill Robinson said after game one. "We're in for a tough series. We have never been bumped around quite so much."

The scene shifted to Montreal for game two, where the reconstituted Royals earned Quebec's first victory in a Memorial Cup final series 5–3. "The Royals, bolstered by the return of three players who missed the first game, were much stronger than the club which bowed 4–2 in the initial meeting," Canadian Press reported.

But the Rangers regained the series lead with a 6–4 victory before almost 9,000 fans at Maple Leaf Gardens. Spare leftwinger Louis Medynski, considered out for the season when he suffered a severe facial cut during a practice in the western final, was the hero of the night. He broke a 4–4 tie with a goal at 18:36 of the third.

Not done yet, the Royals came back to tie the series in game four in Montreal, posting a dramatic 4–3 victory on two last-minute powerplay goals.

The nail-biting series went back to Toronto for a fifth and deciding game. Maple Leaf Gardens had been a comfortable home away from home for the Rangers so far, both of their wins having taken place there. The Gardens ice proved lucky for a third time, as the Winnipeg club won 7–4 to claim the Memorial Cup.

"The Rangers gained their triumph on the great offensive play of Robinson, centre on their first line, and one of his linemates, Les Hickey," according to Canadian Press. "Although they couldn't have won without the work of the Robinson-Hickey combination, it was just as true that Royals would have won had it not been for the spectacular goaltending throughout of Thompson of the Rangers."

Winnipeg Rangers (l to r): Lawrence Northcott (coach), Joe Peters, Hugh Millar, Glen Harmon, Bernie Bathgate, Bill Heindl, Sammy Fabro, Les Hickey, Bob Ballance, Hubert Macey, Manning "Babe" Hobday, Lou Medynski, Earl Fast, Doug Baldwin, Bill Mortimer, Alan Hay, Bill Robinson, Hal Thompson. MA/N3907

Winnipeg coach Northcott agreed. "We had eighteen good men to start with," he stated, "and we were able to throw in replacements at any time without weakening our team. Our defencemen were better because they could score. On the whole, however, the balance of power rested in goaltending."

The Royals' Ken Mosdell won four Stanley Cups with the Montreal Canadiens during a sixteen-year NHL career. Among the top Rangers players, Hugh Millar skated briefly with the Detroit Red Wings in 1947, while Doug Baldwin served stints for Toronto, Chicago and Detroit. Glen Harmon played nine years for the Montreal Canadiens, winning Stanley Cups in 1944 and 1946. Hubbert "Hub" Macey also skated briefly with the Montreal Canadiens and the New York Rangers. Winnipeg's Manning "Babe" Hobday proceeded not to the NHL but into the Canadian army. Tragically, he lost his life serving with an armoured unit in Normandy. Many junior hockey players coming of age in the early 1940s would meet the same fate.

The **1942** Memorial Cup

Thirteen years after winning the Memorial Cup as a player, Charlie Conacher was in the hunt for the trophy again as co-coach of the Oshawa Generals. The team was back in the Memorial Cup final for the fourth time in five years. Conacher served with manager Matt Leyden, who took over behind the bench after regular

Generals coach Tracy Shaw was suspended indefinitely by the CAHA after being involved in an altercation with a referee.

The formidable Generals, led by veterans Albert "Red" Tilson, Ron Wilson, Ron Nelson and Floyd Curry, swept the Montreal Royals in the best-of-seven eastern final en route to the national championship. While Memorial Cup play was nothing new to the team from Oshawa, it was to their opponent.

The Portage La Prairie Terriers, under coach Addie Bell and manager Jack P. Bend, had emerged as the Ollie Turnbull champions of Manitoba before clinching the west. The Terriers, based in a small town 77 kilometres west of Winnipeg, depended largely on homegrown talent. Half the team were local boys.

In fact, the nucleus was a family affair, with Coach Bell's two sons, goaltender Gordon and leftwinger Joe, both establishing themselves as NHL prospects. Manager Bend's son John was an alternate captain and the holder of an MJHL scoring record.

The Terriers marched into Memorial Cup battle with twenty-two straight victories under their belt, eleven in the playoffs. They started the best-of-five final against Oshawa without Joe Bell, who had a bladder infection. "I think we will win the series and I think it will go only four games," predicted the Generals' veteran rightwinger Ron Wilson.

But Portage La Prairie surprised many of the 5,000 fans in attendance at the Winnipeg Amphitheatre with a 5–1 victory in game one. Although no one kept official track of the shots on goal, sixteen-year-old Gordon "Tinkle" Bell was credited with almost 50 saves in a brilliant performance. The game also featured a new innovation, as noted by the Canadian Press. "Under new Canadian Amateur Hockey Association rules, the ice was flooded in between periods," Canadian Press reported, "enabling the players to skate their fastest on a smooth sheet."

The Terriers skated past the Generals 8–7 in game two. Portage La Prairie launched a 3-goal attack in an eighty-eight-second span while Generals captain Bill Mortimer sat out on a penalty. Under 1942 rules, a player sat out the entire two minutes of a minor penalty, whether the opposition scored or not.

Now it was Terriers Coach Addie Bell's turn to exhibit hubris to the press. "We're going to finish the series in game three," he stated. "We'll have Joe back and that will give us our two regular forward lines. That will make plenty of difference."

The recovered Joe Bell did return to the lineup for the third game and scored twice, but the Terriers' winning streak ended at twenty-four games. The Generals posted an 8–4 victory before another capacity crowd. It was only the first time in thirty-two games that the Terriers had lost by more than 1 goal.

Canadian Press staff scribe Marshall Bateman wrote, "Facing elimination after losing the first two encounters, coach Charlie 'The Bomber' Conacher's eastern Richardson Trophy titlists outchecked, outskated and trimmed Terriers at their own game of a good offensive is better than cautious defensive action."

The day before game four, H.A. Jones of Winnipeg arrived at the Amphitheatre at 4:00 a.m. He wanted to be first in line for tickets to what could have been the deciding game. By the time the box office opened shortly after 9:00

Portage La Prairie Terriers. Top row (l to r): Bill Gooden, Wally Stefanew, Jack McDonald, Gordon Bell, Joe Bell, Lin Bend, Bobby Love. Second row: Jack P. Bend (manager), George Jones (president), Addie Bell (coach). Third row: Ed Calder (executive), Sam Green (executive), G.G. Grigg, Bert Wynne (vice president), Lindsay McDougall (trainer), Jim W. Cook (executive), James Hamilton (executive). Bottom row: Don Campbell, Jack O'Reilly, Bill Heindl, Bud Ritchie, Lloyd Smith, Bryan Bell (mascot). MA/N3913

a.m. on April 20, an estimated 4,000 people were waiting with cash in hand.

The next day, more than 5,000 fans witnessed the Terriers whip the Generals 8–2 to win the series. "A great hockey team won," Generals coach Conacher conceded. "They were really flying out there." Center Red Tilson added, "They were just too good for us and they deserved to win."

Portage La Prairie schools closed and business establishments declared a half-day holiday on April 22, as the town went deliriously mad with joy. The Mayor was among hundreds of people milling around the Grand Trunk Pacific Railway Station to welcome home their local heroes.

From the Portage La Prairie Terriers, Billy Gooden, Lin Bend, Jack McDonald, Joe Bell and goaltender Gordon Bell all spent less than two years with the New York Rangers. Rightwinger Don Campbell also had a short-lived career with the Chicago Blackhawks. From the Generals, Ken Smith played seven seasons for the Boston Bruins and Floyd Curry played ten seasons with the Montreal Canadiens, winning the Stanley Cup in 1953, 1956, 1957 and 1958.

The 1943 Memorial Cup

For the fifth time in six years, the Oshawa Generals reached the Memorial Cup championship series. This time, the Charlie Conacher-coached team found themselves up against the Winnipeg Rangers, who had won the 1941 championship.

The Rangers were coached by Bob Kinnear and featured a core of strong prospects led by captain Bill Boorman and centre Calvin "Red" Gardner. Ottawa relied on their flashy rightwinger Floyd "Busher" Curry and gritty but smooth centre "Red" Tilson, the OHA scoring leader of 1942–43.

The Generals dismantled the Montreal Junior Canadiens in straight games to advance out of the east, while the Rangers got past the Saskatoon Quakers to qualify for the junior final, played at Maple Leaf Gardens. For the first time, a best-of-seven format was introduced.

Conacher, a pioneer in the field of pre-series head games, refused to name his starting goaltender, an odd gambit in an era when virtually every team relied exclusively on one netminder. He also casually admitted that he didn't know much about the Rangers. "We don't need to scout them anyway," Conacher said. "They'll have to be pretty good to catch up to my kids, I think. Our formula will be speed and plenty of it."

Coach Kinnear's response was terse. "Regardless of all the reports we have heard about Oshawa's power," he said, "our boys are certain to make it a real series."

The Rangers put Kinnear's words into effect in the first game, prevailing 6–5 before 12,739 fans. "The fast-skating Winnipeg squad backchecked the eastern Canadian Richardson Trophy champions dizzy almost from bell to bell," the Canadian Press reported, "and cut loose with an all-out offensive in the second period of a thrill-packed game to score 4 goals which clinched the victory."

A chastened Conacher admitted his club had suffered from overconfidence going into game one. "They probably thought that all they had to do was go through the motions," he said, "particularly after they moved into a 2–0 lead in the first period."

Oshawa got back on track on April 19, whipping the Rangers 6–2 before 9,402 fans. After the game, Conacher echoed his earlier pronouncement. "Wait until we win in that Memorial Cup final game and then you'll hear some real shouting," he advised. The Generals did go up 2–1 on April 21, posting a 5–3 victory on the strength of a hat trick by Bill Ezinicki. "That was a real hockey game out there," Conacher said. "You couldn't have watched better hockey in a Stanley Cup final. I'm proud of the way my kids came through. But they've still got a tough fight on their hands. These Ranger boys don't quit—they fight until they're ready to drop."

Thirteen thousand eight hundred and sixty-eight spectators crowded Maple Leaf Gardens for game four. The freewheeling Rangers roared to a 7–4 victory, backstopped by strong goaltending by Doug "Stonewall" Jackson. "That's one of the hardest games I've ever played," Jackson said. "They've certainly got a good team, but we whipped them and we can do it enough times to win the series."

The tireless Rangers were smelling victory. They overpowered the Generals 7–3 in game five to take a 3–2 series lead. Winnipeg then seized the Memorial Cup with a 6–3 win in game six. The winning goal was scored by Joe Peterson, who broke a 3–3 tie in the third period despite playing with his wrist in a cast. 14,485 fans watched the game. Paid attendance for the six games was 73,867, an average of 12,311. This was a record for amateur hockey in Canada.

From the Oshawa Generals, Bill Ezinicki played with the Maple Leafs, Bruins and Rangers, winning the Stanley Cup three times with Toronto in 1947, 1948 and 1949. Floyd "Busher" Curry, who spent much of the Memorial Cup final on the injured list, played ten seasons in the NHL with the Montreal Canadiens. He won four Stanley Cups with the Habs. The team's most outstanding prospect, Red Tilson, enlisted in the Canadian army and was killed in Holland in October 1944. The Red Tilson Trophy, awarded to the outstanding player in the Ontario Hockey League, was established in his honour.

From the Rangers, Eddie Kullman spent six seasons on the New York Rangers' right wing while teammate Church Russell served three years in the Big Apple. Frank Mathers, who was kept out of the final by a broken ankle, and Tom Fowler both saw limited action in the NHL, Mathers in Toronto and Fowler in Chicago. Winnipeg's most prominent player, Calvin Gardner had a solid pro

Winnipeg Rangers. Seated on rail (l to r): Vern Smith (stick boy), Joe Peters, Frank Mathers, Ben Juzda, Jack Irvine, Bill Tindall, Stan Warecki, Ritchie McDonald, Bill Boorman, Spence Tatchell, Tommy Fowler, Cal Gardner, Jack Taggart, Bill Vickers, Joe Peterson, Church Russell, Eddie Kullman, Doug Jackson. Standing: Johnny Gross (trainer), Henry Borger (vice president), A.V. Chipman, (president), Lawrence Northcott (executive member), Bob Kinnear (coach). MA/N3908

career with the New York Rangers, Maple Leafs, Blackhawks and Bruins from 1946 to 1957. He won the Stanley Cup playing with Toronto in 1949 and 1951, and had three sons, Dave, Paul and Bill, who also played in the NHL. Ironically, Dave Gardner won the Red Tilson Trophy with the Toronto Marlboros in 1971. "I played against the guy in the 1943 Memorial Cup," Cal Gardner later recalled, "and almost thirty years later my son wins his trophy."

The **1944** Memorial Cup

"Oshawa by a mile."

So predicted Bob Kinnear, who had coached the Winnipeg Rangers to the 1943 Memorial Cup title. The Oshawa Generals had won the Ontario title for the seventh straight season and were heading into their sixth national final in seven years.

Arguably as good as any junior team to play in the final, the 1943–44 Generals were bolstered in their playoff run by some additions from Toronto's St. Michael's College. Gus Mortson, David Bauer and "Terrible" Ted Lindsay helped make the team an eastern all-star juggernaut. Facing off against Oshawa were the Trail Smoke Eaters, whose players were on average two years younger than the Generals. Trail was the first team from British Columbia to reach the Memorial Cup final.

Oshawa met some determined resistance from the Montreal Royals in the eastern final, but defeated them 3–1 in a best-of-five series. The Smoke Eaters, meanwhile, took a crazy road to the final. They dispatched the Port Arthur Navy in straight games after defeating the Regina Commandos in a bizarre best-of-five that went eight games. The first three games ended up being tossed out when Paul Mahara, a Trail player, was found to be ineligible. The CAHA ultimately suspended Mahara from organized hockey for three years for "twice falsifying baptismal papers." The Smoke Eaters then fell behind by two games before winning three in a row to advance.

The best-of-seven Memorial Cup final opened at Maple Leaf Gardens before 14,643 fans. The Generals took the first game in a 9–2 victory. "Oshawa Generals had too much power, speed and polish," the Canadian Press reported. "Smoke Eaters fought gamely, but appeared nervous and were unable to keep up with the Generals on their fast ganging attacks."

In the Oshawa dressing room, coach Charlie Conacher—never one to overestimate his opponents—reached the same conclusion as Bob Kinnear did. "I think we can take them in four straight," he said.

In game two, the Generals went up 2–0, thanks to a 5–2 victory before 7,474 fans. "It seems they're in on me all the time," said shell-shocked Trail goalkeeper Bev Bentley. "Their shots aren't so tough, but when everyone piles in front of the net I can't see the puck. Oh well, you can't stop them all. Really 5–2 wasn't bad."

Ted Lindsay

"Terrible" Ted Lindsay, star of the 1944 Memorial Cup-winning Oshawa Generals, went on to accumulate many points and penalty minutes playing for Detroit and Chicago in the NHL.

"You can tell the folks back home that we're not beaten yet," Trail coach Gerry Thompson said defiantly. "The Generals have a strong club, but we were in a tough spot against Regina when we had to win three straight and the kids came through," he told Canadian Press.

But the Generals were just warming up. They wheeled into high gear in game three, blitzing the Smoke Eaters 15–4 in front of 7,138 fans. The Generals, who had 67 shots on goal, held a slim 3–2 lead after one period but erupted for 9 second-period goals, including 4 in a seventy-second stretch.

To add to their troubles, the Smoke Eaters' lineup was decimated by injuries. The CAHA allowed the team to help themselves to a trio of players from St. Michael's Majors, turning the final game into something resembling a St. Mike's inter-squad match. Nevertheless, Oshawa swept the series with an 11–4 victory on April 24, and took the Memorial Cup. Oshawa thereby became the first team to win the junior championship three times. It was also the last Oshawa team to win the Memorial Cup until the era of Eric Lindros.

Trail Smoke Eaters alumni Bev Bentley, Roy Kelly, Frank Turik, Harvey Ross, John "Dick" Butler and Mark Marquess all had professional minor league careers, with Butler and Marquess enjoying brief NHL stints with Chicago and Boston respectively. While in Toronto, Turik was plucked from Trail by St. Michael's College, and he helped them to the 1945 Memorial Cup.

From the Oshawa Generals, Ken Smith played seven seasons with the Boston Bruins, while goalie Harvey Bennett also played with Boston in 1945. Bob Dawes skated with Toronto, where he won the Stanley Cup, as well as the Montreal Canadiens. Defenceman Bill Ezinicki spent nine seasons in the NHL, with the Maple Leafs, Bruins and New York Rangers, winning the Stanley Cup three times with the Leafs.

Oshawa Generals. Back row (l to r): Sam Johnson (trainer), Matt Leyden (manager), Neil Hezzelwood (secretary), S.E. McTavish (treasurer), Charlie Conacher (coach), T.H. Coppin (executive). Middle row: Fred Petsura, Johnny Marois, Dave Bauer, Ted Lindsay, Al Shewchuk, Gus Mortson, Floyd Curry, Bob Dawes, Jack Taggart, Bob Porter. Front row: Murdie McMillan, Ken Smith, Bob Love, Bill Ezinicki, J.B. Highfield (president), Bill Barker, Don Batten, Johnny Chenier, Harvey Bennett. On ground in front: Red Fleury (mascot).

Of the three players Oshawa borrowed from St. Michael's, Ted Lindsay became a Hall of Famer, collecting many points and penalty minutes over seventeen years with Detroit and Chicago. He won four Stanley Cups with the Detroit Red Wings. Gus Mortson won the same number with Toronto, but not before returning with St. Michael's to contend for the 1945 Memorial Cup. David Bauer, better known as Father Bauer, emerged as one of Canada's great amateur coaches. He coached St. Michael's to a Memorial Cup victory in 1961, the same year that the Trail Smoke Eaters won the world hockey championship on behalf of Canada. In 1962, he organized and coached Canada's first national team, a program he would be involved in for many years. Father David Bauer was inducted into the Hockey Hall of Fame as a builder in 1989.

The 1945 Memorial Cup

The 1945 Memorial Cup was a showdown between two hockey greats. "Gentleman" Joe Primeau, a former member of the Toronto Maple Leafs' Kid Line of the 1930s was at the helm of the Toronto St. Michael's Majors. Roy Bentley, one of the famed hockey-playing brothers from Delisle, Saskatchewan, was behind the bench for the Moose Jaw Canucks. Moose Jaw came into the final, a best-of-seven at Maple Leaf Gardens, with a playoff record of fifteen wins and one loss. Led by Bert Olmstead, Metro Prystai and Gerald "Doc" Couture, they scored victories over the Prince Albert Black Hawks, Edmonton Canadians and Winnipeg Monarchs. St. Michael's College also advanced to the championship series by defeating future NHL superstar Doug Harvey and the Montreal Royals in six games for the eastern Richardson Trophy. The St. Michael's lineup included Tod Sloan, Gus Mortson and Jimmy Thomson.

Heading into the Memorial Cup final, the Moose Jaw Canucks were concerned that they had lost their best player, Doc Couture. A medical student at the University of Saskatchewan in Saskatoon, Couture was expected to stay behind to write exams. But he surprised everyone by showing up in Toronto, although not with the Canucks. The Detroit Red Wings, who were fighting for the Stanley Cup with the Maple Leafs, recruited the centre at the last moment. "He is a good boy and we were hard up," Detroit coach Jack Adams explained.

Couture's absence did not bode well for Moose Jaw, who lost game one by an 8–5 count before 12,420 fans. "Beaten only four times in thirty-eight previous starts this season, coach Primeau's class-laden collegians struck swiftly for 2 goals in the first eight minutes, held Moose Jaw at bay through a bristling second period and sealed the issue with 3 rapid-fire goals early in the third," reported the Canadian Press. Moose Jaw turned the tables in game two, however, with a 5–3 victory. In game three, St. Michael's overwhelmed Moose Jaw with a 6–3 victory, giving them a 2–1 edge in the series. The Canucks, already stung by the loss of Couture, were further hampered by injuries to other key players.

St. Mike's took a 3–1 series lead in game four with a 4–3 victory. The Toronto club, which hadn't won the national title since 1934, thrilled the crowd of 12,740 with a come-from-behind victory. The next night, the Majors wrapped it up with a 7–2 win. "Canucks knew that they were at the end of the trail very soon after the puck was dropped," wrote Dave Dryburgh of the *Regina Leader-Post*. "They tried to break into a gallop, found that the old zip was missing and all the encouragement that 14,000 spectators provided failed to produce the spark that would make the red-and-white Moose Jaw flyers flame again." Paid attendance for the five games was 65,437, which exceeded the Maple Leaf Gardens' junior record set in 1943.

Joe Primeau coached the senior Toronto Marlboros to the Allan Cup in 1950. The next year, the Toronto Maple Leafs named Primeau their coach and, in his first season behind the bench, Toronto won the Stanley Cup. Primeau remains the only coach in hockey history to win all three championships.

St. Michael's graduates Gus Mortson and Jimmy Thomson both played for Toronto and Chicago in the NHL. Johnny McCormack played with Toronto, Montreal and Chicago, Leo Gravelle spent five years with Montreal and Detroit, and Johnny Arundel saw action in Toronto. All of these players except Gravelle and Arundel won Stanley Cups. Tod Sloan and Les Costello returned to the 1946 Memorial Cup before graduating to the big league.

From the Moose Jaw Canucks, Metro Prystai spent a decade in the NHL with Chicago and Detroit, winning the Stanley Cup with the Red Wings. Ralph

Toronto St. Michael's College. Top row (l to r): Frank Turik, Pat Boehmer, Ted McLean, Jim Thomson, Bob Gray, Joe Sadler. Second row: John Blute, Les Costello, Father H.V. Mallon (director of athletics), John Arundel, Bob Paul. Third row: Leo Gravelle, John Frezell (manager), Doug Wallace (assistant manager), John McCormack. Bottom row: Phil Samis, John Morrison, Joe Carruthers (trainer), Joe Primeau (coach), Gus Mortson, Tod Sloan.

Nattrass played in Chicago for four years while Dick Butler had a seven-game stint with the Blackhawks. Mark Marquess also saw limited NHL action in Boston. Bert Olmstead won five Stanley Cups, four with Montreal and one in Toronto. The rugged leftwinger was later inducted into the NHL Hall of Fame. As for Doc Couture, his Red Wings were no more successful in Toronto that year than the Canucks, bowing to the Maple Leafs in seven games. Couture did capture the Stanley Cup with the Red Wings in 1950, however. It was the highlight of an NHL career spanning nine seasons, in which he also played for Montreal and Chicago.

The **1946** Memorial Cup

1946 marked the first time in six years that junior hockey players did not face the prospect of going to war. The Memorial Cup final that spring seemed to reflect the release of tension of a society heading into a more affluent, self-confident era. Two strong teams, the Winnipeg Monarchs and St. Michael's College of Toronto, faced off in one of the best finals to date, held before the largest crowds yet.

Joe Primeau led St. Michael's into the OHA final against his old Maple Leaf linemate Charlie Conacher and the Oshawa Generals, in a closely followed series that drew crowds of more than 13,000 to Maple Leaf Gardens. The St. Michael's squad fell behind two games to one before rallying for three straight wins and the series victory.

This set up an eastern best-of-five showdown final between defending Memorial Cup champion St. Michael's and the Montreal Junior Canadiens. A three-game sweep by St. Michael's was the result. In the western Abbott Cup final, the Monarchs, coached by former Olympic team member Walter Monson, eliminated the Edmonton Canadians in five games.

The 1946 Memorial Cup series was later described by Foster Hewitt as one of the best finals he had ever seen at any level. It opened on April 13, with 14,012 fans in attendance. The Monarchs, paced by Don "Red" McRae and Harry Taylor and backed up impressively by goalkeeper Jack Gibson, narrowly defeated St. Michael's 3–2 in game one. Toronto rallied in the second game, skating to a 5–3 victory. They took the series lead in game three, defeating the Monarchs 7–3 in front of 14,794 fans.

In the fourth game, the Monarchs came back with a 4–3 win. Winnipeg's Harry Taylor and Toronto's Tod Sloan emerged the stars of the series in this outstanding game. Thrilling the crowd of 14,371 with his clever playmaking and dogged determination, Taylor bagged a pair of goals, including the winner. He assisted on another, maintaining his position as the leading point-getter of the series. With 5 goals and 4 assists, Taylor had one more point than the sharpshooting Sloan.

But Winnipeg lost momentum in game five, looking shaky in a 7–4 loss to the collegians. It was Sloan's turn to shine, firing 5 goals including 1 on a penalty shot. The defeat seemed to signal the end for the Monarchs, but they rallied and took the next game by a 4–2 score.

The seventh and deciding game was tied at 2 early in the third period when George Robertson, the Monarchs' fast-skating forward, scored the go-ahead goal at 7:51. Winnipeg clung to the lead until Robertson struck again, providing some insurance with only forty-seven seconds left. Winnipeg bagged a 4–2

Winnipeg Monarchs coach Walter Monson beams as he holds junior hockey's most coveted prize.

Winnipeg Monarchs captain Al Buchanan accepts the 1946 Memorial Cup on behalf of his team.

victory and the third Memorial Cup in their history. Programs, hats, toilet tissue, ticker tape and even a corset were thrown onto the ice by Winnipeg supporters.

The seven-game final had generated over 102,575 paid admissions, the largest turnout in the history of junior hockey. The deciding game drew 15,819 fans to Maple Leaf Gardens—the largest crowd ever to see an amateur hockey game in Canada.

The top scorers for each team—Harry Taylor of Winnipeg and Tod Sloan of Toronto—were both drafted by the Maple Leafs. Taylor won the Stanley Cup with Toronto in 1949. Sloan, the Red Tilson Trophy winner in 1946, went on to a strong thirteen-year pro career, culminating in a Stanley Cup victory with the Chicago Blackhawks in 1961. Toronto's Les Costello, Ed Sandford, Fleming Mackell and Ed Harrison all returned for one more Memorial Cup final before moving on to the NHL, while four more Monarchs saw brief action as pros: George Robertson with Montreal, Al Buchanan with Toronto, Clinton Albright with the New York Rangers, and Gord Fashoway with Chicago.

Ted McLean, who wore number 2 for St. Michael's, later recalled the closeness of the 1946 series against the Monarchs, and the size and intensity of the crowds. "We played them in two exhibition games at Christmas time in Winnipeg and split those," he remembered, "and we were even after six games in the finals and tied after two periods in the seventh game. There was a great deal of pressure because the large crowds were very much divided. The St. Mike's kids and their parents would come out with the school cheer, but all the Protestants were cheering against us."

McLean was offered an NHL contract from the Detroit Red Wings, but turned it down. "I had only played hockey for fun," he said, "and I knew I wanted to become a priest."

The Winnipeg Monarchs celebrate after their 1946 Cup win. Coach Walter Monson is at bottom centre.

The **1947** Memorial Cup

The 1946–47 season was a sweet one for Joe Primeau and his St. Michael's Majors. The Toronto team, which included future Hall of Famer "Red" Kelly, whirled through their regular OHA season, winning all but three games.

They capped a playoff drive to the Memorial Cup final with a sweep of the Montreal Junior Canadiens, outscoring Montreal 37–4, including a 21–0 tally in the third game. This ranks as the most lopsided win in the history of the Richardson Trophy series. St. Michael's moved on to face the Moose Jaw Canucks, who had survived a gritty western final with the Brandon Elks that went eight games.

The 1947 Memorial Cup series moved out of Toronto for the first time in several years, and was held instead in three western cities: Winnipeg, Moose Jaw and Regina. In Winnipeg, St. Michael's picked up with Moose Jaw where they had left off with Montreal, romping to a 12–3 victory.

"A milling crowd that had literally clawed its way to the wickets in an all-day demand for pasteboards, saw a disappointing Moose Jaw outfit hold on for one brief period before the magic sticks of the eastern powerhouse went to work with a vengeance," Scotty Melville wrote in the *Regina Leader-Post*. Toronto's line of "Big Ed" Sandford, Les Costello and Fleming Mackell "passed the disc around like a hot biscuit to collect a baker's dozen in scoring points," he added.

The teams then headed for Moose Jaw, Saskatchewan for game two. The site was different but the result the same, as the Majors skated to a 6–1 triumph. Vince Leah of the *Winnipeg Tribune*, himself a noted amateur coach, wrote that Toronto skipper Primeau had "the softest job in the world. My four-year-old son Donald could lead St. Mike's to the Memorial Cup. That's how competent the youthful easterners are."

Game three was played in Regina's Queen City Gardens before 5,959 fans. The match was halted with just under seven minutes left in the third period due to bottle-throwing fans. St. Michael's was awarded a 8–1 victory.

The vulgar display by fans actually began late in the second period following a Moose Jaw penalty. Because the ice had to be cleared, the second period was halted and the time remaining in it was tacked on to the third. "The hoodlums took over after seven minutes of the third period, another Moose Jaw penalty bringing several bottles over the board," Scotty Melville recorded for posterity. "One Canuck and two players from the Toronto club were struck glancing blows by the missiles. The ice was cleared, but again bottles and other odds and ends were heaved to the ice while the referees tried vainly to face off in the southeast corner of the rink."

Frustrated officials got on the arena loudspeaker and threatened to call the game. When the problems continued, play was stopped for good. "The ice was swept four times and half an hour in all was required to clean up the debris," according to Melville. "Hundreds of fans, ashamed and disgusted at the stupidity of the irresponsible few, streamed away from the national final long before it was halted."

Three nights later in Regina, a smaller but hooligan-free crowd of 2,186 saw St. Michael's wrap up their third Memorial Cup championship with a 3–2 victory.

The 1947 St. Michael's College Majors saw a total of nine members reach the NHL as coaches or players. Red

St. Michael's College Majors star Red Kelly went on to enjoy a spectacular twenty-year career in the NHL.

Toronto St. Michael's College. Left column (top to bottom): Ed Harrison, Harry Psutka, Howard Harvey, Rudy Migay. Middle group (clockwise from centre): Ed Sandford, Father H. Mallon (director of athletics), Joe Carruthers (trainer), Arnold Teolis (associate manager), Fleming Mackell, John McLellan, Joe Williams, Len "Red" Kelly, Les Costello, Clare Malone (manager), Joe Primeau, (coach). Right column (top to bottom): Benny Woit, Warren Winslow, Ray Hannigan, Bob Paul. HHF

Kelly was the most prominent, playing in a spectacular twenty-year career before moving on to coach in Los Angeles and Toronto. He won eight Stanley Cups with Detroit and Toronto, as well as the first-ever Norris Trophy. He won the Lady Byng Trophy four times, was the runner-up for the 1954 Hart Trophy and was inducted to the Hall of Fame in 1969. If that wasn't enough, he also enjoyed a term in Ottawa as a Liberal Member of Parliament.

Other notable St. Michael's graduates include Fleming Mackell, who spent twelve years with Toronto and Boston, while Ed Sandford spent most of a nine-year career with the Bruins. Mackell won the Stanley Cup with Toronto in 1949 and 1951. Ray Hannigan and Les Costello both saw brief ice time with the Leafs, and Costello was able to hang around long enough to snatch a Stanley Cup in 1948. Ed Harrison spent most of four NHL years in Boston. Benny Woit and Rudy Migay competed for the 1948 Memorial Cup with the Port Arthur West End Bruins before heading to the NHL. John McLellan did not play in the NHL, but he did precede his junior teammate Red Kelly as coach of the Maple Leafs in the early 1970s.

The **1948** Memorial Cup

When the Port Arthur West End Bruins met the Lethbridge Native Sons en route to the Memorial Cup championship, they faced what many observers felt was certain elimination at the hands of a team with the highest-scoring junior hockey line that season. Eddie "Pistol" Dorohoy, Freddie Brown and Bill Ramsden accounted for 418 points in sixty-three games on behalf of the Native Sons. Ramsden, who surprisingly never made it to the NHL, accounted for a mind-boggling 104 goals and 57 assists by himself.

But Lethbridge was stopped in seven games by Port Arthur. The seventh was played in Toronto—a most inappropriate location for a western final—with the West End Bruins flooring the mighty Native Sons 11–1.

So Port Arthur advanced to the Memorial Cup final for the first time in twenty-one years. This time, the opposition was the Barrie Flyers, coached by Barrie native Leighton "Hap" Emms. The Flyers had never reached the championship final before, but they had an easy time taking the eastern Richardson Trophy. First, they bounced the Windsor Spitfires and then the Montreal Nationales to advance against Port Arthur in the Memorial Cup championship.

The Bruins opened the best-of-seven final with a 10–8 victory at Maple Leaf Gardens. The Flyers' lineup was racked with injuries but they put up a hard-nosed fight before 13,075 spectators. "If the guys out west who holler about rough play had seen the game, they'd seek a court injunction to halt the series," mused Dave Dryburgh in the *Regina Leader-Post*. "Even those who like their hockey in the raw thought there was too much charging and boarding and the referees have been instructed to clamp down."

"We can't come back," coach Emms moaned to the press with dubious sincerity. "The team has too many injuries. No, I don't think we can come back and I wouldn't be saying so if I thought differently."

The Bruins romped to an 8–1 win in game two. Chippiness on the ice spread to bitter post-game comments. "We can't complain, but I've seen better officiating," Port Arthur coach Ed Lauzon said. "It was the first time I have ever seen a player banished for taking a swipe at the puck and clipping an opponent's boot tops in the process."

The Bruins closed to within one game of the title with a 5–4 victory in game three. "The Flyers kept pace with the slick West End Bruins almost throughout," Canadian Press reported, "and came from behind three times to tie the score. Barrie, however, didn't have the extra punch and drive to take over the lead anytime."

After the third game, Emms announced that his Flyers wouldn't play the Bruins in a fourth game without a change of referees. Vic Lindquist of Winnipeg and Ken Mullins of Montreal had handled the first three games. "If they don't give us different referees, we won't show up," Emms said. "They can suspend me or do anything they want, but we won't play."

CAHA President Al Pickard dismissed Emms's threat. "The fourth game will go on as scheduled," he announced the next day, "and with the same referees."

The *Regina Leader-Post*'s Dave Dryburgh wrote, "It doesn't matter if [Emms] does drop out because he won't win the Cup anyway, but why he should insult the referees is beyond us. They've been extremely lenient with his Flyers who play in such robust fashion that it is evident they gave the rule book only a cursory glance. What is annoying Emms is that the West End Bruins have taken a liking to playing it he-man style, too."

The West End Bruins captured the Memorial Cup in game four, lacing the Flyers 9–8 in overtime before 13,053 fans. "The game was the most bitterly contested that was seen in Toronto junior hockey in years," reported Canadian Press. "The lead changed hands several times as both clubs went all out for victory. Tempers flared and sticks crept high and referee Lindquist, of Winnipeg, was attacked by a Barrie player in the overtime session."

Alfie "Chick" Guarda was given a match penalty for administering a light mauling to Vic Lindquist after the official assessed a penalty to the Flyers. Barrie, having fallen behind in the extra session, scored shorthanded to tie the score, but gave up the winner to Danny Lewicki. "It was a tough game to win and a tougher

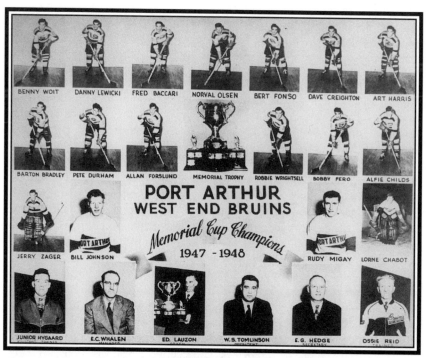

Port Arthur West End Bruins. Top row (l to r): Benny Woit, Danny Lewicki, Fred Baccari, Norval Olsen, Bert Fonso, Dave Creighton, Art Harris. Second row: Barton Bradley, Pete Durham, Allan Forslund, Robbie Wrightsell, Bobby Fero, Alfie Childs. Third row: Jerry Zager, Bill Johnson, Rudy Migay, Lorne Chabot. Bottom row: Junior Hygaard (trainer), E.C. Whalen (manager), Ed Lauzon (coach), W.S. Tomlinson (president), E.G. Hedge (secretary), Ossie Reid (trainer).

one to lose," coach Lauzon said, dripping with as much perspiration as any of his players.

Players from the 1948 Port Arthur team who went on to solid NHL careers include Lewicki, Benny Woit, Rudy Migay and David Creighton. Creighton had a twelve-year stint with the Bruins, Maple Leafs, Blackhawks and Rangers. His son Adam won the Memorial Cup in 1984 with the Ottawa 67's before also moving on to the NHL. Migay played ten seasons with the Toronto Maple Leafs, while Woit had seven seasons in the NHL with Detroit and Chicago, winning the Stanley Cup three times with the Red Wings. Lewicki played nine seasons with the Leafs, Rangers and Blackhawks, winning the 1951 Stanley Cup with Toronto.

The only Barrie Flyer to win the Stanley Cup was Paul Meger, who spent five seasons with the Montreal Canadiens and tasted hockey supremacy in 1953. Goaltender Gilles Mayer, defenceman Stan Long and centre Sid McNabney all played in a handful of playoff games for the Habs in the early 1950s. Gerry Reid also suited up for a couple of playoff games for the Detroit Red Wings in 1949. Ray Gariepy played in one season for Boston and later had a one-game stint with the Maple Leafs.

The **1949** Memorial Cup

In 1931, Bill MacKenzie and Tag Millar met in the Memorial Cup final, MacKenzie as captain of the victorious Elmwood Millionaires and Millar as a player with the Ottawa Primroses. Eighteen years later, the two faced each other again, this time as coaches in a classic best-of-seven series that went eight games. The Montreal Royals, coached by Millar, were determined to defeat the Brandon Wheat Kings and thereby give the province of Quebec its first-ever national junior hockey championship. MacKenzie, who had played in the NHL with the Montreal Maroons, New York Rangers, Chicago Blackhawks and Montreal Canadiens, piloted a powerful Wheat Kings roster including Joe Crozier and Glen Sonmor. The season-long predictions of western hockey experts came one step closer to realization when the Wheat Kings trampled the Calgary Buffaloes to move on to the Memorial Cup final in Winnipeg.

On the eastern playoff trail, the Montreal Royals eliminated teams featuring prominent future NHLers: Bernie Geoffrion's Montreal Nationales and the Leo Boivin-led Inkerman Rockets. The Royals, whose roster included future NHL great Dickie Moore, clinched a berth in the final by sweeping the Barrie Flyers. This gave the city of Montreal its first Memorial Cup finalist since 1941. The Royals' thirteen-win playoff run tied the consecutive playoff victory record set by St. Michael's College in 1934.

More than 5,000 fans were on hand for the Memorial Cup opener, a gruelling, hard-hitting affair won 3–2 by the Royals at the Winnipeg Amphitheatre. The series shifted to Brandon for game two, where Ray Frederick's goaltending led the Wheat Kings to a 3–2 victory at the Wheat City Arena. The loss ended Montreal's record-breaking winning streak at fourteen games.

By now it was apparent that this was going to be a tight series. The Canadian Press reported that bookies were "finding customers hard to locate. Bettors on the contest are few and far between. The report sent to Montreal for even bets was returned without a taker."

The third game, played in Brandon before more than 4,800 fans, ended in a 3–3 overtime tie. Brandon had allowed a third-period 3–1 lead to slip away, and there was no scoring in the fixed overtime session. Each team had 40 shots on goal, and both goaltenders, Frederick and the Royals' Bobby Bleau, were at the top of their games.

The series returned to Winnipeg for game four. Royals captain Bobby Frampton scored the only goal in a 1–0 Montreal victory. The low score belied a thrilling match, in which more than 5,000 fans were treated to numerous end-to-end rushes and superb goaltending. "Good Lord, are they all going to be like this?" wondered the diminutive coach Millar. "I simply can't go through many more of these." The intensity of the series was draining the Montreal coach, who had been suffering from poor health.

Game five was played in Brandon and, for the fifth straight game, the Royals scored first. They went on to a 7–4 victory and took a commanding series lead of three games to one, with one tie.

But the Wheat Kings rebounded with a 2–1 victory in game six before more than 4,800 howling home-ice fans. It was another superb performance for goaltender Ray Frederick, who kicked out 37 shots, 7 in the final two minutes.

The seventh game, also held in Brandon, was hotly anticipated. Prior to the match, scalpers were asking $5 for tickets priced at $1.75 and $2. The sell-out crowd definitely got their money's worth though, as the home team forced an eighth game by delivering a 5–1 victory. "The boys did a wonderful job," coach MacKenzie said. "We've got ten first-year juniors on our club and they deserve a world of credit."

The CAHA ordered the series to resume on neutral ice at the Winnipeg Amphitheatre. If the two teams were to play to a tie—through three regulation periods and three ten-minute overtime periods—a ninth game was scheduled. The deciding game was played on May 16, the latest into spring that any series had gone. The final was attracting so much national attention that CBC Radio broadcast the eighth game with Foster Hewitt calling the plays.

Brandon led by 4–2 three minutes into the third period, but couldn't hang on. Montreal ended up scoring the game's final four goals and won 6–4 before more than 5,000 stunned fans. Quebec had its first Memorial Cup champions.

"Son of a gun! What do you know? This is what we've been dreaming about for years," yelled a jubilant Dickie Moore as he hoisted the Memorial Cup trophy in the Montreal dressing room. "It was a great series and boy, am I glad we won," said Tag Millar. "We won from a great club too. That's all the comment you need from me."

The closeness of the series was reflected in the total goals scored: Montreal 24, Brandon 23.

From the champion Royals, Bobby Frampton, Frederick "Skippy" Burchell and Tom Manastersky later made the NHL, all serving briefly with the Montreal

Montreal Royals. Top row (l to r): Tommy Manastersky, Eric Appleby, Gus Ogilvie (general manager), William Northey (director), Donat Raymond (hon. president), Ernie Hamilton (president) Victor Fildes, Roland Rousseau. Second row: Walter Wells (director), Robert Bleau, Gordon Knutson, Neale Langill, Gordon Armstrong, S.J. Langill. Third row: Matthew Benoit, John A. Hirschfeld, J.T. Millar (coach), R.M. Ferguson (junior manager), Richard Moore, Robert Frampton. Bottom row: William C. Rattray, J. Cadger (trainer), Donald Rose, Frank J. Selke (managing director), Peter Larocque, Mike Darling, Frederick Burchell.

Canadiens. Dickie Moore went on to become one of the Habs' great stars, but first returned to Memorial Cup competition in 1950 with the Montreal Junior Canadiens.

From the Brandon Wheat Kings, Reg Abbott and Frank King skated briefly with the Montreal Canadiens, while Ray Frederick served a short stint with Chicago. Robert Chrystal played two seasons with the New York Rangers. Joe Crozier played five games with the Maple Leafs, and Glen Sonmor also played a couple of games with the New York Rangers. Both men enjoyed impressive coaching careers in both the NHL and World Hockey Association during the 1970s and 1980s. Unfortunately the strain of the Memorial Cup series took a tragic toll on Montreal coach Tag Millar. Millar was ill throughout the finals and died of a kidney ailment and pneumonia on October 21, 1949. He was only thirty-six years old.

The
1950s

It was not uncommon in the 1930s and 1940s for a single game in the Memorial Cup final to attract crowds of 13,000 or 14,000 to Maple Leaf Gardens. By contrast, three games played at the Gardens in 1952 drew a combined total of only 15,000. Although Canada was enjoying a level of peace and prosperity for the first time in two decades, the national junior championship had fallen on hard times.

For many, the answer lay in the belief that the real national championship series was the Richardson Cup final. Western junior teams, once able to face the east on even terms, were becoming less and less competitive. Between 1950 and 1956, teams from the west won only three games in seven best-of-seven finals.

Eastern powerhouses like the 1952 Guelph Biltmore Mad Hatters and the 1955 and 1956 Toronto Marlboros presented formidable opponents, but the east and west had developed markedly different styles.

"They play it like the pros," Stafford Smythe remarked of the eastern juniors, who hit hard and shot often, while the western teams were prone to excessive "dipsydoodling." But the decade wore on, the west began to play it like the pros as well, resulting in some tough finals to set the stage for the 1960s.

The influence of the NHL was not confined to the style of play. The big league had cultivated a system of drawing its players from a web of affiliated junior clubs, as opposed to today's universal amateur draft. For example, the nucleus of the early 1950s Biltmore Mad Hatters became the core of the late-fifties New York Rangers. Players from the Ottawa-Hull Junior Canadiens and Regina Pats of the late 1950s became the cornerstone of the Montreal Canadiens in the 1960s.

On the whole, the game resembled today's hockey, although the juniors still hadn't abandoned fixed overtime sessions in favour of sudden death elimination. Most recognizable to hockey fans are the players from this era who earned their spurs in Memorial Cup competition. Dickie Moore, Andy Bathgate, Bob Pulford, Pierre Pilote and Don Cherry are only a few of the Memorial Cup veterans who poured into the steadily burgeoning professional ranks.

Guelph Biltmores captain Andy Bathgate dominated play in the 1952 Memorial Cup series.

The 1950 Memorial Cup

It may have taken thirty years for a team from Montreal to claim the Memorial Cup, but it only took one more to repeat the feat. Hot on the heels of the 1949 victory by the Montreal Royals, the trophy returned to Quebec when the Montreal Junior Canadiens defeated the Regina Pats in a best-of-seven series.

The Pats were supposed to be rebuilding, and didn't clinch a playoff berth until a week before the regular season ended, finishing one game below .500. They caught fire in the western playoffs, however, and won fourteen of eighteen playoff games against Moose Jaw, Lethbridge, Prince Albert and Port Arthur before moving on to the championship round.

The Montreal Junior Canadiens eliminated the Quebec Citadels in the Quebec Junior Amateur Hockey Association final series before squaring off against the Maritime champions from Nova Scotia. The Halifax St. Marys were no match for the Junior Canadiens, and the series was discontinued after two blowouts in Halifax that Montreal won by scores of 11–3 and 10–1. Montreal, coached by Sam Pollock and Billy Reay, then finished off Guelph—who had the Bathgate brothers Andy and Frank on their roster—to earn a spot in the best-of-seven Memorial Cup final.

The championship series was scheduled to open in the Montreal Forum, with a battered Regina outfit travelling east to face the Junior Canadiens. All three members of Regina's top line—rightwinger Eddie Litzenberger, centre Paul Masnick and leftwinger Gordon Cowan—were on the limp. They had been the highest scoring line in the WCJHL during the regular season.

Dickie Moore, in his second Memorial Cup final after capturing the trophy a year earlier with the Montreal Royals, grabbed the spotlight when he contributed 2 goals in the series opener, helping to spark the Junior Habs to an 8–7 victory. Art Rose and Don Marshall also had 2 goals each for the Junior Habs. 10,414 fans watched a freewheeling game in which 10 third-period goals were scored.

"Art Rose, a speedster from the Lakehead, was the big man in the Montreal cast," Harvey Dryden wrote in the *Regina Leader-Post*. "But don't overlook this Moore. His most fervent admirer will admit he's a showoff and that he plays it rugged now and then, but there's no denying that he can dangle when he wants to."

Montreal scored a 5–2 victory in game two, taking a 2–0 lead in the series. "Moore, who turned in a stellar performance in the first game of the series, was closely checked all night and was held to an assist on his team's first goal," the Canadian Press reported. "This caused him to display his feelings, which netted him five trips to the penalty box including one major for roughing."

Game three was scheduled for Toronto. Coach Pollock, who was dissatisfied with his team's play in game two, ordered his players to leave immediately after the game rather than spend the weekend with friends and family. Some observers wondered what he would have done had Montreal lost the game.

Pollock's discipline had the desired results, as Montreal went up three games to none with a 5–1 victory at Maple Leaf Gardens before 8,429 fans.

"For two periods the Toronto crowd, which had come to cheer the Pats, thrilled to a gritty display by the youthful westerners who threw their best licks at the Junior Canadiens," Dryden wrote, "but their Sunday punch couldn't produce a goal and the crafty eastern Richardson Trophy champions capitalized on three quick openings early in the third period to walk off with a 5–1 victory. Pats had no answer for that outburst."

It was back to Montreal for game four, where the Pats were able to save some face with a gritty 7–4 victory, coming from behind to overcome a Montreal 4–1 edge midway through the game. "This time we'll have to do it the hard way," said Pats winger Lorne Davis. "We'll take one game at a time."

But Montreal, playing at home, plowed to a 6–3 victory in the fifth game on the strength of a hat trick by Billy Goold. Art Rose ended a standout tournament performance with an exclamation point, firing 2 goals just six seconds apart in the second period. The swashbuckling centre Rose led the series with 8 goals.

"We were beaten by a better team and we have no alibis," admitted Regina coach Murray Armstrong. "Our guys gave their best but the Junior Canadiens were too good for us."

The *Montreal Star* summed up the Pats' main weakness as that they "dipsy-doodled too much with the passing pattern in the enemy zone and didn't shoot

Montreal Junior Canadiens. Top row (l to r): Ernie Roche, Bob Dawson, Theo Mathieu (president), W.H. Northey (vice president), Donat Raymond (hon. president), Frank Selke (managing director), Gordon Hollingworth, Kevin Conway. Second row: Art Rose, Bill Goold, Dick Moore, Sam Pollock (coach), Bill Reay (coach), Jacques Nadon, Don Marshall, Kevin Rochford. Third row: Roger Morissette, Herb English, Dave McCready, Bill Sinnett. Bottom row: Gerry Roche (trainer), Charles Hodge, Reg Grigg, Doug Binning, Brian McKay, Frank Le Grove (manager).

enough." The fashion-conscious *Star* also found space to comment on the Pats' uniforms. "Typical of western junior invaders," the newspaper lamented, "Pats were attired in uniforms that had seen better days—with tape holding parts of pants and sweaters together."

The Regina Pats' Paul Masnick won a Stanley Cup with the Montreal Canadiens in 1953 during a six-year NHL career. Teammate Lorne Davis also spent six seasons in the NHL with Montreal, Chicago, Detroit and Boston. Eddie Litzenberger played twelve years with Montreal, Chicago and Toronto. As team captain, he won the Stanley Cup with Chicago in 1961, and earned three more with Toronto from 1962 to 1964.

From the Montreal Junior Canadiens, Gordon "Bucky" Hollingworth, Ernest Roche, Charlie Hodge, Don Marshall and Dickie Moore graduated to the NHL. Moore became a Hall of Famer, playing fourteen seasons in the Montreal Canadiens, Toronto Maple Leafs and St. Louis Blues. He was a two-time Art Ross Trophy winner and a member of six Stanley Cup winners with the Canadiens between 1953 and 1960. Hodge played the bulk of his career with the Habs, winning the Stanley Cup in 1965. Don Marshall, whose nineteen-year career was spent largely with the Habs and the Rangers, won five Stanley Cups in Montreal between 1956 and 1960. Roche also played in Montreal, but only for a handful of games. Bucky Hollingworth spent four seasons in Chicago and Detroit.

The 1951 Memorial Cup

The Winnipeg Monarchs made their last appearance ever in a Memorial Cup final in 1951, having won three Memorial Cups in four trips to the championship. The longstanding western powerhouse battled a newly established eastern force, the Barrie Flyers. The Flyers were making their second appearance at the final, having bowed out to the Port Arthur West End Bruins in 1948.

Barrie moved to the final after prevailing in a bitterly fought Richardson Trophy series with the Quebec Citadels, who had future NHLers Jean Beliveau and Camille "The Eel" Henry on their roster.

The eastern championship rotated from the 4,200-seat capacity Barrie Arena to the Maple Leaf Gardens and the Quebec Colisée, which both attracted crowds of over 14,000. The seven-game series was plagued with arguments, peppered with penalties and marred by Quebec's refusal to play the final game on Barrie ice. It was held at Maple Leaf Gardens as a result.

Meanwhile, coach Walter Monson's Monarchs faced the Regina Pats in a hard-fought Abbott Cup final that went eight games. It was the first time a Winnipeg junior hockey team had met Regina in the western final since 1931. Winnipeg ultimately proved superior in the marathon series and advanced to the Memorial Cup final.

The Monarchs knew they would be in tough against Barrie, a team coached by the legendary "Hap" Emms. The Flyers boasted a forward line of leftwinger and captain Real Chevrefils, centre Leo Labine and rightwinger Jack White. Their lineup also included future pros like Doug Mohns, Jim Morrison and Jerry "Topper" Toppazzini.

The best-of-seven Memorial Cup final opened at the Winnipeg Amphitheatre with Barrie scoring a 5–1 victory. "The well-conditioned Barrie club passed the Monarchs dizzy for the first two periods," the Canadian Press reported, "and only in the last session did the Regals show any resemblance to the form which carried them to the western Abbott Cup title."

The Flyers recorded their second straight 5–1 victory in game two. Emms coyly suggested that his Flyers were "playing away above their heads. Can't tell what will happen with the way those Monarchs skate." The teams moved to Brandon and the Wheat City Arena for game three, but the outcome was the same. Barrie won 4–3. The series was scheduled to move back to Winnipeg for the fourth game, a prospect that didn't overjoy coach Emms. Of the old Amphitheatre he said, "Barrie has better sheds than this."

The building, which was showing its age, had begun to disgruntle players from both teams, who complained the ice was heavy. Flyers netminder Lorne Howes was wringing water from his pads at the end of each game there. To make matters worse, the fourth game was postponed by one day due to ammonia fumes leaking in the Amphitheatre.

Leo Labine played centre on the 1951 Memorial Cup-winning Barrie Flyers' formidable forward line.

The delay didn't take any edge off Emms' team, however, as the Flyers completed a sweep in game four, winning 9–5. "Nothing to be ashamed of against a club like that," Monarchs coach Monson said of his team's defeat. After the game, Emms announced that he was considering making this series his last as a coach. In reality, he would stay in the Memorial Cup hunt until 1968.

A number of the 1951 Barrie Flyers played in the NHL. Real Chevrefils, Leo Labine and Topper Toppazzini skated with the Bruins and Red Wings, and

Barrie Flyers. Back row (l to r): Hank Partridge, Daniel O'Connor, Jerry Toppazzini, George Stanutz, Ralph Willis, Jack McKnight, Paul Emms, Lloyd Pearsall, Dr. Neil Laurie (team physician). Middle row: Real Chevrefils, Jack White, Jim Morrison, Archie Marshall, Hap Emms (coach), Charlie Christie, Bill Hagan, Lionel Barber, Doug Mohns. Front row: Chuck Wood, Doug Towers, Lorne Howes, Howard Norris, Marvin Brewer, Don Emms, Leo Labine.

Toppazzini also saw duty with the Blackhawks. Doug Mohns stayed in Barrie long enough to win the 1953 Memorial Cup with the Flyers before embarking on a lengthy NHL career. Defenceman Jim Morrison spent twelve seasons in the NHL between 1952 and 1971 with Boston, Toronto, Detroit, the New York Rangers and Pittsburgh.

From the Winnipeg Monarchs, Gerry James became a two-sport star in hockey and football. The Toronto Maple Leafs, who were affiliated with the Monarchs, pulled James east to the Toronto Marlboros, with whom he won the 1955 Memorial Cup. He played with the Maple Leafs from 1955 to 1960, also joining the Canadian Football League for eleven seasons with the Winnipeg Blue Bombers and Saskatchewan Roughriders. Bill Burega made a brief NHL appearance with the Maple Leafs.

The **1952** Memorial Cup

Hockey purists who lament that custom has increasingly taken a back seat to commerce might be surprised to find that things haven't changed that much. The sponsor of Guelph's junior hockey team in the 1950s was the Biltmore Hat Company, and as a result, the 1952 Memorial Cup featured a team whimsically dubbed the Biltmore Mad Hatters. This powerful squad faced the more traditionally titled Regina Pats in a best-of-seven series held at Maple Leaf Gardens.

Although their nickname was eccentric, the Biltmores were consistent and focussed, toppling scoring records in their march to the OHA title. As a team, they scored 341 goals in a 54-game schedule, 34 more than the previous recordholders. Their leading scorer, Ken Laufman set an OHA scoring record with 139 points.

Coached by former New York Ranger Alfred "Alf" Pike, Guelph was chock-full of future NHLers like captain Andy Bathgate, Lou Fontinato, Dean Prentice, Ron Murphy, Bill McCreary, Harry Howell, Ron Stewart, Aldo Guidolin and William "Chick" Chalmers.

The Mad Hatters defeated the Montreal Junior Canadiens in six games in the eastern final, while coach Murray Armstrong's Pats advanced to the Memorial Cup final with a victory over the Fort William Hurricanes. Armstrong, himself a veteran of the 1933 Memorial Cup final as a Pat, was well aware of Guelph's powerful lineup. But he pointed out that six members of his team were taking their second crack at the junior championship, the Pats having lost out to the Montreal Junior Canadiens in 1950.

"We're a mature hockey club," he said. "We like to play it rough, our players are big and I don't think the east will push us around." The Pats were led on the ice by Eddie Litzenberger, Doug Killoh and Bob Turner, who would later coach the Pats franchise to the 1974 Memorial Cup.

The Memorial Cup final opened in Guelph's new 4,247-seat arena on April 25. The Mad Hatters posted an 8–2 victory, outshooting the Pats 46–10. "Regina lacked the smooth team play of the Biltmores," the Canadian Press reported. "They relied mostly on individual efforts, and a great deal of the time they were overhauled by the flying Bilts." The teams then moved to Maple Leaf Gardens for the remainder of the series. 7,333 fans watched Guelph post a 4–2 victory in game two. Bathgate scored Guelph's first and last goals, and Murphy and McCreary added one each.

The Pats spent the following evening watching Barbara Ann Scott's ice show in Maple Leaf Gardens, but the respite didn't help them in game three. Regina was bounced 8–2 before 4,270 fans, falling behind 3–0 in the series. Again, Bathgate dominated the play, scoring a hat trick, as did Ron Murphy.

"Currently in the process of presenting the Guelph Biltmore Mad Hatters with their first Memorial Cup in history," Ned Powers wrote in the *Regina Leader-Post*, "Murphy and Bathgate are writing a glorious end to their junior hockey days before taking the big jump to the National Hockey League warfare next winter." Coach Armstrong philosophized, "It is a tall order to win four straight games from a good hockey club like Guelph, but stranger things have happened."

Guelph won game four by 10–2 to complete the sweep. The Mad Hatters had outscored Regina 30–8 over the four games. "Boy, am I glad that's over," Pike said, putting the victory in perspective. "Now I can go fishing." Armstrong acknowledged that the Mad Hatters were simply too much for his team. "I had heard they were good," he allowed. "But I didn't realize that they were that good. They're by far the best club I've seen all season and one of the best clubs I've ever seen. They would have beaten us even at our best."

The attendance at the 1952 tournament was disappointing, to say the least. About 15,000 people attended the three games in Toronto, with a meagre 3,447 turning out for the final game. Many attributed this statistic to the lack of parity between eastern and western champions.

A number of players on the Biltmore Mad Hatters went on to impressive careers in the NHL. Andy Bathgate, Harry Howell, Dean Prentice and Ron Murphy laid the foundation for rebuilding the New York Rangers. The NHL team returned to respectability in the late 1950s after spending most of the first half of the decade in or near the cellar. Bathgate and Stewart moved on to Toronto, winning the Stanley Cup with the Leafs in the early sixties, while Murphy became a Stanley Cup champion with the Blackhawks in 1961. Howell played more games than any other defenceman in the history of major league hockey. He and Bathgate were eventually inducted into the Hockey Hall of Fame.

Bill McCreary spent nine years with the Rangers, Red Wings, Canadiens and Blues, and also served stints behind the bench with St. Louis, Vancouver, and the California Golden Seals. Ron Stewart spent twenty-one years in the NHL, most of them with Toronto and the New York Rangers. He won the Stanley Cup three times with the Leafs between 1962 and 1964. Aldo Guidolin and Chick Chalmers both saw action with the Rangers in the early 1950s.

From the Regina Pats, Eddie Litzenberger won the Calder trophy in his first full NHL season in 1954–55. He went on to a twelve-year career that included stops in Chicago, Detroit and Toronto, winning a Stanley Cup with the Blackhawks in 1961 and three more with the Leafs from 1962 to 1964. Defenceman Bob Turner played eight seasons with Montreal and Chicago, winning Stanley Cups with the Canadiens from 1956 to 1960.

Guelph Biltmore Mad Hatters.

The **1953** Memorial Cup

The Barrie Flyers had good reason for optimism going into the 1953 Memorial Cup final. Not only had eastern teams won the last four titles, but the west hadn't even won a game in the final since 1950. Furthermore, the Flyers had established themselves as one of the dominant junior teams of the era, and could rely on the experience of a core of players who had captured the Cup in 1951, as well as the proven helmsmanship of coach Hap Emms.

Their opponents were the St. Boniface Canadiens, making their first appearance in the final since a 1938 triumph.

St. Boniface, coached by Bryan Hextall, had defeated the Lethbridge Native Sons to take the Abbott Cup in the west, while the Flyers eliminated the Quebec Citadels in the east. First, Barrie defeated St. Michael's College in a tough eight-game Ontario championship series culminating in a classic display of Emms' cockiness. His team leading in the closing minutes of the final game, Emms sent a gift box to St. Michael's coach Charlie Cerre. Fans and players alike watched as

Don McKenney was part of the strong Barrie Flyers team that brought home the Memorial Cup in 1953.

Cerre opened the box to find a book entitled *How to Coach Hockey*.

Hap Emms' team included a couple of future NHL coaches, Don Cherry and Orval Tessier, as well as NHL regulars like Doug Mohns, Don McKenney, Larry Thibault and goaltender Marv Edwards, who was picked up from the St. Catharines TeePees. The Canadiens were captained by Syd White and powered by a line dubbed the "Weston Whizzers" consisting of Cecil Hoekstra, Ab McDonald and Leo Konyk. Weston was a section of Winnipeg where Canadian Pacific Railway employees lived and worked for the "Weston shops" responsible for repairing the locomotives and boxcars. In addition to McDonald and Hoekstra, the Canadiens had future pros Al Johnson and Gary Blaine.

The 1953 championship was played at the Winnipeg Amphitheatre with the exception of game two, which was scheduled for the Wheat City Arena in Brandon. The series opened with Allen "Skip" Teal posting 2 goals and 2 assists in a 6–4 Barrie victory. The Canadiens led 3–1 after the first period and 4–2 after the second, but gave up 4 third-period goals.

The Canadiens jumped to another 3–2 lead early in game two, but gave up 4 straight goals and lost 6–3, leaving a crowd of 4,900 Brandonites stunned. "We beat ourselves in that game," Hextall lamented, "and now we have got to get the next one."

But Barrie increased their series lead to 3–0 instead, winning game three by a score of 7–5. The Flyers were anchored by fine goaltending from Marv Edwards.

While many were predicting a sweep at this point, the Canadiens stayed alive with a 7–4 triumph in game four. The win broke the east's twelve-game Memorial Cup winning streak. Not consoled by his team's three-to-one series lead, Emms blasted officials McDonald and Lecompte of Ottawa as "the worst I have ever seen." He also hammered away at another favourite target, the Winnipeg Amphitheatre. "It was just a pool of water," he complained. "In fact, the whole setup at this barn is a disgrace."

Nevertheless, it was at the soaking old barn that Emms captured his second Memorial Cup title on May 6. Barrie nailed down a game five victory of 6–1 before another capacity crowd of more than 5,000. After a promising start, ill will set in and the game spun out of control. Twenty-four penalties were handed out, including four majors and two misconducts. Don Cherry, who scored goals in games four and five, picked up a major after squaring off against the Canadiens' Frank Holliday.

From the St. Boniface Canadiens, Ab McDonald played with Montreal, Chicago, Boston, Detroit, Pittsburgh and St. Louis from 1959 to 1972 before moving to Winnipeg of the World Hockey Association. He won the Stanley Cup three times, twice in Montreal in 1958 and 1959 and once in Chicago in 1961. Cecil Hoekstra and Gary Blaine each skated briefly for Montreal, as did Al Johnson before playing for the Red Wings from 1961 through 1963. Leo Konyk didn't follow his linemates into the NHL; instead he enrolled at McGill University. As a student of dentistry, he learned to repair teeth rather than loosen them.

From the Barrie Flyers, Don Cherry went on to a solid minor league career punctuated by a one-game stint in the NHL with the Boston Bruins. He later coached the Bruins for five seasons, including runs to the Stanley Cup finals in 1977 and 1978, losing both times to Scotty Bowman's Montreal Canadiens. Cherry then spent one year behind the bench of the Colorado Rockies before giving up coaching for a broadcasting career.

The Flyers' Orval Tessier played with the Boston Bruins and Montreal Canadiens before becoming a successful junior coach. He led the 1972 Cornwall Royals to the Memorial Cup, and later coached the Chicago Blackhawks from 1983 to 1985.

Don McKenney enjoyed a thirteen-year career in the NHL, with Boston, New York, Toronto, Detroit and St. Louis, winning the Stanley Cup with the Maple Leafs in 1964.

Barrie Flyers. Back row (l to r): Tim Hook, Don McKenney, Doug Mohns, Larry Thibault, Bob White, Don Cherry, Jack Higgins, Ken Robertson. Middle row: Harry Partridge (trainer), Jim Robertson, John Martin, Orval Tessier, Fred Pletsch, Howard Norris (manager), Ralph Willis, Orin Carver, Allen "Skip" Teal, Tony Poeta, Archie Campbell (trainer). Front row: Marv Edwards, Charlie Christie (president), Archie Marshall (secretary-treasurer), Bill Harrington, "Hap" Emms (coach), Dr. Neil Laurie (team physician), George Cuculick.

Like Don Cherry, three other Flyers made one-game appearances in the NHL as players: Skip Teal with Boston, and Hill Menard and Anthony Poeta with Chicago.

Doug Mohns, who had also won the Memorial Cup in 1951, spent twenty-two seasons in the NHL from 1954 until 1975. He played for Boston, Chicago and the Minnesota North Stars, among other teams. Mohns later reminisced about his junior coach, Hap Emms, to the *Globe and Mail*. "He was the one who developed my talents and skills," he told Paul Patton. "He was a real disciplinarian. We didn't like it at the time, but we appreciated it afterwards."

The 1954 Memorial Cup

The St. Catharines TeePees of 1954 may have started to figure they were a team of destiny while in the early stages of their OHA championship semi-final with the St. Michael's Majors of Toronto. With his team down by 1 goal late in a game, St. Catharines coach Rudy Pilous pulled netminder Marvin Edwards even though the faceoff was in the TeePees' end.

"All of their players headed for the empty net," Pilous told Paul Patton of the *Globe and Mail* in 1987, "and when we won the faceoff, they only had Marc Reaume back." Hugh Barlow scored the tying goal with twenty-eight seconds remaining, and the TeePees went on to win the series. "We squeezed 4,200 people into the Garden City Rink for that game," Pilous recalled. "But I've met 40,000 since who said they saw it."

The TeePees got past the Toronto Marlboros in seven games to win the OHA championship, then defeated the Quebec Frontenacs for the eastern title. They reached their first Memorial Cup final since their formation as the St. Catharines Falcons in 1943. Led by defensive standouts Pierre Pilote and Elmer "Moose" Vasko, the TeePees also had Brian Cullen, who set OHA records with 68 goals and 93 assists for 161 points, breaking the previous marks for all three totals. Cullen played on the "CBC line" with his brother Barry and Hugh Barlow.

The western champion Edmonton Oil Kings had won sixty-one of sixty-five games during the regular season with future pros Norm Ullman and John Bucyk. Having defeated Fort William in the Abbott Cup series, they waited in Toronto for more than two weeks to meet the eastern champions. When the Oil Kings journeyed east for the Memorial Cup final, they didn't leave anything to chance. They even brought their own water. "We've got four gallons here now and six more are on their way from Edmonton," coach Ken McAuley said. "The players claimed they suffered cramps in out-of-town games from drinking other water and they didn't want to take any chances."

The prairie water made no difference in game one. Jack Armstrong scored three times to propel his team to an 8–2 win over the rusty Oil Kings at Maple Leaf Gardens. "TeePees, clicking on every turn, put on the pressure from the opening and handed the Oil Kings their worst defeat of the season," reported the Canadian Press. "We expect a lot of opposition yet," Pilous said. "They're a good bunch of boys, they should improve."

The Oil Kings shook off the cobwebs in game two, jumping to a 2–0 lead on goals by Bucyk and Ullman. But St. Catharines counterattacked with 4 third-period goals and snatched a 5–3 win. The game was played before 3,680 fans, one of the smallest crowds in years to see a Memorial Cup playoff game in Maple Leaf Gardens.

An even sparser crowd of 3,030 was on hand for game three. St. Catharines placed a stranglehold on the series with a 4–1 victory over an Oil Kings team that Canadian Press called a "ragged-looking band." Brian Cullen led the victors with three goals, setting up another by Barlow. "My club will win Saturday night—we'll win it in four straight," Pilous predicted. He added that the Oil Kings "just don't play in the same kind of a league. That club couldn't win sixty games in a season in the OHA."

"What do you expect?" McAuley fired back. "We went sixteen days without a game before we started this series. The boys are making mental mistakes which could be cured, but they've been off the ice so long you can't talk them into it. The only way the east wins this thing is by stalling the west." The Oil Kings managed to fight the TeePees to a 3–3 tie in game four, but St. Catharines wrapped it up the next day, posting a 6–2 victory before only 2,848 fans. Brian Cullen led the TeePees with two goals and two assists. Ullman and Bucyk replied for the Oil Kings. "It's been a good series," Pilous said. "But I honestly believe we have the better hockey team."

From the St. Catharines TeePees, Pierre Pilote played most of an outstanding NHL career with the Blackhawks, as did Elmer "Moose" Vasko, who also spent two full seasons with the Minnesota North Stars. The pair were defensive stalwarts on a Blackhawks team that captured the Stanley Cup in 1961. Pilote had a stranglehold on the Norris Trophy from 1963 to 1965 and was later inducted into the Hockey Hall of Fame.

The Cullen brothers, Barry and Brian, also turned pro. Barry played portions of five seasons with the Maple Leafs from 1956 to 1959, and in 1960 he played for Detroit. Brian enjoyed seven seasons with Toronto and the New York Rangers. Goaltender Marv Edwards spent time with the Penguins, Maple Leafs and California Golden Seals. Ian Cushenan saw ice time with the Blackhawks, Canadiens, Rangers and Red Wings. Hank Ciesla had four seasons in Chicago and New York, while Cecil Hoekstra saw action with Montreal in 1960.

From the Edmonton Oil Kings, both John Bucyk and Norm Ullman reached the Hockey Hall of Fame. Bucyk spent twenty-three seasons in the NHL with the Red Wings and Bruins, winning the Stanley Cup with Boston in 1970 and 1972 and establishing NHL career and single-season records for most points and assists by a leftwinger.

The career marks would still be standing at the turn of the century. Ullman played for the Red Wings from 1956 to 1968 before moving on to Toronto, where he stayed until 1975. He rounded out his career back in Edmonton with the Oilers in the World Hockey Association. Three other Oil Kings, Gord Strate, Billy McNeill and Gerry Melnyk, also played with the Red Wings in the late 1950s and early '60s, and Melnyk also did stints in Chicago and St. Louis.

St. Catharines TeePees.

The **1955** Memorial Cup

"If we don't win the series in five games, I might be looking for a new job. The pattern lately has been the east in five and I might get thrown out if I let the side down."

The comments were made by Turk Broda, and he didn't let anyone down. Having taken the coaching reins of the Toronto Marlboros halfway through the 1954–55 season, Broda found himself leading a talented group against the Regina Pats in the Memorial Cup final. The Marlboros featured players Al MacNeil, Bobby Baun, Billy Harris and Bob Pulford. They had eliminated the defending national champion St. Catharines TeePees in the OHA final, and defeated the Quebec Frontenacs for the Richardson Trophy.

In western Canada, the Abbott Cup championship saw the Regina Pats and Winnipeg Monarchs squaring off in the last playoff series ever held in the Winnipeg Amphitheatre. Regina claimed their eighth Abbott Cup, wrapping up the series in five games. The Pats were coached by Murray Armstrong, who had faced Broda as a rival netminder in the 1933 Abbott Cup championship between Regina and Brandon. The roster of the 1955 edition included Bill Hicke, Bill Hay and Murray Balfour. Twenty-one-year-old Bob Turner, playing in his fourth season with the Pats, served as team captain.

The Marlboros travelled by train to Regina, where the Memorial Cup final was to be held. The ride west raised the ire of Marlboros president Harold Ballard, indignant that his players had been given tourist class tickets while CAHA officials, press and broadcasters were housed in a private car. "I asked the CAHA if their delegates to various meetings travelled tourist class," Ballard grumbled. "When they stickhandled around that one, I told them we would pay our own way. We've always done things first class and we certainly don't plan to change now."

In keeping with this high standard, Ballard made a notable contribution to junior hockey: he

Bob Pulford was a major contributor to both the 1955 and 1956 Memorial Cup victories for the Toronto Marlboros.

suggested hosting a Memorial Cup dinner. When the Marlboros made the Memorial Cup final again in 1956, he organized the second annual Memorial Cup dinner. This pre-tournament feast has remained part of Memorial Cup tradition ever since.

The Pats opened the final series with a 3–1 victory in Exhibition Stadium, giving western fans some hope they might snatch the junior crown from the east for the first time in the decade. "Pats were outshot and outweighed," wrote Ernie Fedoruk in the *Regina Leader-Post*. "But Armstrong's troops didn't let the coach down in vital departments. He expected hustle and desire. He got that and an excellent defensive and backchecking display which proved to be the big factor in an important contest."

Coach Armstrong had so far refused to use the three additions from other teams allowed under CAHA rules. "We'll play it the same way Saturday," he said of the upcoming second game, "with the same lineup."

The Marlies tied the series in game two, scoring a 5–2 decision with four powerplay goals. Toronto led 3–0 halfway through the game and was rarely threatened. "It was a dandy hockey game," Broda said, hoping his team was beginning to hit its stride. "Still, the boys didn't play as well as they could. Their checking has improved and after another game, we will be hard to beat."

Armstrong announced that for the next game, he would dress Murray Balfour, who had missed the first two games with a knee injury, as well as Lethbridge additions Earl Ingarfield and Les Colwill. These reinforcements didn't help the Pats too much as Toronto managed a 3–2 victory.

Despite trailing two games to one, the Pats and their supporters were surprisingly upbeat. "Pats outskated, outshot and outchecked the heavier Toronto team," the *Regina Leader-Post* reported on game two. "Regina spotted Dukes a 2–0 first-period lead, then came back to stage a display that had Marlboros hanging on the ropes." Armstrong blurted, "They're not half as tough as we're going to be." Broda was actually worried by his team's play. "They were terrible," he said. "That was the worst game of hockey I've seen them play all winter."

The fourth game was pivotal. Trailing 2–1 in the final minute of play, Regina sent the game into overtime when Balfour scored with thirteen seconds remaining. The 5,378 fans in attendance went into hysteria. "When the going gets tough and the games get bigger, then Billy Harris gets us the big goals," Ballard had commented earlier in the series. Now his words proved to be prophetic, as Harris scored the winning goal after forty-four seconds of overtime. Harris had also assisted on the Marlies' other two goals.

"I think we played our best hockey game, but winning that way is awfully bad for the heart," Broda said. "Sure, we only need one more, but it'll be just as hard to get."

They got it in game five, winning another overtime match 8–5. Harris scored the game clincher again. "Pats, great in defeat, blew a 3–0 first period lead and the hard-hitting Dukes exploded for 3 goals in a minute and 27 seconds midway in the third period to send the game into overtime," Fedoruk wrote in the *Leader-Post*. "Pats were powerful," Ballard allowed. "Make no bones about it. If the breaks in those three games fell in favour of Regina, all this noise you hear would

Toronto Marlboros.

be coming from the Pats' dressing room instead of ours." The attendance at game five brought the series total to 25,821, an increase of almost 8,000 over the 1954 Memorial Cup final.

The Toronto Marlboros' Pulford, Baun and MacNeil returned to the Memorial Cup final in 1956 while Billy Harris graduated to the NHL, where he enjoyed a twelve-year NHL career. Ten of those years were spent with the Maple Leafs, with whom Harris won the Stanley Cup in 1962, 1963 and 1964.

From the Regina Pats, Bob Turner won the Stanley Cup five times with Montreal from 1956 to 1960. He rounded out an eight-year career in Chicago. Gary Aldcorn spent most of his five-year pro career with Toronto and Detroit. Captain Mike Nykoluk, Gerry James and Ken Girard all saw action with the Maple Leafs, while Glen Cressman enjoyed a brief stint as a Montreal Canadien. Of the players picked up by the Pats from Lethbridge, Les Colwill spent a season with the Rangers, and Earl Ingarfield spent thirteen seasons with the Rangers, Pittsburgh, and Oakland/California.

The **1956** Memorial Cup

"I guess if you are big enough, tough enough and can skate you can play hockey," Regina coach Murray Armstrong said after watching the Toronto Marlboros defeat the Montreal Junior Canadiens in the eighth and deciding game of the 1956 eastern final. "The players lean on one another and that type of hard checking doesn't enable a good junior team to cut loose with pleasing, wide-open plays."

The Regina Pats and Toronto Marlboros were back for a rematch of the 1955 junior championship. Armstrong's comments reflected the divide between the styles favoured by eastern and western junior teams in the first half of the 1950s. They may also have reflected some frustration that the rougher, more straightforward eastern style had consistently proven too much for western teams to handle. Things would be no different in 1956.

With Turk Broda still behind the bench, the Marlboros had a cast of players who would figure prominently in the NHL for decades to come: Bob Nevin, Carl Brewer, Bob Pulford, Bobby Baun, Harry Neale, Charlie Burns, Wally Boyer and team captain Al MacNeil. Regina's roster included captain Harry Ottenbreit, Bill Hicke, Murray Balfour and goaltender Hank Metcalf. They also picked up three players for the final: Len Lunde from the Edmonton Oil Kings, Johnny "Kayo" Kowalchuck from the Fort William Canadiens and Stewart McNeill from the Port Arthur North Stars.

Bob Baun skated with the Toronto Marlboros for both their 1955 and 1956 Memorial Cup victories.

In the Abbott Cup series, the Pats withstood a close seven-game affair with the Port Arthur North Stars, winning the deciding game 4–3 in overtime.

The Memorial Cup series was held at Maple Leaf Gardens, opening with a 4–4 stalemate on April 27 before a meagre showing of 3,855 fans. Two nights later, with 8,463 in the seats, the Marlboros breezed to a 5–1 victory. Pulford, who came into the final with 18 goals in fourteen playoff games, struck for two. "They weren't shooting," coach Armstrong said of his team's effort. "Pats are getting better," offered his rival Broda. "They're starting to look like big leaguers. I did expect Regina would be a great deal stronger, and I still say it's going to be a good series."

But the Marlboros won the second game as well, beating the Pats 4–2 on the strength of another 2-goal performance from Pulford. Toronto then moved to within one victory of their second straight championship with a 6–1 whipping of Regina before 2,470 fans. Pulford was again a key factor, scoring a hat trick in an effort described by Broda as the Marlboros' best of the series.

Armstrong was predictably disappointed in his team's showing, and aware that their shot at a championship was rapidly slipping away. "That was the key game and we weren't even in it," he lamented. Maple Leaf Gardens President

Stafford Smythe scoffed, "I defy any ordinary citizen to know what the Pats are supposed to be playing. They're supposed to like this type of hockey in the west. That's why they keep losing the Memorial Cup. The Marlies play it like the pros and that's why they're winning. I don't blame the boys. It's the officials above them."

The Marlboros wrapped it up in the fifth game, defeating the Pats 7–4 before 3,601 fans. The red-hot Pulford led the way with his second hat trick in as many games, giving him 10 goals in the series. "It was Regina's best showing," Broda said. "They played a good game and have the nucleus of a good team. They tell me that only two of the Regina players are overage for the 1957 season. If that's the case, then they could quite easily win the 1957 Memorial Cup next year. Isn't Saskatchewan supposed to be next year country?"

Broda became only the second coach to win back-to-back Memorial Cup titles, the other being Tracy Shaw with the 1939 and 1940 Oshawa Generals. Armstrong experienced a total of five Memorial Cup finals, four as coach, but he never managed to attain the championship.

From the 1956 Toronto Marlboros, Bob Pulford spent sixteen years in the NHL with Toronto and Los Angeles, while Bob Baun spent seventeen seasons with Toronto, Oakland and Detroit. The pair won the Stanley Cup with Toronto in 1962, 1963, 1964 and 1967. Pulford, a Hall of Fame inductee, went on to a coaching career with the Los Angeles Kings and Chicago Blackhawks, where he also reached the position of general manager.

Bob Nevin enjoyed a solid 19-year pro career, most notably with the Maple Leafs and Rangers, winning the Stanley Cup with the Leafs in 1962 and 1963.

Toronto Marlboros. Back row (l to r): Bill Stevens, Jim Murchie, Gord Haughton, Stan Buda, John Perdue, Walter Boyer, Carl Brewer, Ron Farnfield, Karl Elieff. Middle row: Art Marshall, Jim Crockett, Charlie Burns, Bill Kennedy, Len Broderick, Ken Girard, Harry Neale, Bob Nevin, Archie French. Front row: Gary Collins, Bob Baun, Walter "Turk" Broda, Stafford Smythe, Al MacNeil, Harold Ballard, Dr. J. Leo Hall, Bob Pulford, Ron Casey.

Carl Brewer played 13 years in the NHL, primarily with Toronto, where he took the Stanley Cup three times between 1962 and 1964.

Harry Neale never played in the NHL but enjoyed great success as a coach in the World Hockey Association with Minnesota and New England. He later stepped over to the NHL, where his work behind the bench and as general manager in Vancouver culminated in a drive to the Stanley Cup final in 1982. He then coached in Detroit before joining fellow Memorial Cup champion Don Cherry in the broadcast booth. Al MacNeil enjoyed an eleven-year career in the NHL as a defenceman, mostly with Toronto and Chicago. He won a Stanley Cup as coach of the Montreal Canadiens in 1971, and also spent time behind the bench in Atlanta and Calgary, where he took the general manager's reins in the mid-1990s.

From the Regina Pats, Murray Balfour went on to eight years in the NHL after returning to Memorial Cup competition in 1957 with another Montreal-affiliated junior team, the Ottawa Canadiens. Bill Hicke, with two Memorial Cup finals under his belt, also returned for another in 1958 before moving on to the big league.

The **1957** Memorial Cup

The 1957 Memorial Cup final marked the first time since 1948 that the trophy was taken home by a team from western Canada. It was not one of the traditional western powerhouses that ended the era of eastern supremacy, but a group of workmanlike players from a town that had never sent a team to the final before.

The Flin Flon Bombers had not previously won their league championship, but they put together a banner season leading up to the 1957 playoffs, winning forty-eight of fifty-five regular-season games in the Saskatchewan Junior Hockey League. Under coach Bobby Kirk, they defeated the Edmonton Oil Kings in the western semi-final, then swept Fort William in four straight to reach the 1957 Memorial Cup.

Their secret, according to Kirk, was balance. "I have three lines and anyone can come up with a goal," he said. The team had eight players with at least 25 goals on the season. If the Bombers had a dominant line, it consisted of Ted Hampson, Mel Pearson and Pat Ginnell, with George Konik leading the team on the blueline. They also picked up three players for the final: Orland Kurtenbach from Prince Albert, and defenceman Jean Gauthier and goaltender Lynn Davis from Port Arthur.

The Ottawa Canadiens, who eliminated the Guelph Biltmores to win the Richardson Trophy, were run by a duo destined to make a lasting impression on the NHL: coach and general manager Sam Pollock and assistant manager Scotty Bowman. On the ice, the junior Canadiens included team captain Ralph Backstrom and Murray Balfour, who had played with the Regina Pats during the previous two seasons. Gilles Tremblay patrolled the left wing and Claude Ruel was on the Ottawa defence.

The Memorial Cup final was scheduled to take place in Flin Flon and Regina. The Canadiens touched off somewhat of a furor when they arrived in Flin Flon too late to play the first game, causing it to be rescheduled. This gaffe stoked local feelings of indignation over suggestions by easterners that the northern Manitoba mining community of 12,000 was not up to scratch in its ability to host the Memorial Cup.

Bombers executive president Jimmy Wardle said, "Flin Flon citizens are up in arms over criticism levelled at the town and its facilities by Ottawa officials who do not recognize, apparently, any part of Canada west of Ottawa. We feel that the nationally known, warm-hearted hospitality and a fine hockey club make up for the lack of a Chateau Laurier and what they amusingly call an 'ice palace' in Ottawa."

But the 2,000 fans who packed the Whitney Forum in Flin Flon for the rescheduled first game didn't stay upset for long. They were treated to a 3–1 Bomber win, fuelled by two goals from George Konik and a solid performance by netminder George Wood. The Bombers also appeared to have the second game in hand. But another packed house was stunned when Ottawa scored 2 goals in the final thirty-three seconds to snatch a 4–3 victory.

In game three, Ottawa made it two out of three in Flin Flon with a 5–2 victory, as Balfour erupted for 3 goals. The junior Canadiens' stay in northern Manitoba was turning out more pleasant than they had expected. "Well, Balfour came through tonight," Sam Pollock said. "Those were his first goals of the play-offs and they couldn't have come at a better time. It also shows that we can come from behind in the worst places in the world."

The teams then headed for Regina, where the Bombers pulled even with a crucial 3–1 game four victory in front of 5,118 fans. Flin Flon's big line—Hampson, Pearson and Ginnell—scored all three Bombers goals, each skater tallying one in the third. Wood was again strong in goal for Flin Flon, making a notable save on a Billy Carter breakaway to keep his team in the game. By now it was clear that the 1957 final would not be another easy win for the eastern team. "After Ottawa took those two in Flin Flon," New York Rangers' general manager Muzz Patrick said, "I thought, without seeing the teams, that it was the same old story, too much balance by the eastern teams. I changed my mind. This western club can win it."

The Bombers took a 3–2 series lead with a 3–2 victory in front of 4,913 fans. It was a heated match, from which Sam Pollock was ejected. Ernie Fedoruk wrote in the *Regina Leader-Post* that Pollock had "questioned the ancestry of the referees following the second period and wound up as a spectator. Assistant Ottawa manager Bowman took over after Pollock was ejected. Bowman managed to last through the third period but he, too, took after the officials, Curly Breault and Dutch Van Deelan, both of Edmonton, as soon as the final buzzer sounded."

The Bombers appeared to have the initiative in the series, but a see-saw struggle continued, with Ottawa rebounding for a 4–2 victory in game six. Ralph Backstrom led the Canadiens with 2 goals. "It's too bad that they can't divide the Memorial Cup," Pollock said. "These two clubs out there both deserve it."

One of the great Memorial Cup series finally ended on May 8, before 4,500

Regina fans. Again, the Bombers line of Hampson, Ginnell and Pearson played a key role, the latter two firing for a pair of goals within a one-minute span late in the first period. Ottawa closed to within 1 late in the second, but Hampson restored the Bombers' 2-goal lead midway through the third period. The Canadiens did score a late goal, but fell short by a score of 3–2.

"It's the greatest thrill of my life," coach Kirk said. "We won the Memorial Cup because an inspired, determined hockey club fought when the chips were down and never gave up."

On Saturday, May 11, hordes of Flin Flonners converged on the Canadian National Railway station to welcome home their victorious Bombers. An estimated 4,000 people cheered as the players, dressed in their traditional maroon blazers and grey slacks, were led to the station platform by the Hudson Bay Mining and Smelting Pipe Band. The sixty-three-piece Flin Flon School Band and local Navy Cadet drum and bugle outfit played music as local dignitaries congratulated "the greatest amateur hockey team in Canada."

From the 1957 Flin Flon Bombers, Ted Hampson enjoyed a sixteen-year career in the NHL and WHA with stops in New York, Detroit, Oakland and Minnesota. Mel Pearson played six pro seasons, most of them in New York and Minnesota. Jean Gauthier played ten years in the NHL including six in Montreal, where he won the Stanley Cup in 1965. Orland Kurtenbach played thirteen pro seasons with the Rangers, Boston and Vancouver. He was the first-ever captain of the Canucks franchise, and later coached the NHL team between 1976 and 1978.

Flin Flon Bombers. Back row (l to r): Mel Pearson, Jean Gauthier, George Konik, Rod Lee, George Woods, Duane Rupp, Mike Kardash, Orland Kurtenbach, Pat Ginnell, Ken Willey, Ronnie Hutchinson, Wayne Sproxton, Barry Beatty, Lynn Davis. Front row: Carl Forrester, Teddy Hampson, Doug Dawson (manager), Bob Kirk (coach), Hec McCaig (trainer), Harvey Flemming, Cliff Lennartz.
MA/N3914

From the Ottawa Canadiens, Backstrom, Rousseau and Tremblay went on to the big league, but they would first return for another crack at the Memorial Cup. Murray Balfour began an eight-year NHL career in Montreal, but hit his stride in Chicago, where he won the Stanley Cup in 1961. Claude Ruel served as coach of the Montreal Canadiens in 1968–71 and 1979–81, winning the Stanley Cup in 1969.

Sam Pollock managed the Montreal Canadiens to nine Stanley Cup victories between 1965 and 1978. His coach for four of those victories was Scotty Bowman, who added another for the Habs in 1979. Bowman, who had previously taken the St. Louis Blues to the Stanley Cup final three times, also coached or managed the Pittsburgh Penguins to the 1991 and 1992 Stanley Cups and the Detroit Red Wings to the 1997 Cup. Both men have been inducted into the Hockey Hall of Fame.

The 1958 Memorial Cup

The National Hockey League of the late 1950s was dominated by one of the greatest dynasties in hockey history. The Montreal Canadiens won five straight Stanley Cup championships from 1956 to 1960, a feat never duplicated. The reign of the Canadiens also extended to the junior ranks, as they developed some of the best talent of the era through their affiliated junior teams. Fittingly, the Canadiens' two top junior farm teams met each other in the 1958 Memorial Cup. The Ottawa-Hull Junior Canadiens of Sam Pollock and Scotty Bowman faced the Frank Mario-coached Regina Pats in a showcase of Habs prospects.

The Pats had dethroned the defending champion Flin Flon Bombers before moving past the Edmonton Oil Kings in straight games in the western semi-final. This victory moved the Pats into the 1958 Abbott Cup championship against the St. Boniface Canadiens, whom they defeated in six games.

Ottawa-Hull, without a home in any major junior league, had spent the winter of 1957–58 playing a patchwork schedule of games against senior teams, minor professional teams and some OHA Junior A teams. Although they did not take part in the regular Junior A playoffs, they were slated to meet the Junior A champions of eastern Canada for the right to represent the east in the 1958 Memorial Cup final.

The Junior Canadiens' first playoff opponents were the Cape Breton All-Stars. In a best-of-seven series, the Junior Canadiens twice hammered Cape Breton by scores of 18–3 and 12–2. The rest of the series was cancelled. The Junior Canadiens then ran up against the Toronto Marlboros. The OHA champion Marlies vehemently protested the Junior Canadiens' use of goaltender Bruce Gamble. Ottawa had borrowed him from Guelph after their regular netminder was lost for the season due to illness. The protest was ignored, and the Junior Canadiens prevailed in five games, advancing to the Memorial Cup final.

Montreal Canadiens fans of the 1960s would have a field day with a program from a 1958 Memorial Cup final game. The Pats featured players like Terry

Ottawa-Hull Canadiens' captain Ralph Backstrom won the NHL's Calder Trophy in 1959 playing with Montreal.

Harper, Red Berenson, Bill Hicke and Dave Balon, while Ottawa-Hull's roster included Jean-Claude Tremblay, Ralph Backstrom, Bobby Rousseau and Gilles Tremblay. Habs scouts were especially interested in two players regarded as the pro team's brightest prospects: Ottawa-Hull's Backstrom and Regina's Hicke.

The best-of-seven series was played entirely in the east, with Ottawa and Hull sharing the games.

It opened in Ottawa on April 25, with 4,500 fans in attendance. The Pats got off to a strong start with a 4–3 win behind three goals from Hicke and some great goaltending from Ken Walters. "The performance by Walters was phenomenal," a *Regina Leader-Post* reporter enthused, "completely overshadowing the work of his more publicized rival, Gamble, at the other end of the rink. Time and again the lean little goaler came up with spectacular saves to frustrate the efforts of a classy pack of enemy snipers."

The Junior Canadiens evened things up in game two, posting a 4–2 victory in Hull. They came out at full throttle, opening up a 4–0 lead only twelve minutes into the game. Backstrom and Gilles Tremblay scored once each, with Billy Carter adding a pair. The *Regina Leader-Post's* Hank Johnson noted that coach Sam Pollock was in a "better frame of mind after the game, taking the padlock off his dressing room door." Pollock said, "We should have kept pouring the coal to them but we let up badly."

The Junior Canadiens roared out of the gates again in game three, skating to a 3–0 lead in the first thirteen minutes. Backstrom struck for a hat trick, while Carter delivered another 2-goal performance in the 6–2 Ottawa-Hull victory.

Backstrom and Carter now had five goals each in three games. "They just kept slaughtering us in that first period," coach Mario lamented. "I thought we were going to be all right in this one, but our defence lets up and it's 3–0 before we know we're in a hockey game."

Mario did some line juggling prior to game four, including moving Hicke from right wing to the left side in an attempt to wring more offence from his best sniper. Hicke had 4 of Regina's 8 goals, but 3 had been in game one. This tinkering paid off, as the Pats won the fourth game 4–3 in overtime before 3,500 fans. Bill Saunders scored the winner from a pass by Hicke at 2:13 of the extra period. "It's a shame they couldn't play some of these games in Toronto," said Maple Leafs coach Billy Reay, a spectator at the contest. "A terrific game like that would pack Maple Leaf Gardens."

Ottawa-Hull moved up three games to two with a 6–3 victory in Hull. Again, the Junior Canadiens demonstrated an explosive offence, salting the game with 3 goals in one minute and twenty-seven seconds during the second period.

The Junior Canadiens carried their momentum into the sixth game, building another early lead and coasting to a 6–1 victory. 4,675 fans packed the Ottawa Auditorium to watch their team claim the Memorial Cup.

Ralph Backstrom, Bobby Rousseau, Gilles Tremblay and J.C. Tremblay all enjoyed lengthy pro careers, and all spent the majority of their ice time with the Habs. Both Backstrom and Rousseau started out their careers with a bang, Backstrom winning the Calder Trophy in 1958–59 and Rousseau collecting it three seasons later. From 1959 to 1969, Rousseau won four Stanley Cups with Montreal, Backstrom won six times and Gilles Tremblay won twice. Jean-Claude

Ottawa-Hull Canadiens. Back row (l to r): Lou Passador, Bob Boucher, John Annable, Bob Olajos, Harold White, Dick Dawson, Claude Richard, Claude Fournel, Paul Gauthier. Middle row: Bruce Gamble, Gilles Tremblay, André Tardif, Jacques Begin, Nick Murray, Terry Gray, Jean C. Tremblay, Claude Cyr. Front row: Bob Rousseau, Bill Carter, Sam Pollock, James P. McCaffrey, Ralph Backstrom, Donat Vien, Scotty Bowman (coach), John Longarini, Claude Ruel.

Tremblay won the Stanley Cup five times with the Canadiens between 1965 and 1971, and also won the 1977 Avco Cup with the Quebec Nordiques of the WHA.

From the Regina Pats, Terry Harper spent nineteen years in the NHL, mostly with Montreal, Detroit and Los Angeles. Red Berenson began a seventeen-year career with the Habs, although it was in St. Louis and Detroit that he blossomed. Bill Hicke enjoyed fourteen years in the NHL and WHA with Montreal, the Rangers, and Oakland/California. Dave Balon played the better part of a fifteen-year career with the Rangers and Canadiens. All four ex-Pats won the Stanley Cup—Harper five times, Hicke and Balon twice, and Berenson once—all with Montreal during the late 1950s and the 1960s. Autry Erickson, who had been picked up by the Pats from Prince Albert for the 1958 Memorial Cup final, had six spotty seasons in the NHL with Boston, Chicago and Oakland/California. He also played briefly for the Toronto Maple Leafs in the 1967 playoffs, earning his name on the Stanley Cup.

The 1959 Memorial Cup

Twenty-five-year-old Scotty Bowman made his third trip to the Memorial Cup final in 1959. The first two times, he had been an assistant to Ottawa-Hull manager and coach Sam Pollock. This time, Bowman held the reins of the Peterborough Petes, who were facing a tenacious Winnipeg Braves team.

The Braves had eliminated the Flin Flon Bombers in an all-Manitoba western final that went six games. The series was clinched at the Winnipeg Arena before 9,018 fans, the largest crowd to witness a junior game in western Canada.

The Petes, known as the TPT Petes because of their sponsorship by Toronto Peterborough Transport, were in their third season in Peterborough, having moved from Kitchener. The transplanted club finished last in the seven-team OHA in their first season under coach Baldy McKay. The following year, they moved up to fifth under coach Teeder Kennedy, and finished second in 1959 under Bowman.

The Petes pushed past a veritable Who's Who of prominent junior clubs in playoff action, eliminating the Barrie Flyers, Guelph Biltmores and the St. Michael's Majors to move out of the OHL. They then eliminated Sam Pollock's Ottawa-Hull Junior Canadiens in the eastern final.

The Petes had Wayne Connelly, their leading scorer, as well as Jim Roberts and Barclay Plager. Winnipeg was powered by a line of Al LeBlanc, Bobby Leiter and Laurie Langrell, the MJHL scoring champion. The Braves also featured future NHL notables Gary Bergman and Ted Green, the latter added from St. Boniface. "It's got to be hustle, hustle, hustle if we're going to win," Braves coach Bill Allum said. "I don't know anything about this Peterborough team, but they must be good to beat Ottawa-Hull."

The Memorial Cup final was held in Winnipeg and Brandon. Game one was played in Winnipeg on April 24, before 6,239 fans. It was a hard-hitting, fast-skating match from which the Petes wrested a 5–4 win. "I think that the Langrell-LeBlanc-Leiter trio are the best junior line we've come up against this year,"

Bowman said. "They were a threat every time that they were on the ice."

The Braves tied the series in game two, posting a 5–2 victory before 9,171 fans at the Winnipeg Arena. The Canadian Press reported, "Braves showed some of the speed up front that won them the western Abbott Cup title as they beat the Petes to the puck while their defence and goalie Wakely left little to be desired."

In the third contest, Winnipeg went up two games to one, prevailing 5–2 before 7,939 fans. Their big line did the main damage again. Langrell had his third straight 2-goal game, while LeBlanc added a single. Braves captain Wayne "Keeper" Larkin also scored twice.

Ted Green went on to play eighteen years in the NHL and WHA, after winning the Memorial Cup with the Winnipeg Braves in 1959.

The Braves then took a commanding 3–1 series lead in the fourth game, winning 5–3 before 8,375 fans. "What can a guy do?" Bowman asked, upset with referee Len Corriveau. "We play our best game of the series and a couple of bad breaks cost us a chance of drawing even."

"We'll wrap it up on Friday," coach Allum predicted, looking forward to the fifth game. "They had us on the run in the early stages but the fellows never quit trying and it paid off. You can't let up against them—they proved it tonight." But Bowman was unwilling to throw in the towel. "Don't forget we've been down worse than this. St. Mike's had us 3–1 with one game tied and we bounced back. We'll do it again, just watch."

But the Petes' comeback never materialized. The Braves wrapped it up in five in Brandon's Wheat City Arena, getting 3 goals from Alan Baty in a 6–2 victory. A capacity crowd of more than 4,000 people attended. "The rugged game almost got out of hand in the third period," Canadian Press reported, "when coach Bowman of the Petes was first given a bench penalty for slapping a stick on the boards, then ejected from the game for pulling out his wallet and appearing to offer money to referee Corriveau."

Before securing the city of Winnipeg its first Memorial Cup since the Monarchs had won in 1946, the Braves had squandered a 2–0 lead in the first period. They rallied to score the game's final 4 goals. Bowman returned at the end of the game to congratulate Allum and the Braves, satisfied that his own team's effort had been solid. "I've never seen a team play so well and lose—but someone has to lose," he philosophized.

Bowman also acknowledged the superiority of the Braves. "They were better around the net and their goalie played well this game," he said. "Scotty's been in the Memorial Cup final three years in a row and that's a record that no one else has," noted Sam Pollock, on hand for the series.

From Bowman's Peterborough Petes, Jim Roberts emerged as a durable NHL winger, splitting a fifteen-year career between St. Louis and Montreal. He won the Stanley Cup five times with the Canadiens. Barclay Plager spent a ten-year pro career patrolling the St. Louis blueline and his number, 8, has been retired by the Blues. Petes captain Bill Mahoney—who missed the final with a broken ankle—coached in the NHL with the 1984 and 1985 Minnesota North Stars.

From the Winnipeg Braves, Gary Bergman played twelve years with Detroit, Minnesota and Kansas City, while Ted Green spent eighteen years in the NHL and WHA with Boston, New England and Winnipeg. The hard-nosed defenceman won the Stanley Cup with the Bruins in 1972, as well as the Avco Cup in both of his WHA stops. He later won five Stanley Cups as an assistant coach with the Edmonton Oilers.

Winnipeg Braves. Back row (l to r): Laurie Langrell, Ted Green, Paul Sexsmith, Allan Ingimundson, Gerry Kruk, Ted Knight, Pat Angers, John Sutherland. Second row from back: Ray Brunel, Allan LeBlanc, Bobby Leiter, Ed Bradawski, Ken King, Howie Hughes, Don Atamanchuk. Third row from back: Bill Allum (coach), Doug Munro, Gary Bergman, Wayne Winston, John Rodger, Alan Baty, Lew Mueller, Jim Drury (trainer). Front row: Jack Perrin (president), Ernie Wakely, Wayne Larkin, Zenon Moroz, Bill Addison (manager). MA/N9094

The
1960s

While players graduating from Canadian junior teams in the 1950s set their sights on a six-team National Hockey League, their 1960s counterparts found an increasing array of opportunities at their disposal. The sport had more exposure than ever in Canada and was also becoming regionally entrenched in areas of the United States. The minor pro leagues were stocked with some solid talent and the junior leagues, bolstered by the growth of the game and simple demographics, were producing more and more players. All of this enabled the NHL to double its size in 1967. Within a few years, the World Hockey Association would offer even more choices for players.

By this era, it was not just a few standouts who went on to pro careers, but a significant number of journeymen. This fact makes the names of many alumni of 1960s Memorial Cup teams recognizable to the modern hockey fan. Moreover, the decade saw some rough finals—the era of soft western teams being pushed aside by more aggressive eastern squads was ending—and the players who emerged as leaders in the championships were often the grinders.

Hard rocks such as Glen Sather and Pat Quinn played major roles in taking the Edmonton Oil Kings to their first Memorial Cup victory in 1963. The tenacious Terry Crisp and scrapping Derek Sanderson helped power the 1965 Niagara Falls Flyers to a championship. Rick Ley, the archetypal hockey workhorse, captained the same Flyers to a victory in 1968. Nonetheless, players like Bobby Orr, Gerry Cheevers and Brad Park gave junior hockey fans plenty of chances to see pure skill.

The 1960s brought an end to the era of junior teams being sponsored by NHL parent clubs. The universal draft was introduced instead. The formation of the Western Canada Junior Hockey League in 1967 was a bold and important stride for western junior hockey. Initially, the new league and its teams were shunned by the CAHA and prevented from competing for the Memorial Cup. But the new league expanded and persevered, becoming what is now known as the Western Hockey League.

Bobby Orr is one of the best players in hockey history, and arguably the greatest to play in a Memorial Cup final. GA/HHF

The **1960** Memorial Cup

The combatants in the 1960 Memorial Cup final took a precarious road to the championship. The final series was a wild-scoring affair with 63 goals scored, an average of more than 10 per game. The St. Catharines TeePees, on one side of the shootout, were bent on snatching their second Memorial Cup championship from the Edmonton Oil Kings.

Oil Kings coach Harry Allen admitted he was not counting on moving past Flin Flon in the western semi-final or the Brandon Wheat Kings in the Abbott Cup championship. Nonetheless, Edmonton sidelined a strong Wheat Kings team in seven games to head to the Memorial Cup for the fourth time in the city's history. The TeePees were involved in an even tighter series with the Brockville Canadiens to decide the eastern champion. The TeePees took a 3–0 game lead only to have Brockville come back to score three wins and a tie. The series was decided in an eighth game and St. Catharines moved on to the final for the first time since 1954.

The Oil Kings included players like Larry Lund, Ed Joyal, Bruce MacGregor and Don Chiz. Chiz, who had toiled in MacGregor's shadow for all their years of Edmonton minor hockey, led the club in scoring in 1960 and picked up the league's most gentlemanly player award to boot. MacGregor, hampered by injuries for most of the season, regained his old form in the playoffs and along with Joyal and Chiz, spearheaded Edmonton's drive to the final.

Coached by Max Kaminsky and managed by Rudy Pilous, the TeePees were an impressive group that included captain and OHA scoring leader Ronald "Chico" Maki, goaltender Roger Crozier, Bob Maki, Vic Hadfield, Pat Stapleton, George "Duke" Harris, Ray Cullen, John Brenneman, Murray Hall, Bill Speer and Doug Robinson. Their big line consisted of Chico Maki, Cullen and Hadfield.

"In order to win at the other end of the country, you've got to have a powerhouse," Edmonton manager Leo LeClerc said. "I figure we have to be 25 percent better at least, and after watching that St. Catharines club in action against Brockville, I'm very doubtful."

The series opened in St. Catharines with the Oil Kings getting off to a good start. They took game one 5–3 on the strength of a goal from Flin Flon pickup Cliff Pennington. The hero, however, was Edmonton goaltender Russ Gillow. Cut over the left eye for eight stitches early in the game, the maskless Gillow was a standout. "This guy Gillow is the best goalkeeper the TeePees have faced all season," offered Rudy Pilous.

The teams played game two in the Maple Leaf Gardens, where the TeePees knotted the series with a 6–2 victory before 5,833 fans. When Gillow experienced swelling around his eye, the Oil Kings had to resort to backup goaltender Dale Gaume. Game three saw 10,666 fans turn out to the Gardens, attracting the largest crowd to see a Memorial Cup game in fourteen years. They watched the TeePees bury the Oil Kings 9–1. St. Catharines opened the scoring forty-two seconds into the game and went on to fire 54 shots at Gillow, who was back in net for Edmonton. Cullen scored twice and set up 2 other goals. Hall also had 2 goals, with defenceman Stapleton adding another and 2 assists.

"I could hardly see out of my eye," Gillow complained. "Only 2 of those St. Catharines goals were good, the others were flukes."

"Too many things went wrong for us out there," coach Allen said. "Our club has been up and down all year and I think we're at the bottom right now. But before this thing ends, St. Catharines will know that they were in a series."

The Oil Kings made good on this vow, roaring back in game four to hammer the TeePees 9–3 before only 2,344 fans. The small crowd had arrived at Maple

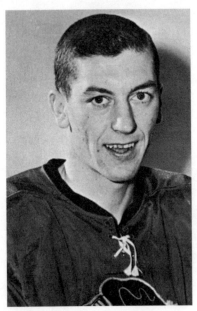

OHA scoring leader Ronald "Chico" Maki led the St. Catharines TeePees to Memorial Cup victory in 1960.

Leaf Gardens expecting St. Catharines to skate easily to their third straight victory, but the Oil Kings closed out a roughhouse third period with a 4-goal splurge. The star of the game was Joyal, who fired 4 markers behind St. Catharines netminder Crozier.

The game featured plenty of rough play and fighting. By the middle of the third, it had degenerated into a maze of clutching, high sticking and fisticuffs. Oil Kings defenceman Wayne Muloin was hit on the head by Bob Maki's stick, causing a wound that required five stitches to close. "Those TeePees are real butchers," declared an irate Harry Allen. "When players try to maim other players, there is something wrong with the management or the coach. If they want to play that kind of hockey, which doesn't draw crowds in any rink, then let them go to it. My boys are no patsies."

Both teams reserved their sticks for goal scoring in game five. For the third time in a row, the winning team scored 9 goals as the TeePees skated to a 9–6 victory before 4,014 fans. Gillow stopped 47 in a losing effort while Crozier's 21 saves were good enough for the win. "They outhustled us," Allen admitted. "But Sunday afternoon will be another game."

However, Edmonton did not rebound. The TeePees took a first-period lead in the sixth game and never looked back, winning 7–3 in front of 8,000 fans. Edmonton was within striking distance entering the third period, but Maki, Harris and Robinson each scored in a span of less than three minutes to clinch the second Memorial Cup for St. Catharines.

For TeePees coach Max Kaminsky, who had played in the NHL in the 1930s in addition to managing, coaching and scouting at various levels of the game, the 1960 Memorial Cup was a glorious finish to a successful career. Less than a year after his championship triumph, he died of cancer at the age of forty-nine. Kaminsky had an OHA trophy named after him, originally awarded to the most gentlemanly player. After the 1970 season, the trophy was presented to the most outstanding defenceman during the regular season.

Many of Kaminsky's St. Catharines TeePees enjoyed success in the NHL and WHA. Chico Maki followed up his Memorial Cup season with a Stanley Cup championship in 1961. Although he played only one post-season game with the Blackhawks that year, Maki went on to play fourteen seasons with Chicago. Pat "Whitey" Stapleton spent fifteen years in the NHL and WHA, mostly with the Blackhawks. Vic Hadfield had sixteen NHL seasons with the Rangers and

St. Catharines TeePees.

Penguins while defenceman Bill Speer played six years in the NHL and WHA, winning the Stanley Cup in 1970 with Boston.

Murray Hall played in the NHL with Chicago, Detroit, Minnesota and Vancouver before moving on to Houston of the WHA. He helped the Aeros claim two Avco Cup championships in 1974 and 1975. George "Duke" Harris split one year in the NHL between Minnesota and Toronto, and then divided three WHA seasons between Houston and Chicago. Ray Cullen spent six years in the NHL, playing mostly in Minnesota and Vancouver, while Doug Robinson played for six years with the Blackhawks, Rangers and Kings. John Brenneman spent five years as a pro in five different cities: Chicago, New York, Toronto, Detroit and Oakland.

From the Edmonton Oil Kings, Larry Lund celebrated two Avco Cup championships with Houston in the WHA, where he played for six years. Eddie Joyal had a solid thirteen-year pro hockey career, spending most of his time with Detroit and Los Angeles in the NHL and Edmonton in the WHA. Bruce MacGregor played fourteen years in the NHL with Detroit and the Rangers, plus two in the WHA with Edmonton.

The **1961** Memorial Cup

In 1944, a leftwinger named David Bauer was plucked from the Toronto's St. Michael's Majors to aid the Oshawa Generals' drive to the Memorial Cup title. In 1961, Father Bauer was back in the national final again, this time spearheading a drive by St. Michael's.

The Bauer-coached team sidelined the defending champion St. Catharines TeePees early in the playoffs. They then swept the eastern final against the Moncton Beavers. Out west, the Oil Kings were again the dominant team, winning sixteen of their nineteen playoff games and defeating the Winnipeg Rangers in the western championship.

The Oilers romped to their second straight Abbott Cup with Don Chiz, Johnny Muloin, Bobby Cox, Larry Lund, Dennis Kassian, goalie Paul Sexsmith and the hard-hitting Tom Burgess on board. Edmonton added defenceman Ken Stephanson of the Winnipeg Braves, Dave Richardson from the Winnipeg Rangers and centre Bryan Hextall Jr. of the Brandon Wheat Kings. But Oil Kings coach Russell "Buster" Brayshaw said he would only use these players in the event of trouble. Richardson and Hextall would provide scoring prowess in reserve, while fighter Stephanson added toughness and intimidation.

St. Michael's featured captain Terry O'Malley along with the Draper twins, Bruce and Dave, Larry Keenan, Arnie Brown, Billy MacMillan, André Champagne, Terry Clancy—the son of hockey legend "King" Clancy—and goal-tenders Gerry Cheevers and Dave Dryden. Cheevers, an outstanding junior prospect, spent eight games playing on left wing during the regular OHA season, picking up a single assist.

The series was held in Edmonton, opening in the old Gardens. Cheevers posted a 4–0 shutout in front of 6,674 fans in game one. "He's all they said he was," Father Bauer remarked, not of Cheevers but of Edmonton goalie Paul Sexsmith. "I thought we should have been ahead 3–0 by the end of the first period but for him." Many observers felt the Cheevers/Sexsmith contest would decide the Memorial Cup.

Edmonton manager Leo LeClerc gave assurances that the Oil Kings "could not be that bad again." Father Bauer asked, "Didn't I tell you before everybody in the east wanted a crack at us in the playoffs? We're not great but just seem to keep plugging along."

Toronto did just that in the second game, taking a 4–1 victory in front of 6,200 customers. Clancy scored twice while Burgess scored Edmonton's goal near the end of the third period to end Cheevers' shutout string at 113 minutes and 25 seconds. "We played well enough to win," moaned coach Brayshaw. "We couldn't beat that Cheevers. The kid was uncanny. He pulled off a couple of saves bordering the impossible."

Father Bauer's team pushed the Oil Kings to the edge in game three with a 4–2 victory. Osborne scored three goals and set up another while Hextall and Chiz scored for Edmonton. Sexsmith was impressive again, even in defeat. "Ridiculous," Edmonton star Chiz grumbled to Ron Glover of the *Edmonton Journal*. "It's ridiculous, nothing else, for a team to come in here and beat us four times in a row."

The Oil Kings turned their injured pride into motivation in the fourth game, and gave their faithful followers reason for hope by scoring a 5–4 victory before 4,864 fans. The first period was highlighted by a collision between Burgess and Cheevers which left the latter with a slight rib injury and needing minor repairs to his face. Burgess earned two minutes in the penalty box.

Cheevers returned to the game and made 27 stops, while Sexsmith stopped 32. The Oil Kings jumped to a 3–0 second-period lead and held on for the victory.

"We've certainly got our backs to the wall," Brayshaw said, "but we looked a bit more like the old Oil Kings and, if we carry on this way, St. Mike's are in for a good series." Father Bauer credited the Oil Kings for their performance. "From the coach out, they wanted to win more than we did," he said. "If we repeat this kind of game, who knows what might happen."

What might happen did, in game five. The Oil Kings, riding another strong performance by Sexsmith, continued along the comeback trail by winning 4–2 before 6,114 fans. Dennis Kassian, scoring twice, finally got untracked in the series. "We have no false illusions," Brayshaw cautioned. "We know it will take plenty of hard work, but Sexsmith is our meal ticket. If he's hot, we just might force the series to seven games." Bauer agreed. "He handled everything we could throw at him," he said, "although we had some defensive lapses."

But Sexsmith couldn't carry his team any further. St. Michael's scored a game six 4–2 victory at Edmonton Gardens to claim their fourth Memorial Cup. Jack Cole, Bruce Draper, Paul Conlin and André Champagne scored for the winning team while Hextall and Lund replied for Edmonton. Champagne was the leading goal scorer in the series with 4 goals and 5 assists. The 1961 victory was the last for St. Michael's. The relentless grind and hard travel of the Ontario junior circuit, in addition to the influence exerted by the NHL, was being seen in an increasingly negative light by the school.

The decision was predicted in a letter sent by Father Bauer to the Toronto Maple Leafs' Conn Smythe, owner of the team that most benefitted from the talent developed at the college. "My opinion is that sooner or later, they [the college] will see fit to discontinue in the Junior A series because of its growing professionalism, its long schedule and rough play which so often results in unfavourable publicity difficult for the educational institution to handle gracefully."

The Maple Leafs attempted to deal with the problem by aiding the development of the Metro Junior A Hockey League after the 1960–61 season. This was a more geographically focussed league designed to alleviate some of the scheduling problems experienced by St. Michael's. But by 1963, the school discontinued its hockey program altogether and the team was relocated to Neil McNeil High School in Toronto. St. Michael's College returned to the OHL in 1997–98 with former Toronto Marlboro Mark Napier acting as coach.

Father Bauer was transferred to St. Mark's College and the University of British Columbia, where he coached the UBC Thunderbirds hockey team before building Canada's Olympic hockey program. He was inducted into the Hockey Hall of Fame in 1989.

From the 1961 St. Michael's Majors, Gerry Cheevers emerged as one of hockey's great netminders. He began his pro career with one season as a Maple Leaf but made his mark in Boston, where he played for fifteen years. This stretch was punctuated by a four-season interregnum with Cleveland in the WHA. Cheevers backstopped the Bruins to the Stanley Cup in 1970 and 1972, and was inducted into the Hockey Hall of Fame.

Dave Dryden played nine years in the NHL with the Rangers, Chicago, Buffalo and Edmonton, plus five years with Edmonton in the WHA. Arnie Brown, who broke into the NHL with the Maple Leafs, played most of his twelve years in the league with the Rangers, Red Wings, Islanders and Atlanta Flames before finishing his career in the WHA. Like Brown, Billy MacMillan started in the NHL with the Maple Leafs, although not until the 1970–71 season. He

Toronto St. Michael's Majors.

played seven seasons with the Maple Leafs, Atlanta Flames and New York Islanders. Larry Keenan played six years in the pros with Toronto, St. Louis, Buffalo and Philadelphia. Bruce Draper played one game with the Leafs in 1962–63, and André Champagne played two games with the Leafs during the same season, returning to win the Memorial Cup with the Toronto Marlboros in 1964.

From the Edmonton Oil Kings, Larry Lund celebrated two Avco Cup championships with Houston in the WHA, where he played for six years. Johnny Muloin played in the NHL with Detroit, Oakland and Minnesota, and in the WHA with Cleveland and Edmonton. Dennis Kassian played a season with the Alberta Oilers in the WHA.

Bryan Hextall, picked up from the Wheat Kings for the 1961 final, played eight seasons in the NHL with the Rangers, Pittsburgh, Atlanta, Detroit and Minnesota. Fellow add-on Dave Richardson of the Winnipeg Rangers went on to a four-year NHL career with the Rangers, Blackhawks and Red Wings.

The **1962** Memorial Cup

By 1962, it looked as though the decade was going to belong to the Edmonton Oil Kings, as far as western junior hockey was concerned. However, Edmonton was still looking for their first national title. Defeated in the 1960 and 1961 tournaments, the Oil Kings hoped that their third attempt in a row would prove lucky. But their opponents in the final, the Hamilton Red Wings, had beginner's luck on their side.

With Russell Brayshaw still behind the bench, the Oil Kings took out the Brandon Wheat Kings in the Abbott Cup final. Meanwhile, the Red Wings, coached by Eddie Bush, sidelined eastern Canada's best junior clubs with relative ease. The vanquished included the St. Catharines TeePees, Niagara Falls Flyers, St. Michael's Majors and Quebec Citadels. The Red Wings lost only one game during their playoff run.

Hamilton featured a multitude of future NHL and WHA regulars, including Pit Martin, Paul Henderson, Bryan Campbell, Bob Wall, Earl Heiskala, Ron Harris, Wayne Rivers, Howie Menard, Jimmy Peters, Lowell MacDonald and Roger Lafreniere. Edmonton, led by captain Wayne Muloin, boasted Glen Sather, Larry Hale, Norm Beaudin and Butch Paul.

Originally scheduled at Maple Leaf Gardens, the first game was redirected by the CAHA to Hamilton, with the next three games to take place in Guelph. A fifth game, if necessary, would be played in Kitchener. This change of plans was the result of a hassle over television rights by Hamilton and Toronto stations. Part of the series was being televised in the Toronto–Guelph–Kitchener area by a local CTV affiliate, a milestone for Memorial Cup media coverage.

Hamilton scored a 5–2 victory in game one before 3,275 onlookers. A 3-goal Red Wings outburst in the second period and a hat trick by Lowell MacDonald paced Hamilton to the win. Afterwards, Eddie Bush added insult to injury by dismissing the Oil Kings as "the scruffiest-looking team I have ever seen in a Memorial Cup final. They all need haircuts, their uniforms were dirty and full of holes and on top of that they came to the Forum in windbreakers."

Edmonton general manager Leo LeClerc fired back, choosing the 3,800-seat Forum as his target. "This place looks like a converted factory chimney," sneered LeClerc, who had wanted to play all the games in Maple Leaf Gardens. "You don't play the Grey Cup in a cow pasture."

Guelph played host to the second game, and 2,800 fans watched the Red Wings take a 2–0 series lead with a 4–2 victory. In an effort to turn the series around, Brayshaw cobbled together a line consisting of Butch Paul between Marc Dufour—a late addition from the Brandon Wheat Kings—and Norm Beaudin. In game three, the line responded with 3 goals, 2 of which came from Beaudin over a twenty-seven-second span in the second period. This sparked the Oil Kings to a 5–3 victory.

"Edmonton played much better and we were due for a letdown," Bush admitted. "The whole team had it all at once and I hope they got it out of their system." For his part, Brayshaw felt that his club was finally in gear. "They played more like the club that won the western Abbott Cup championship," he said. "If we play that well again this could be a long series yet."

But the Red Wings responded with hardened resolve in game four, shutting out Edmonton 3–0 in Guelph. Hamilton scored 2 powerplay goals thirty-six seconds apart in the third to put the game away. Goaltender John Blom blocked 26 Edmonton shots. The contest attracted 4,215 fans, the first sellout of the 1962 Memorial Cup. "We played well enough to win but we didn't score," Brayshaw said. "If we play that way we should take game five. The breaks have got to come our way sometime soon."

But the breaks continued to go to the Red Wings. A total of 7,071 fans crammed Kitchener's Memorial Auditorium to watch Hamilton post a 7–4 victory. The Red Wings fired in 3 goals within 1:20 of the third period to sink the Oil

Kings and take the championship. According to the Canadian Press, a raucous Kitchener crowd greeted every score "with a barrage of eggs, paper cartons and programs and other debris, causing numerous delays in the contest."

MacDonald and Rivers each scored twice for Hamilton with singles coming from Menard, Martin and Henderson. Dufour, Bourbonnais, Paul and Downey scored for Edmonton. The clubs played to packed houses for two consecutive games, establishing cash records for both the Guelph and Kitchener hockey facilities. The joyous Red Wings, winners in their debut appearance in the national final, picked up coach Bush and hurled him in the air three times after the presentation of the Memorial Cup.

Eleven members of the Hamilton Red Wings graduated to either the NHL or the WHA. Bryan Campbell played five years in the NHL with Chicago and Los Angeles. From 1973 to 1978, he skated in the WHA with the Philadelphia Blazers, Cincinnati Stingers, Indianapolis Racers and Edmonton Oilers. Wayne Rivers saw action with the Bruins from

Paul Henderson of the 1962 Memorial Cup champs, Hamilton Red Wings, is probably most famous for his last minute series-winning goal for Team Canada in the 1972 "Summit Series" against Russia.

1964 to 1967, the Blues in 1968 and the Rangers in 1969. He subsequently played with the New York Raiders, New York Golden Blades, New Jersey Knights and San Diego Mariners in the WHA. Defenceman Bob Wall started his pro career with the Detroit Red Wings from 1965 to 1967, before moving to Los Angeles, where he was the first captain in the history of the Kings organization. He played three seasons with the Kings before concluding his NHL years with Detroit and St. Louis. Wall headed to the WHA as an original Alberta Oiler in 1973 before finishing his career in San Diego.

Lowell MacDonald, after breaking in with Detroit in 1962, remained a Red Wing in a utility role through the 1965 season. He was chosen by the Kings in the 1967 expansion draft and stayed with them until the 1969 season. He then headed to the Pittsburgh Penguins, where he played for seven seasons. Ron

Harris skated for four different pro teams from 1963 to 1976, first as a Red Wing and then with the Oakland Seals, Atlanta Flames and New York Rangers.

Earl Heiskala played in the NHL with Philadelphia and Los Angeles from 1969 to 1974. Howie Menard played portions of the four seasons with Detroit, Los Angeles, Chicago and Oakland. Roger Lafreniere played part of the 1963 season with Detroit, and part of the 1973 season in St. Louis. Jimmy Peters played with Detroit and Los Angeles from 1965 to 1975.

Pit Martin had an impressive seventeen-year pro career, beginning in 1962. He joined Wayne Rivers and Lowell MacDonald in Detroit the same year they won the junior championship. Martin stayed with Detroit until the 1966 season, when he became a Boston Bruin. After a year in Boston, he played eleven seasons with Chicago before closing out his career with the Canucks.

Paul Henderson enjoyed an eighteen-year career in the NHL and WHA. He debuted with the Red Wings in 1963, also playing for Toronto from 1969 to 1974. Henderson played in the WHA with Toronto and Birmingham for five years before returning to the NHL to finish his career in Atlanta. Henderson made a further mark with his brilliant performance in the 1972 Canada-Russia "Summit Series." In one of the most famous moments in hockey history, he scored an exhilarating series-winning goal with thirty-four seconds remaining in the final game.

From the Edmonton Oil Kings, Larry Hale skated with Philadelphia from 1967 to 1972. He then played with the Houston Aeros in the WHA for six years,

Hamilton Red Wings. Back row (l to r): Joe Bujdoso, Lowell MacDonald, Wayne Rivers, Harvey Meisenheimer, Ron Harris, John Gofton, Earl Heiskala. Middle row: Eddie Bush, Jack Wildfong, Larry Ziliotto, Paul Henderson, Roger Lafreniere, Bryan Campbell, Jim Peters, Syd Bibby. Front row: Bob Hamilton, John "Bud" Blom, Hubert "Pit" Martin, Jim Skinner, Howie Menard, Kenneth D. Soble, Bob Wall, Larry Harrop, Bob Dean.

winning the Avco Cup in 1974 and 1975. Norm Beaudin enjoyed a brief stint with the St. Louis Blues in 1968 and the Minnesota North Stars in 1971 before moving on to the WHA. He joined the Winnipeg Jets, playing on their Avco Cup championship team in 1976. The most notable Oil King of 1962, Glen Sather, would make a strong mark on the NHL, but not before helping to lead Edmonton in two drives to the Memorial Cup finals of 1963 and 1964.

The **1963** Memorial Cup

The Edmonton Oil Kings were beginning to look like perennial bridesmaids by 1963. The team still had nothing to show for its three consecutive trips to the finals. Nevertheless, Oil Kings coach Buster Brayshaw felt the latest edition was his strongest team yet. The 1962–63 Oil Kings were an aggressive unit capable of playing what Brayshaw termed "eastern style" hockey. They would need all the muscle and tenacity they could muster in facing Hap Emms and his hard-nosed Niagara Falls Flyers team in the final.

The Oil Kings defeated the Brandon Wheat Kings for the Abbott Cup while the Flyers deposed the defending champion Hamilton Red Wings en route to an eastern final triumph over the Espanola Eagles. The Flyers' victory marked the return to Memorial Cup competition of Hap Emms for the first time in ten years. Emms was now owner–manager of a team that had moved from Barrie to Niagara Falls in 1960.

Emms' Flyers, coached by Bill Long, were not short on toughness either. Led by captain Terry Crisp and Gary Dornhoefer, Niagara Falls also featured OHA scoring champion and Red Tilson Trophy winner Wayne Maxner, plus Bill Goldsworthy, Ron Schock, Ted Snell, Don Awrey and goaltender George Gardner.

The Oil Kings had captain Rick Bourbonnais, Glen Sather, Pat Quinn, Bert Marshall, Butch Barber and Harold Fleming. The last two were borrowed from Lethbridge. "This is the biggest club overall that I have taken to the final," Brayshaw said. "It has more weight because I've found that our light clubs in past years have run out of oomph as the season wears on."

The championship final was held in Edmonton's Arena Gardens. Niagara Falls roared to an 8–0 victory in a physical game one before 6,785 fans. Snell and Maxner scored twice each, with Gardner posting the shutout. "They had an off night," Emms said of the opposition, taking no comfort in the margin of victory. "It's going to be a tough series yet." Brayshaw was not ready to sound any alarm bells. "They certainly aren't 8 goals better than us," he said.

His team proved him correct, rebounding in game two with a 7–3 victory to even the series. Butch Paul, an eighteen-year-old centreman from Red Willow, Alberta, was outstanding for the Oil Kings, scoring twice and setting up 3 other goals. "Technically, it was our finest hour," said Brayshaw. "It was a great effort."

The Oil Kings carried the momentum into game three, exploding for 4 second-period goals en route to a 5–2 victory. Paul offered a 2-goal showing in another strong performance. The Flyers' Dornhoefer was lost for the series, suffering a broken leg when he was blindsided by Pat Quinn. Quinn was given a major penalty for charging on the play.

But the roughhouse style seemed to be paying off for Edmonton. For the first time in four years, the Oil Kings held the lead in a Memorial Cup final, and they upped their edge to 3–1 in game four with a 3–2 victory before 6,719 fans.

Niagara Falls refused to die, however, and stayed in the series with a 5–2 victory in the fifth game. The Canadian Press reported that the Flyers, "showing much more drive than they have in any other game this series, took a physical beating from the hard-hitting and sometimes brutal Oil Kings." Terry Crisp, Gary Harmer, Bill Glashan and Don Awrey—who was having a superb series on defence—pitched in goals for the Flyers.

For Crisp, the game was his best of the series so far, bearing out Emms' praise of his burly pivot. "He's by far the best captain I've had in my fifteen years in the game," Emms said. "He's the man who carried the club this far. His drive and spirit on and off the ice is something to behold."

Harmer was the second Flyer to suffer a broken leg in the series, which threatened to become a war of attrition. Emms, who had arrived west with nineteen players, complained that ten of his players were injured in the first five games. Not that he was writing off his team. "I said if the Oil Kings lost the fifth game, they'd lose the series," he said. "Our boys appear more accustomed to the Alberta climate and the altitude, and have regained their strength."

The Flyers fought hard in game six, but Edmonton prevailed, posting a thrilling 4–3 victory before 6,700 fans. Edmonton had piled up a 4–0 lead early in the third period, but Niagara Falls scored midway through and tenaciously fought back to within 1 goal. The Flyers swarmed around the Edmonton net for the rest of the game, getting goals from Schock at 12:09 and Crisp at 18:21, but they weren't able to pull even. Russ Kirk made the game's biggest save on Maxner with about five minutes left. Crisp, who continually picked up his club when it seemed that the Flyers were running out of gas, just missed scoring the tying marker with ten seconds left.

Edmonton claimed the team's first Memorial Cup in seven trips to the final. "I never thought anything could give me the thrill that I got last year when a bunch of fuzzy-cheeked kids carried us to the 1962 Memorial Cup final," Brayshaw said. "But this club did better. It's a great feeling, a better thrill than I got from anything I ever did as a player or coach anywhere."

Brayshaw and LeClerc were lifted onto the Oil Kings' shoulders and given three rousing cheers. A tumultuous roar reverberated through Edmonton Gardens as fans swarmed around both clubs and lifted Kings goalie Kirk, defenceman Quinn and centre Bourbonnais to their shoulders.

It was only the second time that a team from Alberta had claimed the Memorial Cup, the other being the Calgary Canadians in 1926. This was also the first time that a club from west of Manitoba had grabbed the title since the Regina Pats had won in 1930.

"Brayshaw is the greatest coach in the world," defenceman Bob Falkenberg said. "He taught me more about hockey in six months than I have learned in sixteen years." An exhausted and dejected Terry Crisp mused, "I guess we just didn't go to church often enough."

Glen Sather returned to the Edmonton Oil Kings in 1963–64, while Pat Quinn took his bruising style into the pro ranks. He spent nine years as an NHL defenceman with Toronto, Vancouver and Atlanta. Quinn went on to an outstanding coaching career with the Philadelphia Flyers, Los Angeles Kings and Vancouver Canucks, where he also served as general manager for over a decade. He twice won the Jack Adams trophy as coach of the year, with Philadelphia in 1979–80 and Vancouver in 1991–92, and twice took his teams to the Stanley Cup final, Philadelphia in 1980 and Vancouver in 1994.

Bert Marshall, another of the Oil Kings' big defencemen, played fourteen years in the NHL with Detroit, Oakland, the Rangers and the Islanders. Like Edmonton teammates Sather and Quinn, he coached in the NHL, spending time behind the bench of the Colorado Rockies. Oil Kings captain Rick Bourbonnais spent three years in the NHL with the St. Louis Blues. Butch Barber saw action in the WHA, mostly in Chicago. Bob Falkenberg and Ron Anderson would both return for three more runs at the Memorial Cup before moving on to the big league.

From the Niagara Falls Flyers, Gary Dornhoefer played fourteen years in the NHL, the first three in Boston and the rest in Philadelphia. He helped the Flyers win the Stanley Cup in 1974 and 1975. Don Awrey played sixteen years in the NHL with Boston, St. Louis, Montreal, Pittsburgh, Colorado and the Rangers. He won the Stanley Cup with the Bruins in 1970 and 1972. He also played with the Montreal Canadiens in 1976, when they swept the Philadelphia Flyers in four straight, but did not participate in post-season action.

Ron Schock played fifteen years in the NHL with the Bruins, Blues, Penguins and Sabres. Ted Snell spent two pro seasons in three cities—Pittsburgh, Kansas

Edmonton Oil Kings.

City and Detroit—while Wayne Maxner played two seasons with the Boston Bruins. Goaltender George Gardner played seven seasons in the NHL with Detroit, Vancouver and Los Angeles. He also spent two seasons in the WHA with the 1972–73 Los Angeles Sharks and 1973–74 Vancouver Blazers. Flyers captain Terry Crisp and rightwinger Bill Goldsworthy both moved on to impressive professional careers, but not before returning to Memorial Cup competition with Niagara Falls in 1965.

The **1964** Memorial Cup

It took the Edmonton Oil Kings seven trips to the final before they finally won the Memorial Cup in 1963. The following season, they discovered it was just as tough to keep the trophy as it had been to win it. The Toronto Marlboros, never far from contention in any year, returned to the forefront of junior hockey with one of their strongest teams ever.

In spite of a string of western successes, the Oil Kings were not automatic choices for the Abbott Cup. But they were able to defeat Scotty Munro's Estevan Bruins in the western final. The Marlies, on the other hand, were everyone's pick to represent the east in the Memorial Cup final. Coached by Jim Gregory, the Marlboros finished first during the OHA regular season, then pushed aside some strong eastern rosters en route to the final. They swept the defending champion Niagara Falls Flyers, then took on Yves Nadon's Montreal Junior Canadiens, a power-packed squad including Serge Savard, Yvan Cournoyer, André Lacroix, Rogie Vachon and OHA scoring leader André Boudrias.

The Marlboros won the best-of-seven series with four consecutive victories after being held to a 5–5 tie in the series opener. They then demolished the North Bay Trappers before sweeping Scotty Bowman's Notre Dame de Grace Monarchs in the eastern final. This chain of victories brought the team to the Memorial Cup series for the first time since 1956. They still hadn't lost a game in the playoffs. The Marlboros were hitting on all cylinders. They were a strong offensive team led in scoring by centre Peter Stemkowski. Captain Grant Moore, Mike Walton, Ron Ellis, André Champagne, Wayne Carleton and Brit Selby added depth and balance to the forward ranks. Defensively, the Marlboros were anchored solidly by goaltender Gary Smith as well as defencemen such as Rod Seiling and Jim McKenny.

Smith, Walton, Champagne, Seiling, McKenny, Gary Dineen, Ray Dupont and Bill Henderson had all been members of the Neil McNeil High School Maroons of the Metro Junior Hockey League in the 1963 season. The team had been formed from the discontinued St. Michael's hockey program. These players, as well as Maroons coach Jim Gregory, jumped over to the Marlboros before the 1964 season. They formed what some consider the strongest junior A team in recent hockey history.

The Oil Kings boasted a sharp-shooting forward trio of captain Glen Sather, Butch Paul and Max Mestinsek. They could also count on the experience of

A member of the 1964 Memorial Cup-winning Toronto Marlboros, Peter Stemkowski went on to play fifteen years in the NHL.

eleven holdovers from the defending 1963 Memorial Cup championship team. Edmonton brought along three recruits from the SJHL: Fran Huck of the Pats, a prolific sniper who scored 86 goals in league play, rightwinger Larry Mickey of the Moose Jaw Canucks and leftwinger Ron Boehm of Estevan.

The series opened at Maple Leaf Gardens with the Marlboros posting a 5–2 victory. Ron Ellis delivered a 2-goal performance. "This is the first time that I have seen them play," Gregory said of his opponents. "But from what I have heard about them and from what I saw today, I know that they can play much better than they did."

"I am disappointed, but we can play better hockey than you saw out there," Edmonton coach Brayshaw agreed, "and we'll have to if we want to beat the Marlboros. We're not shooting enough and our point men were trying to make too many fancy plays."

Fran Huck, who was supposed to help the Oil Kings match the offensive firepower of the Marlboros, was kept off the scoreboard. Brayshaw shifted the busy little centre to different lines in a fruitless effort to find a scoring combination. "He carried the Regina team on his shoulders throughout the season and didn't have wingmen to pass to," the Edmonton coach said. "Now he is having trouble adjusting to our style."

Only 3,573 fans attended game two, in which the Marlboros posted a 3–2 win thanks to third-period goals a minute and a half apart from Walton and Stemkowski. Gary Smith made some key saves, allowing the Marlies to snatch the victory. "It will take until tomorrow until the Oil Kings are accustomed to Toronto," coach Gregory said, anticipating a tougher game three. "The three-hour difference in time can have a big effect on a team."

Brayshaw felt his club had played better, but knew they still had some distance to go. "If you don't shoot, how do you expect the puck to go in?" he asked. "They just weren't shooting as much as I would have liked them to."

"We stopped playing hockey for a couple of minutes, they bang in 2 goals and that's the game," Edmonton's Butch Paul grumbled. By now, the Oil Kings were physically hurting too. Their top line of Paul, Mestinsek and Sather was on the limp, all three having suffered leg injuries.

Toronto went up 3–0 with a 5–2 victory. A mere 2,204 fans attended, the smallest crowd of the series. Selby and Stemkowski got 2 each for the winning team. Edmonton goaltender Kirk faced 36 shots as the Marlboros raised their level of play a notch. "They're not giving the puck away like they were in the first games," Gregory said of his players. "I thought my penalty killers—Watson, (Nick) Harbaruk, Champagne and Selby—played a great game. Everybody played a good game, for that matter."

Toronto completed the sweep with a tour de force blowout, whipping the Oil Kings 7–2 at Maple Leaf Gardens. They fired 49 shots on Kirk with seven different shooters—Stemkowski, Moore, Seiling, Harbaruk, Walton, Dineen and Champagne—scoring for Toronto. Mestinsek scored both Edmonton goals. In the second period the game was picked up by the CTV network, becoming the first Memorial Cup final to be broadcast live across Canada.

"Too much quality and too much quantity," was how Brayshaw described his victorious rivals. "Every line they threw at us was as good as the one that went off. We've been in the finals now for five years, and the Marlies are so far ahead of any of the other four teams we've played that they have to be the greatest. There's nothing they can't do."

"I am happy, I am proud and I am tired," said Gregory as he was carried off the ice by his elated players. "We won because we have more good hockey players than any other team." Stafford Smythe, the Maple Leaf Gardens President opined, "This is the greatest team we've assembled since the St. Mike's of 1934." Vice president Harold Ballard went even further. "It's the best ever," he said.

Predictably, a number of graduates from the 1964 Toronto Marlboros enjoyed success at the professional level. Pete Stemkowski played for fifteen years in the NHL, most of them with the Maple Leafs, Red Wings and Rangers. Ron Ellis enjoyed an outstanding sixteen years with the Leafs while Mike "Shakey" Walton played fourteen years in the NHL, mostly in Toronto, Boston, Vancouver, and with Minnesota in the WHA. Ellis, Stemkowski and Walton all helped the Maple Leafs capture the Stanley Cup in 1967, with Walton winning one more Cup as a member of the 1972 Bruins.

Brit Selby was named NHL Rookie of the Year in 1965–66. He played briefly with the 1967 Maple Leafs, but missed most of the season with a broken leg. Selby also skated with Philadelphia and St. Louis in the NHL, as well as Toronto, Quebec and New England in the WHA. He helped the New England Whalers win the Avco Cup in 1973.

Jim McKenny played more than ten seasons in the NHL, mostly with the Maple Leafs. Fellow defenceman Rod Seiling enjoyed seventeen years in the pros, mostly with the New York Rangers, although he also played in Toronto, Washington, St. Louis and Atlanta. Wayne Carleton started with the Maple Leafs before spending a couple of seasons in Boston, where he won the Stanley Cup in 1970. Carleton later played for several WHA teams, including Ottawa, Toronto and New England. Nick Harbaruk played in the NHL for five years with

Pittsburgh and St. Louis.

The flamboyant Gary "Suitcase" Smith bounced around the NHL with the Maple Leafs, Oakland Seals, California Golden Seals, Blackhawks, Canucks, North Stars, Capitals and Jets. He finally won a championship after jumping to the WHA. Beginning the 1979 season with the Indianapolis Racers, he was picked up by the Winnipeg Jets in February 1979 and played on their Avco Cup championship squad. He and Tony Esposito shared the Vezina Trophy with Chicago in 1972.

From the Edmonton Oil Kings, Glen Sather spent ten seasons in the NHL as a player. He skated with Boston, Pittsburgh, St. Louis, Montreal, Minnesota and the New York Rangers from 1967 to 1976 before jumping to the WHA. Sather played one season with Edmonton in 1977 before taking over coaching duties with the Oilers. He then proceeded to build some of the greatest teams ever in professional hockey. He coached and/or managed the Edmonton Oilers to five Stanley Cups in 1984, 1985, 1987, 1988 and 1990, also serving as team president. Butch Paul's pro career wasn't anywhere near as flamboyant as his junior years, lasting only three games with the Detroit Red Wings.

All three players picked up by the Oil Kings graduated to the NHL, although Fran Huck served with the junior team again in 1965. Larry Mickey spent eleven years in the big league, playing most of his games in Toronto, Montreal, Los Angeles and Buffalo. Ron Boehm played one season with the Oakland Seals.

Toronto Marlboros.

The **1965** Memorial Cup

"This isn't hockey, it's war."

With these words, Hap Emms summed up the 1965 junior championship. While the Memorial Cup finals of the 1950s had often involved freewheeling western teams stopped by tougher eastern squads, the 1960s saw the west dominated by a series of increasingly pugnacious Edmonton Oil Kings teams. Edmonton had claimed their first championship in 1963 with a bruising triumph over the Niagara Falls Flyers. In 1965, the Oil Kings and Flyers were given a rematch, and the result was a violent, brawl-filled series in which the tables were turned.

Niagara Falls dethroned the defending Memorial Cup champion Toronto Marlboros on their way to the eastern title. Still managed by Hap Emms and coached by Bill Long, the Flyers included Gilles Marotte, Steve Atkinson, Rick Ley, Bill Goldsworthy, Ron Snell, Jim Lorentz, Rosaire Paiement, Derek Sanderson, Jean Pronovost, Brian Bradley, Boris Debrody, Barry Wilkins, and goaltenders Bernie Parent and Doug Favell.

The Oil Kings were making their sixth consecutive appearance in the championship. They had lost many of the players who formed the core of the team over the first part of the decade, and went into the final under some difficult circumstances. Coach Russell Brayshaw had moved out from behind the bench only weeks before, when his son was killed in an automobile accident. The team was taken over by Harry Allen.

Edmonton also faced an uncertain goaltending situation, as their regular netminder, Garry "Moose" Simmons, had suffered an eight-stitch cut on his right kneecap late in the regular season. The wound didn't heal properly, and the team had to conscript goaltender Wayne Stephenson from the Winnipeg Braves for the series. Edmonton's first line was Ron Anderson, Graham Longmuir and Greg Tomalty, but the Oil Kings also featured future NHL winger Garnet "Ace" Bailey. Their favourite mercenary, Fran Huck of the Pats, was back for another final and defenceman Jim Cardiff of the Weyburn Red Wings was brought in to supplement blueline regular Bob Falkenberg.

As in 1963, the series was played in Edmonton. The visiting team opened with a 3–2 victory before 4,676 fans. The Flyers held command most of the way, combining slick skating and passing with a robust, hard-hitting defence. There were several skirmishes, but nothing serious.

The Oil Kings emerged from game one with some injury concerns. All three players on their highest scoring line were injured: Ron Anderson with a sore knee, Graham Longmuir with a back aggravation and centre Greg Tomalty with a shoulder injury. "I think we played pretty well, considering this was the opener," Harry Allen said. "But it was far from our best. We're bound to improve."

There was no improvement in the second game, as the Flyers skated to a 5–1 victory before 4,957 Edmonton fans. Centre Debrody led the charge with two goals while Sanderson, Goldsworthy and John Arbour completed the Niagara Falls scoring. Once again, the Flyers were the more aggressive team, taking fourteen of twenty-five penalties handed out. They played two men short three times, but Edmonton only capitalized once with the two-man advantage.

Despite his team's success, Emms was his usual cantankerous self. He complained bitterly about the refereeing. "That guy is worse than the one we had two years ago in Edmonton in 1963," Emms said of referee Jim McAuley. "We play just as hard in the OHA but the penalty box isn't always full."

"This club is standing around as if they're going to learn something. No club of mine has ever checked this badly," Brayshaw griped, having returned behind the Edmonton bench as Allen's assistant. He acknowledged the team's inexperience, but felt his players were simply not rising to the occasion. "We're not fuzzy-cheeked any more," he said. "We've had six tough months of competition."

Both teams emerged from the second game physically unscathed, although it appeared that Flyer defenceman Ley had been injured in the second period. The stocky fifteen-year-old returned after missing a few shifts. "I was speared," he said. "I won't tell you who it was but I got his number, and you'll find out who it was when he gets carried off before the end of the 1965 series."

By now, the flu bug was making its way through the Oil Kings' roster, adding to their problems. "This cannot be considered a reason why we have looked so bad on the ice," manager Leo LeClerc said. "We may be inexperienced but we are the western Abbott Cup champions, and we have to go out there and play like champions."

Edmonton regained their footing with a 5–1 victory in game three. The undercurrent of chippiness that had run through the series finally erupted into ugliness as 3,403 fans looked on and in some cases participated. The first sign this game was heading out of control came midway through the first period. Derek Sanderson and Doug Favell tangled with Oil King Brian Bennett near the Flyers' net. Edmonton fans along the boards became involved, grabbing at sticks, which resulted in some verbal exchanges with Niagara Falls players.

Real trouble started as the first period ended, when the Flyers' Goldsworthy threw Oil King Ross Perkins into the boards after the whistle. In retaliation, Goldsworthy was promptly thumped and speared in the stomach by Oil King defenceman Bob Falkenberg, who drew a five-minute penalty. Fans continued to mix it up with the Flyers as they left the ice. Eleven policemen on regular duty at the Gardens tried to help linesman Ken Reid restore order.

"A player tried to get at one of the fans with a stick and I tried to protect the fan," said Reid, who was injured in the crossfire. Edmonton city police reinforcements had to be called in to quell the increasingly tense crowd.

There was little trouble between the second and third periods, as police surrounded the area from the dressing rooms and blanketed the player benches and penalty boxes. The Oil Kings built a strong lead on the scoreboard, although Bernie Parent—who replaced Favell in net after the first period—was greeted with the occasional egg from the rowdy Edmonton crowd. The game was delayed several times to clear eggs and rubbish from the ice. Hostilities resumed early in the third period when the Flyers' Ley and the Oil Kings' Anderson received majors and match penalties for a stick-swinging duel. At 16:30 of the third period, Hamilton tangled with Paiement at the Niagara Falls blueline, and the game—5–1 in Edmonton's favour—simply fell apart. In a matter of minutes, bedlam reigned supreme, with fights breaking out all over the ice.

In the most serious incident, Falkenberg was taken to hospital after being knocked unconscious by a sucker punch from Derek Sanderson. Sanderson, who had earlier been given two minors, a misconduct and a major, was assessed another major for intent to injure as well as a match misconduct. As he made his way to the dressing room, he was jumped by a group of spectators. They dragged him into the first aid room to administer a beating. Edmonton police intervened and roughly hauled Sanderson to the Flyers' dressing room.

Art Potter, the president of the CAHA, ordered McAuley to stop the game. The referee had dished out thirty-three penalties, including three match penalties, nine majors and three misconducts. Potter described the brawl as "the most brutal I have ever seen." Hap Emms candidly admitted that both teams were to blame for the fracas, and recommended that the series be moved to a neutral site for the remaining games. He described the donnybrook as "one of the worst things I've seen in my hockey career."

The next day, CAHA secretary–manager Gordon Juckes announced that Anderson and Ley had been handed one-game suspensions for their stick-swinging episode, and that Sanderson had been suspended indefinitely for deliberate injury of a player. His suspension, a notable blow to the Flyers given Sanderson's goal-per-game pace in the series, was later reduced to two games after Matt Leyden, President of the OHA, appealed the original verdict.

Contrary to Emms' advice, the series stayed in Edmonton. Extra police were on hand for game four, but they weren't needed.

NHL Hall of Famer Bernie Parent tended goal for the Niagara Falls Flyers during 1965, the year they won the Memorial Cup.

The Flyers roared back with an 8–2 victory, in a relatively civil contest. Brian Bradley struck for 5 goals while Goldsworthy tallied twice, opening and closing the scoring on unassisted breakaway plays.

The win gave Niagara Falls a 3–1 stranglehold in the series, and they wrapped it up with an 8–1 victory in game five. It was the third time that Hap Emms had won the Memorial Cup, the others being in 1951 and 1953 with the Barrie Flyers. For Niagara Falls players Arbour, Snell and Goldsworthy, it was sweet revenge. They had all played on the 1963 Flyers team that lost to the Oil Kings.

Emms paid tribute to his goaltender Parent, who finished the Memorial Cup final with an outstanding 1.57 goaltending average. "You know what was the biggest single thing we had going for us in this series?" he asked. "There he is— Parent. He kept us in the games. He's the best junior goalie I've ever had."

Parent went on to an equally outstanding NHL career, playing fourteen years in Boston, Toronto and Philadelphia. He was instrumental in clinching the Stanley Cup for the Flyers in 1974 and 1975. In 1984, he became a member of the Hall of Fame. A slew of his Niagara Falls teammates also enjoyed success at the professional level. Bill Goldsworthy played fifteen years in the NHL and WHA, most notably as a member of the Minnesota North Stars. He also spent time with the Bruins and Rangers, as well as Indianapolis and Edmonton of the WHA.

Niagara Falls Flyers. Back row (l to r): Mike Sherman, Ricky Ley, Bobby Ring, Jim Lorentz, Rosaire Paiement, Don Marcotte, Steve Atkinson, Brian Bradley, Andre Lajeunesse. Middle row: Barry Wilkins, Derek Sanderson, Bill Goldsworthy, Dr. M.F. Williams (team physician), "Hap" Emms (owner and manager), Dr. Gord Powell, Guy Allen, Jean Pronovost, Bud Debrody, Barry Keast (trainer). Front row: Bernard Parent, Bill Long (coach), John Arbour, Ted Snell, Dave Woodley, Gilles Morotte, Doug Austin (sports editor), Doug Favell.

Don Marcotte played fifteen solid seasons with the Boston Bruins, winning the Stanley Cup in 1970 and 1972. His teammate for both of those victories was Derek Sanderson, who played nine partial seasons with the Bruins, winning the Calder Trophy in 1967–68. He also served stints with the Rangers, Blues, Canucks, Penguins and the Philadelphia Blazers of the WHA.

Sanderson, whose notoriety in the 1965 final would not prove out of character for the controversial player, surprisingly contributed to one of hockey's more poetic moments. In the 1970 NHL playoffs, he worked a sublime give-and-go with Bobby Orr on the great defenceman's electrifying Stanley Cup-winning overtime goal against the St. Louis Blues.

Joining Marcotte and Sanderson in the Bruins' 1970 Stanley Cup victory was Jim Lorentz, who played ten seasons in the pros, mostly with Boston, St. Louis and Buffalo. Jean Pronovost enjoyed an excellent fourteen-year NHL career, ten with the Penguins and the other four split between the Atlanta Flames and Washington Capitals. Rosaire Paiement played five seasons with Philadelphia and Vancouver before jumping to the WHA, where he played in Chicago, New England and Indianapolis.

Gilles Marotte served with Boston, Chicago, Los Angeles, St. Louis and the New York Rangers for a total of twelve NHL seasons. Brian Bradley played three seasons in the WHA, with New York/New Jersey and San Diego while Ron Snell played a pair of NHL seasons with Pittsburgh and a pair of WHA seasons with Winnipeg. Rick Ley and Steve Atkinson would return for one more run at the Memorial Cup before moving on to the NHL.

From the Edmonton Oil Kings, Wayne Stephenson spent ten years in the NHL with St. Louis, Philadelphia and Washington. He played with the Flyers from 1975 to 1979, winning the Stanley Cup in his first year as backup to his 1965 Memorial Cup rival, Bernie Parent. Ron Anderson played five years with Detroit, Los Angeles, St. Louis and Buffalo, and another two in the WHA with Alberta and Edmonton. Jim Cardiff played three years in the WHA with Philadelphia and Vancouver.

The **1966** Memorial Cup

There are many who contend that Bobby Orr was the greatest hockey player in history. While fans of Gordie Howe and Wayne Gretzky may argue the point, fewer would dispute that Orr was the best player to appear in a Memorial Cup final. Before he led the Boston Bruins out of the NHL wilderness, Orr took the Oshawa Generals—a dominant junior franchise in the late 1930s and early 1940s—back into Memorial Cup contention after a two-decade absence.

The Generals dumped Kitchener four games to one to win the OHA championship. Then they faced the North Bay Trappers, who were the Junior A champions of Northern Ontario. The Generals won in four straight, outshooting the Trappers 232–96 in the series and outscoring them 44–8. Orr scored 8 goals and assisted on 14 to average more than 5 points per game. Oshawa then defeated the Shawinigan Bruins in a best-of-five eastern final to claim their first Richardson Trophy in twenty years.

The Abbott Cup final was a clash of junior titans, with the Estevan Bruins— managed by Scotty Munro and coached by Ernie "Punch" McLean—meeting the Oil Kings. Edmonton was coached by Ray Kinasewich and managed by Bill "Red" Hunter. Edmonton made it to their seventh Memorial Cup finals in a row when they eliminated the Bruins in six games. The Oil Kings featured captain Bob Falkenberg, Garnet "Ace" Bailey, Ross Perkins, Al Hamilton and goaltender Don "Smokey" McLeod. They added three Estevan players to their roster for the national final: forwards Jim Harrison, Ross Lonsberry and Ted Hodgson. Hunter also picked up Weyburn Red Wings goaltender Don Caley.

The Oshawa Generals were coached by Armand "Bep" Guidolin and managed by Wren Blair. They were far from being a one-man show. In addition to Orr, the Generals' lineup included Wayne Cashman, Nick Beverley, Danny O'Shea, Bill Heindl and Barry Wilkins, who had moved over from the defending Memorial Cup champion Niagara Falls Flyers. O'Shea and Cashman, who formed Oshawa's most potent forward unit with Chris Hayes, went into the final with 21 playoff goals apiece.

All games in the final series were scheduled for Maple Leaf Gardens. Edmonton opened the series by thrashing Oshawa 7–2 in front of 4,500 fans. The Oil Kings outshot the Generals 52–20. The high-scoring Perkins netted 2 goals for Edmonton and each of the three Estevan players also figured in the scoring. Orr supplied most of the flourish for Oshawa, firing at least 10 shots on goal and scoring once. Six players picked up fighting majors in a rough third period. The altercation started when Harrison crashed into Bobby Orr and was immediately confronted by Oshawa's Billy White. Orr, who picked up one of the majors, proved to be as adept at fisticuffs as stickhandling.

Edmonton coach Kinasewich accused the Generals of head hunting, telling the Canadian Press that the Generals couldn't take his team's persistent body checking.

"I like a rough, hard-checking game," Kinasewich said, "and if they can't take it, then let them go home." Guidolin countered, "We didn't see one good check all night, and you can tell them to stop sending busters after Orr." On the topic of the score, the Oshawa coach admitted that his club had been soundly trounced and offered no excuse. "We came to play hockey but we ended up watching a game," he said. "We didn't skate, we didn't check, we didn't hit."

Oshawa tied the series in game two, riding a 3-goal performance from O'Shea to a 7–1 victory. Most of the 7,210 fans in attendance were from the Oshawa area. Cashman, a real sparkplug out front, had a goal and 3 assists. The Oshawa scoring attack was matched by a brilliant defensive effort by Nick Beverley. Bobby Orr, handicapped with a groin injury, was used only sparingly, leaving the other defencemen to fill his shoes.

Referee Frank Daigneault called twenty-four penalties in a game that was more frisky than wild. But no one was forgetting what had happened in Edmonton a year earlier. "He's going to lose control," Kinasewich warned, accusing Oshawa's O'Shea of some nasty stickwork, "and that won't be good for the players or the fans."

The Generals took a the series lead in game three by winning 6–2. Once again, O'Shea was prominent, scoring twice. Goaltender Ian Young, playing with a badly bruised catching hand, had his second strong outing for the Generals. Orr was confined to the bench for the second consecutive game because of his groin injury. He made a few brief appearances on the powerplay, but it now looked doubtful that he would be fit for the rest of the series.

Oil Kings goalie Smokey McLeod was removed at the end of the first period, after the Generals had scored 4 goals on their first 7 shots. McLeod steered the first one in with his skate. "You don't expect that a fellow who's played well all season will choke up all of a sudden," Kinasewich said. "But that's what he's done." Red Hunter planned a team meeting on the off day to reinvigorate his Oil Kings, while Guidolin mused about where his team would be if he had a healthy Orr. "If this guy was going well," Guidolin said pointing to his star defenceman, "wouldn't it be great?"

McLeod vindicated himself in game four by backstopping a regrouped Edmonton unit to a 5–3 victory. Trailing going into the third period, the Oil Kings exploded for 3 goals, the winner coming with under four minutes remaining. Orr took a regular shift for most of two periods, but left the game in the second frame and took his gear off. His groin injury had been aggravated when he was checked into the boards by Perkins.

"We blew it," Guidolin said. "We didn't skate. You gotta skate. If you don't, you're dead." Kinasewich thought it was simply Edmonton's turn. "Don't you think we were due?" he asked. "We couldn't get much worse than in the second and third games."

The fifth game saw the Generals outplayed in every department. With Orr far from healthy, the Oil Kings crushed Oshawa 7–4. Craig Cameron scored 3 goals and had 1 assist while Perkins—the Oil Kings' leading scorer throughout the season—scored twice and picked up 4 assists. Young faced 52 shots while Edmonton's McLeod had 33 levelled at him.

Game six was almost as much a victory for the Estevan Bruins as for the Oil Kings. Two Estevan recruits, Hodgson and Harrison, beat the Generals almost singlehandedly before 5,018 fans. They got both Edmonton goals in the 2–1 Oil Kings win, Hodgson scoring the series winner on a blistering slapshot from just inside the blueline. Young didn't even see the puck.

Both goaltenders stopped 37 shots, but the hero was McLeod, who had been so severely criticized in game three. "They owe it all to the goalie, who they said choked," Bep Guidolin said in the Oshawa dressing room. "What are they saying about it now?"

"You are looking at the finest goalie in junior hockey," said Edmonton manager Red Hunter. "When he gets that look in his eye, you just know that nobody's gonna beat him." Guidolin stated the obvious when he pointed to Orr's injury as a major factor in the series, with Young's ailing glove hand adding to the problem. "We don't want to make excuses. But we were hurting bad and that made a big difference."

The win marked the first time a western team had won the championship in an eastern rink since the Port Arthur West End Bruins in 1948.

From the Edmonton Oil Kings' Memorial Cup team, Garnet "Ace" Bailey spent ten years in the NHL with Boston, Detroit, St. Louis and Washington and one season in the WHA with Edmonton. He helped the Bruins win the Stanley Cup in 1972, also playing with Boston in 1970 but not taking part in the post-season action. Bob Falkenberg played for five years with the Detroit Red Wings before jumping to the WHA for six years, mostly in Edmonton and San Diego. Ron Anderson played five years with Detroit, Los Angeles, St. Louis and Buffalo before rounding out his career in the WHA with Alberta and Edmonton. Ross Perkins played three years in the WHA with Alberta and Edmonton. Al Hamilton played six seasons in the NHL with the Rangers and Buffalo and eight in the WHA with Alberta and Edmonton. Craig Cameron skated for nine seasons in the uniforms of Detroit, St. Louis, Minnesota and the New York Islanders.

Goaltender Don "Smokey" McLeod played with the Red Wings and Flyers before moving on to the WHA, where he spent most of his time in Houston, Vancouver and Calgary. He won the Avco Cup with the Houston Aeros in 1974. All three of the players picked up by the Oil Kings from Estevan went on to NHL or WHA careers. Ross Lonsberry played fifteen years in the NHL with Boston, Los Angeles, Philadelphia and Pittsburgh, winning the Stanley Cup with the Flyers in 1974 and 1975. Jim Harrison enjoyed eight years in the NHL, mostly with Boston, Toronto and Chicago, plus three seasons in the WHA with Alberta, Edmonton and Cleveland. Ted Hodgson started with the Boston Bruins, but played most of his big league games with Cleveland and Los Angeles in the WHA.

Edmonton Oil Kings. Back row (l to r): Don Caley, Jim Schraefel, Kerry Ketter, Brian Bennett, Ron Anderson, Craig Cameron, Eugène Peacosh, Harold Myers, Brian Hague. Middle row: "Swede" Knox, "Red" Simpson, Doug Barrie, Ross Lonsberry, Garnet Bailey, Ron Walters, Ted Hodgson, Galen Head, Jim Harrison, Ted Rogers, Borden Lypowy (manager and coach), Waldo Serdiak (equipment manager). Front row: Don McLeod, Dr. Neil Cuthbertson (team physician), Al Hamilton, Ray Kinasewich (coach), Bob Falkenberg, William Hunter (president and general manager), Dave Rochefort, Jim Mitchell (trainer), Ross Perkins, Jim Knox. On floor in front: Murray Pierce (stick boy).

From the Oshawa Generals, Wayne Cashman played over a decade and a half with the Boston Bruins, winning the Stanley Cup in 1970 and 1972. Nick Beverley played more than ten years in the NHL with Boston, Pittsburgh, Minnesota, Los Angeles, Colorado and the Rangers. Danny O'Shea played five years in the pros with Minnesota, Chicago and St. Louis, and a year with Minnesota in the WHA. Bill Heindl had a handful of games with Minnesota and the New York Rangers before playing a year in the WHA with Cleveland. Barry Wilkins began his NHL career with the Bruins before playing six seasons with Vancouver and Pittsburgh, as well as a couple in the WHA with Edmonton and Indianapolis. He holds the distinction of scoring the Vancouver Canucks' first-ever NHL goal.

Bobby Orr played twelve years in the NHL, almost all of them with the Boston Bruins. He led the team to the Stanley Cup in 1970 and 1972. Individual trophies won by Orr include the Hart (three times), Art Ross (twice), Norris (eight times), Conn Smythe (twice), and Calder. He was inducted into the Hockey Hall of Fame immediately after he retired in 1979.

The **1967** Memorial Cup

Canada's centennial was a great year for Toronto hockey teams. The Maple Leafs scored an upset Stanley Cup win over the Montreal Canadiens. The Leafs' premier junior farm team, the Toronto Marlboros, brought the era of professional sponsorship of junior teams to an end with a Memorial Cup championship. For the first time in eight years, the national junior final did not feature the Edmonton Oil Kings.

The 1966–67 season saw a significant shakeup of junior hockey in western Canada. A group of owners from the SJHL joined two teams in Alberta—the Calgary Buffaloes and Edmonton Oil Kings—and executed what was basically an expansion of the SJHL into Calgary and Edmonton. It was a controversial move greeted with considerable argument and legal wrangling. But it was undertaken successfully, and the Canadian Major Junior Hockey League, now known as the Western Hockey League, was born.

The CAHA vehemently protested this move, so the rebels from Saskatchewan simply split from its jurisdiction. The CMJHL was prohibited from competing for the 1967 Memorial Cup, so teams like the Estevan Bruins, Regina Pats, Moose Jaw Canucks, Saskatoon Blades, Weyburn Red Wings, Calgary Buffaloes and defending Memorial Cup champion Oil Kings—all members of the new CMJHL circuit—were ineligible to compete for junior hockey's top prize.

With the Edmonton Oil Kings' vice grip on the Abbott Cup no longer in place, it was the Port Arthur Marrs who emerged as western champions. They defeated the New Westminster Royals in the western final after surviving a semi-final matchup against a tough Flin Flon Bomber team led by Bobby Clarke and Reggie Leach.

The Marrs, sponsored by W. H. Marr, a tractor-trailer equipment company, had suffered only five defeats in twenty-eight games as they won the Thunder Bay Junior Hockey League regular season championship. Much of the Port Arthur offence was generated by the line of captain Ray Adduono between Chuck Kelner and Tim McCormack. Coached by Albert Cava, the Marrs also featured Bob Kelly and Vic Venasky. They picked up Juha "Whitey" Widing and Bill Fairbairn from Brandon, and defenceman Gerry Hart from Flin Flon.

Meanwhile in the east, the Marlboros were back in the hunt. They moved to the top of the OHA after sidelining Claude Ruel's Montreal Junior Canadiens and the Hamilton Red Wings. Toronto then played the Thetford Mines Canadiens, a team that included Gilbert Perreault, Marc Tardif, Réjean Houle and André "Moose" Dupont. The Marlies prevailed and moved on to meet Port Arthur in the Memorial Cup final. The Marlboros were coached by Gus Bodnar, a twelve-year NHL veteran who made the record books by assisting on all 3 goals of fellow Chicago Blackhawk Bill Mosienko's phenomenal twenty-one-second hat trick in 1952. Among the many stars on Bodnar's Marlies were captain Brian Glennie, Brad Park, goaltender Gary Edwards, Mike Byers, Gerry Meehan, Mike Pelyk and Terry Caffery.

All games in the 1967 final were set for the Fort William Gardens in Thunder Bay, Ontario. The series opened with a 6–3 victory by the Marlboros, paced by the prolific line of Doug Acomb, Frank Hamill and Mike Byers. Acomb scored twice, as did Gerry Meehan. An overflow crowd of 5,364 was crammed into the 4,600-seat Gardens.

"I was pleased with the way our kid line played," coach Bodnar said, referring to Acomb, Hamill and Byers. "Marlboros are just about what I expected them to be," Albert Cava told Gordon Walker of the Toronto *Globe and Mail*. "Our fellows can play better than they did today, but I expect we'll have to play at our maximum to beat the Marlboros."

The Estevan Bruins' Scotty Munro, a spectator at the game, put it a different way. "Four zip," he predicted. "The Marrs can't skate with them." Neither Toronto manager Jim Gregory nor coach Bodnar was willing to knock the Marrs, though. "Those new boys they picked up [Widing, Fairbairn and Hart] haven't had a chance to get working together," Bodnar said diplomatically. "They've got the pressure on them," Gregory said of the Marlboros. "Sure, it's nice to have almost 6,000 fans cheering you on, but don't forget when things go bad they scream at them."

The Marlboros maintained their pace in game two, taking a convincing 8–4 victory before more than 5,300 fans. Meehan and Acomb bettered their previous 2-goal performances with a hat trick each.

The Marrs headed into the third game knowing they had to stop Acomb and Caffery, who had 15 points between them in a mere two games. Port Arthur responded with some offence of their own, and won the third game 6–4. Widing and Fairbairn—both 140-plus point men in the regular season—bagged a pair of goals each.

Referee John McEvoy called twenty-nine penalties during the rough contest, including seven majors for fighting. Bob Kelly was handed a one-game suspension for leaving the bench to enter an altercation at 19:59 of the third period. The next day, Bodnar, Cava and McEvoy were read the riot act from CAHA representative "Bones" McCormack and OHA official Matt Leyden, who wanted no part of a repeat performance of the 1965 Memorial Cup fiasco. The next night, in front of another capacity crowd of more than 5,300, the Marlboros moved to within one victory of the junior title. Martin and Bayes scored twice each in the 6–0 rout while Acomb and Caffery added the other goals. The Marlies scored three times on the powerplay.

The Marlboros wrapped up their fifth Memorial Cup with a 6–3 victory in game five. Bayes, Meehan and Martin, with 2 goals each, were the Toronto marksmen. Ray Adduono scored all 3 goals for the Marrs, making him Port Arthur's series leader with 4 goals and 3 assists in the five games. For the Marlboros, twenty-one-year-old centre Caffery topped all point getters with 4 goals and 10 assists.

"It is the biggest thrill of my life," said coach Bodnar of his club's Memorial Cup victory. "This is the best hockey club I've ever played with," captain Brian Glennie added.

Glennie enjoyed ten years in the NHL, mostly patrolling the Maple Leafs' blueline. Gerry Meehan also enjoyed a ten-year career in the NHL and WHA, breaking in with the Leafs but spending most of his time with the Sabres and Capitals. He also served as the Sabres' general manager from 1987 to 1993. Mike Pelyk spent a couple of years in the WHA and another eight with the Maple Leafs. Mike Byers, who also broke in with the Leafs, divided eight years between the NHL and WHA, mostly with Los Angeles, Buffalo and New England. He helped the latter win the Avco Cup in 1973. One of Byers' teammates in New England was Terry Caffery, who spent three years with the Whalers and two with Calgary in the WHA after playing a handful of NHL games with Chicago and Minnesota.

Goaltender Gary Edwards played more than ten years in the NHL with a number of teams. Most of his games were played for Los Angeles, Cleveland and Minnesota, while fellow Marlboros goalie Bob Whidden played four years with Cleveland in the WHA. A third Marlboros goaltender, Cam Newton, also played with the WHA's Cleveland franchise at the end of his career. Before that, he net-minded for Chicago of the WHA after breaking in with the Pittsburgh Penguins.

Another Toronto Marlboro who played professionally was Chris Evans, who divided eight years between the two leagues, mostly with the St. Louis Blues and Calgary Cowboys. Fred Barrett went on to record thirteen NHL seasons for Minnesota and Los Angeles. John Wright played three years in the NHL, mostly with Vancouver and St. Louis. Steve King and Tom Martin had two and three years respectively in the WHA. The most notable Marlboro of 1967 was Brad Park, a future NHL Hall of Famer who slipped past the Maple Leaf scouts and spent an outstanding decade and a half with the New York Rangers, Boston Bruins and Detroit Red Wings.

From the Port Arthur Marrs, players who graduated either to the NHL or WHA include netminder John Adams, who played a pair of seasons with the Bruins and Capitals. Vic Venasky spent seven years with the Los Angeles Kings

Toronto Marlboros. Back row (l to r): Tom Smythe (assistant manager), Bob Smith (publicity), Gary Edwards, Fred Barrett, Ken Kelly, Gord Davies, Austin Kimmis (statistician), Phil Forsdike (equipment manager). Second row from back: Bob Davidson (chief scout), Norm Mackie (trainer), Steve King, John Wright, Doug Acomb, Richie Bayes, Jim Blain, Dave Mintz (assistant trainer), Dr. Leo Hall (team physician). Third row from back: Frank Hamill, Brad Park, Mike Byers, Cam Crosby, Mike Pelyk, Chris Evans, Tom Martin, Terry Caffery. Front row: Bob Whidden, Jim Gregory (general manager), Gerry Meehan, C. Stafford Smythe (managing director), Brian Glennie, Harold Ballard (president), Al Osborne, Gus Bodnar (coach), Cam Newton.

while Ray Adduono played five years in the WHA, mostly with San Diego and Minnesota. Ted Tucker served a brief NHL stint with the California Golden Seals. Bob Kelly put in six seasons with St. Louis, Pittsburgh and Chicago.

Of the players picked up by Port Arthur en route to the final, Whitey Widing played nine years in the NHL and the WHA, mostly with the LA Kings. Bill Fairbairn spent eleven years in the NHL, most of them with the New York Rangers. Gerry Hart enjoyed a fifteen-year pro career with Detroit, Quebec, St. Louis and the New York Islanders. Ron Busniuk played a few games with the Buffalo Sabres before heading to the WHA where he divided four seasons between Minnesota, New England and Edmonton.

The **1968** Memorial Cup

Any Memorial Cup final that had Hap Emms on one side and Punch McLean on the other had to be an eyebrow-raiser for junior hockey fans. As owner and manager of the Niagara Falls Flyers, Emms had already forged a cantankerous reputation while McLean, the coach of the Estevan Bruins, was just beginning to fashion his. McLean's team went into the final with a reputation for rough play, foreshadowing the style of his squads in the 1970s. The Flyers were set to cap their impressive showing throughout the '60s with one more Memorial Cup triumph.

The Bruins began the season with twenty-two straight wins and later put together a twenty-five-game streak in the early playoffs, winning their last nine games of the regular season and romping through five playoff series with only one loss. In the OHA final, the Flyers took eight games—four wins, three losses and a tie—to eliminate coach Wally Kullman's stubborn Kitchener Rangers. Niagara Falls then got past the Verdun Maple Leafs in a best-of-five series. The Flyers' lineup included Rick Ley, a veteran of three Memorial Cup finals, Steve Atkinson, Brad Selwood, Phil Roberto, Don Tannahill and goalie Phil Myre. By this time, Hap Emms had handed over the coaching reins to his son Paul.

In 1957, Roderick "Scotty" Munro had almost singlehandedly built junior hockey in Estevan, a southeastern Saskatchewan city of 10,500. In the franchise's infancy, the 2,200-seat Civic Auditorium was full for most home games. Munro enlisted Ernie "Punch" McLean as coach and the pair built the Bruins into a contender. The 1968 team included notable players Jim Harrison and Danny Schock. For the final, they also picked up Pats forward Ron Garwasiuk and two defencemen, Joe Zanussi of the Swift Current Broncos and Kerry Ketter of the Edmonton Oil Kings. Estevan topped off their additions with goaltender Ken Brown from the Moose Jaw Canucks.

All of the final series games were scheduled for the Niagara Falls Memorial Arena with the exception of game two, which was to be played at the Montreal Forum. Rather comically, the first game was delayed by ten minutes because both teams came to play in identical stockings and similar sweaters. Historically, both clubs had been farmhands of the Boston Bruins and wore variations of the Bruin yellow, black and white. The CAHA ordered the hometown Flyers to change their garb, so the players went back to their dressing room and returned minutes later in road sweaters.

Despite their gear, the Flyers were on home ice, where they were tough to beat.

The Bruins found out just how tough, as they were dumped 7–4 before 3,000 cheering fans. Estevan played a typically physical game, taking 89 of the 111 penalty minutes assessed. Most of these originated in a brawl that broke out in the final minute and spilled over into the stands behind the Bruins' bench.

Phil Roberto and Garry Swain led the Niagara Falls attack with 2 goals each, while Atkinson scored once and assisted on 3 others. "We took a lot of penalties before the fight started and we don't usually play that brand of hockey," Munro said, his tongue firmly in his cheek. He allowed that the refereeing was "all right," but complained that fans were baiting his players at their bench.

Hap Emms said he didn't expect the Estevan club "to be so easy next time. You know they had an easy series for the western Canada Abbott Cup title with Penticton, and then they've been sitting around here since, waiting for us to finish off Verdun."

Sure enough, Estevan rebounded to win game two 4–2, enjoying the neutral ice in Montreal. Danny Schock, the Bruins' captain from Terrace Bay, Ontario scored a goal and set up 2 others to lead the scoring attack, while Ken Brown took over from Gordie Kopp in the net. "It was the greatest moment in my career, and the only thing that will ever be bigger is to take the Memorial Cup back west," Schock said.

CAHA officials had hoped to draw a crowd of 7,000 to the Forum, but had to settle for a disappointing turnout of only 1,849. "I'm not worried about losing money," Punch McLean told a Canadian Press reporter. "If the CAHA decides to play the rest of the games here, we'll just have to sell a few more bales of hay." The venue wasn't the only thing different about game two, as the Flyers had been forced to suit up in the uniforms of the Montreal Junior Canadiens, a move which did not amuse the NHL Canadiens' manager Sam Pollock.

For game three, the series reverted back to Niagara Falls. This time, the Flyers wore the St. Catharines Black Hawks' sweaters. Niagara Falls staged a repeat of their game one performance, winning 7–4 as Atkinson scored 2 goals and assisted on 2 others. The speedy little Atkinson, a 160-pound veteran, was one of only two players remaining from the 1965 Flyers team, Ley being the other. Atkinson was emerging as the key player in the series. With 4 goals and 4 assists in the first three games, he furnished offence to burn, even passing up a hat trick near the end of the third game when he elected to pass to teammate Don Tannahill for an empty-net goal.

Facing a critical game four, the Bruins came out hitting but ran into penalty trouble. Nonetheless, Estevan goalie Brown came just short of robbing the game outright from the Flyers by prolonging a 3–3 tie deep into overtime until OHA scoring champion Tom Webster finally beat him at 12:56 of the fifth period.

Munro was upset with referee McAuley over the fact that thirty of forty-four penalties went to the Bruins. He felt that his key players were physically spent for the overtime due to their strenuous penalty-killing efforts during regulation. The Bruins, badly outplayed in the first two periods, ended up taking only 31 shots to the Flyers' 63. A fatigued but exhilarated Niagara Falls team saluted the opposing goaltender. "He was just fabulous," Tannahill offered. "He's got a lot of heart."

The loss seemed to demoralize the Bruins. Now down 3–1 in games, Estevan could not mount a comeback of any kind. The Flyers posted a 6–0 shutout in game five to claim the Memorial Cup. Niagara Falls Memorial Arena was thick with fog during the entire contest. Centre Doug Brindley paced the Flyers' attack with 2 goals. With the final minutes ticking away in the third period, Paul Emms sent each of his lines to the dressing room as they came off the ice. Each player changed out of his St. Catharines uniform and reemerged in the familiar yellow and black to receive the Memorial Cup. A sweaty crowd of 3,813 sent up a victorious roar as the final bell sounded. Several hundred fans ran onto the ice to mob backup goaltender Dave Tataryn, who had been sent out in the final eighty seconds to replace Myre.

"This is not as balanced a club as the one that won the 1965 Memorial Cup," Atkinson admitted. "But we must be good to win the title." Fellow veteran Rick Ley commented on the camaraderie of the 1968 squad. "I don't want to compare the two teams," he said of the 1965 and 1968 winners, "but I will say that this is the greatest bunch of guys I ever played with." The leader in the series scoring was Atkinson with 5 goals and 7 assists. Estevan's Gregg Sheppard had 5 goals and 2 assists.

After the Bruins returned to Saskatchewan from the 1968 Memorial Cup series, the Abbott Cup mysteriously disappeared for a short time. After an intense search, Estevan police located the hardware in Punch McLean's house. McLean later explained that he had been searching for the storied trophy himself, and eventually remembered that he hid it in his own basement!

Rick Ley spent four years with the Toronto Maple Leafs before jumping to the WHA. He played for the New England Whalers for seven years, and then returned to the NHL for two seasons with the Hartford Whalers. Ley would go on to a coaching career with the Whalers and the Vancouver Canucks. Brad Selwood sandwiched seven years in the WHA with New England between two years with the Maple Leafs and one with the Los Angeles Kings. Tom Webster played six years with New England as well as some time in the NHL, mostly with Detroit and California. Before he returned to the NHL as coach of the Los Angeles Kings, he coached the Windsor Compuware Spitfires to the 1988 Memorial Cup, losing to the Medicine Hat Tigers.

Ley, Selwood and Webster all played on the New England Whalers team that won the World Hockey Association's first Avco Cup in 1973.

After playing one game with the Boston Bruins in the 1968–69 season, Steve Atkinson played five terms with the Sabres and Capitals. He rounded out his career with the Toronto Toros in the WHA. Phil Myre enjoyed a solid fourteen-year career in the NHL with Montreal, Atlanta, St. Louis, Philadelphia, Colorado and Buffalo. Phil Roberto played eight years in the NHL, mostly with Montreal,

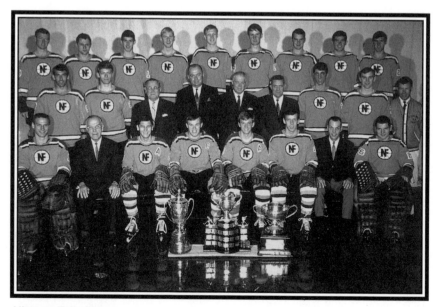

Niagara Falls Flyers.

St. Louis, Detroit and Kansas City, before finishing his career with one season in the WHA. He was a member of the 1971 Canadiens team that won the Stanley Cup. Don Tannahill played a couple of seasons with the Vancouver Canucks before moving to the WHA, where he divided three years between Minnesota and Calgary.

From the Estevan Bruins, Jim Harrison played twelve years in the NHL, mostly with Boston, Toronto and Chicago. He also spent four years in the WHA with Alberta, Edmonton and Cleveland. Danny Schock played a handful of games with the Boston Bruins and Philadelphia Flyers in the 1970–71 season after making his NHL debut during their Bruins' run to the Stanley Cup the previous spring. Greg Polis became a ten-year pro with Pittsburgh, St. Louis, Washington and the New York Rangers. Of the players added by the Estevan Bruins for the final, Kerry Ketter and Ken Brown each enjoyed one or two seasons in the WHA. Joe Zanussi spent two years in the WHA with Winnipeg and split another three between Boston and St. Louis in the NHL. Ron Garwasiuk returned to the 1969 Memorial Cup championship with the Regina Pats. Gregg Sheppard had a ten-year NHL career with the Bruins and Penguins. Dale Hoganson was an NHLer for eight seasons, suiting up for Los Angeles, Montreal and Quebec.

The 1969 Memorial Cup

The 1960s closed with two junior teams from traditional hockey strongholds vying for the Memorial Cup. The Regina Pats were returning to the national final for the first time in a decade to face an outstanding Montreal Junior Canadiens team.

With thirteen rookies in its lineup, Montreal defeated the Sorel Black Hawks for the Richardson Cup, taking the best-of-five series in four games. Meanwhile, Regina claimed the Abbott Cup after a seven-game series against the Dauphin Kings. The two finalists prepared for a series to be played in Montreal and Regina.

Coached by Roger Bédard, the Junior Canadiens featured a strong collection of Quebec talent, including Réjean Houle, the OHA scoring champion, Red Tilson Trophy winner and most gentlemanly player that year, as well as Gilbert Perreault, Richard Martin, Marc Tardif, Bobby Lalonde, Guy Charron, Jocelyn Guèvremont, André "Moose" Dupont, Norm Gratton, Jean-Pierre Bordeleau, Richard Lemieux and Bobby Guindon. In goal were Wayne Wood and Ted Tucker. The Junior Canadiens also picked up netminder Jim Rutherford from the Hamilton Red Wings, a move that irritated Regina coach and manager Bob Turner. He felt that the Wood/Tucker tandem, having allowed the least number of goals during the OHA regular season, should have sufficed. The Pats countered this formidable Montreal lineup with some good players of their own, including captain Ron Garwasiuk, Butch Goring, Don Saleski, Larry Wright, Barry Cummins and goalie Gary Bromley.

The first game was a 5–3 Montreal victory before a Forum crowd of 8,821 fans. Rutherford was outstanding between the pipes. "We would have had a 2–0 lead at the end of the first period if it hadn't been for the big saves by Rutherford," coach Turner said. Charron paced the Habs' attack with 3 goals, while Tardif and Perreault added singles. Murray Keogan and Larry Wright replied for the Pats with a pair and a single respectively.

In the next game, Montreal whipped Regina 7–2 to conclude Montreal's home portion of the series. Twenty game misconduct penalties were assessed after a wild free-for-all broke out at 16:14 of the third period. The match attracted a healthy crowd of 10,662 customers.

For game three, the teams travelled to Regina, where the visitors won 5–2 before 5,120 fans. The 5'5" Bobby Lalonde, a seventeen-year-old rookie, turned in a stellar performance during the loosely-played contest at Exhibition Stadium. He had 6 shots on goal and scored with his first 4.

Montreal showed more explosive offence in game four. Down 5–1 early in the second period, the Junior Canadiens rallied to tie the game and force overtime. They scored twice in the fixed-time extra frame to defeat Regina 8–6 and claim the Memorial Cup. A crowd of 5,223 Regina fans looked on in bewildered disappointment.

Montreal had been trailing by 4 goals in the second period when coach Bédard elected to shake things up by replacing leftwinger Bobby Guindon with Marc Tardif on the Habs' production line. Tardif's linemates Perreault and Houle responded almost immediately, and a comeback was mounted. "I started to switch lines when we were behind 5–1 and I guess it paid off," Bédard told Mal Issac of the *Regina Leader-Post*.

Tardif scored for the Junior Canadiens, as did Arthur Quoquochi, Richard Martin, Norm Gratton and André Dupont, who netted a pair. Guy Charron also scored twice, nailing the overtime winner. He emerged as the top scorer of the series with 6 goals and 4 assists.

Over the four games, the Pats' leading scorer was Ron Garwasiuk, who tallied 2 goals and 4 assists. Butch Goring, who played only the last two games in the series, was a close second with 3 goals and 2 assists. Goring had been added to the Pats roster from the Dauphin Kings of the MJHL.

It was the first time a team from Montreal had won the Memorial Cup since 1950, when the Montreal Junior Canadiens prevailed under the stewardship of Sam Pollock and Billy Reay. Such was the depth of the 1969 Junior Canadiens that a number of the strongest prospects returned to contend for the 1970 Memorial Cup. Many would graduate to impressive professional careers.

Réjean Houle played fourteen years with the Montreal Canadiens in the NHL and Quebec Nordiques in the WHA. He won the Stanley Cup with the Habs in 1971, 1973, 1977, 1978 and 1979. Houle took over as manager of the Canadiens in 1995. Marc Tardif began his professional career with five seasons in Montreal, winning the Stanley Cup in 1971 and 1973. He then played a season with Los Angeles in the WHA before returning to Quebec, where he enjoyed a number of impressive seasons with the Nordiques in both the WHA and NHL. Tardif was a member of the Nordiques team that won the Avco Cup in 1977.

Gil Perreault led the Montreal Jr. Canadiens to Memorial Cup victory in 1969 and 1970, and later became a legend in Buffalo, playing for the Sabres.

Guy Charron played in the NHL for more than a decade with Montreal, Detroit, Kansas City and Washington. André Dupont spent about the same number of years in the pros, mostly with St. Louis, Quebec and Philadelphia, where he won the Stanley Cup in 1974 and 1975. J. P. Bordeleau played eight years with the Chicago Blackhawks. Wayne Wood spent five years in the WHA, mainly with Toronto and Birmingham. Jim Rutherford had an impressive ten-year career with Detroit, Pittsburgh, Toronto and Los Angeles.

From the Regina Pats, Butch Goring enjoyed more than ten years with the Los Angeles Kings, winning the Lady Byng and Masterton Trophies in 1977–78. He was just getting warmed up. Goring went on to become a key member of the New York Islanders dynasty of the early 1980s, winning four Stanley Cups with the team from 1980 to 1983. He was the Conn Smythe Trophy winner in 1981. Don Saleski played nine years in the NHL, mostly with the Philadelphia Flyers. He won the Stanley Cup with his Memorial Cup rival André Dupont in 1974 and 1975. Larry Wright played parts of five seasons in the NHL, mostly with Philadelphia and Detroit. Barry Cummins enjoyed a year with the California Seals and Ron Garwasiuk had a season with Los Angeles of the WHA. Pats goaltender Gary Bromley played six years in the NHL with Buffalo and Vancouver and two in the WHA with Calgary and Winnipeg.

The 1969 Junior Canadiens were the first team from Montreal to win the Memorial Cup since 1950.

The
1970s

The 1970s were pivotal years for the Memorial Cup championship. In 1972, the first round robin tournament was played, with the major junior league champions of Ontario, Quebec and western Canada participating. The Memorial Cup became an "event," combining the allure of an all-star game with the intensity of a championship final.

The round robin format drew higher attendance and increased television coverage to the games. It also brought a larger pool of junior talent and a diversity of coaching styles. The format rewarded stamina; teams could only get to the tournament by endurance of a marathon of league playoffs. A team that was able to execute in key games could find themselves well placed to claim the title.

No longer a single battle between east and west, the Memorial Cup tournament became a three-way competition between regions, reflecting the fact that the game's roots were spreading out.

The spark of the Quebec Remparts offence, Guy Lafleur went on to become one of the greatest players ever to put on a Montreal Canadiens uniform. MONTREAL GAZETTE

The **1970** Memorial Cup

With many of the key players from the 1969 Montreal Junior Canadiens return-ing in 1970, it was little surprise to see the Junior Habs re-emerge as Memorial Cup favourites. Led by the formidable Gilbert Perreault, the 1970 Montreal team seemed to gain strength throughout the playoffs.

The Junior Canadiens finished first in the OHA and defeated the Ottawa 67's and St. Catharines Black Hawks en route to a meeting with the Toronto Marlboros in the OHA championship series. This Montreal vs. Toronto matchup, parallel to the traditional NHL rivalry between the Canadiens and the Maple Leafs, was surrounded by fanfare and excitement. The Marlboros' impressive lineup included Steve Shutt, Dale Tallon, Fred Barrett and Steve Vickers. Played in the Montreal Forum and Maple Leaf Gardens, the semi-final was a classic that went seven games and drew large crowds.

In the end, Montreal prevailed and went on to play the Sault Ste. Marie Greyhounds of the Northern Ontario Hockey League. Montreal began the series with a 6–2 win, but the Greyhounds surprised the powerful Quebec team with a 5–4 victory in game two. It was the first time in the eight-year history of the NOHA that one of its teams defeated an OHA club. A vengeful Montreal squad won the next three games by scores of 10–1, 9–2 and 20–1 before moving on to a Richardson Trophy final against the Quebec Remparts. Quebec had just defeat-ed the Prince Edward Islanders in a bitter and raucous series.

The Remparts finished first in the Quebec Junior Hockey League that sea-son, with budding superstar Guy Lafleur accounting for an astounding 103 of the team's 323 goals. The Quebec-Montreal rivalry was every bit as intense as the Toronto-Montreal competition. Lafleur and the rest of Maurice Filion's Remparts were out to dismiss suggestions by Montreal players that their QJHL success was cheap currency when compared to the higher level of OHA competition. The best-of-five series drew crowds of over 14,000 in Quebec and over 18,000 in Montreal. It ended in a three-game sweep for the Junior Canadiens.

Meanwhile in the west, a team new to Memorial Cup competition emerged to face the rolling Montreal juggernaut. The Weyburn Red Wings beat out the Moose Jaw Canucks and Regina Pats in the SJHL playoffs before eliminating the BC champion Vernon Essos, Alberta's Red Deer Rustlers and the Westfort Hurricanes of the Thunder Bay Junior Hockey League. Weyburn travelled north by bus to Melville, Saskatchewan and boarded the eastbound Canadian National train to Montreal.

The Red Wings, who hailed from a prairie town of fewer than 8,000 resi-dents, were not picked by many to win the Memorial Cup. But coach Stan Dunn vowed that his team would win at least one game from the host Montreal squad. Weyburn hoped to use tough forechecking to derail the Junior Canadiens' free-wheeling forwards.

The Red Wings picked up Rod Norrish, Scott Smith, Gary Leippi and goalie Gary Bromley from the Pats, and two other players from Edmonton and Moose Jaw. Weyburn's hopes were dealt a blow from the outset, when Smith was sidelined for the duration with an injury. Smith had scored 22 goals and 28 assists for Regina in the 1970 playoffs, and his absence left Weyburn sniper Calvin Booth, who had netted 32 goals in twenty-eight playoff games, with a heavy burden to bear alone. Booth and the Red Wings were up against a formidable array of Montreal artillery. There was captain and Red Tilson Trophy winner Gilbert Perreault, Richard Martin, Bobby Guindon, Normand Gratton, Bobby Lalonde, Jocelyn Guèvrement, Richard Lemieux, Serge Lajeunesse and Ian Turnbull. Montreal had also added Peterborough goaltender John Garrett, who led the OHA in goals-against average, to complement their regular netminder Wayne Wood.

The series opened in Montreal, where Richard Martin scored 4 goals to lead the Junior Canadiens to a 9–4 victory. Perreault did not score but collected a pair of assists. Wood started in net for Montreal and Jerome Mzarek, a pickup from Moose Jaw, worked the game for Weyburn.

Two nights later, a crowd of 4,100 fans showed up to watch Montreal take a 6–2 victory. Guindon got 2 goals and Lajeunesse, Lalonde, Gratton and Lemieux added singles for Montreal. Garrett was solid in net. "We were much sharper and, if we had received an all-out effort from everyone on the club, it would have been a much closer hockey game," Weyburn coach Dunn said.

Game three was a tight contest before 4,030 fans. For a while it appeared that the Red Wings would eke out their first win of the series. But with only thirty-three seconds left, a forty-footer from defenceman Serge Lajeunesse found its way through a maze of legs and past Bromley, giving Montreal a 5–4 victory. The winning goal came only three minutes after Gilbert Perreault had sent the sparse crowd into a frenzy by tying the game with his second goal of the night. Mzarek had started for the Red Wings but was replaced by Bromley after taking a shot to the head early in the third. "Weyburn gave its ultimate effort and lost," said Richard Martin, who also scored for Montreal. "I am sure we can win in four."

The Junior Canadiens were not a team that lacked killer instinct. They proved it two nights later with a 6–5 win before 4,561 fans. Gratton scored 3 times while Perreault racked up a goal and 3 assists. Lalonde and Monahan each scored singles.

Once again Weyburn had fought hard, coming back from a 2-goal deficit in the second period to take a 4–2 lead. But Montreal tied the score with 2 goals in the last two minutes of the second period and then surged ahead in the third. Monahan's goal at 14:16 proved to be the Memorial Cup winner. Mzarek blocked 42 of 48 shots by the Junior Canadiens while Garrett and Wood combined to turn aside 30 of 35 Weyburn drives.

For ten Junior Canadiens—Guèvremont, Gratton, Guindon, Lajeunesse, Lalonde, Lemieux, Martin, Moreau, Perreault and Wood—it was their second consecutive Memorial Cup. This was only the third time that a team had won two consecutive championships, the first two being the 1939 and 1940 Oshawa Generals and the 1955 and 1956 Toronto Marlboros.

Soon after the Junior Canadiens had won the 1970 national title, the Flin Flon Bombers offered a second straight challenge for the Memorial Cup. The Bombers operated in the independent Western Canada Hockey League, still not recognized by the CAHA. "We are not interested in any more games," replied Phil Wimmer, general manager of the Junior Canadiens. "We're finished for the year."

Many Junior Canadiens players went on to outstanding professional careers, the most notable being Gilbert Perreault. He became a Hall of Famer on the strength of a brilliant seventeen-year career with the Buffalo Sabres. Perreault won the Calder Trophy in his first year in the NHL, and led the Sabres to the Stanley Cup final in 1975. His Junior Habs teammate Richard Martin joined Perreault in Buffalo, playing with him and René Robert on the famous "French Connection" line, one of the most potent trios in the NHL. Martin had a productive decade with Buffalo before finishing his career in Los Angeles.

Bobby Lalonde played for more than ten years in the NHL with Vancouver, Atlanta and Boston. Jocelyn Guèvremont also spent the better part of a decade in the big league, chiefly with the Canucks and Sabres. J. P. Bordeleau played nine seasons with the Chicago Blackhawks and Richard Lemieux spent most of five seasons with Vancouver and the Kansas City Scouts before finishing off in Calgary of the WHA. Serge Lajeunesse enjoyed pro stints with Detroit and Philadelphia. Norm Gratton spent time in the NHL with New York, Atlanta, Buffalo and Minnesota, while Bobby Guindon spent most of his pro years in the WHA with Quebec and Winnipeg.

Ian Turnbull made his mark mainly with the Toronto Maple Leafs, where he brought an offensive flair to his blueline position for nine seasons. Goaltender Wayne Wood spent five years in the WHA, mostly with Vancouver, Calgary and Toronto. John Garrett enjoyed more than ten years in the pros, playing in Minnesota, Toronto, Birmingham and New England in the WHA, and Hartford, Quebec and Vancouver in the NHL. After his playing career ended, Garrett

Montreal Junior Canadiens.

joined fellow Memorial Cup alumni Don Cherry and Harry Neale in the *Hockey Night in Canada* broadcast booth.

From the Weyburn Red Wings, Larry Giroux played seven years in the NHL, mostly with Detroit, St. Louis and Hartford. Wendall Bennett and Gene Sobchuk each played a year in the WHA, Bennett with Phoenix and Sobchuk with Cincinnati. Regina Pats pickup Rod Norrish served a brief NHL tour with Minnesota, while Port Arthur pickup Vic Venasky played seven years with the Los Angeles Kings.

The **1971** Memorial Cup

The 1971 Memorial Cup championship held some radiance and some infamy. On one hand, the final offered Canadians their first bright glimpse of Guy Lafleur. On the other, it was almost derailed by violence and inter-league bickering. The eastern championship between the St. Catharines Black Hawks starring Marcel Dionne and the Quebec Remparts led by Guy Lafleur held the promise of brilliance. But it was abandoned partway through in the midst of bitter controversy. The Memorial Cup final itself was jeopardized by haggling over player eligibility and travel allowances. In the end, the Remparts and the Edmonton Oil Kings faced each other in an abbreviated final series.

In the OHA playoffs, the Frank Milne-coached Black Hawks eliminated the Kitchener Rangers, the defending Memorial Cup champion Montreal Junior Canadiens and the Toronto Marlboros to claim the OHA crown. Marcel Dionne's output during this run measured a breathtaking 2-goals-per-game clip. Dionne, who had led the OHA in scoring with 143 points during the 1971 season, was flanked by leftwinger Brian McKenzie and rightwinger Bobby MacMillan. With George Hulme in goal, the Black Hawks were anchored on defence by Dave Fortier, Bob McMahon and Brian McBratney.

The Remparts, under coach and manager Maurice Filion, had concluded their regular-season campaign with fifty-four wins and seven defeats. Quebec scored a total of 437 goals including 130 by Lafleur, who also added 79 assists. Like St. Catharines, there was more to the Remparts than their superstar. The team also boasted André Savard, Jacques Richard and Richard Grenier. In goal, Michel Deguise had been picked up from Sorel. During their Quebec playoff run, the Remparts quickly pushed aside the Verdun Maple Leafs and Trois-Rivieres Draveurs. They defeated the Shawinigan Bruins in five games for the provincial title.

The Black Hawks-Remparts contest was an intense rivalry on many levels. The series inevitably had some Quebec vs. Ontario and French vs. English undertones. In addition to the potent matchup between Dionne and Lafleur, there was some unfinished business between Dionne and the Remparts coach–manager. Dionne had been coached by Filion as a member of the 1968 Drummondville Rangers but left the Quebec league to compete in the OHA. He felt that the Ontario league offered a higher level of competition and a better chance to develop his skills. This defection rankled Filion, who had vowed to defeat Dionne and his OHA club with a team from Quebec.

The first game was played in St. Catharines and ended in a 4–2 victory for the Remparts. Lafleur and Richard both scored twice, while Dionne and Clyde "Chief" Simon scored for the Black Hawks. More spectators saw the match in Quebec than in Ontario. The game was shown on closed-circuit TV in Quebec City, where 5,540 fans watched, and in Verdun, where 2,540 fans paid to see televised action in the auditorium. Although pleased with the win, Filion was not happy with the work of referee Tom Brown. "Every time we tried to talk to him, he said nothing," Filion complained, "but Dionne can talk to him all night."

The next evening, the Black Hawks evened the series with an 8–3 trouncing of the Remparts. Dionne fired 4 goals with 3,321 St. Catharines fans roaring in support. The aggressive Black Hawks outshot Quebec 61–24.

The series returned to Quebec City for the third game. A crowd of 13,896 packed the 10,240-seat Colisée to cheer on the Remparts to a 3–1 win. Lafleur scored twice and Jacques Locas added a single. Referee Marcel Vaillancourt handed out 102 minutes in penalties, 77 to the Black Hawks. Brian McBratney and Brian McKenzie of St. Catharines were penalized for belligerency with the linesmen, McKenzie receiving a one-game suspension. "It's his last year in junior," CAHA president Earl Dawson said. "I made it quite clear that if anything like that happened again, I would have him suspended and remove his name from the draft list so he wouldn't be able to play hockey next year."

One night later, the series got even uglier. The Remparts crushed the Black Hawks 6–1, Lafleur netting a hat trick before another overflow crowd. As the game moved further out of reach, the St. Catharines players—heavily penalized by referee Jack Bowman—began to manhandle the smaller Remparts. Scrap after scrap broke out, with Black Hawk Mike Bloom exiting the penalty box to re-enter the fray more than once.

Their team leading on the scoreboard but losing in the fisticuffs, the Colisée fans became increasingly volatile. St. Catharines coach Milne later complained that his players were pelted with potatoes, tomatoes, eggs, bolts from seats, golf balls, debris and at least one knife. The St. Catharines team left the ice for their dressing room at the end of the game under an escort of Quebec City policemen. A spectator succeeded in spitting on Bloom, who replied by blindly swinging his stick—hitting one of the constables in the face and sending him to hospital for three stitches.

Things were no better outside the building. A cordon of policemen escorted the young Black Hawks to their team bus which had been taken around to the back of the Colisée. A large, ornery mob had gathered and was throwing bottles and pounding on the sides of the vehicle. The St. Catharines players, becoming genuinely frightened, lay face down on the floor of the bus as five police cars, sirens wailing, cleared a path for the vehicle. Fans in their cars later circled the club's motel until the early hours of the morning.

The next contest was held on neutral ice at Maple Leaf Gardens before 15,343 fans. The St. Catharines crew stuck strictly to hockey and handed a decisive 6–3 setback to the Remparts. Lafleur scored a goal while Dionne managed two assists. The Black Hawks now trailed three games to two. But the series suddenly ground to a halt. The Black Hawks would not return to Quebec City. "The parents of the kids refuse to send them into such a violent atmosphere," Milne announced. The Black Hawk ownership offered to play the last two games at the Montreal Forum in Quebec. "Absolutely not," was the reply from Filion. "We will not switch from our rink."

The game four story had taken on a life of its own. Not only were parents of the St. Catharines players reading lurid press accounts of the last game played in Quebec City, but new suggestions of threats and assaults against Dionne and his relatives began to surface.

There were further stories of threats made against St. Catharines players by the Front de libération du Québec or FLQ, the separatist sect that had kidnapped the British trade commissioner and a Quebec cabinet minister only six months earlier. When the FLQ murdered the minister, the federal government responded by introducing the War Measures Act. The stories about FLQ threats to the Black Hawks, genuine or not, further convinced the St. Catharines camp not to return to the Quebec capital.

"We've had this thing before," said CAHA president Dawson, who felt that the eastern championship must go on. "Last year for instance, it was Charlottetown." He was referring to a similar incident the year before when the Remparts played against the Charlottetown Islanders.

J. E. Turcotte, president of the Remparts, said that he was very hopeful the Black Hawks would reconsider and return to Quebec City. "I am very disappointed that they have cancelled the game," he told Gordon Walker of the *Globe and Mail*. "It is not a businesslike way of doing things. This is no credit to St. Catharines at all. We have good people in Quebec City as they have in Toronto and St. Catharines, although we have a few trouble makers as they have."

Nevertheless, things remained at a stalemate. Dawson finally declared Quebec the series winners after receiving official notice from St. Catharines that their team would not go back to Quebec City. The Remparts were promptly challenged by the Edmonton Oil Kings, but there was now controversy about the refusal of the QJHL and the OHA to play in a national final against the Western Canada Hockey League. Although the WCHL was no longer operating outside the jurisdiction of the CAHA, western teams were granted certain privileges. They were allowed to use four over-age players and received $10,000 in travel expenses compared to $6,000 for eastern teams. The eastern leagues objected to these allowances.

"The burning ambition of every Canadian boy is to play for the Memorial Cup as a junior and the Stanley Cup as a pro," declared Bill Hunter, coach and general manager of the Oil Kings. "If the Prime Minister wants to do something right for the west for a change, he'll use the War Measures Act to enforce a Memorial Cup final."

Drastic measures weren't needed and neither was Pierre Trudeau. The differences between the leagues were reconciled, and the Remparts prepared to play the Oil Kings in a shortened best-of-three series for the Memorial Cup.

The Edmonton Oil Kings had reached the final bracket of the WCHL by eliminating the Saskatoon Blades, Calgary Centennials and Flin Flon Bombers. Edmonton boasted a strong-skating club with captain Ron Jones, Darcy Rota, Phil Russell, Tom Bladon, Dave Kryskow and Alfred John Rogers. They immediately set out for Quebec City, where they were politely received by fans.

The final series opened at the Colisée, and the Remparts seized the first game with a 5–1 win. Centre Michel Brière scored twice and Lafleur had a goal and 3 assists. The series was over two nights later when Quebec won 5–2 to the delight of 11,401 fans celebrating the city's first-ever Memorial Cup triumph. Landry and leftwinger Richard scored 2 goals each while Savard notched a single. Lafleur was held scoreless and uncharacteristically received a ten-minute misconduct in a game that was chippy but brawl-free. As the final seconds ticked off, Colisée fans gave the Remparts a standing ovation, singing the Remparts team song "Ils Sont En Or" in unison.

The atmosphere in the two games in Quebec City had been buoyant and intense. Fans stood, clapped, sang and danced. Whenever Quebec scored, the hometown crowd erupted into an ovation of "de Ralliement des Remparts—Ils Sont En Or." Once, on the occasion of a Lafleur goal, the ice was covered by a shower of debris that included a black bra.

Holding the Memorial Cup Trophy high over his head, Guy Lafleur made a triumphant lap around the rink, hailed by the adoring public. They were already calling him the greatest player in hockey.

Guy Lafleur went on to become one of the Montreal Canadiens' definitive players, a superstar to rank with Habs greats Maurice Richard and Jean Beliveau. Combining panache with an unerring instinct for the game, Lafleur won the Stanley Cup five times with the Canadiens in 1973, 1976, 1977, 1978 and 1979. His individual awards include the Art Ross trophy (three times), the Hart (twice) and the Conn Smythe. After retiring at the end of the 1984–85 season, he returned to play with the New York Rangers in 1988–89. Lafleur finally ended his career with two seasons back in Quebec City.

The Flower was not the only Rempart to enjoy success at the professional level. Jacques Richard spent ten seasons in the NHL with Atlanta, Buffalo and Quebec. Richard Grenier played a year with the New York Islanders and a year in the WHA with Quebec. André Savard would move on to an NHL career, but first he returned to Memorial Cup competition in 1973, as did Charlie Constantin. After being absent from the QJHL since the 1984–85 season, the Quebec Remparts returned in 1997–98 when the Beauport Harfangs moved to Quebec City.

From the Edmonton Oil Kings, Rota, Russell and Bladon would be back in the 1972 Memorial Cup tournament. Dave Kryskow played four years in the NHL with Chicago, Washington, Detroit and Atlanta and two more in the WHA with Calgary and Winnipeg. Ron Jones spent part of five pro seasons with Boston, Pittsburgh and Washington. Alfred John Rogers returned to the Memorial Cup tournament in 1972. He later played a handful of NHL games with Minnesota before spending a year with Edmonton in the WHA.

From the St. Catharines Black Hawks, Dave Fortier played four seasons with Toronto, the New York Islanders and Vancouver, as well as a year with Indiana

Quebec Remparts.

in the WHA. Bob McMahon played three NHL seasons with Pittsburgh and one in the WHA with New England. Brian McKenzie played a handful of games with the Pittsburgh Penguins before playing with Edmonton and Indiana in the WHA. Mike Bloom played a season with San Diego in the WHA before spending three years with Washington and Detroit in the national league.

Marcel Dionne spent eighteen years in the NHL with Detroit, Los Angeles and the New York Rangers. Only two players in NHL history, Wayne Gretzky and Gordie Howe, have scored more goals, assists or points. Dionne's individual trophies include the Art Ross and Lady Byng (twice). Like his junior rival Guy Lafleur, he was ultimately inducted into the Hockey Hall of Fame.

The **1972** Memorial Cup

The Memorial Cup of 1972 represented the beginning of a new era in the junior hockey championship. For the first time, the competition format was a round robin, which brought the Peterborough Petes, Cornwall Royals and Edmonton Oil Kings together in Ottawa to vie for the top prize.

Back for their second straight run at the title was Edmonton, coached by Brian Shaw and managed by Bill Hunter. The core of the team, including captain Tom Bladon and his two alternates, Phil Russell and Darcy Rota, returned from the 1971 final. In the western playoffs, the Oil Kings took out Punch McLean's New Westminster Bruins and the Calgary Centennials before eliminating the Earl Ingarfield-coached Regina Pats.

Coached by Roger Neilson, the Peterborough Petes were led in scoring by Doug Gibson. They also had Bob Gainey, Colin Campbell, Bob Neely, captain Ron Lalonde, Jim Jones and goalie Mike Veisor. Neilson had moulded the Petes into a prototype of defensive prowess and discipline that would become his hallmark in the NHL. A high school teacher in Peterborough, he built a Petes team that could throw its weight around—each player in the lineup was over 190 pounds—but could also stick to a game plan. Neilson developed an excellent penalty-killing unit that allowed his team to play a physical game with some impunity. The Petes finished third in regular season play and defeated the St. Catharines Black Hawks in the first round of the playoffs. This moved them into a semi-final matchup with the first-place Toronto Marlboros.

Many scouts regarded the Marlboros, featuring the record-setting line of Billy Harris, Dave Gardner and Steve Shutt, as the best junior team in the country.

The Petes won their series with Toronto four games to one, taking the final game 6–4 after the Marlboros had opened up a 4–0 lead. In the OHA championship series, Peterborough defeated the Ottawa 67's. It was their first OHA title since 1959, when Scotty Bowman led the Petes past St. Michael's College in a rousing eight-game series.

The Cornwall Royals, under the direction of coach Orval Tessier, finished first in the Quebec Major Junior Hockey League, leading the league in both offence and defence. In the playoffs, the Royals eliminated the Verdun Maple Leafs and Shawinigan Bruins before defeating the defending Memorial Cup champion Quebec Remparts. Cornwall was backstopped by the goaltending of Richard Brodeur and had a healthy mix of scoring and grit reflected in players such as Blair MacDonald, John Wensink and Al Sims. Before the Memorial Cup series began, two of the three competing teams picked up goaltenders to reinforce their squads. Edmonton added John Davidson from the Calgary Centennials, who had finished the season with a goals-against average of 2.37 and accumulated eight shutouts. Peterborough recruited two netminders: Michel "Bunny" Larocque from the 67's and Gilles Gratton from the Oshawa Generals.

"It will be a classic, one of the best junior finals ever played, and the Edmonton Oil Kings of the Western Canada Hockey League will win it," said Del Wilson, president of the Regina Pats and a scout for the Montreal Canadiens. The Petes' victory over the Marlboros appeared to have opened the field, leading to a consensus among many of the scouts that the Oil Kings were going to take home their third Memorial Cup. "Edmonton should go home a winner if they play Davidson," said Chicago Blackhawks scout Jimmy Walker.

"Edmonton should whip both these teams," said Bob Turner, a California Golden Seals scout and former Pats defenceman. "Edmonton has the best talent in the tournament," concurred another California scout, George Agar. "About the only thing you can say for Peterborough," said Jerry Blair, a scout from the Minnesota North Stars, "is that they never quit." Nicknamed the TPT Petes for their Toronto-Peterborough Transport sponsorship, the team was known during the tournament as Tenacious, Persistent and Tough.

No one even mentioned the Royals.

Cornwall and Peterborough were first to square off. The Petes recorded a 4–2 victory on the strength of Veisor's goaltending. The crowd of 7,893 seemed to have adopted the underdog Royals as their favourites. Ron Lalonde scored twice for Peterborough and Doug Gibson scored his sixteenth of the playoffs. "Veisor was the difference," coach Neilson told Ross Peterkin of the Ottawa *Citizen*. "Our goalie Brodeur was not at his best," Cornwall coach Tessier admitted. "He was a little tense out there. We didn't get too much hockey out of our veterans, but I think we surprised a few people."

The next challenge for the Petes came in the form of the Oil Kings. Peterborough became the first team to qualify for the final game in the new format with a controversial 6–4 win. Edmonton had taken a 2–1 lead into the second period, when they were overtaken by a 3-goal Peterborough outburst in a three-minute span.

Neilson changed the tide by moving Ron Lalonde, his best checker, against Brian Ogilvie, who had scored for the Oil Kings. This move seemed to slow Edmonton's momentum. "After a couple of shifts," Neilson explained, "I noticed that Ogilvie was one of their better centres, so I played Lalonde against him."

Having taken the lead late in the second, the Petes appeared to be skating away from Edmonton, but they ran into penalty trouble and fell two men short. Within a minute and a half, the Oil Kings had tied the score on goals by Don Kozak and Darcy Rota.

At the end of the second, Neilson called for a measurement of Darcy Rota's stick. It was ruled illegal, and Rota was assigned to the penalty box for the first two minutes of the third period.

It was the turning point of the game. Only sixty-three seconds into the frame, Oil Kings defenceman Phil Russell received a hooking penalty, and with the Oil Kings two men short, Gibson scored at 1:55 to give Peterborough the game winner. The Petes employed their patented checking game to protect the 1-goal lead and it worked to perfection. The Oil Kings managed only 2 shots on net in the third period, the first at 12:13.

To make matters worse, the Petes later called for another stick measurement, this time on Ogilvie's lumber. It was also ruled illegal, and he was penalized with just under three minutes left. This virtually ruled out any possibility of an Edmonton comeback. Jim Jones scored the insurance marker at 18:53 of the final stanza.

"They took the game away from the players and decided it on a technicality," fumed a livid Bill Hunter. "It's the cheapest way that I know of to win a hockey game."

Neilson saw the move as a matter of good strategy. "When we were leading 4–2, I wasn't concerned," he said, "but when Edmonton came back to tie the score, I requested Vaillancourt to take a measurement at the end of the second period. I felt it would throw Edmonton off a bit and the penalty might just pick us up."

"It was a cheap way to win a hockey game," Hunter repeated to Bob Mellor of the Ottawa *Citizen*. "The Oil Kings have never once protested a stick and never will. I believe in retribution. That guy upstairs will be watching too. We'll win it on the ice."

Edmonton coach Brian Shaw, while peeved with the stick measurement, acknowledged that the Petes had played a sound game. "That's the best checking team we've run across so far this season," he said. "It has to be the best coached team in Canada. They're extremely well disciplined."

The Petes had made it to the final, leaving the Royals and Oil Kings to play each other for the right to face them. The underappreciated Royals rose to the occasion, eliminating Edmonton with an emphatic 5–0 shutout. Dave Johnson and Gary MacGregor scored twice each, and Gerry Teeple added the other goal. Brodeur earned his shutout by blocking 40 Edmonton shots while Cornwall fired 39 at Davidson.

"We didn't skate and we didn't hit," Hunter moaned to Gord Walker of the *Globe and Mail*. "That's our game, skating and hitting. When we didn't do either, we were gone. We were well-beaten by Cornwall and we had no excuses. I just want to say that I am proud of the job done by our coach."

The Royals took on Peterborough for the Memorial Cup trophy in a one-game make-or-break effort. To the surprise of the pundits, Cornwall won 2–1 in an endurance test before 10,155 fans.

The first period took sixty-three minutes as referee Cassidy assessed twenty-one penalties, seventeen of which came before the nine-minute mark. He handed out a total of eighty-six penalty minutes in the first period. There was plenty of fighting but no scoring, prompting some of the fans to chant, "We want hockey!"

The Royals got on the board with a strange goal early in the second period. Brian Bowles let rip a slapshot from the blueline which sailed over the net and off the end glass. When it bounced back in front, Veisor was unable to corral it and it ended up in the net. "That break decided the game," Neilson said.

Peterborough tied it before the end of the second period and the teams headed into the third in a deadlock. Their players appeared to be tiring, undoubtedly enhanced by the high humidity and 28-degree Celsius temperature in the Civic Centre.

The Royals, playing what many considered the most disciplined junior team in the country, exercised some discipline of their own. They used a two-man forechecking game to press the Petes' defence into making mistakes. This tactic paid off when Gary McGregor scored on a turnover early in the final period. From there, the Royals followed their system and relied on Brodeur to make big saves.

Both goaltenders were superb and had plenty of work, with the Petes outshooting the Royals 47–38.

Neilson felt that Brodeur's performance had won the game. "Cornwall outhustled us a little—it was a goalkeepers' duel," he said. It was only the Petes' third loss of the playoffs.

It was also the first time that a Cornwall team had won the Memorial Cup. For the Royals, who had finished last in league play the previous year, it was a Cinderella story. "This is my greatest thrill in hockey," said Orval Tessier, whose teammates threw him into the showers fully clothed after the game.

From the Cornwall Royals, Bob F. Murray went on to play fifteen NHL seasons with Chicago. Richard Brodeur played seven seasons with Quebec in the WHA, winning the Avco Cup in 1977. He also spent nine seasons in the NHL, mostly in Vancouver. Al Sims played the better part of ten seasons in the big league, most of them in Boston and Hartford. John Wensink played eight NHL seasons. Like Sims, he played most of his games with Boston and participated in the 1977 and 1978 Stanley Cup finals. Blair MacDonald played six years with Edmonton and Indianapolis of the WHA and four with Edmonton and

Cornwall Royals.

Vancouver in the NHL. Before Canadian hockey fans had ever even heard of Jari Kurri, MacDonald scored 46 goals and 94 points playing on Wayne Gretzky's right wing in 1979–80.

From the Peterborough Petes, Bob Gainey played sixteen excellent seasons with the Montreal Canadiens, winning the Stanley Cup five times between 1976 and 1986. He also won the Selke Trophy four times and the Conn Smythe in 1979. Gainey went on to coaching and managing duties with Minnesota and Dallas. Colin Campbell played a year in the WHA before spending eleven more in the NHL with Pittsburgh, Edmonton, Vancouver, Detroit and the Colorado Rockies. He later coached the New York Rangers.

Mike Veisor played ten years in the NHL, mostly in Chicago and Hartford. Ron Lalonde spent seven years with Pittsburgh and Washington. Bob Neely played most of five seasons on the Maple Leafs blueline while Jim Jones spent two years with Vancouver of the WHA and three with the Leafs. Doug Gibson played three NHL seasons with Boston and Washington while Steve Lyon and Danny Gloor enjoyed brief stints with Pittsburgh and Vancouver respectively.

From the Edmonton Oil Kings, Darcy Rota went on to an impressive eleven-year NHL career with Chicago, Atlanta and Vancouver. Phil Russell played fifteen years with Chicago, Atlanta, Calgary, New Jersey and Buffalo. Tom Bladon spent nine years in the NHL, mostly in Philadelphia—where he won the Stanley Cup in 1974 and 1975—and Pittsburgh. Don Kozak was a big-leaguer for seven seasons with Los Angeles and Vancouver. Terry McDonald made a brief appearance with the Kansas City Scouts.

Backup goaltender Doug Soetaert played twelve years with the Rangers, Winnipeg and Montreal, supporting Patrick Roy in the Canadiens' drive to the Stanley Cup championship in 1986. John Davidson played the better part of a decade in the pros, first with St. Louis and then New York, where he was instrumental in taking the Rangers to the 1979 Stanley Cup final. Davidson's backup that year was Doug Soetaert.

Of the coaches, Roger Neilson and Orval Tessier both moved on to the NHL,

Tessier with Chicago and Neilson with Toronto, Buffalo, Vancouver, Los Angeles, New York and Florida. Neilson guided the Vancouver Canucks to the Stanley Cup final in 1982. Richard Brodeur, Colin Campbell, Darcy Rota and Blair MacDonald were all on that Canucks team.

The **1973** Memorial Cup

There were no upsets in the 1973 Memorial Cup championship. "We lost only seven games all season," Glenn Goldup of the Toronto Marlboros recalled. "In the past, the Marlies always had one strong line and played it to death, but George Armstrong was our coach and he used all three lines on the powerplay and to kill penalties. And it didn't matter if we were down 3 or 4 goals going into the final period, we were always confident we could pull it out."

As Goldup confirmed, the 1973 Marlboros were a confident and well-coached group. The Memorial Cup tournmanent was held in the Montreal Forum that year and, although Toronto faced two solid teams in the Quebec Remparts and Medicine Hat Tigers, the Marlboros were favoured going in.

The Marlies, under rookie coach and former Maple Leafs great George Armstrong, had dominated the OHA regular season, setting records for goals and points. They also demonstrated that they could play defence, posting the league's best goals-against average. The team was a high-profile gate attraction, featuring players like Mark and Marty Howe, Paulin Bordeleau, Bob Dailey and rookie goaltender Mike Palmateer. They also possessed great depth and balance. Although there were eleven rookies on the team, seven players topped the 30-goal mark and eleven scored more than 55 points during the season. The big line featured Mark Howe, Glenn Goldup and Wayne Dillon, a trio that broke records set the previous year by Steve Shutt, Billy Harris and Dave Gardner.

Toronto moved past St. Catharines and Ottawa in the first two rounds of the playoffs, to bring about an OHA final with the Peterborough Petes. It was a tough matchup that went seven games, the last game drawing the largest-ever crowd—16,485—for a junior hockey game in Maple Leaf Gardens. Toronto, leading in series points with three wins and two ties, needed only another tie to advance, and got it in dramatic fashion on a Bordeleau penalty shot with a minute left. This gave them a 5–5 draw and the OHA title.

In the QMJHL, the Quebec Remparts emerged as the dominant team under Orval Tessier, who had moved over from behind the bench of the Cornwall Royals. In the playoffs, the Remparts defeated the Trois-Rivieres Draveurs and Sherbrooke Beavers in straight games. They had more trouble in the QMJHL final, where they met the defending champion Royals. But the Remparts won in seven games and prepared to make their second Memorial Cup appearance in three years. Five players from the 1971 Remparts returned in 1973, including André Savard and Charlie Constantin, while the team also featured newer players such as Guy Chouinard and André Deschamps.

In the WCHL, coach Jack Shupe's Medicine Hat Tigers emerged to challenge for the Memorial Cup. They had won the league championship in only their third season by defeating the Calgary Centennials, Edmonton Oil Kings and Saskatoon Blades. Dubbed the "Gassoff Gang" after their scrapping trio of Bob, Brad and Ken Gassoff, the Tigers were powered by the offensive talents of Tom Lysiak, Lanny McDonald and Boyd Anderson. Lysiak and McDonald were first and third respectively in WCHL scoring while Anderson finished ninth.

The first game of the Memorial Cup series featured the Marlboros playing the Remparts. Paulin Bordeleau fired three goals to lead Toronto to a 5–2 triumph. Toronto had jumped to a 4–0 lead by the second period and although the Remparts were able to close the gap, they could not muster a comeback. Coach Tessier noted that the offensive power wielded by the Marlboros was even superior to what had been displayed in the 1972 tournament when he faced them as the coach of the Royals. "I think the competition in the QMJHL is not as tough as in the OHA, except for one or two teams," he said.

The Marlboros faced Medicine Hat in the next game. This time, some aggressive checking and hitting provided the Tigers with a 3–2 victory. Of the 6,088 fans in attendance, nearly 500 had travelled from Alberta for the game. Brad Gassoff broke the 2–2 deadlock midway through the third. The Lysiak–McDonald–Anderson line had an off night; the trio was on the ice for both Toronto goals. "They can play better and dirtier," Calgary Centennials owner Scotty Munro said of the Tigers. Marty Howe had a different point of view. "I don't think they're really dirty," he commented. "It's just that they like coming at you. I found that our biggest trouble was getting the puck and holding on to it. The passes weren't clicking and we had a hard time getting good rushes organized."

"The Marlies are a good solid hockey team," coach Shupe told the Canadian Press. "I think they gave us one of the toughest games we've had in a long while."

Having beaten the powerful Marlboros without any production from their best line, the Tigers seemed nicely placed going into their second game. But Medicine Hat was taken by surprise when the Quebec Remparts exploded out of the gate, roaring to a 6–1 first period lead. The end result was an 8–3 rout. Chouinard and Savard led the way with 2 goals apiece, but a full team effort secured the win before a crowd of 12,699. "We did everything tonight that we didn't do against Toronto," an elated Jacques Locas said. "We showed them right at the start that we wouldn't back down if they tried to rough us up and it worked."

From the start of the game, referee Jim Lever of the OHA let both teams know that he wouldn't stand for any nonsense. He called fifteen minor penalties in the first period alone.

Quebec, Medicine Hat and Toronto all ended the round robin with a victory and a loss, meaning that the two finalists were decided on goals differential. Quebec had scored 9 and given up 8, Toronto 7 and 5, and Medicine Hat 6 and 9. Consequently, Quebec and Toronto would play each other in the deciding match.

Touted as the best team in the country for much of the season, the Marlboros left no room for doubt in the Memorial Cup final. They recorded a 9–1 victory in front of 9,762 spectators. Toronto's offence was invincible, getting 4 goals on the powerplay and 3 short-handed. Glenn Goldup and Peter Marrin, both doubtful starters due to injuries, led the way offensively with 2 tallies apiece while Mark Howe collected 3 assists.

The Remparts scored first, taking a 1-goal lead at the two-minute mark. But it was all downhill from there. "We went out there and took a 1–0 lead and tried to nurse it," Tessier said. "Then we just relaxed." The Quebec coach showed some class by refusing to lay his team's defeat at the feet of the officials. "Some of my players decided to take cheap penalties and it hurt us," he said. "I'm not blaming the referee. He called an excellent hockey game."

Of the Marlboros' output with a man advantage, George Armstrong said, "I know that a lot of people think our powerplay is no good. But it has never had to be good."

The shots on goal in the final game bore this out. The Marlboros posted 53 to the Remparts' 20. For

Before he grew his bushy moustache—a trademark during most of his sixteen NHL years—Lanny McDonald was a fresh-faced member of the Medicine Hat Tigers.
MORLEY L. FACH

Armstrong, the victory was a continuation of the outstanding success he had enjoyed with the Maple Leafs. "I was surprised to realize that I liked the Marlies' coaching job as much as I did," he recalled. "It's like having a big family I guess. It can be a very rewarding experience."

Among those in attendance at the May 12 game was Mark Howe's father, Gordie. "The kid played well," the senior Howe said. "Toronto players told me before the game that they felt they could handle Quebec and they did."

From the 1973 Toronto Marlboros, Mark and Marty Howe began their careers in the WHA, spending four years with Houston and two with New England. Their father Gordie played with them during this period, forming the core of two Avco Cup-champion Houston Aeros teams in 1974 and 1975. Mark Howe went on to play more than fifteen years in the NHL with Hartford, Philadelphia and Detroit. A leftwinger in junior, he eventually became an all-star defenceman in the NHL. Marty spent six years in the NHL with Hartford and Boston.

Paulin Bordeleau spent three years with Vancouver and three in the WHA with Quebec. He helped the latter team win the Avco Cup in 1977. Bob Dailey played nine years in the NHL with Vancouver and Philadelphia. Glenn Goldup's professional career also spanned nine seasons, starting in Montreal and finishing in Los Angeles. Wayne Dillon spent three years in the WHA with Toronto and Birmingham, and four in the NHL with the Rangers and Jets.

Mike Palmateer backstopped the Maple Leafs for six seasons and the Capitals for two. John Hughes spent five years in the WHA, mostly with Phoenix, Cincinnati and Houston. He also had a pair of NHL seasons in Vancouver and Edmonton. Dennis Owchar played six years with Pittsburgh and the Colorado Rockies. Tom Edur played three years in the WHA with Cleveland and two in the NHL with the Colorado Rockies. He finished his career in Pittsburgh.

From the Medicine Hat Tigers, Lanny McDonald became a Hall of Famer. He played sixteen outstanding seasons with the Maple Leafs, Rockies, and Flames, winning the Stanley Cup with Calgary in 1989. Tom Lysiak also enjoyed solid

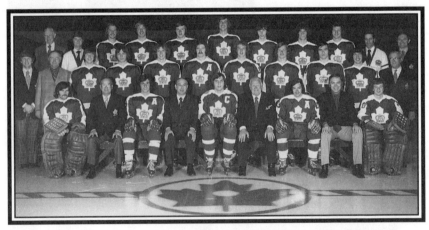

Toronto Marlboros. Back row (l to r): Dr. Leo Hall (team physician), Pat Reilly (trainer), Marty Howe, Tom Edur, Jim Clarke, Dick Decloe, Wayne Dillon, Brad Winton, Dennis Owchar, Dan Lemelin (trainer), Karl Elieff (physiotherapist). Middle row: Paul McNamara (administrator), George Hannah (equipment manager), Bruce Boudreau, Geoff Green, Dan Glugosh, Glenn Goldup, Jeff Woodyatt, Mark Howe, John Hughes, Kevin Devine, Austin Kimmis (statistician). Front row: Kevin Neville, Jack White (assistant manager), Peter Marrin, Frank Bonello (general manager), Bob Dailey, Harold Ballard (president), Paulin Bordeleau, George Armstrong (coach), Mike Palmateer.

success in the pros, playing thirteen seasons with Atlanta and Chicago. Eddie Johnstone had a ten-year career with Detroit and the New York Rangers. As for the Gassoffs, Bob and Brad each played four years in the NHL, Bob with St. Louis and Brad with Vancouver. Bob Gassoff's career was cut short when he was killed in a motorcycle accident in May 1977.

From the Quebec Remparts, André Savard played twelve seasons with Buffalo, Boston and Quebec. Charlie Constantin played four seasons with Quebec and Indianapolis in the WHA, winning the Avco Cup with the Nordiques in 1977. Real Cloutier and Guy Chouinard would return to Memorial Cup competition in 1974.

The **1974** Memorial Cup

The 1974 Memorial Cup saw the Quebec Remparts, the St. Catharines Black Hawks and the Regina Pats convene in Calgary to decide the junior championship. For the Remparts and the Black Hawks, it was a rematch of the bitter 1971 Richardson Cup series, while the Pats were seeking a return of the title for the first time in forty-four years.

The Pats seemed to get stronger as they moved through the playoffs. They needed seven games to overcome the Saskatoon Blades, then six to defeat the Swift Current Broncos. The western final against the Calgary Centennials was a four-game Regina sweep. Coached by former Montreal Canadien Bob Turner, the Pats featured the scoring prowess of junior sensation Dennis Sobchuk along with Clark Gillies, Rick Uhrich, Glen Burdon and defenceman Greg Joly. Garth Malarchuk of the Centennials and Larry Hendrick of the Edmonton Oil Kings were added to their goaltending roster for the final. But neither was needed, as regular netminder Eddie Staniowski proved to be up to the task.

While the Pats shifted into playoff gear gradually, the Black Hawks were unstoppable from the beginning. St. Catharines eliminated their OHA opponents without a single loss, taking out the Oshawa Generals, Toronto Marlboros and Peterborough Petes. The team was coached and managed by Paul Emms. Their leading forward unit was known as the "Gas Line": Dave Gorman, Rick Adduono and Dave Salvian. Captain Rick Hampton and Wilf Paiement supplemented the Black Hawks' offence. Adduono, Gorman and Paiement had all finished in the top five of the OHA regular season scoring race. St. Catharines picked up Frank Salive from Peterborough to back up their regular netminder Bill Cheropita.

The Quebec Remparts, coached by Marc Picard and managed by Paul Dumont, emerged as the premier team in the QMJHL. They were competing for the Memorial Cup for the third time in four years. Backstopped in goal by Bob Sauve and led by Memorial Cup veterans Real Cloutier and Guy Chouinard, Quebec pushed aside the Shawinigan Dynamos, Laval Nationals and Sorel Black Hawks.

The first game of the 1974 tournament featured St. Catharines and Quebec. The St. Catharines Black Hawks scored a 4–1 victory before 6,577 fans in the

Calgary Corral. Hampton, a seventeen-year-old centre and sometime defence-man, scored twice in the lugubriously-paced game. Many fans left the Corral after Hampton put St. Catharines ahead 3–1 halfway through the third period. The following night, with 7,415 in the seats, Eddie Staniowski blocked 29 shots and led Regina in a 4–0 whipping of St. Catharines. In a commanding perfor-mance at both ends of the ice, Pats defenceman Joly notched 2 goals, one with his team two men short.

It was a brawl-studded game. Fights dominated the first two periods with the teams accumulating a total of 11 majors. The worst altercation resulted in game misconducts assigned to the Pats' Robbie "Rough House" Laird, who had earlier contributed a goal, and the Black Hawks' Greg Craig, who had accumu-lated only six minutes of penalty time in 67 regular-season games. Things settled down in the third period as the Pats laboured to preserve the shutout for Staniowski.

Impressive as their win over the Black Hawks was, Regina was unable to carry the momentum into its subsequent meeting with the Remparts. Guy Chouinard scored twice in pacing Quebec to a 5–3 victory.

With the teams knotted at 3 going into the final period, this game was the tightest of the tournament. Late in the second, the red light came on after Sobchuk banged at a rebound during a scramble in front of the Remparts' net, but referee Bob Nadin ruled no goal. The next chance went to Quebec when defenceman Jean Gagnon flipped a low shot past Staniowski in the early minutes of the third period. This proved to be the winning goal.

With each team now 1–1 in wins, Regina proceeded to the final on goals dif-ferential while Quebec and St. Catharines, still deadlocked, had to play one more game to determine the other finalist.

Quebec seized the moment in an explosive way. They stopped the Black Hawks cold with an 11–3 pounding, handily earning the right to meet the Pats. Chouinard was lethal, contributing a goal and 4 assists, but the real offensive weapon for the Remparts was Cloutier, who tallied a hat trick. Jacques Locas and Daniel Beaulieu added 2 each, while singles were scored by Richard Perron, Michel Lachance and André Perreault. The Remparts were particularly danger-ous on the powerplay, scoring five times with the man advantage.

On May 12, the Pats claimed their first Memorial Cup since 1930 in front of 7,382 fans at the Corral. This time it was Sobchuk's turn to show some offence. He ended his standout junior career by collecting 3 goals and 1 assist in the 7–4 victory.

The Remparts had been leading the game 3–0 at 11:26 of the first period. They took a 3–1 lead into the second but Sobchuk caught fire in the middle frame, scoring twice in the midst of a 4-goal run by the Pats. Quebec pulled to within 1 with five minutes left in the third, pressing hard for the equalizer. But with two minutes left, Glen Burdon replied to give the Pats some insurance before Sobchuk hit an empty net in the final minute.

Coach Bob Turner admitted his team had been "shook up pretty good" when they fell behind by 3 goals. He felt that a second-period scrap between Clark Gillies and Richard Nantais had been the catalyst for his team's resurgence. Gillies also contributed a goal while Greg Joly—easily the top defenceman in the three-team tournament—earned 3 assists. Locas scored twice to lead the Remparts and Charlie Constantin and Perreault scored once each. Apart from the single fight, the game had been played clean. Referee Kerry Fraser earned praise for letting the two teams play hockey.

Despite surrendering 3 first-period goals, Regina netminder Staniowski had been steady under pressure. He had little to do in the last two periods as the Pats outshot the Remparts 52–31. Sauve was brilliant in a losing cause, however, and was named to the tournament all-star team. Other all-stars included the Remparts' Richard Perron on defence and Real Cloutier on left wing. From the Pats, Greg Joly took the other spot on defence and Rick Uhrich and Glen Burdon were chosen at right wing and centre respectively. The Remparts' Chouinard was named top player in the series.

Hot on the heels of the 1973–74 season, Dennis Sobchuk signed a contract with Cincinnati of the WHA for more than $1,000,000. Even so, he played with Phoenix in 1975–76, as Cincinnati had not yet set up shop. Sobchuk played four seasons with Cincinnati and Edmonton in the WHA before rounding out his career with two NHL seasons with Detroit and Quebec.

Greg Joly played for a decade with Washington and Detroit, while Ed Staniowski enjoyed a solid pro career with St. Louis, Winnipeg and Hartford. Clark Gillies had an outstanding fourteen-year career with the New York Islanders and Buffalo Sabres. Combining toughness and fire power, he established himself

Regina Patricias. Back row (l to r): Glen Burdon, Drew Callander, Mike Wirchowski, Mike Harazny, Rob Tudor, Kim McDougal, Jon Hammond, Dave Thomas. Middle row: Wayne Zurowski (assistant trainer), Clark Gillies, Bill Bell, Dave Faulkner, Mike Wanchuk, Jim Minor, Rob Laird, Dennis Sobchuk, Norm Fong (trainer). Front row: Eddie Staniowski, Bob Turner (coach), Greg Joly, John Weber (assistant manager), Dr. Jim Chatwin (team physician), Rick Uhrich, Del Wilson (general manager), Bob Leslie. On floor in front: Randy McCormack, Ken Gilson (stick boys).

as a key player in the Islanders' four-year Stanley Cup dynasty from 1980 to 1983.

From the Remparts, Guy Chouinard enjoyed a productive decade with Atlanta, Calgary and St. Louis. He hit the 50-goal mark in 1978–79. Real Cloutier twice led the WHA in scoring with the Quebec Nordiques, winning the Avco Cup in 1977. He maintained a good scoring touch with the NHL Nordiques and Buffalo Sabres as well. Bob Sauve became an outstanding NHL goaltender, playing more than ten years with Buffalo, Chicago and New Jersey. He led the NHL in goals-against average with the Sabres in 1979–80.

From the Black Hawks, Wilf Paiement had a solid career with Kansas City, Colorado, Toronto and Quebec. Rick Hampton played a couple of pro seasons with each of California, Cleveland and Los Angeles. Rick Adduono played a season with Birmingham in the WHA, plus a handful of NHL games with Boston and Atlanta. Dave Gorman spent five years in the WHA with Phoenix and Birmingham and served a brief NHL stint with Atlanta. Dave Salvian played one game with the New York Islanders.

The **1975** Memorial Cup

There was something old and and something new in the Memorial Cup championship of 1975. The Toronto Marlboros, carrying almost a half century of tradition, ran up against the New Westminster Bruins and Sherbrooke Beavers, who were making their first appearances in the national final. Punch McLean had moved his Estevan Bruins from Saskatchewan to New Westminster, British Columbia in 1971, so the Bruins were not exactly new kids on the block. But they did represent the first team from BC to compete for the junior championship since the Trail Smoke Eaters lost in 1944.

New Westminster finished third in the western division of the WCHL, but they were able to sideline the first-place Victoria Cougars and second-place Medicine Hat Tigers in the playoffs. The Bruins completed their charge to the western title with a seventh-game victory over the Saskatoon Blades. New Westminster had earned a reputation as a team that won by physical intimidation and also boasted a strong lineup with a number of future NHLers including Barry Beck, Brad Maxwell and Mark Lofthouse. Gord Laxton was their regular goaltender, and McLean picked up Ed Staniowski for good measure.

After finishing first overall in the QMJHL, Sherbrooke polished off the Hull Festivals and Chicoutimi Sagueneens in opening rounds before eliminating Mike Bossy and the Laval Nationals in the championship final. Coached by Ghislain Delage, the Beavers' prominent players included future NHLers Claude Larose and Bobby Simpson.

In Ontario, the Toronto Marlboros cruised to first place in the regular season but encountered some adversity a couple of months before the playoffs. Rightwinger Mark Napier announced he would circumvent the NHL amateur draft, having signed a contract with the Toronto Toros of the WHA. The ensuing publicity served as a distraction to the team. As the post-season began, the tension was exacerbated when John Tonelli announced that he had a contract with the Houston Aeros of the WHA to commence in August.

Tonelli's case was more complicated, as it meant that he would sit out all of Toronto's games after he turned eighteen on March 23. He didn't want to risk jeopardizing his chances of playing professionally with the Aeros in the 1976 season. Tonelli, who contributed leadership, toughness and defensive smarts to the Marlboros, not to mention 49 goals and 86 assists on the season, was lost for the playoffs. Initially, Toronto looked like they would falter, pushed to the brink of elimination by the eighth-place Kingston Canadians in the first round. The Canadians had finished the season 45 points behind Toronto, but the Marlboros had to come from behind to snatch a playoff victory in eight games. Toronto went another eight games against the fifth-place Sudbury Wolves, winning the final game in sudden death overtime.

Less than fifteen hours after leaving Sudbury, Toronto won the opener of the OHA finals against the Hamilton Fincups. "That Sudbury series was unbelievable," Marlboros defenceman Mike Kitchen said. "Those were eight of the toughest games I've ever played. We didn't get home until this morning and Hamilton had been off four days. I didn't think we could take them."

The Marlboros defeated the Fincups and proceeded to the Memorial Cup tournament. Although Tonelli was out of the picture, Toronto still boasted an impressive lineup. In addition to Napier and Kitchen, they had captain Bruce Boudreau, who finished the regular season with 68 goals and a league-leading 165 points. John Anderson, Mike Kaszycki and Mike McEwen were also offensive threats.

Displaying their new-found knack for dramatic comebacks, the Marlboros faced Sherbrooke in the first game of the tournament. They scored a 5–4 overtime victory before 3,162 fans at the Kitchener Memorial Auditorium.

The Beavers had built up a 3–0 lead early in the second period but the Marlboros fought back to square the score. Napier, Toronto's best player of the night, put them ahead for the first time midway through the third, scoring his second goal on a great solo rush. From there, the Marlboros appeared on their way to victory. But with the Beavers employing a sixth attacker, Claude Larose knocked a rebound past Gary Carr at 19:31 of the third frame.

Toronto's Lynn Jorgenson ended a wide-open but erratic overtime by tipping Mike Kitchen's blueline shot behind Sherbrooke goalie Nick Sanza from the crest of the goalmouth. Sherbrooke coach Delage blamed foolish penalties for his team's mid-game collapse, but he wasn't about to criticize WCHL referee Murray Harding. "I don't want to put the blame on the referee. He has a job to do."

Jorgenson commented, "They thought they could outhit us, but once they realized we were going to give it right back to them, they played hockey again."

The Beavers let another lead slip away in the second game of the tournament against New Westminster. The Bruins overcame a 3-goal deficit after the first period to claim a 7–5 victory. They scored 5 unanswered goals in the second and hung on for the win. The game lasted almost three hours and was marred by 102 penalty minutes including 14 five-minute majors. The Bruins got the better of most of the scraps, but Sherbrooke were able to expose a sluggishness in the Bruins that would later be exploited by the Marlboros.

New Westminster then clinched a spot in the final with a 6–2 victory over Toronto. The Bruins focussed on solid physical play without resorting to brutal intimidation. Toronto goaltender Carr appeared unsteady at times, stopping 17 of 23 shots. Laxton was forced to make several outstanding saves including a breakaway skate save on Napier when the Marlboros were shorthanded in the second.

For the second consecutive game, the Bruins called on an array of talent for their goal scoring. Clayton Pachal, Brian Shmyr, Steve Clippingdale, Mike Sleep, Fred Berry and Rick Shinske all scored for New Westminster. It was their first fight-free match of the tournament, although the Bruins were still tagged with more minor infractions than the Marlboros.

McLean saw penalty killing as the key to his club's win. "Toronto is supposed to have the best powerplay in the east," he told Dennis Passa of the Canadian Press. "But we've got a fine bunch of penalty killers ourselves." Gord Laxton said he didn't care which team his club played in the final. "We beat them both," he said. Bruins captain Barry Smith asked, "Are we the favourites now? If we are, it will be the first time all season."

The Bruins' win left the Marlboros and Beavers facing each other in a semifinal. The winner would move on to meet New Westminster in the deciding game. The Marlboros came through in the clutch and made a strong statement, hammering Sherbrooke by a score of 10–4. The game was close going into the third period, with Toronto holding a 5–4 lead, but the Marlboros pulled away to record a resounding win.

The victory centrepiece was a 5-goal performance by Bruce Boudreau—a Memorial Cup record. Boudreau had not scored a goal in the tournament since the third game of the Marlboros' series against Hamilton—a six-game famine. "I can't remember ever going that long without scoring in my three years of Junior A hockey," said Boudreau. "Tonight was just one of those nights when God was looking down on me."

"The momentum that George Armstrong has put into the team is unbelievable," said Sherbrooke coach Guilbault. "They play very disciplined hockey and are a talented hockey team. We had to play catch-up hockey all night and, as you've seen, you're definitely not able to do that in a Memorial Cup tournament."

The Marlboros carried their momentum into the final game at the Kitchener Memorial Auditorium. Although they fell behind early, Toronto managed to erase a 2–0 deficit. In the second period, they scored 2 goals twenty-four seconds apart to break a 3–3 tie. The Marlies surged on to claim the Memorial Cup with a 7–3 victory over the Bruins.

Kaszycki and Anderson scored 2 each while Napier, Boudreau and Jorgenson scored singles for Toronto. Harold Phillipoff, Kelly Secord and Mark Lofthouse scored the Bruins' goals. It was a clean game, with referee Marcel Vaillancourt calling just ten minor penalties, five to each team.

In the traditional post-victory hijinks, the Marlboros threw coach George Armstrong into the shower and then into the hotel swimming pool. Armstrong admitted that before the game, he had been concerned his Marlboros wouldn't be able to hold their ground with the bigger New Westminster players. Kitchen, who handed out numerous checks at the Toronto blueline, maintained that forechecking was the key to the Toronto victory. "We were digging out here today," Kitchen told the Canadian Press. "The last time we played them, we shied away in the corners."

"I could see from the start it was going to be completely different from the first matchup," Marlboros general manager Frank Bonello said. "We were standing up to their little shots and we were skating. We were moving and they were chasing us." According to Punch McLean, New Westminster's three-day layoff gave Toronto an edge. "The Marlies got a few lucky bounces at the wrong time for us and that's all you need in junior hockey in a one-shot deal." For the Marlboros, this was their last Memorial Cup, setting a record at seven that would stand into the next century.

From the 1975 Toronto Marlboros, Mark Napier played three years with Toronto and Birmingham in the WHA prior to eleven productive NHL seasons with Montreal, Minnesota, Edmonton and Buffalo. He was a member of the Stanley Cup champion Canadiens in 1979 and Oilers in 1985. Starting his career in the Toronto and Chicago organizations, Bruce Boudreau became a high-scoring superstar in the minor-pro leagues while Mike Kitchen played eight years

Toronto Marlboros. Back row (l to r): George Hannah (equipment manager), Trevor Johansen, Mark Murphy, Mike Kaszycki, Ed Saffrey, Ron Wilson, Brian Crichton, Lynn Jorgenson. Second row from back: Bruce Kennedy (assistant trainer), Bill Wells, Jim Kirkpatrick, Mike McEwen, Bernie Johnston, Steve Harrison, Dan Lemelin (trainer), Paul McNamara Jr. (administrator). Third row from back: Dr. L. Hall (team physician), Craig Crawford, Al Cameron, Mark Napier, Mike Kitchen, John Smrke, John Anderson, Austin Kimmis (statistician). Front row: Steve Bosco, Jack White (assistant manager), Frank Bonello (general manager), Bruce Boudreau, Harold Ballard (president), George Armstrong (coach), Gary Carr.

with the Colorado Rockies and New Jersey Devils.

John Anderson enjoyed a solid NHL career, playing a dozen seasons with Toronto, Quebec and Hartford. Ron Wilson divided fourteen seasons between Winnipeg, St. Louis and Montreal. Mike Kaszycki played five years with the New York Islanders, Capitals and Maple Leafs. Trevor Johansen divided five seasons among Toronto, Colorado and Los Angeles. Mike McEwen played twelve years in the big league, mostly with the Rangers, Islanders and Hartford Whalers. He helped the Islanders to the Stanley Cup in 1981, 1982 and 1983.

From the Sherbrooke Beavers, Claude Larose played four years with Cincinnati in the WHA and one season with the Rangers. Bobby Simpson played four years with Atlanta, St. Louis and Pittsburgh. Peter Marsh recorded five NHL years in Winnipeg and Chicago.

New Westminster goaltender Gord Laxton spent four seasons with the Pittsburgh Penguins while Barry Smith played three years with Boston and Colorado. Much of the team would return to Memorial Cup competition, as the Bruins were back in the hunt for the championship for the next three years.

The **1976** Memorial Cup

The Montreal Forum was an inspiring setting for the 1976 Memorial Cup. The Quebec Remparts, Hamilton Fincups and New Westminster Bruins all had an opportunity to contribute to the mystique of one of hockey's great buildings. The Bruins were back with a team considered by many, including their coach Punch McLean, to be their best ever. But the Fincups were determined to bring the Steel City its first Memorial Cup in fourteen years.

Hamilton finished first in the Ontario Major Junior Hockey League's Hap Emms division, and suffered only one loss in their OHA playoff run against the Kitchener Rangers, Toronto Marlboros and Sudbury Wolves. Under the direction of coach Bert Templeton and general manager Dave Draper, the Fincups featured notable future NHLers Dale McCourt, Al Secord, Ric Seiling and Willie Huber.

Like the Fincups, the New Westminster Bruins were an imposing playoff force, losing only one game in eliminating the Victoria Cougars, Brandon Wheat Kings and Saskatoon Blades. The core of the 1975 Memorial Cup team had returned. The Bruins boasted four 50-plus goal scorers—Fred Berry, Rick Shinske, Steve Clippingdale and Mark Lofthouse—as well as talented grinders Harold Phillipoff and Stan Smyl. On defence, the Bruins relied on the powerful duo of Barry Beck and Brad Maxwell. Rounding out the lineup was netminder Glen Hanlon, borrowed from Brandon after the Bruins' regular goaltender Blaine Peterson broke a collarbone in the western final.

Representing the QMJHL were the Quebec Remparts, back for their third crack at the Memorial Cup in five seasons. Quebec eliminated the Sorel Black Hawks, Cornwall Royals and defending provincial champion Sherbrooke Beavers. Under coach and general manager Ron Racette, the Remparts included Eddy Godin, Jean Savard, Val James and goaltender Maurice Barrette. They may have boasted the fewest big names of the three teams, but the Remparts began the round robin with a 4–3 victory over Hamilton. Goalie Barrette was the star of the game on the strength of a 45-save performance. "I want to see my name on the Memorial Cup," he said.

Remi Levesque, Jean Gagnon, Eddy Godin and Yvan Hamelin scored for the Remparts, who held a 3–0 lead after two periods and added another goal in the third. Two goals by Hamilton's Steve Hazlett and 1 by Ric Seiling cut the lead to 1 with just over five minutes left, but the Fincups could not pull even. The game was a rough affair slowed down by several penalties. But the 7,983 fans saw the action intensify toward the end when Hamilton pressed vainly for a tie.

The Remparts met the Bruins in the second game of the tournament. New Westminster played a trademark physical game in dumping Quebec 4–2. The Bruins jumped out to a 4–1 lead, and lived up to their reputation by manhandling the Remparts for the last two periods. An attack of appendicitis suffered by goalie Maurice Barrette compounded the Remparts' problems. The sudden departure of Barrette, who needed an operation, greatly diminished Quebec's chances of moving into the final.

In their next game against the Fincups, New Westminster came out hitting, but they ran into penalty trouble. The Fincups fired 7 powerplay goals en route to an 8–4 victory. Referee Marcel Vaillancourt handed out twelve fighting majors in the first period alone, and the two teams accumulated seventy penalty minutes. Most of the infractions were called on the Bruins, and Hamilton took advantage by whipping up a 6–1 lead before the first intermission.

The Fincups ran up a 5–0 score against New Westminster's starting goaltender Carey Walker before he was replaced by Hanlon.

Centre Joe Contini scored a first-period natural hat trick with 3 explosive goals in a minute and ten seconds. He also added 3 assists. Other Fincups scorers included rightwinger Seiling with 2 goals and 4 assists, Steve Hazlett with a pair, and Cal Herd with a single. The Fincups' victory over New Westminster earned them a place in the Memorial Cup final, based on goals differential.

"Everybody says our powerplay isn't worth a damn," coach Templeton scoffed. McLean, fuming at his club's loss, termed Vaillancourt "incompetent." He later asked the CAHA to bar the Sherbrooke official from working any more games.

Meanwhile, the Bruins prepared to meet Quebec in the semi-final match. The Bruins settled down for this game, smashing the Remparts on the scoreboard rather than the ice. Lofthouse scored 4 times and Harold Phillipoff and Smyl each tallied twice in a 10–3 plastering. The other New Westminster marksmen were Clayton Pachal and Clippingdale. Val James, Michel Frechette and Jean Savard scored for the Remparts, with all Quebec goals coming in the first period.

McLean yanked Hanlon and replaced him with Walker at 4:05 of the first period, when the Bruins were leading 2–1. Walker was beaten by Savard forty-two seconds later, and the New Westminster coach reverted to Hanlon. The latter didn't give up another goal. "I took Hanlon out because I wanted to talk to him," McLean explained. "He was very nervous and I wanted to calm him down. Then the puck bounced on Walker for another goal."

Dale McCourt played seven seasons in the NHL with Detroit, Buffalo and Toronto after winning the Memorial Cup in 1976 as captain with the Hamilton Fincups.

The Bruins did not receive a single major penalty in the game, bearing out their coach's assertion that they could play more than one style and win. "They can play tough, they can play rough and they can play disciplined hockey," McLean stated.

The New Westminster Bruins and Hamilton Fincups came face to face in the final game of the Memorial Cup tournament. The Fincups emerged victorious, claiming a 5–2 victory before 4,350 fans at the Forum. The city of Hamilton captured its first junior title since the Red Wings won in 1962.

The Fincups used a tenacious forechecking game to create scoring chances. They beat the Bruins by taking dead aim at the westerners' greatest strength: the imposing defensive pairing of Beck and Maxwell. "We tried to give Beck the puck and then put pressure on him," Templeton explained to Alan Halberstadt of the *Globe and Mail*. "We would then anticipate him throwing it over to Maxwell."

It was a line of relative paperweights—Ed Smith, Archie King and Mike Keating—that created the most havoc in the New Westminster zone. Keating scored the opening goal at 2:40, backhanding a shot past Hanlon after some vigorous corner work by his teammates. Hazlett and King added goals later in the period after the Bruins had climbed to within 1. Contini and Joe Kowal also scored for the Fincups, while Allen Fleck and Stan Smyl replied for the Bruins.

"We knew if we stayed on top of them, they'd give the puck up," Smith said. "They aren't used to that style. They're used to being able to wheel it right out of their own zone."

Hamilton outshot the Bruins 21–7 during the second period, played almost exclusively in the Bruins' zone. Only some acrobatic goaltending by Hanlon kept them from breaking the game open. "They beat us to the puck, that's all there is to it," Hanlon said. Hamilton outshot the Bruins 37–22 on the night.

Templeton believed hard work all season long made the difference in the Fincups' win. "We're small in size, but I don't think there is a club in Canada that practises harder," he said. "I firmly believe we're the best conditioned club in

Canada." McCourt, a tireless skater at centre for the Fincups, stated the Bruins' reputation for roughness failed to intimidate the Hamilton team. "Intimidation is a pretty big word," the tournament's Most Valuable Player said. "We aren't afraid of anybody, no matter how tough they are. When it came down to the final, they couldn't play tough or they would have hurt themselves."

Ironically, it was a Bruin, Rick Shinske, who won the George Parsons Trophy for most sportsmanlike player. Remparts goalie Maurice Barrette won the Hap Emms Memorial Trophy as outstanding goaltender.

From the 1976 Hamilton Fincups, Dale McCourt played seven seasons in the NHL with Detroit, Buffalo and Toronto. Al Secord contributed physically and statistically during an impressive pro career, dividing twelve years between Boston, Chicago, Toronto and Philadelphia. Willie Huber played a decade in the big league, mostly with Detroit and the New York Rangers. Ric Seiling served ten solid seasons with Buffalo and Detroit. Joe Contini played two seasons with the Colorado Rockies, while Jay Johnston and Joe Kowal had brief stints with Washington and Buffalo respectively. Mike Keating saw brief action with the Rangers, as did Steve Hazlett with the Canucks.

From the Quebec Remparts, Eddy Godin played two seasons with the Washington Capitals, while Jean Savard spent a couple of years in the NHL, mostly in Chicago. Val James skated a handful of games with Buffalo and Toronto. Mario Marois punched in for fifteen NHL seasons for Vancouver,

Hamilton Fincups. Back row (l to r): Mino Piconi, Ric Seiling, Mike Federko, Rob Mierkalns, Joe Kowal, Willie Huber, Mike Keating, Bill Reilly, Ted Long, Rob Street, Bud Mountain. Middle row: Bill Dynes, Steve Hazlett, Archie King, Sean Sullivan, Denis Houle, Al Secord, Ron Roscoe, Ed Smith, Cal Herd, Mark Perras, Andy Alway. Front row: Al Jensen, Joe Sinochio, Ron Cupido, Danny Shearer, Bert Templeton (coach), Dale McCourt, Dave Draper, Joe Contini, Mario Cupido, Dr. E.V. Ellis, Mark Locken.

Quebec, Winnipeg, St. Louis and the New York Rangers.

From the New Westminster Bruins, Clayton Pachal played three NHL seasons with Boston and Colorado. Harold Phillipoff enjoyed a three-year gig with Atlanta and Chicago, while Rick Shinske spent three seasons in Cleveland and St. Louis. Steve Clippingdale made a brief showing with Washington and Los Angeles, and Fred Berry saw action briefly with Detroit. Many Bruins would return to the Memorial Cup final in 1977.

The **1977** Memorial Cup

Once the capital of British Columbia, the city of New Westminster sits beside the Fraser River, tucked in close to Vancouver. In the 1970s, New Westminster combined traces of its prominent history with working class grit. It was a fitting home for the Bruins team that had emerged by mid-decade as the scrapping dynasty of western junior hockey. The Memorial Cup tournament of 1977 was the first ever held in BC.

The Bruins took out the Victoria Cougars, Portland Winter Hawks and Brandon Wheat Kings in the WCHL playoffs, winning each series by 4–1. Although there had been some turnover from the team that went to the 1976 final, New Westminster could count on a number of seasoned veterans including Mark Lofthouse, Stan Smyl and the dynamic defensive duo of captain Brad Maxwell and Barry Beck. New players Miles Zaharko, Ray Creasy and John Ogrodnick added to the mix. "I've been a bridesmaid two years running," coach Punch McLean said. "Of course I don't want to be one again. But what I want isn't all that important—it means far more to the kids. Winning the Memorial Cup would be a great experience for them, especially the ones who turn pro. Winning and leadership in junior hockey carries over to the pros."

The Ghislain Delage-coached Sherbrooke Beavers of the QMJHL eliminated Mike Bossy's Laval Nationals, the Cornwall Royals and the Quebec Remparts to claim the provincial championship. With solid netminding from Richard Sevigny, the Beavers also featured Rick Vaive, Jere Gillis, Ron Carter and Daniel Chicoine.

Making their first trip to the Memorial Cup tournament were the Ottawa 67's. They took out the Sault Ste. Marie Greyhounds and Kingston Canadians before defeating the London Knights for the Ontario championship. Coached by Brian Kilrea, the 67's featured some superb prospects including Bobby Smith, captain Doug Wilson, Tim Higgins, Ed "Boxcar" Hospodar and goaltender Pat Riggin, an addition from the London Knights.

The 1977 tournament marked the first time that a double round robin format, where each team plays each other twice before the playoffs, was used. Fans numbering 9,160 were entertained by a close, high-scoring opening match between Ottawa and New Westminster. Mark Lofthouse tallied 2 goals and 2 assists as the Bruins edged out a 7–6 win at Vancouver's Pacific Coliseum. Centre Ray Creasy, who had arrived just an hour before the game from Winnipeg, had 4 assists. He returned to Winnipeg two days later to attend his father's funeral.

Ottawa's offence included a hat trick from Bobby Smith and 2 goals by Tim Higgins.

The Bruins' roll continued the following night as they downed Sherbrooke by a score of 4–2. With just over two minutes left in the game, Brad Maxwell broke a 2–2 third-period tie by going end to end and beating goaltender Richard Sevigny. The loss was a bitter one for Sevigny, who had been outstanding in stopping 50 shots. "We don't want to lose after being here three times," said a determined Maxwell, whose effort on the winner foreshadowed things to come.

Both of the Beavers' goals came from leftwinger and team captain Jere Gillis on the powerplay. Referee Paul Corcoran called 62 minutes in penalties in the first period and 122 in the game including six majors.

Ottawa rebounded from their first-game loss with a 6–1 win over Sherbrooke. The line of Tom McDonnell, Tim Higgins and Shane Pearsall accounted for 4 goals, while Hospodar and Smith pitched in 1 apiece. In the second period, Jere Gillis scored the only Sherbrooke goal, giving him all 3 of his team's goals in the tournament. Pat Riggin's performance in net was solid, but he wasn't severely tested. Sherbrooke coach Delage showed some frustration with his team's lack of offence, complaining that he wasn't getting goals from key players. Ron Carter, a 77-goal scorer in the QMJHL that season, had been blanked in the tournament.

The 67's made it two in a row by scoring a spirited overtime win over the Bruins. Steve Marengere, a speedy rightwinger, scored his second goal of the game at 2:28 of the extra period. The 4–3 victory dismayed many of the 10,522 fans gathered at the Pacific Coliseum. Ottawa had trailed 3–1 late in the third, but fought back and forced overtime with a last-minute marker by defenceman Jimmy Kirkpatrick. The equalizer, Kirkpatrick's second goal of the match, was a shot from the right point that deflected off Maxwell's skate past netminder Carey Walker.

"It was a bad goal," Walker admitted. "I just let all our guys down."

"We beat ourselves," McLean said. "There's no way you should give up 2 goals in the last two minutes of a hockey game."

The loss could have been devastating for New Westminster, but they managed to put it behind them, claiming a 4–2 victory against Sherbrooke. Barry Beck scored 1 goal and set up 2 others as the Bruins tallied 3 times in a seven-minute span of the third period.

The Bruins were trailing 2–1 when Beck assisted on goals by Orleski and Creasy. The 212-pound defenceman then added some insurance with a blazing shot from the point. Lofthouse also scored with his fourth of the series, while Sherbrooke got powerplay goals from Carter and the reliable Gillis.

Creasy's winner at 7:42 was a display of pure tenacity. Before scoring, he was checked head first into the Sherbrooke bench by Raymond Roy. Getting back onto the ice, Creasy was hammered into the boards by Daniel Chicoine. While moving back into the play, he was tripped by Rick Vaive, who drew a delayed penalty. The Bruins pulled goalie Peterson on the delayed call, and the pinball-like Creasy scored when he picked up a Beck rebound off the end boards and fired high into the far corner. The win gave New Westminster a berth in the final against Ottawa. "When I came here from Estevan with the Bruins, we had stories on the back of the sports pages," McLean said. "Now we are front page stuff. It's nice to get the recognition."

The final game of the double round robin was little more than a warmup for Ottawa, as the 67's were already assured a place in the final with the Bruins. A crowd of 4,262 saw the 67's skate to a 5–2 win in a game in which they never trailed. The Beavers got excellent goaltending from Sevigny during the tournament, but they failed to produce the fire power shown in the QMJHL regular season, when they scored 392 goals in seventy-two games.

Ottawa had goals from Smith, centre Warren Holmes, Higgins, McDonnell and Doug Wilson. Smith and Wilson both added assists, sharing the series lead at the end of round robin play with 10 points each.

Ottawa and New Westminster both advanced to the final with 3–1 records, while the winless Beavers were dispatched to the stands to watch the championship game. The assembled Coliseum crowd of 13,460 saw a tight game that went right down to the wire. New Westminster led 2–0 after the first period on powerplay goals from Creasy and Lofthouse, and held a 5–2 lead going into the final period. It appeared that the Bruins were comfortably on their way to the title. However, the 67's caught fire in the third, taking the game to the Bruins in the last twenty minutes. Ottawa fought all the way back to tie the score. But with just over six minutes left, Brad Maxwell scored on a solo rush up the ice to put the Bruins back into the lead. New Westminster hung on to claim the match and their first Memorial Cup.

"Maxwell's goal was a thing of beauty for Bruins fans," Lyndon Little wrote in the *Vancouver Sun*, "as he made a brilliant individual effort on a solo coast-to-coast rush down the left side, beat 67's defenceman Kirkpatrick with a nifty move at the blueline and fired a shot through the legs of goaltender Riggin."

"I didn't think I'd score on the shot," Maxwell admitted. "I just took the shot and was hoping that someone would score on the rebound. We played so well in the first two periods, I thought maybe the two-year jinx was coming back. What makes it so great is that hardly anybody figured we had a chance this year. Last season we had such a powerhouse that everybody picked us to win it all. This year's team had a lot of pride and determination. We didn't have the big stars, but everybody pulled together and worked hard."

"You have to give those guys credit," said Maxwell of his opponents. "You give them an inch and they'll take a mile. When they tied it up at 5–5, I began to think maybe we were jinxed in the Memorial Cup."

"This is an unbelievable experience for not only myself, but also for a great bunch of kids who didn't quit when everyone expected them to," McLean said. Bobby Smith, whose play throughout the tournament had been a treat to watch, was predictably disappointed. "When we tied it up, there wasn't a guy on our bench who didn't think we'd win," he said. "But the Bruins have some great players. I know Beck won the Most Valuable Player award, but I thought Maxwell was the key to their club."

"The Bruins are one helluva team," Ottawa coach Kilrea later said. "When we tied the game 5–5, I figured there was no way we could lose. New Westminster certainly showed character. I'm so proud of our team I'd rather be their coach and lose than be the coach of the Bruins. And that's not a slam against New Westminster."

Riggin, a pickup from London of the OMJHL, stopped 23 shots and was named the tournament's all-star goaltender and outstanding goaltender. Other all-stars were Beck and Maxwell on defence, Mark Lofthouse on right wing, Bobby Smith at centre, and Jere Gillis of Sherbrooke on left wing. Maxwell was handed a gold medal as the first star of the championship game. The seven-game series set a Memorial Cup attendance record of 58,995.

From the 1977 New Westminster Bruins, Barry Beck went on to become an imposing blueline force in the NHL, playing ten seasons with the Colorado Rockies, New York Rangers and Los Angeles Kings. Brad Maxwell also played ten impressive seasons in the pros, mostly with the Minnesota North Stars. Mark Lofthouse spent six seasons with Washington and Detroit while Miles Zaharko played four seasons with Atlanta and Chicago.

From the Sherbrooke Beavers, Richard Sevigny played eight years with Montreal and Quebec. Jere Gillis played ten NHL seasons, mostly with Vancouver, the Rangers and Quebec. Daniel Chicoine saw brief action with Minnesota and Cleveland, as did Ron Carter with the Edmonton Oilers. Rick Vaive played a year in the WHA with Birmingham before moving on to an outstanding thirteen-year NHL career with Vancouver, Toronto, Chicago and Buffalo. He became the first player in Maple Leafs history to score 50 goals in a

New Westminister Bruins. Back row (l to r): Doug Sauter, John Paul Kelly, Carl Van Herrewyn, Doug Derkson, Don Hobbins, Randy Rudnyk, Ray Creasy, Larry Dean. Middle row: Jake Mitchell, Miles Zaharko, Randy Betty, Jerry Bell, Bruce Andres, Dave Orleski, Mark Lofthouse, Brian Young, Dr. Peter Wodynski. Front row: Blaine Peterson, Brad Maxwell, Ernie McLean (coach), Barry Beck, Bill Shinske (general manager), Stan Smyl, Carey Walker.

season, a mark he hit three times.

A number of players from the Ottawa 67's made an impression on the NHL. They include captain Doug Wilson, who served as one of the league's premier defencemen for over a decade and a half. He played fourteen years in Chicago and two in San Jose, winning the Norris Trophy in 1981–82. Tim Higgins also had a strong career, playing eleven years with Chicago, New Jersey and Detroit. Warren Holmes spent three seasons in Los Angeles. Pat Riggin played nine years with Atlanta, Calgary, Washington, Boston and Pittsburgh, after spending a year in the WHA with Birmingham.

Bobby Smith was selected first in the 1978 NHL entry draft and won the Calder Trophy in his rookie season. He went on to an outstanding 15-year career with Minnesota and Montreal, winning the Stanley Cup with the Canadiens in 1986. Smith became the general manager of the Phoenix Coyotes in 1997.

The **1978** Memorial Cup

Some teams make better underdogs than favourites. The 1975 and 1976 Bruins had been considered serious contenders for the Memorial Cup, but it was a less star-studded, more resilient team that finally brought New Westminster the title in 1977. The Bruins' media guide for 1977–78 explained that this would be a rebuilding year. But a late-season drive saw the team in Memorial Cup competition again, this time with the Peterborough Petes and the Trois-Rivieres Draveurs.

Ernie "Punch" McLean had been suspended for twenty-five games in the latter part of the 1977–78 season for punching referee John Fitzgerald, but was back behind the bench when the Bruins marched through two consecutive round robin tournaments for the western championship. The first contest saw the Bruins defeat the Portland Winter Hawks and Victoria Cougars, while they prevailed over the Flin Flon Bombers and the Billings Bighorns in the second. No longer able to rely on NHL graduates Barry Beck and Brad Maxwell, the Bruins received leadership from captain Stan Smyl as well as players like John Ogrodnick, Larry Melnyk and John Paul Kelly.

The Peterborough Petes were coached and managed by Gary Green, a twenty-five-year-old Roger Neilson protégé. Their roster included future NHLers Steve Larmer, Keith Acton, Keith Crowder, Mark Kirton, Tim Trimper and goalie Ken Ellacott. Peterborough finished in second place in the Matt Leyden division of the OHA before heading into the playoffs. They scored a first-round win over the Oshawa Generals and knocked off the defending champion Ottawa 67's before sidelining the Hamilton Fincups in the provincial final.

In the QMJHL, coach Michel Bergeron took his Trois-Rivieres Draveurs to first place overall with 101 points. The Draveurs eliminated the Quebec Remparts, Sherbrooke Beavers and Montreal Juniors without losing a game. Their quest was to become the first club in their league to win the Memorial Cup since the 1972 Cornwall Royals. Backstopped by the goaltending of Jacques Cloutier, the Draveurs were led by Jean-François Sauvé, Richard David,

Normand Lefebvre and Normand Rochefort.

The tournament was divided between the Sault Ste. Marie Memorial Gardens and the Sudbury Community Arena. It opened in the Gardens with Trois-Rivieres posting a 5–2 victory over Peterborough. Thirty-eight seconds into the final period, Normand Lefebvre scored his second goal of the game to spark the Draveurs to the victory.

The Petes had held a 2–1 lead near the end of the first but Lefebvre tied it with two seconds remaining. From there, the Draveurs pulled away from their opponents. "Our guys weren't full of desire," Peterborough coach Green said matter-of-factly.

The Petes rebounded strongly in their next game. They scored a 7–2 victory over the Bruins in the Sudbury Community Arena, jumping to a 6–0 lead after only twenty-five minutes of play. Mike Meeker and Bill Gardner had 2 goals each while Tim Trimper had a goal and 3 assists. Peterborough, having wrapped up a seven-game series with Hamilton only four days before the tournament, managed to overcome their fatigue and were particularly well focussed on the powerplay, where they scored four times. "We never expected to get that kind of a lead," Green said. "I had quite a lot of confidence coming into this game today. The mental attitude was much better today. The thing I was most concerned about was the physical drain." A loss would have ended Peterborough's chances in the double round robin affair. As it was, the win came at a cost. Peterborough centre Keith Acton, already bothered by a knee problem, suffered a separated shoulder. Although he was not lost for the tournament, the injury reduced the forward's effectiveness.

Next, it was New Westminster's turn to show some resilience. They bounced back to defeat the Draveurs 6–4 in Sault Ste. Marie. Stan Smyl, who was appearing in his fourth straight tournament, contributed to 5 of the 6 Bruins' goals, scoring 3 and setting up 2 others. Brian Young, John Ogrodnick and Ken Berry had single goals for the Bruins, who fired 39 shots at Cloutier. Lefebvre scored 2 goals for Trois-Rivieres.

In the next game, Peterborough met the Draveurs in Sudbury. The

Future Vancouver Canucks captain Stan Smyl led the New Westminster Bruins to their second straight Memorial Cup victory in 1978.

Petes showed signs of hitting their stride, claiming their second straight victory. The largest crowd of the tournament, numbering 5,094, watched the Ontario team down Trois-Rivieres 4–0. Kirton opened the scoring midway through the second period, and the Petes protected their slim edge until breaking loose for 3 goals in the final twenty minutes. The loss was even more costly for Trois-Rivieres as defenceman Rochefort and rightwinger Lefebvre, the tournament's leading scorer, were lost due to injuries.

"The defence played really well in front of me," netminder Ellacott said. "They had a few good chances, but we cleared the puck pretty well." The Petes' goalie noted that his team often started slowly, but were used to coming back from playoff deficits. "We feel pretty good right now," he continued, "but it's been like that all season. Every playoff series we've been in this year, we've lost the first game and we've had to come back. We always seem to do it."

The next evening, the Petes clinched a spot in the Memorial Cup final by edging the Bruins 4–3 in a dramatic comeback victory witnessed by 3,641 fans. New Westminster was ahead by 1 goal late in the game, prompting Green to go with six attackers in the last minute. The move paid off as Trimper tied the game at 19:57, forcing an overtime session. Twenty seconds into the extra period, Keith Crowder won the game for the Petes.

"Either one team comes out flat or something," said Green, attempting to explain what happens in overtime. "It just depends on whether one team is up or not. One team will have more desire, or confidence, or whatever."

With the Petes reaching the final on the strength of three wins and a loss, the Bruins and Draveurs were left to battle for the other spot. In the second period of the qualifying game, a tenacious New Westminster club scored 4 times in fifty-two seconds en route to a 6–3 victory. The Bruins' offence was anchored by 2-goal performances from John Paul Kelly and Scott McLeod. "It's always exciting," McLean said, "especially this year when we're not even supposed to be here. Nobody gave us a hope in hell."

With nothing to lose in the Cup final, the Bruins played the style that had been their calling card for the past four years and hit their way to a 7–4 win over Peterborough, recording their second consecutive Memorial Cup triumph.

New Westminster took a 3–1 lead in an abrasive first period but Peterborough stayed in the game and left the Bruins clinging to a 4–3 edge at the second intermission. Scott McLeod completed a hat trick at 5:38 of the third period, giving the Bruins a 5–3 lead. The goal that proved to be the Memorial Cup winner was disputed by the Petes, who said that Bruins winger Ken Berry was in the crease when McLeod put the puck past Ellacott.

"He did just a great job," McLeod said of Berry. "He shot the puck and rammed it into Ellacott. He took Ellacott right out of the play and the puck was just sitting there and there was no way I could miss it. I thought they might call it no goal, because he was standing right in the crease. That is what they were arguing about."

The Bruins got their offence from the grinders. Stan Smyl, nicknamed "Steamer" for his chugging stride and relentless forechecking, scored 1 goal and set up 4 others. His line included McLeod, who scored three times and had 1 assist, and Berry. Ogrodnick had 2 goals and defenceman Boris Fistric a single.

Peterborough fired 39 shots at goaltender Martens while New Westminster had 28. The match attracted 5,898 customers. "It was an aggressive hockey game," McLean said. "I'd hate to be in a seven-game series. We wouldn't have too many players left, either side."

Ken Ellacott was named all-star goalie with the Bruins' Brian Young and the Petes' Paul MacKinnon on defence. The all-star forwards were Kirton of Peterborough at centre, Normand Lefebvre of Trois-Rivieres on left wing and Stan Smyl of the Bruins on the right side. Smyl also took the tournament MVP honours.

From the 1978 New Westminster Bruins, John Ogrodnick played fourteen standout seasons in the NHL, proving himself a consistent point-getter with Detroit, Quebec and the Rangers. John Paul Kelly played seven seasons with Los Angeles while Ken Berry spent four with Edmonton and Vancouver. Larry Melnyk was a defenceman for nine seasons with Boston, Edmonton, the Rangers and Vancouver. Brian Young served a brief stint with the Blackhawks.

Stan Smyl played thirteen years in the NHL, all of them with the Vancouver Canucks. Throughout his career, his grit paid off in consistent offensive production. In 1982, Smyl captained the underdog Canucks on a run to the Stanley Cup final. It was remarkably similar to the New Westminster Bruins' drive of 1978, except for the ending: a defeat at the hands of the New York Islanders.

New Westminster Bruins. Back row (l to r): Doug Sauter, Terry Kirkham, Larry Melnyk, John Ogrodnick, Randy Irving, John Paul Kelly, Bill Hobbins, Scott McLeod, Dave Bensmiller. Middle row: Larry Dean, Carl Van Harrewyn, Kent Reardon, Larry Jones, Neil Meadmore, Dave Orleski, Boris Fistric, Florent Robidoux, Brian Young, Jamie Nash, Bill Smith. Front row: Dr. Peter Wodynski, Richard Martens, Jake Mitchell, Stan Smyl, Ernie McLean (coach), Doug Derkson, Bill Shinske, Carey Walker, Jack Patrick.

Bergeron's Trois-Rivieres Draveurs produced a handful of NHLers. Most notably, goaltender Jacques Cloutier played twelve years with Buffalo, Chicago and Quebec. Jean-François Sauvé had seven seasons with Buffalo and Quebec, while Richard David played a year in the WHA and three in the NHL, all with Quebec. Normand Rochefort enjoyed thirteen years in the pros, mostly with Quebec and the New York Rangers. A defensive stalwart for his entire career, Rochefort was recognized for his hard work when he was named to play for the triumphant Canadian dream team in the 1987 Canada Cup series. Bergeron himself became a coach in the NHL with Quebec and the Rangers.

From the Peterborough Petes, Keith Acton was a reliable NHL performer for fifteen years, mostly in Montreal, Philadelphia and Minnesota. Mark Kirton played over five seasons with Toronto, Detroit and Vancouver, while Greg Theberge spent five in Washington. Bill Gardner enjoyed nine seasons in Chicago. Mike Meeker and Randy Johnston skated briefly with Pittsburgh and the New York Islanders respectively. Jeff Brubaker started in the WHA with New England before playing more than nine NHL seasons, mostly with Hartford, Toronto, Edmonton and the Rangers.

Steve Larmer, an outstanding player at both ends of the ice, averaged over a point per game in a lengthy NHL career. As the NHL "Iron Man," he played eleven full seasons for the Blackhawks without missing any action. His 884 consecutive games placed him third on the all-time Iron Man list behind Doug Jarvis and Garry Unger. Larmer later won the Stanley Cup with the Rangers in 1994. Like Bergeron, Gary Green went on to coach in the NHL. Before taking up the reins of the Washington Capitals, he joined the Petes for another Memorial Cup appearance in 1979.

The **1979** Memorial Cup

Two of the three finalists from the previous year's Memorial Cup tournament were back in 1979. The Peterborough Petes and Trois-Rivieres Draveurs both returned to seek the title snatched by underdog New Westminster in 1978. For the first time in five years, the Bruins did not make the trip to the national championship. It was staged in the three Quebec cities of Sherbrooke, Trois-Rivieres and Verdun. The Bruins' now-familiar role as western representatives was filled by the Brandon Wheat Kings, who were after their first title since 1949.

The Wheat Kings lost only five times during the 1978–79 regular season. They opened the WHL playoffs in a three-team round robin with the Saskatoon Blades and Edmonton Oil Kings. Brandon and Saskatoon advanced, and the Wheat Kings subsequently polished off the Blades in the east division final.

The WHL semi-final featured Brandon, the Portland Winter Hawks and Lethbridge Broncos in another round robin series. The Wheat Kings and Winter Hawks both went 3–1 to advance to the championship final. Portland featured Perry Turnbull, Blake Wesley, Dave Babych, Clint Malarchuk and Jim Benning. The Dunc McCallum-coached Wheat Kings included Laurie Boschman, Brian

Propp, Ray Allison and Brad McCrimmon. Brandon triumphed in six games.

In the OMJHL, Gary Green's Peterborough Petes finished first in the Matthew Leyden division. Their powerful lineup had eleven veterans of the 1978 Memorial Cup tournament, including future NHLers Keith Crowder, Tim Trimper, Jim Wiemer, Bob Attwell and Ken Ellacott. The Petes sidelined the Kingston Canadians, Sudbury Wolves and Niagara Falls Flyers for the Ontario title.

Coached by Michel Bergeron, the Trois-Rivieres Draveurs were anchored by the goaltending of Jacques Cloutier. Jean-François Sauvé and Normand Rochefort were among the team's big producers. Early in the playoffs, Trois-Rivieres dumped the Shawinigan Cataractes, Roger Bédard's Montreal Juniors and the Sherbrooke Beavers.

Despite having sat idle for ten days, Trois-Rivieres got off to a strong start in the championship series. They scored the first of two consecutive wins in a 4–3 triumph over Peterborough. Gaston Douville and Jean-François Sauvé struck for 2 early first-period goals and Michel Normand and Bernard Gallant added 2 more to post the victory. For the Petes, Terry Bovair had 2 goals and Keith Crowder a single.

Coach Green said his Ontario champions could play "at least 50 percent better" than they did in the opener, and promised a noticeable improvement when the two clubs met later in the tournament.

Trois-Rivieres moved on to defeat Brandon 4–1 before 3,105 fans. A brawl erupted during the pre-game skate. "You'll have to go ask Brandon what happened before the game," said an irate Bergeron. "I've seen the Memorial Cup for five years and they do that all the time out west. I'm disappointed by this team and I have no respect for them."

The brawl started with players taunting and jabbing each other with their sticks, and degenerated into a free-for-all with all the players on each side, including the four netminders, throwing punches for a good twelve minutes. Eventually, Trois-Rivieres police rushed to the ice, separating the combatants and sending them to their dressing rooms. Both teams had their warmup time limited to three minutes.

When the hockey finally started, Robert Mongrain scored 3 goals and Douville added a fourth to pace the Draveurs to their second straight tournament victory. Laurie Boschman spoiled Cloutier's shutout bid by scoring with forty-three seconds remaining.

The post-game conversation focussed more on pre-game fisticuffs than on the outcome of the penalty-filled contest. Referee Normand Caisse handed out thirteen majors and a total of 115 minutes in penalties during the game. Wheat Kings coach Dunc McCallum laid the blame squarely on the referee. "There was too much crap after the whistle," he said. "You can't let meetings go on after every whistle or you are going to get into trouble. After the pre-game stuff, I thought my guys were high and ready to go. Then we took a couple of bad penalties."

"If we played these guys sixteen times in a season, we'd likely have fifteen brawls," defenceman McCrimmon told Gregg Drinnan of the *Brandon Sun*.

Each club was fined $1,000 by the disciplinary committee for their part in the pre-game brawl. For the remaining games, neither team was to be permitted within ten feet of the centre-ice circle during the warmup.

Brandon fell further behind overall in their second game, losing 7–6 in overtime to Peterborough. It was a wide-open, nail-biting affair at the Sherbrooke Sports Palace played before only 2,387 fans. The Wheat Kings took a 6–4 lead into the third period only to lose it on Jim Wiemer's second goal at 2:31 of overtime. Wiemer's winner was a knuckler from outside the blueline that eluded goaltender Rick Knickle. The Brandon netminder had withstood a 14-shot barrage from the Petes in the third to extend the contest past regulation time.

"Bill Gardner passed me the puck and we were just supposed to shoot it in," Wiemer said. "I just shot it on the net and it bounced between the goalie's legs."

The next game was also in Sherbrooke. Ellacott turned in his strongest performance of the series, lifting Peterborough to a 3–2 victory over the Draveurs. Chris Halyk's powerplay goal at 6:08 of the third period broke a 2–2 tie. The victory allowed Peterborough to boost their win–loss record to 2–1, identical to Trois-Rivieres.

The Petes' Bovair, who had 19 regular-season goals, was emerging as a clutch goal scorer, tallying four times in three Memorial Cup games. "The puck's really bouncing for me," he said. "But actually, our whole line is playing real well. We're working hard and the puck is going in for me."

Brian Propp, along with Brandon Wheat Kings teammates Brad McCrimmon, Ray Allison and Laurie Boschman, was taken in the first round of the 1979 NHL entry draft.

The next night at the Auditorium de Verdun, the Wheat Kings came alive in a game they desperately needed to win. Brandon thumped Trois-Rivieres 6–1 before 2,300 fans. In the first period, Boschman's pair of goals in a span of fifteen seconds sent the Wheaties on their way to the series' most lopsided triumph. Solidly backstopped by Bart Hunter, they outshot the Draveurs 45–31. A Portland pickup, Hunter had taken over from Knickle in goal.

"Up until tonight's game we had played only one good period out of six," McCallum said. "I couldn't figure out why, but I finally figured out that it was because the kids were tired. With that day off though, it gave the guys a little bit more spring in their legs. I don't think we were ready when we played Trois-Rivieres the first time. We seemed to lack motivation, but we were determined from the start tonight."

With a 1–2 record, Brandon needed a win against the Petes to have any hope of advancing. Again, the evenly matched teams fought to a close result, but Brandon came out on top this time, edging the Petes 3–2.

The two clubs had entered the final period locked in a 2–2 tie. Allison scored a pair of goals for Brandon, and Halyk and Tim Trimper countered for the Petes. Brian Propp scored the winner midway through the third to send the Wheat Kings into the final game.

Watching from the stands, Trois-Rivieres players had been pulling for a Peterborough victory, which would have allowed the QMJHL victors into the championship game. When the Wheat Kings prevailed, Green was left to dismiss suggestions from the Quebec media that the Petes had thrown the game to eliminate the Draveurs. Brandon's win left each of the three teams at 2–2, with Brandon and Peterborough advancing on goals differential.

"We definitely went out there determined to win," Green said of the Petes. "We wanted the advantage of being the home team in the final." Coach McCallum of the Wheat Kings was delighted with the play of Bart Hunter in the nets. "I planned on playing Hunter because of the way he played against us in the western final," he said. "He's a yeller in the dressing room and gets the players up."

The championship game was played at the Auditorium de Verdun before 2,982 fans. It was a classic. The Petes and Wheat Kings staged one of the greatest final games in Memorial Cup history. When it was over, Peterborough had claimed a 2–1 victory in overtime.

Trimper opened the scoring at 8:12 of the first period, deflecting Stuart Smith's drive from the blueline. Hunter had little chance to prevent the goal. Propp tied the score later in the first and the two teams, evenly matched and fighting desperately for victory, locked into a scoreless duel that lasted forty-five minutes and forty-eight seconds.

In overtime, the play that resulted in the winning goal began with the Petes clearing the puck from their zone. Brad McCrimmon chased the biscuit down and played it with the assumption that icing would be called. But the call wasn't made, and Bovair stole the puck, throwing it out to Gardner, who in turn relayed it to Larry Murphy. The defenceman pounded a shot on Hunter, and the rebound was fired home by Bob Attwell at 2:38. The Petes had a 2–1 victory.

"I thought, near the end, that their defence was finally starting to tire," Gary Green said. "We felt that if we were going to get a break, we'd have to work for it. So we just dumped it in. I thought McCrimmon was finally starting to have a bad time. He's an incredible defenceman—he's got an amazing amount of stamina."

"I wasn't tired," McCrimmon insisted. "I wasn't tired until the puck went into the net." He chose his words carefully about the lack of an icing call. "I skated pretty hard for it and it was over the line," he commented. "That's all I'll say." Emotionally and physically spent, McCrimmon was philosophical about the loss. "Everyone on this team showed guts, desire, pride and class. We might not have won it, but we proved ourselves."

"There was a breakdown. There should have been someone there," said Dunc McCallum of the winning goal. "We had three guys standing around the crease. The forwards panicked a little and got in too close, leaving the slot open. One shot. Just one shot and who gets it wins. That's junior hockey."

Bart Hunter was awarded the Stafford Smythe Trophy as the Most Valuable Player in the tournament. He also drew outstanding goaltender honours in winning the Hap Emms Memorial Trophy. The award for most sportsmanlike player went to Chris Halyk of the Petes. Four Wheat Kings—Hunter, McCrimmon, Boschman and Allison—were selected to the Memorial Cup all-star team. Defenceman Normand Rochefort of Trois-Rivieres and rightwinger Tim Trimper of the Petes also made the all-star squad.

From the 1979 Peterborough Petes, Keith Crowder made his mark with nine strong seasons in Boston and one in Los Angeles. Tim Trimper played six years in the NHL with Chicago, Winnipeg and Minnesota. Jim Wiemer spent a decade in the big league, mostly in Boston, while Ken Ellacott had a season with Vancouver. Stuart Smith spent four years with Hartford, and Bob Attwell played two seasons with the Colorado Rockies. Other Peterborough players returned to Memorial Cup competition in 1980.

From the Trois-Rivieres Draveurs, Jacques Cloutier went on to an impressive NHL career, playing over ten seasons with Buffalo, Chicago and Quebec. Jean-François Sauvé served seven seasons with Buffalo and Quebec. Normand Rochefort had over ten solid seasons in the NHL with Quebec, the Rangers and Tampa Bay.

The Brandon Wheat Kings saw four of their players—Laurie Boschman, Brian Propp, Ray Allison and Brad McCrimmon—taken in the first round of the 1979 NHL entry draft. Propp enjoyed a superb career, consistently maintaining a point-per-game output in a decade and a half with Philadelphia, Boston, Minnesota and Hartford. Boschman spent nearly fifteen years in the pros, proving himself a solid performer in Toronto, Edmonton, Winnipeg, New Jersey and Ottawa. Ray Allison split seven seasons between Hartford and Philadelphia. Brad McCrimmon became an outstanding NHL defenceman with Boston, Philadelphia, Calgary, Detroit and Hartford. He won the Stanley Cup with the Calgary Flames in 1989. Steve Patrick divided six seasons among Buffalo, Quebec and the New York Rangers.

Of Brandon's goaltenders, Rick Knickle played backup during two seasons with the LA Kings, while Bart Hunter returned to the 1980 Memorial Cup as an over-age player with the Regina Pats.

Peterborough Petes. Back row (l to r): Carmen Cirella, Jim Pavese, Jim Wiemer, Jeff Beukeboom, Stuart Smith, Keith Crowder. Second row from back: Frank Gurney (trainer), Anssi Melametsa, Veli Kinnunen, Dave Beckon, Dave Fenyves, Greg Theberge, Bob Attwell, Herb Warr (vice president). Third row from back: Dick Todd (trainer), Brad Ryder, Bill Gardner, Mark Reeds, Tim Trimper, Larry Murphy, Terry Bovair, Ed Redmond (vice president). Front row: Rick LaFerriere, Chris Halyk, Bud Robertson (vice president), Gary Green (general manager and coach), Jack Shrubb (president), Ken Ellacott.

The
1980s

In 1983, the Memorial Cup was held in the United States for the first time, when the Portland Winter Hawks hosted a highly successful tournament. Having grown widely within Canada, the junior game was starting to take hold in parts of the USA.

Although Memorial Cup competition was expanding into new places during the eighties, it was disappearing from old ones. The Toronto Marlboros, having collected more championships than any other junior team in history, moved to Hamilton in 1989. The New Westminster Bruins, a west coast dynasty that brought British Columbia its first Memorial Cup, moved to Kamloops and eventually became the highly successful Blazers.

The strong showing of Canadian teams at the World Junior Championships raised the profile of junior hockey and proved that the major junior leagues continued to provide a strong infrastructure for the development of players. This was further borne out by the fact that many American and European players were choosing the Canadian Hockey League as the place to cultivate their skills, a trend that would continue into the nineties.

Product of the Laval Voisins, Mario Lemieux became one of the greatest players ever to compete in the NHL. MONTREAL GAZETTE

The 1980 Memorial Cup

The 1980 Memorial Cup promised to be a battle of wit and strategy between three good coaches but ended in bitterness and accusations. The defending champion Peterborough Petes were making their third consecutive trip to the tournament with Mike Keenan taking over the coaching reins from Gary Green. Matching tact with Keenan were Bryan Murray at the helm of the Regina Pats, and Doug Carpenter steering the Cornwall Royals. The winning team was the dark horse survivor of a controversial round robin, in which Keenan had to fend off charges that he threw a key match.

The Petes finished the OMJHL regular season with a league-leading 95 points. They kept rolling in the playoffs, taking out the Sudbury Wolves and Ottawa 67's, before removing the Windsor Spitfires in four straight games for the Ontario championship. Playing in their third straight Memorial Cup tournament, the Petes had the necessary talent and experience to repeat as champions. Their reliable roster included captain Dave Fenyves, Larry Murphy, Bill Gardner, Mark Reeds, Terry Bovair, Tom Fergus, Steve Smith and goalie Rick LaFerriere, who would play every game in the tournament.

In Regina, manager Bob Strumm and coach Bryan Murray looked like a pair of geniuses after taking the dismal last-place Pats of the season before to first place in the WHL in 1979–80, scoring a league-leading 429 goals. Unlike many teams that make overnight improvements, the Pats were playoff worthy, taking out the Lethbridge Broncos in four straight before heading into a round robin with the Medicine Hat Tigers and Brandon Wheat Kings. With Brandon eliminated, the Pats were left to take on Medicine Hat in a fight-laced divisional final. Regina won in five games, and it took five more to defeat the Victoria Cougars in the WHL final and head to the Memorial Cup championship.

Backstopped by Bart Hunter, a standout with Brandon in the 1979 tournament, the Pats also featured the highly touted draft prospect Doug Wickenheiser. Additional offence was provided by Ron Flockhart and defencemen Darren Veitch and Garth Butcher.

In the QMJHL, Carpenter's Cornwall Royals were an emerging powerhouse. They survived a seven-game opening-round series with the Shawinigan Cataractes, and then eliminated the Chicoutimi Sagueneens and Sherbrooke Beavers. In addition to seventeen-year-old sensation Dale Hawerchuk, the Royals boasted Marc Crawford, Dan Daoust, Fred Boimistruck, Dave Ezard and goalie Ron Scott.

Brandon, Manitoba and Regina, Saskatchewan played host to the Memorial Cup final. The first game in Brandon matched Regina and Peterborough. Mark Reeds scored at 3:52 of overtime to give the Petes a 5–4 win before 4,055 short-sleeved fans at Keystone Centre. The Petes had opened up an early 3–0 lead, but Regina fought back to within 1 after forty minutes. They forced overtime when Brian Varga's goal at 18:36 of the third period equalized the score at 3. Reeds won it for Peterborough with a high slapshot to the stick side, notching their twelfth consecutive post-season victory.

It was Reeds' second goal of the game. Bill Gardner, who had 106 points in fifty-nine games for Peterborough during the regular season, contributed a goal and 3 assists. "We really took it to them in the overtime," Keenan said. "But give Regina credit, they kept coming back. When we got off our game a bit, they played with intensity. We were fortunate to be up 3–0. We capitalized on our opportunities, they didn't."

The Pats' position in the tournament slipped further when they were beaten by Cornwall 5–3 in front of 3,540 Brandon fans. Dale Hawerchuk was the game's first star with 3 assists, and Marc Crawford scored 2 goals. Regina received 2 goals from defenceman Darren Veitch and one from Varga. The Royals outshot the Pats 54–27.

"I don't know if we're pressing and that's hurting us," Murray wondered. "We didn't do the things we normally do. You know the kids want to win, but this isn't the Regina team that I am accustomed to."

"This was a moral victory for us," Carpenter said. "It

Regina Pats captain Garth Butcher went on to play fourteen hard-nosed years in the NHL.

should give us confidence. The fact that we're really not supposed to be here is fine with me. We've had our backs to the wall many times and so far we've proven everybody wrong."

Cornwall met Peterborough in the third game of the tournament, and 3,273 fans saw the Petes down the Royals 8–6. Larry Floyd scored three times for the winners. Gilles Crépeau also scored a hat trick for Cornwall, while Boimistruck scored twice.

The tournament moved to Regina for game four. In the Agridome, a crowd of 6,008 watched their Pats squander a 3–0 third-period lead and drop a 4–3 decision. Peterborough clinched a spot in the final with the victory, in which they scored 4 third-period goals in less than eight minutes.

Keenan showed some wiliness worthy of his predecessor Roger Neilson when he called for an examination of Doug Wickenheiser's glove in the second period. Referee Glen Agar initially ignored the request, but he was pressed so vociferously by Keenan and assistant captain Bill Gardner that he levied a bench minor against the Petes. Ultimately, Agar inspected the glove and discovered a hole at its palm that allowed Wickenheiser to grasp his stick better. The referee then assessed Wickenheiser with a minor penalty and Peterborough scored on the ensuing powerplay.

Regina's next game was a must-win situation against Cornwall. The Pats stayed alive by mounting an 11–2 blitz with 5,884 fans in attendance. Regina's devastating offensive thrust produced 48 shots on Royals netminder Ron Scott, the hapless victim of a reeling defence. The line of Ron Flockhart, Darren Galley and Mike Blaisdell was especially prominent, Blaisdell scoring a hat trick.

"If Peterborough comes to play in their next game with Cornwall, there is no question in my mind that they are 5 to 8 goals better," said Blaisdell, mindful that a Peterborough victory would eliminate the Royals and guarantee the Pats a spot in the final. "If they don't win, it's because they don't want to win."

The Petes, who controlled Regina's destiny as well as their own, looked like they would indeed defeat the Royals in the last game of the round robin. They climbed to a commanding 4–2 lead after two periods, outshooting Cornwall 30–14. But a stunned Regina crowd witnessed the Petes collapse in the third. The Royals outshot Peterborough 21–6 in the final period, scoring 3 unanswered goals to take a 5–4 victory.

The Petes had squandered their lead before the midway point of the final frame. Rod Willard scored the winning goal for the Royals at 9:48. Dave Ezard scored twice for Cornwall, while Mike Corrigan and Hawerchuk added singles.

The Cornwall triumph ended Peterborough's playoff winning streak at four-teen, and secured the second berth in the championship game for the Royals. As for Regina, they suspected that something was rotten, alleging outright that the Petes had thrown the game. Acrimony had been visible as the game wound down. Regina fans had pelted the Petes with soft drink containers, coins, pop-corn and other debris, and a cranky crowd gathered outside the Peterborough dressing room to ensure that its point was made.

A furious Bryan Murray did not mince words afterwards. Calling for stiff sanctions against Keenan and the Petes, he fumed, "The Peterborough coach should be suspended, put out of hockey for a year, the team should be fined, and the Pats and Cornwall should play in the final. But I know that won't happen because no one has the guts to do it. This is a real disappointing day to be involved in junior hockey. It was a mistake that Peterborough were ahead by the third period but they soon corrected it. They avoided moving the puck out of their own zone. It's just a shame that people paid good money to see something like this."

Royals captain Dan Daoust agreed that the Petes did not play especially well in the final period, but stopped short of suggesting a fix. "A lot of people will say Peterborough gave it to us," he said. "Whether they did or not, I don't know." Others felt certain that the victory was on the level. "Personally, I feel it was a fair game," said Marcel Robert, President of the QMJHL. "There's no question in my mind that the Petes played to their full potential," said Dave Branch, commissioner of the OMJHL.

Royals coach Carpenter was asked if he felt the game result was suspicious, but he would not say. "I'm not going to worry about that," he replied. "I'm going to worry about winning the Memorial Cup. We got into the final, and that's what we're here for." As for Keenan, he offered only a few terse words. "I have no comment about tonight's game," he said. "We're preparing for Sunday's championship final game."

If Keenan had hatched a plan to win the Memorial Cup by ensuring that his team played the supposedly weak Royals, it bombed. The Royals stuck with the Petes throughout the match and ultimately won the championship. Defenceman Robert Savard scored in overtime to give Cornwall a 3–2 victory. The unassisted goal, Savard's first of the tournament, came at 1:28 of the extra period when he skated the length of the ice and fired a shot between the legs of Rick LaFerriere. The tally brought a loud cheer from the Regina crowd, and a shower of eggs and soft drink containers toward the Peterborough bench.

"This was the most important goal in my life," Savard said. "I told everybody back home, wait 'til we get into the championship game, I'll score the winner. But to actually do it is just incredible."

Daoust and Ezard scored the first 2 Cornwall goals, both on the powerplay. Steve Smith and Terry Bovair replied for Peterborough. The game was held up periodically as spectators threw eggs at the Peterborough players and bench, forcing cleanup crews to make a series of ice-sweeping trips. Paid attendance for the championship game was announced at 5,736 but as many as 2,000 seats remained empty.

Dave Ezard was named the Most Valuable Player of the tournament, while Dale Hawerchuk was voted most sportsmanlike. Ezard had tied Hawerchuk and Gilles Crépeau for the tournament scoring lead, but he also scored several clutch goals and killed off numerous penalties. LaFerriere was named the best goaltender. The all-star team included LaFerriere, plus Regina's Veitch and Peterborough's Murphy on defence. The all-star forwards were Bill Gardner of the Petes at centre, Mark Reeds of Peterborough at right wing, and Hawerchuk of Cornwall at left wing.

A number of Cornwall Royals players would return to Memorial Cup action in 1981, including Hawerchuk and Crawford. Dan Daoust was an NHL regular for eight years with Montreal and Toronto. Defenceman Fred Boimistruck played two years with the Maple Leafs, while goaltender Ron Scott saw intermittent duty over five seasons with the Rangers and Kings.

From the Peterborough Petes, Larry Murphy went on to become one of the highest-scoring defencemen in the history of the NHL. He enjoyed a lengthy career with Los Angeles, Washington, Minnesota, Pittsburgh, Toronto and Detroit. Murphy won the Stanley Cup with Pittsburgh in 1991 and 1992, and with Detroit in 1997. In 1981–82, he set records for most points and assists by a rookie defenceman. Tom Fergus enjoyed a twelve-year career in Boston, Toronto and Vancouver, while Dave Fenyves became a star defenceman in the American Hockey League, occasionally getting called up to Buffalo or

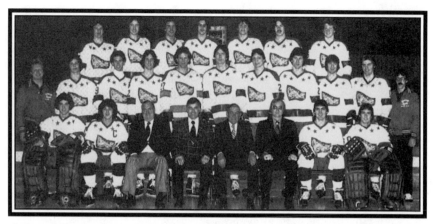

Cornwall Royals. Back row (l to r): Newell Brown, Fred Boimistruck, Craig Halliday, Pat O'Kane, Marc Crawford, Robert Savard, Bobby Hull Jr. Middle row: Steve Ouderkiak (trainer), Dale Hawerchuk, Pat Haramis, Scott Arniel, Mark Corrigan, Fred Arthur, Dan Zavarise, Dan Brown, Gilles Crépeau, Rod Willard, Mario Boisvert (trainer). Front row: Tom Graovac, Dan Daoust, Larry Lascalle (director), Paul Lemard (president), Gus Lebrun (vice president), Doug Carpenter (general manager and coach), Dave Ezard, Ron Scott.

Philadelphia. Steve Smith also played a handful of games over six seasons with Philadelphia and Buffalo. Larry Floyd and goalie Rick LaFerriere both served brief NHL stints, Floyd with New Jersey and LaFerriere with the Colorado Rockies. Mark Reeds participated in parts of eight seasons for Hartford and St. Louis.

The Regina Pats' Doug Wickenheiser was drafted first overall by the Canadiens, and played an unspectacular ten-year pro career, mostly with Montreal, St. Louis and Vancouver. Garth Butcher brought a hard-nosed presence to the blueline for fourteen years with Vancouver, St. Louis, Quebec and Toronto. Rightwinger Mike Blaisdell played nine years in the NHL with Detroit, Pittsburgh, Toronto and the Rangers. Defenceman Darren Veitch spent ten years with Washington, Detroit and Toronto. Ron Flockhart had a nine-year NHL career, mostly in Philadelphia and St. Louis.

All three coaches in the 1980 Memorial Cup tournament went on to the NHL. Doug Carpenter coached the Devils and Maple Leafs, while Bryan Murray performed coaching duties in Washington and Detroit, winning the Jack Adams Trophy as NHL coach of the year in 1983–84. He also served as the General Manager of Detroit and Florida. Mike Keenan worked behind the bench with Philadelphia, Chicago, St. Louis and the Rangers. He took teams to the Stanley Cup finals on four occasions, with the Flyers in 1985 and 1987 (losing to Edmonton on both occasions), with the Blackhawks in 1992 (bowing out to Pittsburgh), and with New York in 1994 (when the Rangers won their first NHL championship since 1940). Keenan won the Jack Adams Trophy in 1984–85.

The **1981** Memorial Cup

While the 1980 Cornwall Royals eked out a surprise Memorial Cup victory, the Royals of the following year were a strong, seasoned group led by returning veterans Dale Hawerchuk and Marc Crawford. The 1981 squad added players like Doug Gilmour and Scott Arniel for offence. Two impressive newcomers to Memorial Cup action, the Victoria Cougars and Kitchener Rangers, challenged the Royals for the top prize.

Mindful of the controversy generated in the 1980 series, when accusations of game-throwing were made, tournament organizers implemented a rule change for 1981. If one team clinched a final berth after four games, the other two would play a two-game total-goal series. If one team clinched after five games, the other two would play a sudden death semi-final.

Dale Hawerchuk led the QMJHL in scoring during the regular season, ringing up 81 goals and 102 assists in seventy-two games. The Royals finished first overall in the league, but ran into some trouble in the playoffs. They were taken to seven games by both the Quebec Remparts and the Sherbrooke Beavers before eliminating the Trois-Rivieres Draveurs four games to one for the league championship.

Cornwall coach Bob Kilger, a former NHL referee, took over the team in the last week of pre-season training camp. Doug Carpenter, who had coached Cornwall to their 1980 Cup victory, had departed to coach the New Brunswick Hawks in the American Hockey League. Nine players returned from the championship team, and the Royals also picked up goaltender Corrado Micalef from Sherbrooke to supplement their regular netminder, Joe Mantione.

In the WHL playoffs, the Victoria Cougars took out the Spokane Flyers and Portland Winter Hawks in four straight games each. Victoria then fell behind three games to one in the western final against the Calgary Wranglers before rallying to win three straight. The seventh game was decided with less than two minutes left, when Terry Sydoryk broke a 2–2 tie at 18:07 of the third period.

The Cougars were coached by Jack Shupe, who had taken the Medicine Hat Tigers to the Memorial Cup in 1973. They boasted some impressive talent, including top-ranked junior goaltender Grant Fuhr and a slew of future NHLers including Barry Pederson, Geoff Courtnall, Paul Cyr, Bob McGill, Torrie Robertson, Tony Feltrin and Stu Kulak.

Although the Kitchener Rangers finished just over .500 in the 1980–81 season, their record marked a drastic turnaround from the previous year's seventeen wins, fifty-one defeats and 34 points. In the OHL, Kitchener defeated the Niagara Falls Flyers, Windsor Spitfires and Sault Ste. Marie Greyhounds to claim the league championship.

The underdog Rangers played under coach and general manager Orval Tessier, who was entering his fourth Memorial Cup final. He had appeared once as a player, with Barrie in 1953, and twice as a coach, with Cornwall in 1972 and the Quebec Remparts in 1973—the only year he lost. Tessier's Rangers were led by sixteen-year-old captain Brian Bellows and included Mike Eagles, Jeff Larmer,

Allan MacInnis, Fred Arthur, Joe McDonnell and goaltender Wendell Young.

The tournament began with the defending champion Royals scoring on Young with their first 2 shots, generating some instant momentum. They took a 6–3 victory over Kitchener with 3,950 fans in attendance at the Windsor Arena. Hawerchuk scored a goal and added 2 assists to pace the Royals' attack and to shatter Kitchener's twelve-game unbeaten streak. After Cornwall bolted to a 4–1 lead midway through the first period, Kitchener coach Tessier sent in backup netminder Steve Bienkowski to replace Wendell Young, who had played the previous eight playoff games for the Rangers. "We wanted to set the tempo of the game," Royals coach Kilger said. "So we came out and did the same thing tonight that we'd been doing all year."

The Rangers fell further into a hole in their second game at Windsor Arena. They were handed a 7–4 defeat by the Victoria Cougars, who got 3 goals from Pederson and 28 saves from Fuhr. Cornwall and Victoria met in the third game, a contest between the tournament's unbeaten teams. The Royals stayed that way with a 3–1 victory. Rookie goaltender Mantione turned back 29 shots in an impressive effort before 3,269 fans. "Joe's a very confident young man," Kilger said, "and if you were to ask him who was the best goalie, he'd say, 'Joe Mantione.'" Cornwall had a 2-goal effort from Crépeau, and Arniel scored the game winner at 1:12 of the second period. Royals captain Marc Crawford added 3 assists, while Mark Morrison replied for Victoria.

The Royals and Cougars came together for a rematch in the next game. Kitchener got back into the series by beating Cornwall 6–4. Bellows netted 3 goals, and Larmer, Mike Moher and Kerry Williston also scored for the Rangers. Hawerchuk also scored a hat trick, while Gilmour added a single for the Royals.

Kitchener had been leading 6–2 when play got rough. Royal Dan Frawley was tripped and crashed into the Rangers' goalpost. Moments later, Gilmour jumped Kitchener's Mike Clayton, while Moher and Robert Savard threw off their helmets and started swinging at one another. "If those masks [the Cornwall players wore a wire cage with their helmets] hadn't been on, there would have been fights," Bellows said. "We're not a dirty club, but those masks made the other team braver, and they were sticking us all night."

The Rangers came full circle one night later, defeating the Cougars 4–2 to even their win-loss record at 2–2. Wendell Young was a standout in the Kitchener net, blocking 40 shots in this must-win game. Bellows, Moher, Kevin Casey and Bob Hicks scored for the Rangers, while Pederson and Daryl Coldwell replied for the WHL representatives, who dropped their second game in a row. Cornwall was now 2–1 and Victoria 1–2 in the series.

Any hope still nurtured by the Victoria Cougars was rudely quashed in their next game.

The Royals helped themselves to an 8–4 victory before 4,086 fans at Windsor Arena. Corrado Micalef started in goal and he was very sharp, especially in the first period when the Cougars fired 20 shots at him. Dale Hawerchuk moved into high gear and hit for 4 goals, 2 of them shorthanded. Fuhr, who allowed 8 goals on 33 shots, did not live up to his number one ranking.

"The fact we gave up those two breakaway goals by Hawerchuk is unbelievable,"

Wendell Young was the starting goalie for the Kitchener Rangers, runners-up for the 1981 Memorial Cup.

Jack Shupe said. "I don't think we gave up a goal like that all year. But that's the way the Royals were playing tonight. They play tight-checking and skate well, and they take advantage of the breaks given to them."

With Victoria eliminated, the championship game featured Kitchener and Cornwall. The Royals scored a 5–2 victory over the Rangers before a sellout crowd of 4,500, becoming only the fifth team in Memorial Cup history to win back-to-back titles. Scott Arniel fired two goals, while the winning goal was scored by Doug Gilmour at 9:57 of the second period. Mike Eagles and Bellows scored the Kitchener goals.

Kitchener goaltender Young was outstanding in a losing cause, blocking 41 shots and keeping the Rangers close. Micalef was solid in the Royals' net, making 35 saves.

Hawerchuk, who had 8 goals and 5 assists in the tournament, was chosen Most Valuable Player. Mark Morrison of Victoria was selected most sportsmanlike player and Micalef was named the top goaltender. The all-star team included Micalef in goal, Fred Arthur and Joe McDonnell of Kitchener on defence, Hawerchuk at centre, Bellows on right wing and Cornwall's Crawford on left wing.

"What a great year for our team," Gilmour later recalled. "I was seventeen years old and we had Hawerchuk, he was our undisputed leader. The tournament was exciting. Coach Kilger put me on the second line with Jeff Eatough for the final game. I think it was 2–0, then they came back to tie, then I scored the winner and never looked back."

Doug Gilmour became one of the most solid all-around players ever to skate in the NHL. He played with St. Louis, Calgary, Toronto and New Jersey, winning the Stanley Cup with the Flames in 1989. Gilmour also won the 1993 Frank Selke Trophy. Scott Arniel played eleven seasons with Winnipeg, Buffalo and

Boston, while Dan Frawley played over five years with Chicago and Pittsburgh. Goalie Corrado Micalef spent five years in the Detroit Red Wings nets, while defenceman Eric Calder played two games with Washington.

Dale Hawerchuk won the Calder Trophy in his rookie pro season of 1981–82. He had a superb career with Winnipeg, Buffalo, St. Louis and Philadelphia. Hawerchuk scored more than 100 points in six different seasons, and scored more than 90 points ten times. Royals captain Marc Crawford saw duty with the Vancouver Canucks over the course of six seasons. But it was as a coach that he enjoyed distinguished NHL success. Crawford won the 1994–95 Jack Adams Trophy for his work with the Quebec Nordiques, and captured the Stanley Cup with the same team playing as the Colorado Avalanche in 1996.

From the Victoria Cougars, Grant Fuhr went on to establish himself as one of the great goaltenders in NHL history, playing with Edmonton, Toronto, Buffalo, Los Angeles and St. Louis. He won the Stanley Cup with the Oilers in 1984, 1985, 1987, 1988 and 1990. Fuhr won the Vezina Trophy for 1987–88.

Barry Pederson averaged almost a point per game over twelve seasons in the pros, mostly with Boston, Pittsburgh and Vancouver. He won the Stanley Cup with the Penguins in 1991. Geoff Courtnall enjoyed a lengthy NHL career with Boston, Edmonton, Vancouver and St. Louis, winning the Stanley Cup with the Oilers in 1988. Bob McGill played over a dozen years in the big league, mostly with Toronto and Chicago, while Torrie Robertson played the better part of a decade with Washington, Hartford and Detroit. Tony Feltrin and Stu Kulak played part of four NHL seasons, Feltrin with Pittsburgh and the Rangers, and Kulak with the Rangers, Vancouver, Quebec and Winnipeg. Mark Morrison served a brief stint with the New York Rangers.

Cornwall Royals.

From the Kitchener Rangers, Joe McDonnell skated with Vancouver and Pittsburgh over a three-year span. Fred Arthur played part of three years with Hartford and Philadelphia, while Russ Adam saw brief action with Toronto. A number of other Kitchener players would return to challenge for the Memorial Cup in 1982.

The **1982** Memorial Cup

In some ways, the 1982 Kitchener Rangers resembled the 1981 Cornwall Royals. They had a strong core of players that had seen Memorial Cup action the previous year, bringing experience and exceptional skills to the team. Like the Royals, Kitchener were more dominant in their second run at the national title.

The Rangers were under the direction of coach and general manager Joe Crozier, who had previous Memorial Cup experience playing for the 1949 Brandon Wheat Kings. It was his first year with the team, having been replaced behind the Toronto Maple Leafs' bench in January 1981. In the OHL playoffs, the Rangers eliminated the Windsor Spitfires and Sault Ste. Marie Greyhounds before defeating the Ottawa 67's in the league championship. Kitchener had lost the final game of the 1981 Memorial Cup to a Cornwall team with more playoff experience. This time, Kitchener had the edge, as a number of Rangers were returning, including Brian Bellows, Wendell Young, Al MacInnis, Jeff Larmer and Mike Eagles. Future NHLers Scott Stevens, Mike Hough and Grant Martin made the club's latest edition all the more powerful.

In the QMJHL, André Boisvert's Sherbrooke Beavers opened the post-season with a fourteen-game, double round robin series involving eight different teams. Sherbrooke, Chicoutimi, Laval and Trois-Rivieres survived the contest and went on in the playoffs. Sherbrooke eliminated the Laval Voisins and Trois-Rivieres Draveurs in succession, needing only four games in both series. Captained by Mario Dore and led by a forward combination of Gerard Gallant, Sean McKenna and John Chabot, the Beavers also included Michel Petit and Paul Boutilier on defence and Michel Morrissette in goal.

The Portland Winter Hawks, fresh from a 46–24–2 regular-season record, steamrolled to the WHL title. They sidelined the first-year Kamloops Junior Oilers and the Seattle Breakers and then met Bill Laforge's Regina Pats in an ugly western final. Three Regina players were suspended and the Pats' trainer fined after a game four altercation in which the Regina bench emptied. The Winter Hawks were cleared of blame and took a 4–1 series victory. Portland thereby became the first American-based team to advance to the Memorial Cup tournament.

Coached by Ken Hodge and managed by Brian Shaw, the Winter Hawks were led by a potent offensive line featuring Ken Yaremchuk at centre, Randy Heath on the left side and Brian Shaw (manager Shaw's nephew) on the right. The defence included captain Glen Ostir, Gary Nylund and Brian Curran. Portland's goaltending was supplied by Darrell May and Mike Vernon, an addition from the Calgary Wranglers and the WHL's best goaltender during the regular season.

Game one pitted Sherbrooke against Kitchener at the Robert Guertin Arena. It ended in a sobering 10–4 rout in favour of the Beavers. The line of Gerard Gallant, Sean McKenna and John Chabot accounted for 8 of Sherbrooke's goals, Gallant scoring a hat trick and his linemates pitching in 2 apiece. Kitchener fired 52 shots at Sherbrooke's Michel Morrissette, beating him only four times. Wendell Young and Darryl Boudreau made 23 saves in 33 shots for the Rangers.

The Rangers cleaned up their act for game two, trouncing Portland 9–2. Eager to erase the embarrassment of their opening loss, Kitchener came out blasting and ran up a 5–1 lead at the end of the first period. Bellows scored just eleven seconds into the game, setting a Memorial Cup record. The previous fourteen-second mark for fastest opening goal was set by the New Westminster Bruins' Mark Lofthouse in 1976. Bellows' linemates were also on the attack, Larmer tallying 2 goals and 4 assists and Grant Martin a pair of goals. Larmer set a Memorial Cup record by scoring all his assists in the same period.

Sherbrooke and Portland met in the third game before 2,517 spectators. The Winter Hawks became the first American-based team to win a game in the Memorial Cup championship when Heath, an 82-goal scorer in the regular season, ripped a rebound into the Sherbrooke goal at 7:33 of overtime, finalizing the game at 6–5. The Beavers had held the lead late in the third, but an unlikely goal allowed Portland to pull even with less than four minutes left. The goal was credited to Brian Shaw but was actually knocked in by Sherbrooke defenceman Michel Petit. He was batting at a loose puck while trying to clear a high rebound from Shaw's slapshot when the puck went in. "I saw it just at the last minute," said a remorseful Petit. "It was just a reflex action."

Richard Kromm led Portland to victory with his first 2 playoff goals of the spring. "We got a little undisciplined, and they were flying," Sherbrooke coach Boisvert said. "Scoring the tying goal in your end is bound to hurt you." Portland rightwinger Brian Shaw commented, "We'll take our goals any way we can get them."

The fourth game saw another impressive showing by Kitchener, as the Rangers shut out Sherbrooke 4–0. Bellows and Al MacInnis each scored twice.

Kitchener players threw their weight around, with physical play reaching a boiling point in the second period. The game was delayed nearly an hour by a bench-clearing brawl, which resulted in the ejection of three players. Some stickwork between the Beavers' Gerard Gallant and the Rangers' Mike Eagles sparked the fighting, which culminated in ninety-three minutes of penalties. The rumble did not faze Young, who blocked 29 shots to earn the only shutout of the 1982 Memorial Cup. He described the outburst as "part of the game."

The Rangers faced the Winter Hawks on the following night. They turned in a less robust performance, going down by a score of 4–2. Portland's line of Yaremchuk, Heath and Shaw underpinned their scoring attack. Each scored once in the first period, as the Winter Hawks opened up a 4–0 lead only twelve minutes into the game. After allowing the fourth goal on Portland's eighth shot, Wendell Young was pulled in favour of Jim Ralph, an Ottawa 67's goaltender picked up by the Rangers. Winter Hawks netminder Darrell May was outstanding, blocking 43 shots and preventing the Rangers from capitalizing during their resurgence later in the game. "We were very strong in the first period," Portland coach Ken Hodge said. "We didn't do much after that."

In the final game of the round robin, Sherbrooke took destiny into its own hands. The Beavers blasted Portland 7–3 and advanced to the Memorial Cup final. Four Sherbrooke goals came on the power play. Chabot and Bachand scored 2 apiece, while single tallies went to Gallant, Gilbert and McKenna.

The game was marred by another brawl. With 3:06 left in the second period, Sherbrooke was up 5–2 when several skirmishes broke out deep in the Sherbrooke end. Fighting escalated as Sherbrooke goaltender Morrissette left his crease to join in.

Referee Phil Desgagnes assessed 132 minutes in penalties, sending both teams to their dressing rooms. The remaining time was tacked onto the start of the third period.

Portland manager Shaw was unhappy with the officiating, but Sherbrooke coach Boisvert dismissed the Winter Hawks' complaints. "They can say what they want to say," he maintained. "We played a hell of a game and they can't take that away from us."

All three teams finished with 2–2 records, so the finalists were decided by goals differential. Thanks largely to their 7–3 loss to Sherbrooke in the final round robin game, Portland was eliminated.

Kitchener and Sherbrooke met for the third time in the championship game played before 4,091 fans. Brian Bellows came to the fore, scoring 3 goals and adding 2 assists in the Rangers' 7–4 victory. It was the city of Kitchener's first Memorial Cup title.

"We knew we had the better club and we took it right to them," Joe Crozier said. "We just borrowed the Montreal Canadiens' defence and cut away the middle of the ice. That kept them to the outside where they couldn't hurt us."

The Rangers led 3–1 after the first period and 5–2 after the second. Mike Eagles scored 2 shorthanded goals fourteen seconds apart early in the third, putting the game firmly out of the Beavers' reach. Grant Martin and MacInnis scored the other goals for Kitchener, while the Beavers got 2 from McKenna and 1 each from Mike Fafard and Paul Boutilier late in the game.

"In my mind, Bellows is a good under-pressure player," Boisvert said. "He proved that today. He made things happen."

Bellows, who won the tournament's Most Sportsmanlike Player award, was edged out as Most Valuable Player by the Beavers' Sean McKenna, a decision that perturbed coach Crozier. Although Bellows had 5 points in the final, all-star balloting was based only on the elimination series. Rightwinger McKenna, who finished with 6 goals and 5 assists, was also named to the all-star team along with three other Beavers: goaltender Morrissette, centre Chabot and defenceman Boutilier. Jeff Larmer and MacInnis, who tied with Gary Nylund for the final spot on defence, were selected from the Rangers. Michel Morrissette was named the outstanding goaltender.

Brian Bellows won the Stanley Cup with the Montreal Canadiens in 1993,

Kitchener Rangers. Back row (l to r): Paul Higgins, Scott Clements, Scott Stevens, John Tucker, Jim Quinn. Middle row: Les Bradley, Brett Johnston, Brad Schnurr, Robert Savard, Bob Ertel, Joe Crozier, Dave Shaw, Dave Nicholls, Grant Martin, Bob Schlieman. Front row: Darryl Boudreau, Mike Eagles, Mario Michieli, Allan MacInnis, Brian Bellows, Joel Levesque, Kevin Casey, Louis Crawford, Wendell Young.

the peak of an exceptional NHL career that also included service in Minnesota, Tampa Bay and Anaheim. Al MacInnis became one of the big league's top defencemen playing for Calgary and St. Louis. He won the Stanley Cup and the Conn Smythe Trophy with the Flames in 1989. Goaltender Wendell Young played in Vancouver, Philadelphia, Tampa Bay and Pittsburgh, winning the Stanley Cup as a backup for the Penguins in 1991 and 1992.

Other Kitchener players who proceeded to the NHL include Mike Eagles, who played a number of years in Quebec, Chicago, Winnipeg and Washington. Jeff Larmer played parts of five seasons with the Colorado Rockies, New Jersey and Chicago. Mike Hough spent more than ten years with Quebec and Florida. Grant Martin saw limited action in Vancouver and Washington, while Mike Moher and Perry Pelensky served briefly in the pros, Moher in New Jersey and Pelensky in Chicago. Scott Stevens emerged as one of the NHL's premier blueliners with Washington, St. Louis and New Jersey, helping the Devils to a Stanley Cup in 1995.

From the Sherbrooke Beavers, Sean McKenna played more than six NHL seasons in Buffalo, Los Angeles and Toronto, while John Chabot spent eight years in Montreal, Pittsburgh and Detroit. Michel Petit joined the Vancouver Canucks in 1982–83, then eventually moved on to the Rangers, Quebec, Toronto, Calgary and Tampa Bay. Paul Boutilier played more than six years in the pros, mostly with the Islanders, with whom he won the Stanley Cup in 1983. Gerard Gallant would return to Memorial Cup competition with the Verdun Juniors.

Defenceman Gary Nylund played more than ten years with Toronto, Chicago and the New York Islanders, and Darrell May served a brief stint in St. Louis. A number of Portland Winter Hawks would be back in the 1983 junior championship.

The **1983** Memorial Cup

There were many firsts in the 1983 Memorial Cup tournament, most of them achieved by a single team. It was the first time a team won the championship without winning a junior league title, as the tournament was the first four-team Memorial Cup. It was also the first time an American team captured the trophy. The Portland Winter Hawks, by virtue of their status as tournament host, were assured a place in the final four from the beginning of the season.

Putting the host team in the tournament was seen as an important fan draw by Memorial Cup organizers. Portland, Oregon was a particularly strong junior hockey market, and the benefit of including the Winter Hawks became evident when the Winter Hawks sold more than 6,500 eight-game ticket packages in advance. The Portland Memorial Coliseum, with a seating capacity of 10,000, was the scene for all tournament games.

Judging by their performance, the Winter Hawks were not undeserving of their guaranteed place in the championship. They finished second in their division with 100 points on the season and proceeded to the league championship by defeating the Seattle Breakers and Victoria Cougars. But the Lethbridge Broncos defeated the Winter Hawks for the western championship in five games. The Winter Hawks were a run-and-gun team. Seven players had 100 or more points in the season: captain Richard Kromm, Ken Yaremchuk, Randy Heath, Alfie Turcotte, Cam Neely, Grant Sasser and Brad Duggan. Ray Ferraro had 90 points in fifty games. There were also nine 20-goal scorers on the team. As a unit, Portland averaged almost 7 goals a game.

Bruno Campese and Ian Wood held down the goaltending duties, but an injury to Wood prompted the Winter Hawks to enlist the services of Calgary's Mike Vernon. The Wranglers netminder was finding a comfortable home away from home with Portland, having made a trip to the 1982 tournament with the team.

Vernon was the centre of some controversy, stemming from his acceptance of the offer to play for the Winter Hawks after he had refused Lethbridge. Vernon had faced the Broncos earlier in the playoffs, and was unwilling to play for their coach, John Chapman. "It's garbage that Vernon should be allowed to play for Portland after he turned us down," said an angry Chapman, whose regular netminder Ken Wregget was unavailable due to injury. "The rules say the league champions get the first pick when adding a goaltender."

The Lethbridge Broncos surprised many by becoming western champions. They eliminated the Winnipeg Warriors and Saskatoon Blades before dumping the Winter Hawks in the league final. Lethbridge lost only three games during the entire run. This was a team that finished fifth in the east division of the WHL and scored 211 fewer goals than Portland. But the Broncos also allowed 116 fewer.

Lethbridge was led by the Sutter twins, Ron and Rich, as well as Ivan Krook, Bob Rouse and Troy Loney. Mark Tinordi and Gerald Diduck were on defence. Goalie Wregget had been a key to the Broncos' success in the playoffs, leading all goaltenders with a goals-against average of 3.02. He would prove to be difficult to replace.

During the regular season, the Paul Theriault-coached Oshawa Generals were led in scoring by Dave Gans. John MacLean, who boasted a league-leading 38 points in the post-season, led during the playoffs. The Generals' lineup also included defencemen Joe Cirella and Todd Charlesworth, as well as goaltender Peter Sidorkiewicz. Captain Cirella had played sixty-five games for the NHL Colorado Rockies in 1981–82, but returned to Oshawa for most of the 1982–83 season.

The Generals eliminated the Belleville Bulls and the Peterborough Petes, before removing the Sault Ste. Marie Greyhounds in four straight for the OHL championship.

The Pierre Creamer-coached Verdun Juniors were led by Pat LaFontaine, coming off a brilliant year with 103 goals and 132 assists. LaFontaine was a strong candidate for first pick overall in the 1983 NHL entry draft but was ultimately taken third after Brian Lawton and Sylvain Turgeon. In the QMJHL playoffs, Verdun pushed aside the Trois-Rivieres Draveurs, Shawinigan Cataractes and Longueuil Chevaliers to claim the league championship. In addition to LaFontaine, Verdun relied on the solid experience of Gerard Gallant, who had previously played in the 1982 Memorial Cup as a member of the Sherbrooke Beavers, defenceman Jerome Carrier, forward Jacques Sylvestre and captain Jean-Maurice Cool.

The first game of the Memorial Cup tournament matched Lethbridge against Oshawa. Broncos' coach Chapman started goalie Dave Ross, who the club had picked up from the Kamloops Junior Oilers. Ross had not played in a month and couldn't hold back a persistent Oshawa team.

The Generals broke open a tight-checking game in the third period, scoring 3 goals in six minutes en route to an 8–2 win. Oshawa's offence was paced by Joe Cirella, who had 1 goal and 2 assists. "We are a lot better hockey club than we showed today," Lethbridge coach Chapman said. "I still feel it will be Oshawa and us in the finals."

In the next game, Portland edged Verdun 7–6, entering the tournament on a winning note before 7,346 enthusiastic home fans. The Winter Hawks jumped to a 4–1 first-period lead and led 7–2 after forty minutes. In the third period, Verdun served notice they couldn't be taken for granted by scoring 4 unanswered goals. Neely and Sasser led Portland with 2 goals apiece, while Gallant scored twice for Verdun. The Juniors carried this late momentum into their second game, defeating Lethbridge 4–3. The loss eliminated the Broncos from the semi-final playoff round. Lethbridge outshot the Junior Canadiens 47–33, but could not finish enough of their chances. Sylvestre scored twice for Verdun, while Daniel Roy and Gallant got singles. The ever-industrious Rich Sutter scored twice, and Ivan Krook netted a single for the Broncos.

The same day, Portland secured a berth in the final game, relying on their formidable offence to bulldoze Oshawa 10–5. The Generals held a 3–2 lead going into the second period, but Portland stormed out and grabbed a 5–3 lead on goals by Kromm, Sasser and Yaremchuk. Oshawa's Cirella and Greg Gravel notched goals within thirty seconds of each other to tie the game at 5–5. Turcotte gave the Hawks a 6–5 advantage skating into the final period.

The third period was all Portland, as Heath and Turcotte each scored twice, turning the match into a rout. Turcotte and Yaremchuk each finished the night with a hat trick and 2 assists.

Oshawa and Verdun were slated to play each other in the tournament semi-final, but there were still two round robin games left. Nothing was at stake in either case except pride. Lethbridge reclaimed some by hammering Portland 9–3 before 8,811 fans, Ron Sutter delivering a hat trick. There was some bad blood between the two teams, as they had been hacking each other through the media since the start of the tournament. But the game stayed under control. Portland sat out Vernon and Yaremchuk, stating that both were nursing minor injuries.

"You saw the way our hockey club played and beat Portland in the WHL final," said Broncos coach Chapman, whose team had won five of their last six games against the Winter Hawks. "I think we showed the other two teams, if they were watching this game, how to beat Portland through forechecking." Chapman also said that he held no bitterness regarding Mike Vernon's refusal to play for the Broncos. "I was wrong," he admitted. "Ross would have rode a bike from New Haven, Connecticut to be in this series."

In a preview of the semi-final game, goaltender Sidorkiewicz kicked out 35 shots in leading Oshawa past Verdun 5–1. Todd Hooey, Gans, Gravel, MacLean and Charlesworth scored for the Generals. LaFontaine, used sparingly by Verdun, scored a powerplay goal in the third, his second of the tournament. LaFontaine had gone to a hospital earlier in the day for injections to control allergy problems.

The semi-final game had Oshawa taking on Verdun again. The smallest crowd of the tournament, totalling 5,173, attended at Memorial Coliseum. The Juniors came out flying, building a 4–1 lead in the first period. But Oshawa struggled back in the second to even the score. At 6:07 of the final period, Norm Schmidt broke the 5–5 tie, moving up from his defensive position to convert a goalmouth pass from Don Biggs. The Generals added an empty-net goal to put the icing on an impressive comeback. Sidorkiewicz bulwarked the revival during the last two periods, making a number of game-savers in the last five minutes. He stopped 46 shots overall.

The victory moved the Generals into the final against the Winter Hawks. This time there would be no comeback. Portland returned to their seemingly

The Portland Winter Hawks' Cam Neely had a brilliant thirteen-year NHL career in Vancouver and Boston.

bottomless offensive well and posted an 8–3 victory to claim the Memorial Cup.

Seventeen-year-old rightwinger Cam Neely scored 3 goals to spearhead the assault. His linemates also enjoyed a productive evening. Heath had a goal and 2 assists, while Yaremchuk had 3 assists. The pair tied Oshawa's Cirella for the tournament scoring lead with 11 points each. "This is a history-making day for everyone connected with the Portland organization," coach Hodge observed. "We wanted to win it for our fans—and ourselves. There has been virtually no turnover, from the general manager to the coach to the scouts to the trainer. We've been here since day one on July 21, 1976. We all share in everything, including the Memorial Cup triumph."

"We're mostly a Canadian team playing in an American city," said Portland defenceman Brian Curran. He acknowledged the outstanding support given to the team by Portland fans over the years. "But just as much as twenty guys deserved to win this tournament, those people deserved it too."

"They beat us twice here so they deserve to be champions," said a gracious Joe Cirella. "The better team won today, but in our hearts we're still winners."

"I've never seen a team skate like that," said Generals defenceman

Joe Cirella, captain of the Memorial Cup runners-up Oshawa Generals, had a strong pro career in New Jersey, Quebec, New York and Florida.

Schmidt. "They are so much faster than any team in the OHL. We couldn't stay with them." Being the first time a team had earned a spot in the tournament by virtue of its host status, and despite the strong showing by the Winter Hawks, there were inevitably some questions about whether Portland had truly earned its place in the final four. "If you want to tarnish the win, go ahead," Hodge offered in response. "But what we have here, we have for a lifetime and our families have for a lifetime. No one can take that away from us."

The final game drew 9,527 chanting fans. The eight games attracted 54,090, second only to the 1977 tournament in Vancouver. The four-team experiment was a winner.

Oshawa's Cirella, MacLean and Sidorkiewicz made the all-star team, as did

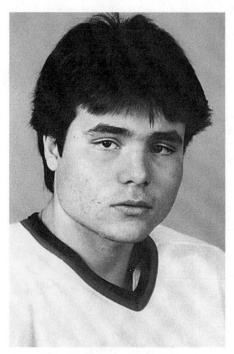

The NHL career of Portland Winter Hawk John Kordic came to a tragic end in 1992 when he died during a scuffle with Quebec City police.

Jerome Carrier from Verdun, and Randy Heath and Ken Yaremchuk from Portland.

A number of players from the 1983 Portland Winter Hawks went on to the NHL. Cam Neely had a brilliant thirteen-year career, beginning in Vancouver and flourishing in Boston, where he combined physical play with goal-scoring prowess. Ray Ferraro was first traded to the Brandon Wheat Kings, where his junior career soared, prior to an exceptional pro career with Hartford, the Islanders, the Rangers and Los Angeles. Brian Curran also enjoyed a long term in the NHL, mostly with Boston, the Islanders and Toronto. Another big, rock-hard Winter Hawk defenceman, Jim Playfair, played a handful of games in Edmonton and Chicago.

Richard Kromm played nine seasons with the Calgary Flames and the Islanders, while Ken Yaremchuk spent six years in

Chicago and Toronto. Alfie Turcotte played parts of seven seasons in Montreal, Winnipeg and Washington. Derek Laxdal, a seventeen-year-old who didn't have much of an impact on the '83 Winter Hawks, later blossomed into an NHL prospect and played games for the Toronto Maple Leafs and New York Islanders. Grant Sasser and Randy Heath saw brief NHL action, Sasser with Pittsburgh and Heath with the Rangers. Gord Walker had stints over four seasons with the Rangers and Los Angeles. John Kordic brawled through six years in the big league, mostly in

Portland Winter Hawks captain Richard Kromm holds the reward for a hard-fought victory over the Oshawa Generals in the 1983 Memorial Cup finals.

Montreal and Toronto. In August of 1992 he died of a cardiac arrest in a Quebec City motel when city police attempted to subdue his drug-induced rage. Mike Vernon went on to become an exceptional goaltender with Calgary, Detroit and San Jose, helping the Flames to a Stanley Cup in 1989 and the Red Wings in 1997.

From the Oshawa Generals, Joe Cirella had a strong pro career with New Jersey, Quebec, the Rangers and the Florida Panthers. Todd Charlesworth played with the Rangers and Pittsburgh, while Peter Sidorkiewicz spent six years with Hartford, Ottawa and New Jersey. John MacLean became a pivotal player with New Jersey, winning the Stanley Cup with the Devils in 1995. From the Verdun Juniors, Pat LaFontaine became an outstanding NHL star with the Islanders and Buffalo, while Gerard Gallant was also a solid performer with Detroit and Tampa Bay for more than ten years.

From the Lethbridge Broncos, the Sutter twins, Ron and Rich, went on to lengthy professional careers. Ron played mostly with Philadelphia and St. Louis,

Portland Winter Hawks. Back row (l to r): Tim Daugherty (director of marketing and public relations), Randy Heath, Ray Ferraro, Brad Duggan, Innes Mackie (trainer), Gordon Walker, Alfie Turcotte, Terry Jones, Brian Lamberton (stick boy), Dr. E. Robert Wells (team physician). Middle row: Dr. Roy Rusch (team physician), John Kordic, Tim Lorenz, Bryan Walker, Brian Curran, Jim Playfair, Derek Laxdal, Cam Neely, Casey Brusse (stick boy), Jann Boss (office manager). Front row: Bruno Campese, Grant Sasser, Curt Brandolini, Ken Hodge (coach), Richard Kromm, Brian Shaw (general manager), Kelly Hubbard, Ken Yaremchuk, Ian Wood.

and Rich mostly with Pittsburgh, Philadelphia, Vancouver, St. Louis and Chicago. Defenceman Mark Tinordi and Gerald Diduck would also enjoy professional success, Tinordi mostly with Minnesota, Dallas and Washington, and Diduck with the Islanders, Vancouver, Chicago, Hartford and Phoenix. Bob Rouse played thirteen years with Minnesota, Washington, Toronto and Detroit, winning a Stanley Cup with the Red Wings in 1997.

Troy Loney's solid NHL career included ten years in Pittsburgh, where he won the Stanley Cup in 1991 and 1992. Goalie Ken Wregget, who was injured for the 1983 Memorial Cup, went on to play many seasons in the pros, mostly with Toronto, Philadelphia and Pittsburgh, where he won the Stanley Cup in 1992.

The **1984** Memorial Cup

While many highly touted junior prospects haven't lived up to expectations in the NHL, there was little doubt that Mario Lemieux would have no such problem. In the 1984 tournament, all eyes were on Lemieux and his team, the Laval Voisins, who were up against the Ottawa 67's, Kitchener Rangers and Kamloops Junior Oilers. But the Voisins ended up sitting out the final game. For the first time since the round robin format had been adopted, two Ontario teams squared off for the championship.

The 1984 Memorial Cup was staged at the Kitchener Memorial Auditorium, so the Kitchener Rangers had a place assured in the tournament. Coached by Tom Barrett, Kitchener had the best regular season record in the OHA, and eliminated Sault Ste. Marie in the playoffs before losing to the 67's in the Ontario final. The Rangers' appearance in the Memorial Cup was their third in four years, this time with a lineup that included John Tucker, Wayne Presley, Shawn Burr, Dave Shaw, David Bruce and goaltender Ray LeBlanc.

Having defeated the Rangers, the Ottawa 67's took their place in the tournament as Ontario champions. Named for Canada's birthday, the 67's served notice they should be taken seriously with an impressive regular season and playoff run. Brian "Killer" Kilrea coached the club to the Leyden division title with a team record of 102 points. The 67's roster included captain Brad Shaw, Adam Creighton, Bruce Cassidy, Don McLaren, Gary Roberts and goalie Darren Pang.

The Laval Voisins dominated the QMJHL with a 54–16 record. In the playoffs, the Jean Begin-coached team swept the Drummondville Voltigeurs and Granby Bisons before removing the Longueuil Chevaliers in six games. Although they were up against some strong teams in the Memorial Cup tournament, the Voisins had a distinct advantage over their opponents: Mario Lemieux. In the Quebec league, the Voisins captain had done what he would later accomplish routinely in the NHL: dominate the scoring race. His mind-boggling 282 points established a longstanding record, and he was maintaining the same pace in the playoffs with 52 points in fourteen games.

What made Laval particularly threatening was that Lemieux was not the only player who could turn on the red light. The Voisins also had a prolific sniper in Vincent Damphousse, plus the talents of defencemen Steve Finn and Bobby Dollas.

Coached by Bill Laforge, the Kamloops Junior Oilers ousted the Seattle Breakers and Portland Winter Hawks before meeting the Regina Pats in a tough western final. In game six, Kamloops found itself on the brink of elimination, behind three games to two and trailing 3–2 with less than a minute left. But centre Dean Evason scored at 19:48 of the third period to force overtime, and Ryan Stewart scored in the extra frame to give Kamloops a 4–3 victory. The seventh game was also tied in the third when Stewart scored to send the Junior Oilers on their way to the Memorial Cup. The Kamloops team also included future NHLers Doug Bodger, Ken Daneyko and fifteen-year-old Rob Brown.

Kitchener got off to an explosive start in the Memorial Cup tournament. They scored 17 goals in opening back-to-back victories over Laval and Kamloops. In their first match, the Rangers held Mario Lemieux in check and demolished the Voisins 8–2. This game marked the first time in eighty-five outings that Lemieux was held pointless. The Rangers marched out to an 8–0 lead midway through their second game against the Junior Oilers. But this one was not so easy to finish.

Trailing 8–2 going into the third, Laforge's troops began to chip away at the deficit. They scored 5 straight goals in the final frame, pulling to within 1 with less than four minutes remaining. The Rangers, however, were able to stem the tide. David Bruce scored a late empty-netter to secure a harrowing 9–7 victory. Kamloops coach Laforge attributed his team's slow start to inexperience. For one thing, the Oilers had ten players under the age of seventeen. "We were nervous," he said. "We're a young team, but once we got our confidence, we were all right and on our way."

In their second game, Laval's record fell to 0–2 thanks to a 6–5 loss to Ottawa. They got off to a strong start, with Lemieux scoring at 1:39 of the first period to end his one-game scoring drought. Twelve seconds later, Michel Mongeau streaked down the right wing and sent a fifteen-foot wrist shot past Pang, who was then replaced by Coram. Ottawa refused to fold, however, and fought back to gain a 6–5 victory. Phil Patterson scored the winner midway through the third period.

"Obviously some of our players thought they were going to pad their totals tonight, because they played as individuals and not as a team," Kilrea said. "I didn't like what I saw from the goaltender out, and I thought I would try to change the momentum."

"I think we stood around and watched Lemieux for the first five minutes," said 67's captain Brad Shaw, who assisted on the winning goal. Bill Bennett scored twice for the 67's and also assisted on the winner.

The next game brought Kamloops together with Ottawa. The 67's scored a 5–1 victory before a crowd of 6,327, stretching their unbeaten streak to fifteen playoff games. Cassidy scored twice for the OHL champs, and Pang was called upon to make only 18 saves. The second period was slowed by some chippiness as the Oilers tried to draw the 67's off their game, but the Ottawa players stayed focussed. Their victory gave Ottawa a 2–0 record matching Kitchener's, meaning the teams would meet later to decide who earned a bye into the final.

Laforge had previously coached the Oshawa Generals in the 1980–81 season, taking a young team not expected to do much and turning it into a contender. During his one-year stay, Laforge's team accumulated almost 2,000 more penalty minutes than the next most penalized team in the OHL. He was suspended by the league after an altercation during a playoff game, and moved to the WHL to coach the Regina Pats the next season.

"We all remember Laforge and we were worried the game might get out of hand," Don McLaren said. "But we kept our cool. We had nothing to gain by going after them."

"I thought we played well, but Kilrea's team was older and stronger than us," Laforge said. "We hope now just to get into the semi-finals and wait for a bounce to come our way and see how far we'll last." Kamloops did go a little further. Facing Laval in their third game, the Oilers earned a semi-final berth with a 4–3 win. Lemieux was again prominent for the Voisins, grabbing 1 goal and 2 assists, but his team exited from the tournament with no wins in three starts.

Kamloops held one semi-final spot. It was up to Kitchener and Ottawa to decide who would get the other and who would secure a direct ticket to the championship game. Kitchener claimed a 7–2 win to move into the final, sending the 67's off to meet Kamloops on a semi-final detour.

Defenceman Dave Shaw and centre Wilks led the Rangers offensively with 2 goals each, while LeBlanc made some key saves early on. His team had secured a 4–1 lead by the end of the first period. "I think revenge played a big part of it, at least for the players," the Rangers' Shaw said. "We were pretty embarrassed losing to Ottawa in the playoffs."

The loss landed the 67's in a semi-final matchup with Kamloops, but Ottawa was not about to let the season slip away. Booed by Kitchener fans in the previous day's loss, a refocussed Creighton ignored the taunts from the local crowd as he led the way with 2 goals and 3 assists. The tall centreman paced his team to a 7–2 victory over the Junior Oilers. "We've played 103 games this season and there haven't been many when the guys didn't go all out," Laforge said of his team's defeat. "The 67's and Rangers are just better than us."

The final game brought the year-long rivalry between the Ottawa 67's and Kitchener Rangers to a head. The teams had met ten times during the year, winning four each and tying twice. With so little talent dividing them, it was predictable the tone of the match would depend on who got the breaks. They went to Ottawa, as the 67's scored early on a couple of oddball plays, earning a 7–2 victory along with their first Memorial Cup.

The Rangers opened the scoring on a goal by Tucker, but the teams were tied late in the first period. Then Kitchener was victimized by 2 bizarre goals. The first came when goaltender Ray LeBlanc was caught away from the net after moving out to clear the puck. His pass was intercepted by Patterson, who scored unassisted. Then, with a mere five seconds left, Ottawa defenceman Bruce Cassidy dumped the puck into the Kitchener end from the centre line. The puck travelled along the end boards and LeBlanc, anticipating that it would circle behind the

Adam Creighton was part of the Ottawa 67's team that beat the Kitchener Rangers for the 1984 Memorial Cup.

goal, went behind the cage in routine fashion. But the puck hit a joint between two sections of the side glass and was deflected toward the vacant net, sliding into the goal before the distressed netminder could scramble back. That goal made the score 3–1 and turned out to be the Memorial Cup winner.

"I don't want to cry about bad bounces, but what can you say?" coach Barrett asked. "It took the starch right out of us. We owned them for the first ten minutes. We should have been ahead 3–0."

The Rangers fought to get back into the game, but Ottawa would not surrender the lead and later pulled away with the blowout. Adam Creighton, the tournament's top scorer with 12 points, was named Most Valuable Player and the all-star team centre, while Kitchener's Brian Wilks was named most sportsmanlike player. The rest of the all-star team consisted of Darren Pang in goal, Brad Shaw and Bruce Cassidy on defence, Jim Camazzola on left wing, and Don McLaren at right wing. Pang was named the outstanding goaltender.

When Adam Creighton's name went on the 1984 Memorial Cup, it joined that of his father Dave, who won the trophy with the Port Arthur West End Bruins in 1948. Like his dad, Adam went on to a lengthy NHL career, playing mostly in Buffalo, Chicago, Tampa Bay and St. Louis. Ottawa captain Brad Shaw spent a number of seasons with Hartford before relocating to Ottawa, while Bruce Cassidy saw spot duty in Chicago over six seasons. Goaltender Darren Pang also played in Chicago for three years. Although Gary Roberts did not create any headlines in the 1984 Memorial Cup, his tenacity impressed the Calgary Flames, who picked him twelfth overall in the subsequent entry draft. Roberts would return to Memorial Cup action in 1986 before entering the NHL.

From the Kitchener Rangers, John Tucker went on to play for over a decade with Buffalo, Tampa Bay, Washington and the New York Islanders. Shawn Burr spent time in Detroit, Tampa Bay and San Jose, while Dave Shaw went on to Quebec, the Rangers, Boston and Tampa Bay. David Bruce played over six years in Vancouver, St. Louis and San Jose, while Brian Wilks spent part of four years in Los Angeles. Mike Stevens saw brief action with Vancouver, Boston, the Islanders and Toronto. Goaltender Ray LeBlanc served a brief stint with Chicago.

Ottawa 67's.

The high-scoring Wayne Presley returned to the Memorial Cup tournament in 1985 with the Sault St. Marie Greyhounds.

From the Kamloops Junior Oilers, Dean Evason played for Washington, Hartford, San Jose, Dallas and Calgary. Ryan Stewart and Jim Camazzola both had short NHL stints, Stewart in Winnipeg and Camazzola in Chicago. Defenceman Ken Daneyko went on to a solid career in New Jersey, winning the Stanley Cup in 1995. Doug Bodger stepped up to become a fine two-way defenceman in Pittsburgh, Buffalo and San Jose. Laforge went on to become one of the biggest coaching failures in the history of the NHL, winning only four of twenty games for the Vancouver Canucks before general manager Harry Neale replaced him.

From the Laval Voisins, Mario Lemieux became one of the greatest players in NHL history with the Pittsburgh Penguins. He completely dominated the league, as he had in his junior days. Lemieux's many individual awards include the Calder, Conn Smythe (twice), Art Ross (six times), Bill Masterton (once) and Hart Trophies (three times). He won the Stanley Cup with Pittsburgh in 1991 and 1992 and retired from the game in 1997. Vincent Damphousse became a reliable point-per-game producer with Toronto, Edmonton and Montreal. He played on the Montreal Canadiens championship team in 1993. Michel Mongeau saw brief action in St. Louis and Tampa Bay. Steven Finn spent a number of seasons in the NHL, mostly in Quebec, while Bobby Dollas put in time with Winnipeg, Quebec, Detroit and Anaheim.

The **1985** Memorial Cup

Reflecting the growing popularity of the Memorial Cup, the location of the 1985 tournament was partly determined by television. The initial site was the Shawinigan Municipal Auditorium, but the building was supported by a number of pillars that interfered with television coverage. As a result, the Centre Marcel-Dionne in Drummondville was selected, and all of the games save the first two were played there.

Although they were playing on home ice for only their first two games, coach Ron Lapointe's Shawinigan Cataractes hosted the tournament. The team finished first in the QMJHL regular season standings with a 48–19–1 mark. In the league final though, they were defeated by the Verdun Junior Canadiens. Shawinigan was hoping to become the first QMJHL club to win the national title since the 1981 Cornwall Royals, and the first Quebec-based team to triumph since the 1971 Quebec Remparts. Up front, the Cataractes featured Mario Belanger, Dave Kasper and Sergio Momesso. With Robert Desjardins in goal, they were led defensively by Yves Beaudoin and Patrice Lefebvre.

The Verdun Junior Canadiens emerged as QMJHL champions after eliminating the Hull Olympiques, Chicoutimi Sagueneens and the Cataractes. The Junior Canadiens were coached by former Laval bench boss Jean Begin, who had taken over from former Montreal Canadien Yvon Lambert. Verdun was led by captain Claude Lemieux, and also included sixteen-year-old Jimmy Carson, Everett Sanipass, Jerome Carrier, Carl Vermette, defenceman Ron Annear and goaltender Yves Lavoie. The general manager of Verdun was Eric Taylor, who had held the same position with the great Montreal Junior Canadiens teams of 1969 and 1970.

Terry Simpson's Prince Albert Raiders were somewhat of a Cinderella story. Only in their third season of major junior league play, the Raiders completed the 1985 season with a 58–11–3 record, the best in Canada.

Led by team captain Dan Hodgson, they were equally formidable in the playoffs, losing only one game in a march past the Calgary Wranglers, Medicine Hat Tigers and Kamloops Blazers. The single loss was an 11–3 thrashing at the hands of the Tigers, who had beaten the Raiders in five of their six regular season meetings. But Prince Albert got the Medicine Hat monkey off its back with four subsequent wins in the WHL east division final. In addition to Hodgson, the Raiders featured Tony Grenier, Dave Pasin, Pat Elynuik, Dave Manson, Ken Baumgartner, Dave Goertz and Emanuel Viveiros.

The Sault Ste. Marie Greyhounds were coached by Terry Crisp, who had won the championship as a player with the Niagara Falls Flyers in 1965. Twenty years later, Crisp steered his Greyhounds to playoff victories over the Kitchener Rangers, Hamilton Steelhawks and Peterborough Petes. NHL prospects on the team included Chris Felix, Bob Probert, Jeff Beukeboom, Rob Zettler, Derek King and Wayne Presley, who had played in the 1984 Memorial Cup with Kitchener.

On May 11, Sault Ste. Marie began the round robin at the Shawinigan Municipal Auditorium. A total of 3,276 fans watched the Greyhounds manage a 4–3 victory over the Cataractes. The first period was rough, but the Greyhounds established control of the contest in the second when the wheels appeared to fall off Shawinigan's skating game. Centre Steve Hollett ripped a high wrist shot past a screened Robert Desjardins to secure the win.

In the next game, Sault Ste. Marie beat Verdun 6–3 at Drummondville. Leftwinger Derek King, the OHL's rookie of the year, scored twice, including the tie-breaker five minutes into the third period. The same day in Shawinigan, the Cataractes whipped Prince Albert 6–2. Referee Jean-Pierre Desaulniers handed out 108 penalty minutes in a rough affair. Alain Bisson had 1 goal and 2 assists.

The tournament then shifted to Drummondville for a match between Prince

Albert and Verdun. Defenceman Dave Goertz scored twice in the 5–3 victory, giving the Raiders some hope. "I have waited three long years for a second chance," said Goertz, a member of the Regina Pats team that lost to Portland in the 1982 WHL final.

One more win would have given the Greyhounds a place in the final game, but the Raiders handed Sault Ste. Marie its first loss of the tournament instead. Dale McFee scored three times and Tony Grenier scored twice in the 8–6 triumph. Hodgson set a tournament record with five assists in one game, giving him eight helpers in just three games. Hodgson's record, like many in the Memorial Cup record books, is unofficial because all records set before the institution of the round robin format in 1972 have not been kept track of. The two teams were tied 2–2 after the first period, but Prince Albert pulled away in the second. They went into the second intermission with a 7–3 lead. The Greyhounds narrowed the gap in the third period but ran out of time.

On May 15, Shawinigan earned a spot in the final with their 5–1 victory over Verdun. The game's first star, goaltender Desjardins, came within a shade of posting the first shutout in Memorial Cup play since 1982. But the 5'5", 130-pound netminder was beaten on a Franco DeSantis slapshot at 18:35 of the third period. The next evening brought the semi-final matchup between Prince Albert and Sault Ste. Marie. The Raiders pulled themselves into the final game by hammering the Broncos 8–3. "When you play a team twice in three nights and they not only beat you both times but score 16 goals in the process," Terry Crisp observed, "you have to give them full credit."

The line of Hodgson, Grenier and Pasin combined for 13 points. Hodgson had a goal and 4 assists, giving him a record-tying 12 assists in the tournament. This equalled the total set in 1982 by Kitchener Ranger Jeff Larmer. Pasin had 2 goals and 3 assists, while Grenier had 2 goals and an assist, giving him a tournament-leading 7 goals. "I think our outstanding player tonight was [goaltender Ward] Komonosky," Prince Albert coach Simpson said. "I'm really happy for him because some of our critics wonder about our goaltending."

For the first time since 1974, a team from Ontario did not have a crack at the Memorial Cup. Prince Albert cruised to their first Memorial Cup in a decisive 6–1 win over the Cataractes. A pro-Shawinigan crowd of 3,865 jammed the Marcel Dionne Centre, equipped with every noisemaking device conceivable. But only fifteen seconds into the game, they were hushed as Dean Braham put the Raiders' first shot past Desjardins. Steve Gotaas scored early in the second period to increase the lead. Shortly thereafter, Ken Baumgartner served notice that the Raiders weren't about to relax. He took on Steve Masse of Shawinigan in a heavyweight scrap between a pair of 6'1", 200-pound defencemen. "Sometimes you've just got to go in there and tune some of the boys in," Hodgson said. "Kenny Baumgartner did that. I thought that was a big part of the game." By picking up 1 more assist, Hodgson finished the tournament with 13, breaking the previous record by Jeff Larmer.

The Raiders scored four times in the second to put the game beyond reach. Mario Belanger spoiled Komonosky's shutout with a powerplay goal early in the third. Nevertheless, Komonosky's performance earned him the Hap Emms

Memorial Trophy as the tournament's outstanding goaltender, as well as the game's first star.

"The big guy slammed the door and kicked the lights out today," said Hodgson of the Raiders' unheralded goaltender. Hodgson's 13 assists and single goal in the tournament earned him the Stafford Smythe Memorial Trophy as Most Valuable Player.

Terry Simpson, who had coached Canada's national junior team to the 1985 world title in Helsinki, Finland, put the Memorial Cup win in a class by itself. "This is much more gratifying because we've spent the last three years building this club," Simpson said. "It's a victory that the entire organization can celebrate."

Shawinigan coach Lapointe, whose club was outhustled and outmuscled by Prince Albert, conceded a hard, tough game was not enough to beat the Raiders. "I think we were the underdog in this tournament from the start," he said. "I think we really showed a lot of guts. We lost the second period today 4–0, and that was the match right there."

Prince Albert and Shawinigan dominated the all-star team, with the Raiders' Hodgson at centre, Tony Grenier at left wing and Dave Goertz on defence. Shawinigan placed Desjardins in goal, Yves Beaudoin on defence and Patrice Lefebvre at right wing. Grenier was named most sportsmanlike player.

In addition to his playoff accolades, Hodgson was named the 1985 CMJHL Player of the Year. He played in four seasons with the Toronto Maple Leafs and Vancouver Canucks, never able to fully elevate his game to the NHL level.

Other Raiders who moved on to the NHL include Ken Baumgartner, who took his aggressive style to Los Angeles, the Islanders, Toronto and Anaheim. Pat Elynuik spent a number of seasons with Winnipeg, Washington, Tampa Bay and Ottawa. Steve Gotaas played three years for Pittsburgh and Minnesota. Dave Goertz had a stint with Pittsburgh, and Emanuel Viveiros saw brief action in Minnesota. Kim Issel, a big rightwinger, became an Edmonton farmhand and made it into some Oilers games in the late

Terry Crisp, coach of the Sault Ste. Marie Greyhounds, went on to the big leagues and lead the Calgary Flames to a 1989 Stanley Cup victory.

1980s. Defenceman Dave Manson enjoyed the most success in the NHL, patrolling the blueline for Chicago, Edmonton, Winnipeg, Phoenix and Montreal.

From the Shawinigan Cataractes, Sergio Momesso went on to regular service in the NHL with Montreal, Vancouver, Toronto, the Rangers and St. Louis.

Claude Lemieux of the Verdun Junior Canadiens became one of the NHL's premier clutch performers, playing with Montreal, New Jersey and the Colorado Avalanche. In his first ten years in the pros, he won the Stanley Cup with every team he played on: Montreal in 1986, New Jersey in 1995 and Colorado in 1996. He was awarded the Conn Smythe Trophy in 1995.

Other pro-bound Junior Canadiens included Jimmy Carson, who went from being one of the most promising young players in the league with Los Angeles, Edmonton and Detroit to a fourth-line journeyman in Vancouver and Hartford. Everett Sanipass played five years with Chicago and Quebec. Derek King would have another stab at the Cup with the Oshawa Generals in 1987.

From the Sault Ste. Marie Greyhounds, Bob Probert enjoyed crunching success on the ice with Detroit and Chicago, becoming one of the NHL's most popular players for his fighting abilities. Jeff Beukeboom patrolled the blueline for a number of years with Edmonton and the Rangers, winning Stanley Cups with the Oilers in 1987, 1988 and 1990 and the Rangers in 1994. Rob Zettler brought his stay-at-home game to Minnesota, San Jose, Philadelphia and Toronto. Chris Felix saw brief action in Washington, while Wayne Groulx and Tyler Larter served stints in Quebec and Washington respectively. Ken Sabourin also saw spot duty with Washington and Calgary. Wayne Presley moved on to a solid NHL career, mostly in Buffalo and Chicago.

Terry Simpson, Ron Lapointe and Terry Crisp all went on to coach in the big league. Simpson stood behind the bench for the Islanders, Philadelphia and Winnipeg. Lapointe had the unfortunate but brief job of coaching the hapless Quebec Nordiques of the late-1980s. Crisp coached the Calgary Flames, with whom he won the Stanley Cup in 1989, and Tampa Bay.

Prince Albert Raiders.

The 1986 Memorial Cup

Three years after first hosting the Memorial Cup tournament, the Portland Winter Hawks were called upon to do it again. The 1986 tournament was originally slated to be hosted by the reborn New Westminster Bruins franchise, but the team pulled out because Expo '86 in Vancouver was expected to place too great a strain on the local hotel facilities. As the WHL team with the best record as of December 15, Portland was awarded the tournament. The Winter Hawks hosted a pair of high-rolling squads in the Kamloops Blazers and Hull Olympiques, as well as the workmanlike and determined Guelph Platers.

Portland finished second to Kamloops in the west division and lost to the Blazers five games to one in the best-of-nine division final. With Ken Hodge still behind the bench, the Winter Hawks were led in scoring by centre Ray Podloski and leftwinger Dave Waldie. Other key players included Dave Archibald, Bob Foglietta and Blaine Chrest.

The Kamloops Blazers finished the regular season in first place with 102 points. Cruising through the playoffs, they eliminated Seattle, Portland and Medicine Hat. The Blazers were a powerful team that included captain Mark Kachowski, Greg Hawgood, Rudy Poeschek, Greg Evtushevski, Robin Bawa and Rob Brown, back for his second Memorial Cup tournament after playing with the Kamloops Junior Oilers in 1984. They were coached by Ken Hitchcock.

Guelph's appearance in the 1986 playoffs was their first since returning to the OHL in 1983. During the 1984–85 season, the Platers had finished with a dismal 47 points in sixty-six games. A year later, their record was 84 points in sixty-six games. Much of the improvement was credited to Jacques Martin, the 1985–86 OHL coach of the year. Brought over from the Peterborough Petes by manager Rob Holody, Martin immediately overhauled the Platers, giving them a sound defensive foundation.

The new approach served the Platers well heading into the playoffs. They went 15–3–2 in the post-season run to the OHL title, defeating the Sudbury Wolves, Windsor Spitfires and Belleville Bulls. Guelph included captain Paul Brydges, defencemen Steve Chiasson and Kerry Huffman, and leftwinger Gary Roberts, who won the Memorial Cup with Ottawa in 1984.

The Hull Olympiques were a high-profile team, coached by Pat Burns and owned by Wayne Gretzky. They had a pair of sharpshooters in Luc Robitaille and Guy Rouleau, both of whom finished at the top of the QMJHL in scoring with 191 points. Rouleau won the crown, as his numbers included 92 goals compared to Robitaille's 68.

"Almost as much as the Oilers are hated, we were just as hated in Quebec," said coach Burns, referring to the swaggering Edmonton Oilers of the 1980s. Hull was riding high in 1986, having scored fifteen consecutive post-season victories over the Shawinigan Cataractes, St. Jean Beavers and Drummondville Voltigeurs. Robitaille scored 44 points over the playoff run. "I think Hull has the team to win the Memorial Cup," said Voltigeurs coach Michel Parizeau after his team's defeat in the Quebec league final. "They have the talent, depth and balance. What they have that the Ontario and west don't have is speed."

On opening day of the 1986 Memorial Cup tournament, Hull used its imposing offence to secure a 7–5 victory over Portland. They outshot the Winter Hawks 56–35. Guy Rouleau tied a mark set by Joe Contini of the 1976 Hamilton Fincups, notching 6 points in the game (3 goals and 3 assists). Luc Robitaille scored twice. On Portland, Bob Foglietta also scored a hat trick and goaltender Lance Carlsen stopped 49 shots in a strong effort. The other opening day matchup had Guelph meeting Kamloops. The Platers defeated the Blazers 5–3 in a close contest. Gary Roberts scored twice for Guelph, who were trailing 2–1 entering the final period. But the Platers dished out some perseverant forecheck-ing, yielding 4 goals. Mike Murray scored the winner with four minutes left. "It was a typical game for us," coach Martin said. "We had to feel the other team out and wait for the opportunities."

In the two games played on the following day, Portland dumped Guelph 6–4 and Hull scored a 5–4 overtime victory over the Blazers. Leftwinger Dave McLay led the Portland attack with 2 goals while Carlsen turned in an acrobatic goal-tending performance, turning back 39 shots. "Guelph is a rugged club and we wanted to play the game in the middle to stay away from their aggressiveness along the boards," coach Hodge said. "It was an important victory for us after los-ing our opening game."

In the Olympiques' victory over Kamloops, Guy Rouleau scored at 1:37 of overtime to give Hull its second win. This assured the Olympiques of moving beyond the round robin portion of the tournament. Rouleau's winner was his sec-ond goal of the game and fifth of the tournament, giving him an incredible 9 points in two games.

The next evening, Hull met the Platers, who showed the first sign that they might cause problems for the Olympiques powerhouse. Guelph implemented a tough, tight-checking game plan and snatched a 3–1 victory. Their defence, anchored solidly by three-year junior veteran Chiasson and the rookie Huffman, drove the opposing forwards to the outside, forcing them to shoot at goalie Steve Guenette from poor angles. Mike Murray scored twice for the Platers, the winner coming at 9:19 of the second period. "We knew Hull was a skating club and we needed to come out hitting," Murray said. "We had a good forechecking game to keep the puck in their end of the rink."

Next, the Winter Hawks and Blazers met before 7,388 Portland fans. With a win, Portland would eliminate the Blazers from the tournament. Kamloops stayed alive, however, with a nail-biting 6–5 victory. Ken Morrison scored at 17:35 of the third period to force another game between the teams.

Taking a 4–1 lead in the second period, Kamloops looked ready to walk away with the win. But a double-minor penalty to Blazer defenceman David Marcinyshyn allowed the Winter Hawks back in, and they scored twice on the power play.

The normally easygoing Hitchcock was so incensed that he punched Marcinyshyn in the face during the intermission. "I've never done anything like that ever before in hockey," Hitchcock said. "I also can't remember the last time we got sucked in like that." Of the match to follow he said, "We've got a few scores to settle early in the game. Portland got away with a few things tonight when the score was close in the third."

Bob Foglietta enjoyed his second 3-goal game of the tournament for the Winter Hawks, while Rob Brown led the Blazers with 2.

In the rematch, Kamloops was disciplined and focussed, hammering the Winter Hawks 8–1. Greg Hawgood contributed 3 goals and an assist to the Blazers' cause. This victory moved the Blazers into the semi-final against Hull. "We weren't 8–1 bad," Hodge said. "They had a hot goaltender who got the job done and ours didn't."

"We scored on our few chances and they didn't when they had good chances," Hitchcock observed. "We're happy to still be here after almost being shown the exit."

In their semi-final match, the Blazers found themselves on the other end of a blowout. They fell 9–3 to the Olympiques—or rather to Robitaille and Rouleau. The two snipers made all the difference for Hull, as Robitaille had 4 goals and 1 assist while Rouleau had 2 goals and 4 assists. This was the second time in the tournament Rouleau had tied the Memorial Cup record of 6 points in a single game.

"We weren't sharp and we weren't aggressive," Hitchcock said. "Guys that normally fill the net were shooting high and all over the place. Burns was smart. He got our best checkers away from his top line, and we couldn't get away with the double line changes like we did earlier in the tournament."

"We haven't even yet played up to our potential," Hull captain Rick Hayward said. "Tonight we showed just some of the things we can do."

Twelve hours later, Hull played the final game of the 1986 Memorial Cup. The players had to wake up early for an 11:00 a.m. start so the Canadian Television Network could run the game in the afternoon for the eastern-viewing audience.

As in these teams' previous meeting, the Platers played the game on their terms, taking the body and displaying tight forechecking, sound goaltending and ruthless opportunism. They defeated the Olympiques 6–2 to win the Memorial Cup in front of 4,166 fans.

Four of Guelph's goals came during two lethal strikes. Rightwinger Luciano Fagioli got 2 goals eleven seconds apart in the opening period, while Mike Murray and Allan MacIsaac scored thirteen seconds apart in the second. Exploiting some fragility in the Hull side, Lonnie Loach and Keith Miller completed the scoring. The Platers fired 37 shots at Hull goaltenders Eric Bohemier and Desjardins, while the Olympiques aimed 33 on the ever-reliable Guenette. Hull received their goals from Benoit Brunet and Robitaille.

"After a four-day layoff, we thought the key to the game would be the first period," Jacques Martin explained. "We broke the period down into four segments of five minutes and our objective was not to get beat in any of those segments. You want to play in their zone against a team like Hull because they are so dangerous in your zone. We had to force the play on them and take the middle away in the neutral zone. We're not pretty or fancy, but we get in your face and go hard. The players all year have had the character and discipline it takes to be a winner."

Pat Burns said he was not looking for an excuse in the lack of time between the semi-final and final games. "There's no reason to be tired when you're winning," he said. "Guelph worked harder than we did today."

Steve Chiasson was named the tournament MVP and Guenette the top goaltender. The all-star team featured Guenette in goal, Chiasson and Blazer Ron Shudra on defence, Guy Rouleau and Luc Robitaille of Hull at centre and left wing respectively, and Portland's Bob Foglietta on the right side. Kerry Huffman of Guelph won the George Parsons Trophy for sportsmanship. Rouleau tied the tournament record of 16 points set by Kitchener's Jeff Larmer in 1982, while Robitaille's 8 goals tied the record set by Dale Hawerchuk of the Cornwall Royals in 1981.

From the Guelph Platers, Steve Guenette saw brief NHL service with Pittsburgh and Calgary. Steve Chiasson established himself as a solid defenceman with Detroit and Calgary, while Kerry Huffman enjoyed a number of seasons with Philadelphia, Quebec and Ottawa. Lonnie Loach served stints in Ottawa, Los Angeles and Anaheim. Gary Roberts emerged as a fierce competitor in Calgary, winning the Stanley Cup with the Flames in 1989 and scoring 53 goals in

Guelph Platers. Back row (l to r): Robb Graham, Luc Sabourin, Bill Loshaw, Luciano Fagioli, Marc Tournier, Lonnie Loach, Rob Arabski, Brian Hayton, Tom Nickolau. Middle row: Kerry Huffman, Denis Larocque, Allan MacIsaac, Paul Kelly, Mike Murray, John McIntyre, Jamie McKinley, Keith Miller, Chuck Edwards (trainer). Front row: Steve Guenette, Jacques Martin (coach), Steve Chiasson, Alex Campagnaro (vice president), Paul Brydges, Robert Holody (general manager), Gary Roberts, Andy Helmuth. Inset: (left) Joseph Holody (president and governor), (right) Alex Dudnick (trainer).

1991–92. John McIntyre, a rookie for the Platers, developed into an NHL role player and played with Toronto, Los Angeles, the New York Rangers and Vancouver.

Luc Robitaille of the Hull Olympiques won the Calder Trophy for the 1986–87 season. He became one of the NHL's most prolific scorers with Los Angeles, Pittsburgh and the Rangers. Benoit Brunet moved on to the Montreal Canadiens' left wing after competing for the Memorial Cup again with Hull two years later. Stephane Matteau played with Calgary, Chicago, the Rangers and St. Louis. Martin Simard saw some pro action in three seasons with Calgary and Tampa Bay and Jean-Marc Routhier had a brief term with the Quebec Nordiques.

From the Kamloops Blazers, Rob Brown saw action with Pittsburgh, Hartford, Dallas and Chicago. In 1988–89, he scored 115 points in sixty-eight games on a line with Mario Lemieux, but his career plummeted from there, eventually landing in the minors. Greg Hawgood wore the uniforms of Boston, Edmonton, Philadelphia, Pittsburgh and San Jose. Rudy Poeschek played with the New York Rangers, Winnipeg and Tampa Bay, and captain Mark Kachowski spent three years with Pittsburgh. Robin Bawa skated with Washington, Vancouver, San Jose and Anaheim. Ron Shudra and David Marcinyshyn each had stints in the NHL, Shudra with Edmonton and Marcinyshyn with New Jersey, Quebec and the New York Islanders.

From the Portland Winter Hawks, Dave Archibald played with Minnesota, the Rangers, Ottawa and the Islanders. Glen Wesley made an impact with Boston, Hartford and Carolina. Jeff Finley became a stay-at-home defenceman for the New York Islanders and Philadelphia Flyers. Ray Podloski saw brief action with Boston.

Both Jacques Martin and Pat Burns coached in the NHL, Martin in St. Louis and Ottawa and Burns in Montreal, Toronto and Boston. A former policeman, Burns took the Canadiens to the Stanley Cup final in 1989. He won the Jack Adams Trophy in 1992–93.

The **1987** Memorial Cup

In 1973, Bryan Maxwell played with the losing Medicine Hat Tigers in the Memorial Cup championship. Fourteen years later, he was behind the Medicine Hat bench, taking on the host Oshawa Generals and Longueuil Chevaliers in the first three-team tournament since 1982.

The OHL Governors chose to have the Leyden and Emms division championship teams meet in a best-of-seven "Super Series," with the winner earning host-team status for the Memorial Cup tournament. After this series, the teams would proceed into the playoffs for the OHA title.

The Super Series pitted the Oshawa Generals against coach Bert Templeton's North Bay Centennials. The Generals prevailed in seven games. Having earned the right to host the Memorial Cup, Oshawa entered the playoffs, defeating the Kingston Canadians and Peterborough Petes. They met North Bay again in the league final and prevailed once more in seven games. Oshawa had a formidable team. Managed by Sherry Bassin and coached by Paul Theriault, the 1987 Generals established a team record with 101 points on the season. They received much of their offence from the "LSD line" of Lee Giffin, Scott McCrory and Derek King, who had played with the Sault Ste. Marie Greyhounds in the 1985 Memorial Cup. McCrory won the OHL scoring title and was voted the league's player of the year. Captained by Jim Paek, the Generals also included Jeff Daniels, Gord Murphy and goaltender Jeff Hackett.

In the QMJHL playoffs, the Longueuil Chevaliers were first-place finishers in the Robert LeBel division. Coached by Guy Chouinard, they survived a first-series round robin that included Laval, Hull and St. Jean. Next, Longueuil met the Laval Titan in a best-of-seven division final. It was an incredible series that saw the Chevaliers lose the first three games, then score four consecutive victories. Longueuil went on to defeat Chicoutimi for the league title. The Chevaliers started the regular season with Guy Lapointe as their general manager, but Lapointe returned to the NHL as an assistant coach with the Quebec Nordiques and was replaced by former Montreal Canadiens' goalie Michel "Bunny" Larocque. The Chevaliers had Robert Desjardins in goal, making his third consecutive appearance in the Memorial Cup after playing with Shawinigan in 1985 and Hull in 1986. Mario Debenedictis, Yves Racine, Ron Stern and high-scoring forward Marc Saumier were other key players in the lineup.

With Bryan Maxwell in his first season as coach, the Medicine Hat Tigers finished on top of the WHL's east division. They were a balanced club, with one 100-point scorer in Mark Pederson and ten players with 64 points or more. Trevor Linden, Rob DiMaio, Dean Chynoweth, Neil Brady, Guy Phillips and goaltender Mark Fitzpatrick were other notable players on the Medicine Hat roster.

The Tigers opened the playoffs against the Moose Jaw Warriors, winning in five games. They moved on to face the Saskatoon Blades, this time going seven games. In the WHL final, Medicine Hat survived another seven-game struggle against the Portland Winter Hawks. The Tigers had faced elimination four times in their last two series, developing a resilience that became a defining characteristic of the team. "It was our never-say-die attitude that prevailed and allowed us to beat Moose Jaw, Saskatoon and Portland," coach Maxwell said.

The Memorial Cup final opened on May 9 at the Oshawa Civic Auditorium. The Generals edged past Longueuil 3–2 before a crowd of 3,555. Jeff Daniels opened the scoring for Oshawa, and Ron Stern replied for Longueuil late in the first period. Oshawa moved ahead on goals by one of Canadian junior hockey's first European imports, Finnish defenceman Petri Matikainen, and Sean Williams, who stuffed a rebound past a sprawled Desjardins for the winner. As the game came to an end, a bizarre free-for-all erupted. Stern jumped Oshawa's Gord Murphy, prompting Shayne Doyle to leave the Oshawa bench and intervene. Things were beginning to settle down when a woman seated behind the Longueuil bench jumped onto the ice and hit Doyle with a hockey glove, followed by a slap to Doyle's face. Ron Stern, who had been on his way to the dressing room, returned to the ice and resumed brawling with the Oshawa players.

"She is lucky she didn't take a punch in the chops," said Oshawa coach

Stopping shots for the Memorial Cup-winning Medicine Hat Tigers, Mark Fitzpatrick was named outstanding goaltender for the 1987 series.

Theriault, who suspected that the woman had some connection to Stern. "Based on the way he reacted, she must have been a relative or girlfriend or something." Stern replied that he had no idea who the woman was and hadn't seen her attack Doyle. "I didn't see any of that," he said. "One of our players was there and there were four or five players after him."

Both the Generals and Chevaliers were fined $250 for the brawl, and the OHL was fined $5,000 for not properly ensuring the security of the players. Doyle and Stern received one-game suspensions.

The Generals notched their second win over Medicine Hat 5–3, with Lee Giffin scoring 2 goals including the winner. The Tigers had held a 3–2 lead at the end of the second, but were called for two penalties in the final minute of the period. The Generals seized this opportunity, scoring with the man advantage forty-four seconds into the third to tie it up, and getting the go-ahead goal one second after the Tigers returned to full strength.

At times, the game was vicious. Referee David Lynch cracked down on both sides, assigning 150 minutes in penalties. Mark Kuntz of Medicine Hat and Tony Joseph of Oshawa both received match penalties and were handed one-game suspensions a day later.

In the next game, Medicine Hat met Longueuil before 3,360 fans. Rob DiMaio scored 3 goals to help the Tigers to a 4–2 triumph. One of the Chevaliers' key offensive players, Marc Saumier, spent more time in the penalty box than on the ice, sitting out a total of eighteen minutes. He was handed a misconduct by referee John Willsie for throwing water on the timekeeper.

The Generals improved their record to 3–0 and earned themselves a bye into the championship game with a 6–3 decision over Longueuil. Late in the second period, Oshawa got 2 goals from Scott McCrory and Scott Mahoney thirty-four seconds apart, breaking open a close 2–1 game. The Chevaliers' Richard Laplante and Real Godin scored twice early in the third to climb back to within 1. But Oshawa put the game out of reach with 2 quick goals from Barry Burkholder and Lee Giffin.

"They showed what they are all about," said Oshawa coach Theriault of the opposition. "It went from 4–1 to 4–3 like that, and all of a sudden, it is a hockey game again."

With Oshawa now moving into the final, Medicine Hat and Longueuil prepared for a two-game, total-goal semi-final. The Tigers went a long way to ensure themselves a spot in the final by running up a formidable 6–0 win in the first game. They were led by Jeff Wenaas with a pair, and Rod Williams, Dale Kushner, Wayne McBean and Guy Phillips added singles. Goaltender Fitzpatrick blocked 19 shots to record the shutout. Faced with a 6–0 goals deficit, the Chevaliers had their work cut out for them heading into the second game against the Tigers. They didn't even come close. The Tigers skated to a 3–1 victory, winning the semi-final by a score of 9–1. Medicine Hat received goals from Scott McCrady, Wenaas and Kushner.

The title match between the Generals and Tigers took place on May 16 at the Oshawa Civic Centre with 3,564 fans in attendance. Trevor Linden, who had just turned seventeen years old, took the first steps toward establishing his reputation as a strong playoff performer. He scored twice to help Medicine Hat to a 6–2 victory and the Memorial Cup. Linden beat Jeff Hackett less than two minutes into the first period, and Guy Phillips followed up with another Medicine Hat marker. McCrory got one back for Oshawa, but Linden fired another before the period ended.

McCrory cut the Tigers' lead to 3–2 in the second, but Kushner tallied a crucial insurance marker at 17:10 on the powerplay. "The fourth goal was the straw

Medicine Hat Tigers.

that broke the camel's back," defenceman Dean Morton said. "It came at a bad time."

"Guys like Pederson, Phillips and Kushner carried us through the playoffs by scoring some big goals," Linden said, "but I guess it was my turn to score today."

"They were tremendous," Theriault said of the Tigers, who had played their third game in four days. "The effort was there, but nothing was happening for us because they were on our tail all game."

In the Tigers' dressing room, an exuberant Bryan Maxwell was drenched in champagne by his players. "It's the highlight of my hockey career," he said. "We played today like we played all year long—with great forechecking and scoring when we got the chances."

"We had a tremendous group of guys and fifteen of them had been disappointed the previous season when we had a good playoff but were eliminated by Kamloops Blazers," Tigers general manager Russ Farwell said. "We had so many returnees from that team and they just weren't going to be denied."

Medicine Hat defenceman Wayne McBean was voted Most Valuable Player, and Mark Fitzpatrick was named the outstanding goaltender. Medicine Hat's McBean, Fitzpatrick, centre Jeff Wenaas, leftwinger Dale Kushner and rightwinger Guy Phillips were selected for the all-star team, as was Oshawa defenceman Gord Murphy. General Scott McCrory was named most sportsmanlike player.

From the Oshawa Generals, Derek King became a reliable performer with the Islanders, Whalers and Maple Leafs while Jeff Daniels played a few seasons in Pittsburgh and Florida. Jim Paek skated with Pittsburgh, Los Angeles and Ottawa, winning the Stanley Cup with the Penguins in 1991 and 1992. Lee Giffin played twenty-seven games for Pittsburgh from 1986–88. Gord Murphy played with Philadelphia, Boston and Florida. Kevin Miehm saw action in St. Louis, while Tony Joseph and Dean Morton both served NHL stints, Joseph with Winnipeg and Morton with Detroit. Goaltender Jeff Hackett became a starter with the New York Islanders, San Jose and Chicago.

From the Longueuil Chevaliers, Yves Racine played in Detroit, Philadelphia, Montreal, San Jose, Calgary and Tampa Bay. Ron Stern brought grit and character to the Canucks and Flames.

The core of the 1987 Medicine Hat Tigers would return to Memorial Cup competition the following year. Graduate Dale Kushner went on to play with the New York Islanders and Philadelphia Flyers in the NHL.

The **1988** Memorial Cup

The 1988 Memorial Cup was held in Chicoutimi, a town of about 50,000 people located in Quebec's Laurentian Mountains. Chicoutimi is the home town of two of hockey's early stars, Georges Vezina, the "Chicoutimi Cucumber," who played goal with the Montreal Canadiens from 1916 to 1924, and Johnny "Black Cat" Gagnon, who played for the Boston Bruins, New York Americans and

Montreal Canadiens in the thirties. The 1988 Medicine Hat Tigers, Windsor Spitfires, Drummondville Voltigeurs and Hull Olympiques sought to make their own history in Chicoutimi.

Chicoutimi had their major junior club, the Sagueneens, but they were not guaranteed a berth in the tournament. The Sagueneens managed to finish first in their division for the regular season, but were eliminated in the QMJHL playoffs. Instead, the Hull Olympiques were Quebec champions heading into the tournament, with the Drummondville Voltigeurs runners-up. Hull had eliminated Granby and Laval to win the Lebel division in the QMJHL playoffs. In the Dilio division, Drummondville took out Victoriaville and Shawinigan. Hull rebounded from a three-games-to-one deficit to score a triumph over the Voltigeurs for the championship.

Coached by Alain Vigneault, Hull finished atop the QMJHL during the regular season. The team's top scorers were Marc Saumier, who had played with Longueuil in the 1987 Memorial Cup, and Benoit Brunet, who participated in the 1986 tournament with Hull. Their lineup included rookie Martin Gelinas, Stephane Quintal, Daniel Shank and goaltender Jason Glickman. Drummondville was backstopped by Frederic Chabot, relying on key players Rob Murphy, Martin Bergeron, Simon Gagne and Mario Mercier.

The Medicine Hat Tigers were returning for a second consecutive run at the championship, this time with a new coach. Bryan Maxwell had left to become an assistant coach with the Los Angeles Kings, and replacing him was former NHL defenceman (and future Kings coach) Barry Melrose.

Medicine Hat's regular-season performance reached a higher level when defenceman Wayne McBean, who had started the year in the NHL with Los Angeles, returned to the Tigers. With McBean in its lineup, Medicine Hat lost only six games, finishing in second place in the WHL's east division. The Tigers took out the Prince Albert Raiders, Saskatoon Blades and Kamloops Blazers in the WHL final. In addition to McBean, the Tigers had a number of players returning from the previous year's championship team, including Trevor Linden, Rob DiMaio, Mark Pederson, Dean Chynoweth and Mark Fitzpatrick.

The OHL champion Windsor Spitfires set seven team records in 1987–88, achieving the best offensive and defensive statistics in their history as well as the most points. Entering the playoffs, the team had won thirty-five of their last thirty-six games and were a lethal 54–0 whenever they took a lead into the third period. The Spitfires were coached by Tom Webster, who had won the Memorial Cup as a player with the 1968 Niagara Falls Flyers. Also aboard were captain Adam Graves, Darrin Shannon, Darryl Shannon and goalie Pat Jablonski. In the playoffs, Windsor polished off the Kitchener Rangers, Hamilton Steelhawks and Peterborough Petes without losing a match. They became the first team in OHA history to sweep their way to the league title. "The only streak I'm concerned about is winning each game," Webster said.

"They have built for this year," said Tigers coach Melrose, unwilling to be intimidated by the formidable numbers generated by the Spitfires. "We can't compare our statistics with theirs." Windsor went up against Drummondville in the first game of the Memorial Cup on May 7. The Spitfires kept their streak alive with an 8–3 win. The hard-hitting game was watched by 2,958 fans. Windsor's Peter DeBoer fired 2 goals as the Spitfires jumped out to a 4–0 lead early in the second period.

Two games were played on the following day. The first had Medicine Hat enjoying a 7–1 rout of Drummondville. The Voltigeurs' Mario Mercier and the Tigers' Darren Taylor squared off in a scrap at the opening faceoff. However, the altercation was upstaged twenty-six seconds later when Medicine Hat's Rob DiMaio scored. The Tigers took a 3–0 lead into the first intermission and did not look back. The second game was a much closer contest, with Windsor edging Hull by a score of 5–4. The Spitfires grabbed a quick 3–0 lead by 4:17 of the first period and hung on for the win.

Medicine Hat kept rolling in their second game. They trounced Hull 7–3 before 2,896 Drummondville fans. "Every time our opposition needs a big goal," Alain Vigneault complained, "they get it." His team was now 0–2 in the tournament, and the coach's frustration was showing. "We just run and run around the net and get nothing." The Tigers played the Spitfires next, in a meeting regarded by many of the 2,000 fans on hand as a preview of the championship game. Windsor scored their twenty-first straight win with a 5–2 triumph, thereby securing a spot in the Memorial Cup final.

The Tigers, trailing 3–2 in the third, got into trouble when they took two major penalties for slashing. First Ryan McGill was sent off for drawing blood after he hacked Adam Graves in the ear. McGill then watched as Brad Hyatt and Ron Jones scored on the ensuing power play, breaking open a previously close game. "When we got those 2 quick goals, that was the turning point," Tom Webster said. Barry Melrose agreed. "You can't kill ten minutes and expect to beat a good club," said Melrose, unhappy with the officiating of referee Dave Jackson. The Medicine Hat coach was also upset with the tournament schedule. "I hope the organizers are happy," he said, pointing out that his team had played three games in three nights. "We had to play the best team the last night. Everything was set up for Windsor to win."

The first team eliminated was the Drummondville Voltigeurs, who bowed out to Hull 5–2 to set up a semi-final rematch between Medicine Hat and Hull, the winner facing Windsor in a one-game showdown. The semi-final at Georges Vezina Arena was a close contest, with the defending champion Tigers pushed to the limit by a determined Hull team. With less than seven minutes left, Darren Taylor broke a 3–3 tie with the game winner, sending Medicine Hat to the title match with a 5–3 victory. Linden opened the scoring, and the teams went back and forth exchanging the lead for some time. By the first intermission, Hull was ahead by 3–2. But Jason Miller tied it for Medicine Hat early in the second, and the teams battled at even terms until Taylor shoved a rebound past Olympiques goalie Jason Glickman to silence the pro-Hull crowd of 2,989 fans. "I'd have to say that was the biggest goal of my life," said Taylor, a defensive forward with 12 goals on the season.

The championship game was one for the ages. A crowd of 3,301 watched the action at Vezina Arena. Flying from the opening faceoff, the Spitfires shot their way to a 3–0 lead only twelve minutes into the game. The Tigers clawed back to

Hull Olympiques' star Martin Gelinas proceeded to the NHL to play for Edmonton, Quebec and Vancouver.

within one by the end of the first, and then took over in the second. They built a 5–4 lead going into the final frame. When the Tigers managed a 2-goal advantage, the momentum and the game seemed to be theirs. But Windsor came back, firing 2 goals to tie the score at 6. With 2:43 left, Mark Pederson scored his second to give the Tigers a 7–6 victory and their second consecutive Memorial Cup.

Other Medicine Hat goals came from Kirby Lindal with two, Mark Woolf, Rob DiMaio and Jason Miller. The Spitfires had a pair from Mike Wolak, the tournament's leading scorer, and singles from Peter DeBoer, Jean-Paul Gorley, Paul Wilkinson and Darrin Shannon. Fitzpatrick, the WHL's second team all-star goalie, was uncharacteristically shaky at the outset but grew steadier as the game went on. "I didn't play well, but the team started to play well," said Fitzpatrick, who was named the tournament's best goaltender. "Somehow or other, I let my concentration slack off in the first period, but I thought I battled back in the second. It was just nerves. I just had to calm down a bit."

Barry Melrose identified a late first-period goal by rookie rightwinger Woolf as the turning point. The goal narrowed Windsor's lead to 3–2 going into the second period. "It gave us time to regroup," Melrose said. "They became unravelled a bit. They hadn't had a team come back on them." While the Tigers' dressing room was awash with champagne, tears flowed in the Spitfires' clubhouse. "I think we're still a better team," said Darrin Shannon. "I can't really believe it. It really hasn't sunk in that we lost."

"The boys are taking it hard," Webster admitted. "It's not easy when you have only lost two games in your last forty. All I can say is we both won a game. I don't think we lost. We ran out of time."

The Memorial Cup triumph capped a remarkable year for a quintet of Tigers. In addition to winning the Memorial Cup twice, DiMaio, Pederson, McCrady, McBean and Linden had earned gold medals with Canada's World Junior Championship team earlier that winter. "It's been a year I'll never forget," DiMaio said. "I have three rings in one year, and that's more than most hockey players get in a career." The tournament all-star team featured the Hat's Mark Fitzpatrick in goal, Linden on right wing, Rob DiMaio at centre and Dean Chynoweth on defence. Windsor's Darrin Shannon was on left wing and Darryl Shannon on defence. Fitzpatrick's award marked the first time in the fourteen-year history of individual trophies that a repeat winner was named, as the Tigers' goalie had also been recognized as the 1987 tournament's best. Rob DiMaio was named Most Valuable Player, with Martin Gelinas voted most sportsmanlike.

From the Medicine Hat Tigers, Trevor Linden was selected second overall in the 1988 NHL entry draft. He became captain of the Vancouver Canucks and played a pivotal role in lifting the team to respectability in the early nineties. Rob DiMaio skated with the Islanders, Tampa Bay, Philadelphia and Boston. Dean Chynoweth saw action with the New York Islanders and Boston. Mark Fitzpatrick played goal with Los Angeles, the Islanders and Florida. Mark Pederson served in Montreal, Philadelphia, San Jose and Detroit.

In 1986, Neil Brady was drafted third overall in the first round by New Jersey. He was given chances with the Devils, Senators and Stars but never established himself as an NHL regular. Wayne McBean also had a relatively disappointing career with the Los Angeles Kings, New York Islanders and Winnipeg Jets. Dan Kordic, a 6'5", 220-pound defenceman, became an intimidating force on the Philadelphia Flyers' blueline. Neil Wilkinson, who had played US College hockey with Michigan State before joining the Tigers, became a solid NHL defenceman with Minnesota, San Jose, Winnipeg, Chicago and Pittsburgh. Ryan McGill skated for Chicago, Philadelphia and Edmonton. Jason Miller went on to see sporadic ice time in New Jersey. Mark Woolf and Murray Garbutt would return to Memorial Cup competition in 1991 with the Spokane Chiefs.

From the Windsor Spitfires, Darrin and Darryl Shannon played in the NHL, with both Winnipeg and Buffalo. While Darrin moved with the Jets to Phoenix, Darryl skated for the Maple Leafs. Pat Jablonski looked after the nets in St. Louis, Tampa Bay and Montreal. Glen Featherstone took his hard-hitting style to St. Louis and Boston. Captain Adam Graves enjoyed an exceptional pro career with Detroit, Edmonton and the Rangers. He won the Stanley Cup with the Oilers in 1990 and with the Rangers in 1994.

Hull Olympiques who proceeded to the NHL include Martin Gelinas, who ground through Edmonton, Quebec and Vancouver. Stephane Quintal skated with Boston, St. Louis, Winnipeg and Montreal. Daniel Shank played in Detroit and Hartford. Rob Murphy of the Drummondville Voltigeurs played in Vancouver, Ottawa and Los Angeles. Goaltender Frederic Chabot was briefly tested in Montreal and Philadelphia.

Tom Webster went on to coach the New York Rangers and the LA Kings. He was succeeded in Los Angeles by Barry Melrose, who guided the Kings to the Stanley Cup final in 1993. Alain Vigneault jumped right into the pressure cooker

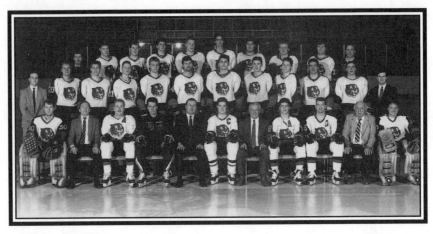

Medicine Hat Tigers.

in 1997, when he began his NHL coaching career with the legendary Montreal Canadiens. In 1990, Medicine Hat Tigers general manager Russ Farwell became the general manager of the Philadelphia Flyers after two very successful years with the WHL's Seattle Thunderbirds. He will always be remembered for being involved in one of the biggest trades in hockey history, obtaining superstar Eric Lindros from Quebec in exchange for Peter Forsberg, five other players, $15 million US and two first-round draft picks.

The **1989** Memorial Cup

On December 30, 1986, a bus carrying the Swift Current Broncos to a game in Regina ran off the road in poor weather. Four players—Scott Kruger, Trent Kresse, Brent Ruff and Chris Mantyka—were killed. The tragedy stunned the country, and left the Swift Current community and the WHL badly shaken. The Broncos were a fledgling organization that had started operation in the fall of 1986, following a twelve-year absence of major junior hockey in Swift Current. The community rallied around the grieving team, and within two years it was ready to claim its first Memorial Cup. The 1989 tournament was played in Saskatoon. The OHL sent the Peterborough Petes and the QMJHL sent the Laval Titan. But it came down to an all-Saskatchewan battle between the Broncos and the host Saskatoon Blades.

The Broncos had the best record in the Canadian Hockey League in 1988–89. They were 33–2–1 on Swift Current ice, setting a WHL record for most wins at home. Five Broncos scored 100 or more points: Sheldon Kennedy, Tim Tisdale, Peter Kasowski, Brian Sakic and defenceman Dan Lambert. Darren Kruger finished with 97 points and set a WHL record with 63 powerplay assists. Kruger's twin brother Trevor was the team's goalie, and their brother Scott was one of the players who died in the 1986 accident. The Broncos became the first team in WHL history to sweep through the playoffs with no losses or ties, sweeping through Moose Jaw, Saskatoon and Portland. "We have the team to do it this year," Tim Tisdale said. "If we can't get up for four games, we don't belong there."

In the regular season, the Marcel Comeau-coached Saskatoon Blades finished second to Swift Current by 25 points and bowed out to the Broncos in the WHL east division final. The Blades' key players included captain Tracey Katelnikoff, defenceman Ken Sutton and goaltender Mike Greenlay. The city of Saskatoon was making its second appearance in the Memorial Cup. In 1936, the Saskatoon Wesleys had bowed to the West Toronto Nationals in the final. The Blades, having been around for more than twenty years without a trip to the national championship, were not favourites in 1989, but they were more than ready to end the drought.

In the OHL, coach Dick Todd's Peterborough Petes sidelined the Belleville Bulls, Cornwall Royals and Niagara Falls Thunder to claim the league title. Peterborough's lineup included defenceman Bryan Hayton, who had won the Memorial Cup with Guelph in 1986, as well as captain Dave Lorentz, Tie Domi, Jamie Hicks, Ross Wilson and seventeen-year-old Mike Ricci.

The Laval Titan were a high-offence team with three 100-point men in Donald Audette, Denis Chalifoux and Claude Lapointe, as well as attack-minded defenceman Patrice Brisebois. In February, the Titan had strengthened their lineup by trading for three players from the Verdun Junior Canadiens. Joining Laval were rightwinger Steve Parent, defenceman Marc Picard and centre Neil Carnes, a third-round pick of the Montreal Canadiens in 1988. Laval was making its first appearance in the Memorial Cup since 1984, when the Mario Lemieux-led team was known as the Voisins. The Titan finished second in the league during the 1989 regular season, 1 point behind the pennant-winning Trois-Rivieres Draveurs. In the playoffs, they eliminated the Granby Bisons, Shawinigan Cataractes and Victoriaville Tigres for the Quebec league title.

The Memorial Cup tournament opened on May 6 with Swift Current facing Peterborough. Sheldon Kennedy led the Broncos with 2 goals as they collected a 6–4 victory. Tie Domi provided much of the Peterborough offence, scoring twice.

In another opening day match, Saskatoon skated to a 5–3 victory over Laval. The Blades jumped out to a 2–0 lead, but the Titan roared back to tie the score. With the benefit of a 2-goal performance from Brian Gerrits, the Blades were able to pull away for good.

The next game matched the Titan and Broncos. Swift Current edged Laval 6–5 in an entertaining shootout before 8,733 fans. In the third period, the Broncos scored 2 goals in six seconds to push past the Titan. Kimbi Daniels and Dan Lambert each scored twice for the Broncos, while Neil Carnes bagged a pair for Laval. Peterborough and Saskatoon met in the hard-hitting fourth game. The Petes took a 2–0 lead and hung on for a 3–2 victory. Ross Wilson scored twice and Andy MacVicar once for Peterborough. Saskatoon received goals from Jason Smart and Ken Sutton.

Winless in two games, Laval managed to stay in the hunt for the title by defeating Peterborough 3–1. A large crowd of 8,517 fans watched the match at Saskatchewan Place. Carnes, Caron and Audette got the goals for Laval, while the lone Peterborough marker was scored by Hicks. It was the first victory of a QMJHL team over an OHL or WHL team since 1986. "They were a desperate team and we didn't show we were determined to put them away," Petes coach Dick Todd told the *Regina Leader-Post*'s Ed Willes.

The next game was a classic battle between the two Saskatchewan teams. Now 2–0 in the tournament, Swift Current had the opportunity to earn a spot in the final. But the Blades snapped the Broncos' fourteen-game winning streak with a thrilling 5–4 upset in front of 8,763 raucous fans. The Broncos ran up a 3–0 lead on goals by Bob Wilkie, Kasowski and Brian Sakic. Although Dean Holoien replied for the Blades, Swift Current was able to take a 2-goal margin into the first intermission.

But the Blades were a team on a mission. Four minutes into the second, Saskatoon tied the score on goals by Jason Smart and Ken Sutton. Sutton scored again to put the Blades in front. The Broncos came back, pulling even on a goal by Kennedy. But Darin Bader scored for Saskatoon late in the period, and this time, despite being outshot 43–26 overall, their lead held. Saskatoon clinched a place in the final, while the Broncos waited to face either the Petes or Titan in the semi-final.

The hardworking Laval team could not get past the Petes, dropping a 5–4 decision. At one point, the Petes led by 4–1. Ricci, recovering from a case of the chicken pox, scored for Peterborough, as did Hicks, Jamie Pegg and Geoff Ingram. The Laval scorers were Chalifoux, Lapointe, Audette and Carnes. Although neither of the local teams was playing, a healthy crowd of 7,016 fans turned out.

With Laval out of the tournament, the Petes met Swift Current in the semi-final. A crowd of 8,378 partisan fans was on hand.

The Broncos opened a 2–0 first-period lead and then stoned the Petes, nailing down a 6–2 victory. Swift Current had outstanding goaltending from Trevor Kruger, who held the fort while his teammates patiently built their lead. The Broncos went into the third period ahead 3–1 and pulled away, although they were outshot 38–23 over the last two periods. For Swift Current, Trevor Sim and Tisdale scored twice, and Daniels and Blake Knox notched singles. Ricci and Wilson scored for Peterborough, which perhaps showed some effect of playing four games in six days and a flu bug that had hampered the team all week.

For the first time, two WHL teams faced each other for the Memorial Cup. The fact that both teams were from Saskatchewan was icing on the cake for the crowd of 9,078 fans who packed Saskatchewan Place. Having already staged one classic game earlier in the tournament, the teams treated their loyal fans to an encore performance, battling into overtime. Tim Tisdale gave Swift Current a 4–3 victory and the 1989 Memorial Cup.

The Broncos took a 2–0 lead early in the second period, courtesy of Kennedy and Knox. As they had done in the previous meeting, Saskatoon ignored this deficit. Blades centre Scott Scissons scored, and then Katelnikoff picked off a Tisdale pass and tied the game with a shorthanded goal. Kory Kocur put Saskatoon into the lead with just seventeen seconds left in the second. Kimbi

Daniels put the Broncos back to even terms early in the third period.

Goaltenders Greenlay and Kruger, both superb throughout the game, duelled in overtime. Just over three minutes into the extra period, Tisdale deflected a shot from the point past Greenlay and into the Blades' net. "There was a big scramble in front," the netminder told Canadian Press. "I'd lost my stick—I can't even remember how—and I saw [Darren Kruger] shoot. I went down on my knees and couldn't see anything any more. The shot came through and it hit a stick, I assume it was Tisdale's, right in front and hit the inside of my leg and went in the net."

"We gave them 2 easy goals on giveaways and I had the goat horns on for a while," said Tisdale, the game's first star. "But I made up for it at the end." Mike Greenlay, the game's second star, was named the top goaltender in the tournament. Swift Current's Dan Lambert, the third star, was voted MVP. Jamie Hicks of Peterborough was named most sportsmanlike player. The all-star team featured Lambert and the Blades' Ken Sutton on defence, Tisdale at centre, Sheldon Kennedy on right wing, and Laval's Neil Carnes on left wing. The nine games attracted a total of 77,296 fans, establishing a Memorial Cup tournament record for attendance.

From the Swift Current Broncos, Sheldon Kennedy went on to play with Detroit, Calgary and Boston in the NHL. Dan Lambert skated for part of two seasons with the Quebec Nordiques. Kimbi Daniels saw action with Philadelphia. Big defenceman Bob Wilkie would play some games for the Detroit Red Wings and Philadelphia Flyers. Geoff Sanderson, a seventeen-year-old Bronco rookie who hadn't yet blossomed into a high scorer, went on to enjoy the most success. Playing for the Hartford Whalers, he quietly became one of the team's Most Valuable Players of the 1990s.

Sheldon Kennedy led the Swift Current Broncos to Memorial Cup victory in 1989.

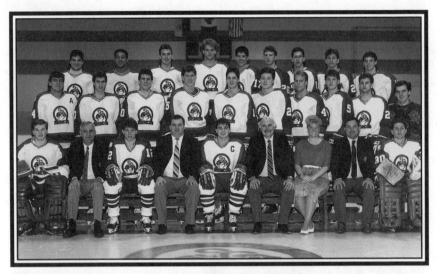

Swift Current Broncos. Back row: Kimbi Daniels, Mark McFarlane, Geoff Sanderson, Trevor Sim, Kyle Reeves, Brian Sakic, Matt Ripley, Darren Kruger, Blake Knox. Middle row: Bob Wilkie, Tim Tisdale, Kevin Barrett, Wade Smith, Peter Soberlak, Chris Larkin, Kevin Knopp, Jeff Knight, Peter Kasowski, Grant Farquhar (athletic therapist). Front row: Don Blishen, John Rittenger (president), Sheldon Kennedy, Graham James (coach and general manager), Dan Lambert, John Foster (public relations), Ramona Schwartz (office manager), Lorne Frey (assistant coach and general manager), Trevor Kruger. Rod Steensland photo.

From the Saskatoon Blades, Ken Sutton played in Buffalo, Edmonton and St. Louis, while goalie Mike Greenlay enjoyed a brief stint with Edmonton.

Tie Domi of the Peterborough Petes made a pugnacious impression with Winnipeg, the Rangers and Toronto. His junior teammate Mike Ricci served with Philadelphia, Quebec and Colorado, winning the Stanley Cup with the Avalanche in 1996.

Members of the Laval Titan who enjoyed professional success include Patrice Brisebois and Donald Audette, the former with Montreal and the latter with Buffalo. Neil Carnes, the tournament's all-star leftwinger and third-leading scorer, was tragically killed in a motorcycle accident later that summer.

A further tragedy involving participants of the 1989 Memorial Cup came to light in 1997. Swift Current Broncos coach Graham James was convicted of the sexual assault of two of his teen-age players on the 1989 team, including Sheldon Kennedy. Over the course of the case it came to light that James had been sexually abusing his players in Moose Jaw, Winnipeg and Swift Current from 1984 to 1995, his entire junior coaching career.

The
1990s

Every year, a new plate bearing the names of the most recent junior champions is added to the Memorial Cup. As the players behind these names create new stories in the National Hockey League and at the international level—or become part of the rich history of amateur hockey in North America—the Memorial Cup itself acquires a new layer of mystique. In this way, the stature and intensity of the tournament keeps growing. The fight to get one's name on this trophy is what makes the Canadian Hockey League a place where not only playing the game, but winning at it, is learned. It gives the Memorial Cup tournament lustre, but also grit and sometimes even ugliness.

When looking at past tournaments, it is interesting to note that players who dominate at the junior level do not necessarily dominate or even play in the NHL. Likewise, some players given little attention at the junior level become key performers later on. Perhaps the Memorial Cup's true value lies in the fact that it is a beginning as well as an ending. It always raises as many questions as it answers.

Eric Lindros became the most highly touted prospect from the Oshawa Generals since Bobby Orr.

The **1990** Memorial Cup

Nearing the turn of the century, only the Toronto Marlboros had won more Memorial Cups than the Oshawa Generals, and only Toronto's St. Michael's College had won as many. The Generals won the trophy in 1939, 1940 and 1944 and were looking for number four in 1990. They faced the Laval Titan, Kamloops Blazers and Kitchener Rangers in a series featuring hockey's "Next One," Eric Lindros.

The Memorial Cup was held in Hamilton, Ontario. Although the Hamilton Dukes, formerly the Toronto Marlboros, were originally slated to be the host team, their poor performance in the 1989–90 season led the team to step aside and clear a place for the OHL champions and runners-up.

The finalists for the OHL title were the Oshawa Generals and Kitchener Rangers. The Generals finished the regular season with 88 points to put them in a first-place tie with the London Knights. In the playoffs, Oshawa defeated the Cornwall Royals, Peterborough Petes and the Rangers to claim the league title.

Coached by Rick Cornacchia, the Generals were a solid team. In addition to seventeen-year-old Lindros, their lineup featured captain Iain Fraser, Brent Grieve, Mike Craig and Jarrod Skalde. Kevin Butt and backup Fred Brathwaite provided the goaltending. Grieve and Fraser were playing in their second Memorial Cup tournament, having competed for the 1987 trophy for Oshawa as well.

The Kitchener Rangers were coached and managed by Joe McDonnell. They had proven themselves capable of going toe to toe with the Generals, having pushed Oshawa to seven games in the OHL final. Captain Steven Rice, Gilbert Dionne (the younger brother of Marcel Dionne), defenceman Cory Keenan and goaltender Mike Torchia led the Rangers on the ice.

The Laval Titan finished the regular QMJHL season with an unexceptional 77 points, tied for fifth place with Hull. Heading into the playoffs, however, Laval caught fire and eliminated the Shawinigan Cataractes and Hull Olympiques. In the league championship, the Pierre Creamer-coached club polished off the Victoriaville Tigres in four straight. The Titan roster included future NHL regulars Patrice Brisebois, Martin Lapointe, Sandy McCarthy and Gino Odjick.

The Kamloops Blazers entered the Memorial Cup tournament as the top-ranked junior team in the country. In the WHL playoffs, Kamloops sidelined the Spokane Chiefs and Seattle Thunderbirds before ousting the Lethbridge Hurricanes in the WHL final. The Blazers boasted an impressive roster including Scott Niedermayer, Darryl Sydor, Paul Kruse, Dave Chyzowski, Mike Needham, Len Barrie and goalie Corey Hirsch. Ken Hitchcock was still behind the bench.

On May 5, Kitchener and Kamloops opened the 1990 Memorial Cup with an overtime shootout before 7,003 fans. Ranger Shayne Stevenson scored the winning goal at 7:41 of the extra period, firing a shot from close range between the pads of Corey Hirsch. "I didn't even see where the goalie was," said Stevenson, who had fired blindly after spinning around on the play.

The game was a seesaw battle. Kitchener, who finished the first period with a 3–2 lead, fell behind 6–4 by the end of the second. Stevenson's winner was his second goal, while Dave Chyzowski and Darryl Sydor also scored twice for Kamloops. The Blazers outshot the Rangers 45–37 overall.

In Copps Coliseum, Oshawa trounced Laval by a score of 6–2. The Generals jumped out to a 5–1 first-period lead and coasted to victory on 2 goals from Cory Banika and singles from Jarrod Skalde, Paul O'Hagan, Grieve and Fraser. Laval had goals from Sylvain Naud and Denis Chalifoux.

On the second day, Oshawa and Kamloops met in a game that many people considered a preview of the final. Kamloops dominated, outshooting Oshawa 50–21. But the Generals stole a 7–6 win on Iain Fraser's goal at 3:55 of overtime.

For the second time in as many days, Oshawa hit for 5 goals in the opening twenty minutes, including a hat trick by Mike Craig. Kamloops trailed 6–2 after two periods, despite outshooting Oshawa 17–3 in the second. The Blazers started connecting in the third. Len Barrie scored his second of the game and Niedermayer further narrowed the gap. With less than three minutes left, Sydor scored to pull Kamloops within one. With thirty seconds remaining in regulation time, Chyzowski completed the rally with his second of the match, a twenty-footer over the left shoulder of Butt.

The Generals regrouped during intermission. They claimed victory when Fraser deflected a point shot behind Hirsch, bringing the pro-Oshawa crowd of 7,500 to their feet. "We're not out of this thing yet," Blazers centre Len Barrie said. The CHL's leading scorer in 1989–90 with 85 goals and 100 assists, Barrie was the focus of a good deal of attention. In addition to contributing 2 goals and 2 assists, he generated numerous scoring chances and engaged in heated verbal sparring with the Generals.

"Things got a little emotional and there was a lot of yapping going on," the Blazer said. "We totally outplayed them and should have won this hockey game. A team that gives up a 4-goal lead doesn't have any character anyway."

"I'd like to take this opportunity to thank Barrie in public," Oshawa coach Cornacchia replied. "He insulted us and said we had no character."

The next match in the tournament was less exciting. Kitchener defeated Laval by a score of 5–3 before 3,249 fans. Ranger Mark Montanari, who had begun the season with the Maine Mariners of the American Hockey League, scored early in the third to break a 3–3 tie. Raymond Firth's empty netter and Torchia's solid play in goal sealed the win for Kitchener.

Kamloops, after firing almost 50 shots per game at the Generals and Rangers, was expected to break out in its match against Laval. The Titan, however, had other plans. They introduced the Blazers to a paralyzing forechecking game and shut them down 4–2.

The Laval scorers were Chalifoux, Patrick Caron, Claude Boivin and Martin Lapointe. Replying for Kamloops were Paul Kruse and Trevor Sim, a Memorial Cup winner with the 1989 Swift Current Broncos. "They're not a skilled team, but they work hard," said Corey Hirsch about the Titan. "I didn't play well at all in the first two games."

With Kamloops banished, the focus shifted to the all-Ontario rivalry between Oshawa and Kitchener. Just as the Saskatoon Blades and Swift Current Broncos had enthralled fans in the 1989 tournament, the Generals and Rangers played a thriller for the fans in Hamilton. Oshawa took a 5–4 decision in double overtime. The game lasted four and a quarter hours, but the crowd of 11,134 were kept on the edge of their seats the whole time.

Both teams had potted 2 goals after 1. Lindros set up Oshawa's only goal of the second, a powerplay marker by Mike Craig. But Kitchener got it back two minutes later on a powerplay goal by Dionne, which sent the teams into the third period tied 3–3. The shots were even at 21 at this point.

Oshawa began the third with some heavy hitting and grabbed a 4–3 lead on a goal by Fraser. The Rangers answered two minutes later, Rice firing a hard, low wrist shot past Butt. After Iain Fraser was foiled by Torchia on two breakaways, the teams went into overtime.

Oshawa dominated the first overtime period, creating several good scoring chances, but Torchia kept the door shut tight. It was a rambunctious period, in which referee Don Van Massenhoven ignored a number of muggings, preferring to let the players decide the game. At 4:16 of the second overtime, Dale Craigwell fired the winning goal. "I would love it to be an all-Ontario final," Cornacchia said. "I hope to see Kitchener on Sunday."

"We know we can beat them, but we have to be ready for Laval," Kitchener coach McDonnell said. "This wasn't a sudden death hockey game—we've still got another shot at doing something here."

Laval came close to being a spoiler, but the Rangers eked out a 5–4 win to move into the final. Centre Mark Montanari scored the winning goal late in the second period, and Kitchener hung on the rest of the way before 10,188 spectators at Copps Coliseum.

Creamer's team could not overcome the Ontario powerhouse, although they did try valiantly to break out of the slump that Quebec-based teams had been mired in since the Quebec Remparts won the junior title in 1971. "Playing in front of their fans was a big help," the Laval coach said. "If we had played even one game at our home rink, I think it would have been a different story."

The Kitchener Rangers and Oshawa Generals, having fought through a seven-game series in the OHL final and played a double-overtime marathon in the round robin, were now set to take the tournament to a spectacular climax. A record crowd of 17,383 filled Copps Coliseum, and they got their money's worth.

The ebb and flow of the game was similar to the teams' previous match. It was another back-and-forth exchange, with one team pulling ahead and the other ready with a quick response. Rangers defenceman Jason York got the scoring underway in the first with a powerplay tally. The Generals' Cory Banika replied less than two minutes later to even the score.

Kitchener regained the lead in the second with a powerplay goal by Joey St. Aubin. Then Kevin Butt took an early exit from the game due to an injury, and was replaced by Fred Brathwaite, who turned in an excellent performance. With less than two minutes left, leftwinger Brent Grieve scored for Oshawa, sending the teams into the final period in a 2–2 deadlock. Early in the third, Grieve found the net again to give Oshawa its first lead of the game. But Gilbert Dionne scored fifty seconds later on the powerplay to pull the Rangers even. The teams went to overtime tied at 3.

The first overtime period ended with the score still tied. At 2:05 of the second overtime session, Oshawa defenceman Bill Armstrong sent a floating shot toward goaltender Torchia that appeared to bounce off a stick before sailing over the Kitchener netminder's glove into the net. The Generals were the new junior hockey champions of Canada. The final game was the fourth overtime match of the tournament, the Generals and Rangers each having played in three. As in the first game between these teams, the players decided the outcome. Referee Steven Walkom called only seven minor penalties.

"It would have been easy to fold, but we have a character group of players," said Rick Cornacchia, the first Generals coach to win the Memorial Cup since Charlie Conacher in 1944. Brent Grieve and Iain Fraser, veterans of the 1987 tournament in which the Generals lost to Medicine Hat, were especially pleased with the outcome. "In 1987, I remember our team coming out flat and they got a couple of quick goals," Grieve said. "When Medicine Hat won, that was one of the worst feelings I've ever had. Winning it feels so much better."

Fraser, who had 3 goals and 7 assists in four games, was voted the Most Valuable Player. Oshawa and Kitchener each picked up three spots on the all-star squad, with the Generals' Eric Lindros at centre, Paul O'Hagan on defence and Fraser at right wing; and the Rangers' Mike Torchia in goal, Cory Keenan on defence and Steven Rice at left wing. The championship game was the thirty-seventh straight start for Torchia, voted top goaltender. Teammate Jason Firth won the award for sportsmanship. Eric Lindros did not dominate play for Oshawa as he would the next year, but he was an integral member of the team and contributed nine assists. He had only played twenty-five games during the 1989–90 OHL regular season after refusing to play for the team that drafted him, the Sault Ste. Marie Greyhounds. The Memorial Cup tournament drew 70,563 spectators, the second-highest total ever after the previous year's attendance in Saskatoon.

Iain Fraser captained the Oshawa Generals to their 1990 Memorial Cup victory.

Eric Lindros became the most highly touted prospect from the Oshawa Generals since

Oshawa Generals. Back row (l to r): Mark Logan (assistant coach), Wade Simpson, Dave Craievich, Eric Lindros, Bill Armstrong, Mark Deazeley, Matt Hoffman, Trevor McIvor, Scott Luik, Bryan Boyes (trainer). Middle row: Colleen Corner (office secretary), Cory Banika, Dale Craigwell, Brian Grieve, Jean-Paul Davis, Craig Donaldson, Brent Grieve, Jarrod Skalde, Mike Craig, Clair Cornish, Scott Hollis, Wayne Daniels (scout). Front row: Fred Braithwaite, Paul O'Hagan, Scott Clark (business manager), Larry Marson (assistant coach), John Humphreys (president), Iain Fraser, Rick Cornacchia (head coach), Frank Jay (director of operations), Ian Young (assistant coach), Joe Busillo, Kevin Butt.

Bobby Orr in 1966. He was selected by the Quebec Nordiques and traded to the Philadelphia Flyers, where he quickly established himself as one of hockey's premier players, winning the Hart trophy in his third NHL season. Generals captain Iain Fraser played with the New York Islanders, Quebec, Dallas, Edmonton, Winnipeg and San Jose. Brent Grieve went on to skate with the Islanders, Edmonton and Chicago. Mike Craig would see action with Minnesota, Dallas and Toronto, and Jarrod Skalde with New Jersey, Anaheim and Calgary. Dale Craigwell played for the San Jose Sharks early in the new franchise's history. Fred Brathwaite tended some goal for the Edmonton Oilers.

Kitchener Rangers captain Steven Rice brought his hard-hitting game to the NHL with the New York Rangers, Edmonton and Hartford. Gilbert Dionne skated in Montreal, Philadelphia and Florida. Mike Torchia played in several games for Dallas.

From the Laval Titan, Gino Odjick became one of the most penalized players in the NHL with the Vancouver Canucks. Sandy McCarthy also became an enforcer for Calgary. Patrice Brisebois, a Montreal draft pick, returned to the Memorial Cup in 1991 with the Drummondville Voltigeurs. Martin Lapointe would play with Laval in the 1993 tournament.

Some Kamloops Blazers players would return to challenge for the Memorial Cup in 1992, including Darryl Sydor and Corey Hirsch. A number would see NHL action, including Paul Kruse with Calgary and the Islanders, Len Barrie with Philadelphia, Florida and Pittsburgh, Mike Needham with Pittsburgh and Dallas, and Dave Chyzowski with the Islanders. Ken Hitchcock left the Blazers to become an assistant coach with the Philadelphia Flyers. In 1996 he was named the head coach of the Dallas Stars.

The **1991** Memorial Cup

Twenty years after the 1971 Remparts won the Memorial Cup in Quebec City, the Drummondville Voltigeurs and Chicoutimi Sagueneens were hoping lightning would strike twice for the Quebec capital. They competed for the 1991 title with the Sault Ste. Marie Greyhounds and the Spokane Chiefs, who were intent on becoming the second American franchise to receive a Memorial Cup coronation. Because the only junior team in Quebec City was the expansion Beauport Harfangs, the QMJHL decided that the two 1991 league finalists would represent the league, rather than having the fledgling Harfangs host the tournament.

The Drummondville Voltigeurs were the first team to qualify, sweeping the College Français de Longueuil to win their division. Chicoutimi edged the Laval Titan four games to three in the other semi-final. The Sagueneens then defeated Drummondville in straight games to win the President's Trophy as Quebec champions. Coached by Joe Canale, Chicoutimi was anchored by the goaltending of Félix Potvin. The team relied on Steve Larouche and Stephane Charbonneau for offence. The Voltigeurs were coached by former NHL defenceman Jean Hamel and they had a roster that included future pros Patrice Brisebois, Ian Laperriere and Denis Chasse.

The WHL was dominated by Kamloops and Spokane. Although the Blazers remained the top-ranked squad in the country, the Chiefs management felt that they could position their team for a serious run at the championship. The Chiefs made some deals during the regular season, trading young prospects to Brandon for all-star netminder Trevor Kidd in late January. From that point on, the club was nearly unbeatable. The Chiefs finished the regular season second to the Blazers, and cruised to their first-ever league championship with a 14–1 post-season ledger. After disposing of Seattle, the Chiefs cleared a huge hurdle by sidelining Kamloops in the division final. Then they swept the Lethbridge Hurricanes for the WHL crown. Bryan Maxwell, who had coached the 1987 Medicine Hat Tigers to a Memorial Cup victory, was behind the Chiefs' bench. In addition to Kidd, he could depend on the quicksilver combination of WHL scoring champion Ray Whitney and Pat Falloon.

This Memorial Cup tournament was supposed to be Eric Lindros' junior swan song, but his Oshawa Generals lost the OHL championship series to the Sault Ste. Marie Greyhounds. Lindros was originally drafted by the Greyhounds but he refused to play for them and was eventually traded to Oshawa. Lindros' snub of Sault Ste. Marie made for an extremely heated series where the angry crowd played a dominant role by loudly jeering the superstar every second he was on the ice. Sault Ste. Marie, which had previously swept the Dukes of

Hamilton and Niagara Falls Thunder, was coached by former NHL leftwinger Ted Nolan and managed by Sherry Bassin. The team's roster included Adam Foote, Mike DeCoff, Denny Lambert, Wade Whitten, Mark Matier and Brad Tiley.

The Memorial Cup opened on May 11 with 3,000 Quebec fans in the seats. Drummondville posted a 4–2 win over the Greyhounds, getting goals from four different players: Hugo Proulx, Patrice Brisebois, Claude Jutras, Jr. and Ian Laperriere. Tony Iob and Rick Kowalsky replied for Sault Ste. Marie.

There were two games the next day. Spokane, playing their first match in eleven days, showed no signs of rust in trouncing Drummondville 7–3. Former Medicine Hat Tiger Mark Woolf got the Chiefs off to a fast start, scoring twice in the first six minutes. Whitney also struck twice and Pat Falloon added a hat trick in the third period. Denis Chasse scored all 3 goals for the Voltigeurs, who

Trevor Kidd matched the best Memorial Cup tournament goals-against average of 1.67 established by Cornwall's Richard Brodeur in 1972.

were outshot 43–26. It was a game full of scraps and cheap shots; referee Michel Lemieux called 206 penalty minutes, many generated from skirmishes after the whistle. The other game that day saw the Greyhounds stymied by a hot goaltender at Le Colisée. Félix Potvin made 33 saves in backstopping Chicoutimi to a 2–1 victory. Stephane Charbonneau and Sebastian Parent scored for Chicoutimi, while Iob replied for the Greyhounds.

Spokane rocked Chicoutimi 7–1 in the fourth game, a match strewn with eight ejections and 226 penalty minutes. Canadian Hockey League president Ed Chynoweth was still sorting out fines in the aftermath of the Spokane–Drummondville game. A crowd of 9,320 watched Brent Thurston and Falloon each score twice, while Woolf, Kerry Toporowski and Whitney padded their points totals for Spokane. Steve Laroche scored the only Sagueneens goal. The victory ensured Spokane a spot in the championship final.

Baseball star George Brett, the co-owner of the Spokane Chiefs, was on hand for the next game. Along with 5,277 fans, he watched his team score on 4 of their first 6 shots on net. The Chiefs built a 5–0 lead by the end of the first period and needed no more, sailing to an 8–4 victory and thereby eliminating the Greyhounds. "We put them further behind the eight ball right off the bat," said Falloon, who scored twice to finish the round robin event with 7 goals. The other top point-getters in the tournament, Whitney and Woolf, scored a goal each.

With the Greyhounds gone and the Chiefs advancing to the championship final, the two Quebec-based teams battled twice in three nights. The last contest of the round robin was little more than a warmup for the ensuing semi-final, with Drummondville taking a 5–3 decision over Chicoutimi. The semi-final game featured a superb 52-save effort by Félix Potvin, but it was all in vain. Drummondville claimed a 2–1 victory after Chicoutimi defenceman Steve Gosselin batted the puck into his own net in overtime. The clubs exchanged

Pat Falloon of the 1991 Memorial Cup-winning Spokane Chiefs, was drafted second overall behind Eric Lindros in the 1991 NHL draft.

goals in the first period, with Proulx of Drummondville and Larouche of Chicoutimi putting their teams on the board. The game then settled into a lengthy deadlock until 11:26 of overtime, when the winner got past a stunned Potvin. Ian Laperriere received the credit, and an anguished Gosselin dropped to his knees, his head in his hands. The Voltigeurs had seven men on the ice thirty seconds before the winning goal, but referee Benoit Lapointe missed the infraction.

Drummondville entered the Memorial Cup final against a team missing its third-leading scorer. Mark Woolf was scratched from the lineup for disciplinary reasons. He had already been sent home late in the season, but Maxwell had allowed the twenty-year-old rightwinger to return for the playoffs. "I had a couple of beers and missed curfew five times," said Woolf of his earlier banishment. "When I left, it was like my dog died." This time, there was no reprieve.

After only fifty-eight seconds of play, Spokane jumped out to an early lead on a goal by Mike Jickling. But Dave Paquet tied the game at 6:34. "That was the only time anybody even tied Spokane," Drummondville coach Jean Hamel later said. The Chiefs had played with a lead throughout the entire tournament. Six minutes later, Murray Garbutt put the Chiefs ahead for good. He scored again with nineteen seconds left in the first period, and Jon Klemm struck in the middle period. These two tallies served to demoralize the Voltigeurs. Pat Falloon rounded out the scoring to claim the top spot in the points race. His 8 goals equalled the record set by Dale Hawerchuk in 1981 and tied by Luc Robitaille in 1986.

"This feels better than winning the world junior," Falloon said. Foxwarren, Manitoba's pride, had been a member of the gold medal-winning Canadian team at the world junior tournament in January. "Now I know what hockey means to these kids," Spokane President Bobby Brett said, "to all Canadian kids." He was moved by the tears pouring down his players' faces during the Cup celebrations. Falloon was a runaway winner of the MVP award. He joined linemate Ray Whitney and Brent Thurston on the all-star team, along with defencemen Patrice Brisebois of Drummondville and Brad Tiley of Sault Ste. Marie. Whitney was also named the tournament's most gentlemanly player, while Félix Potvin of the Sagueneens earned the nod as top goaltender.

Trevor Kidd, who had allowed just 5 goals in three games, matched the best tournament goals-against average of 1.67 established by Richard Brodeur with Cornwall in 1972. In passing Kidd over for top goalie honours, tournament officials clearly felt that Potvin faced more pressure in the Chicoutimi net. With 1987 and 1991 Memorial Cup victories under his belt, Bryan Maxwell became

Spokane Chiefs. Below left on stairs (l to r): Mark Woolf, Murray Garbutt. On ground: Mark Szoke, Rich More, Chris Lafrenière, Trevor Tovell, Jon Klemm, Scott Bailey, Shane Maitland, Bart Cote, Gary Braun (assistant coach). Above, in wagon: Bryan Maxwell (coach), Mike Chrun, Brent Thurston, Trevor Kidd, Geoff Grandberg, Bobby Brett (president), Kerry Toporowski, Frank Evans, Steve Junker, Tim Speltz (general manager), Mike Jickling, Bram Vanderkracht, Calvin Thudium, Pat Falloon, Cam Danyluk, Ray Whitney.

the only person to coach two different WHL organizations to the junior title. The final game drew 8,756 fans, and the pro-Drummondville crowd showed some class by offering polite applause for both teams as the game ended. Overall attendance was 58,316, placing the 1991 event fourth in tournament history behind Saskatoon in 1989, Hamilton in 1990 and Vancouver in 1977.

Pat Falloon was drafted by the San Jose Sharks in 1991, second overall to Eric Lindros. He led the team in scoring during his rookie season. Traded to Philadelphia in the 1995–96 season, Falloon became Lindros's teammate. Ray Whitney was drafted by San Jose in the second round and continued playing on a line with Falloon in California. Trevor Kidd took little time establishing himself in the NHL, becoming the starting netminder of the Calgary Flames. Scott Bailey, Spokane's former starting goaltender who became a fixture on the players' bench after the Kidd trade, would make it into a number of NHL games with the Boston Bruins. Captain Jon Klemm joined the Quebec Nordiques organization, moving with the team to Colorado and winning the Stanley Cup in 1996.

From the Drummondville Voltigeurs, Patrice Brisebois developed into a regular blueliner with Montreal. Ian Laperriere played with the Los Angeles Kings, New York Rangers and St. Louis Blues, while Denis Chasse served with St. Louis, Washington, Winnipeg and Ottawa. The outstanding graduate of the 1991 Chicoutimi Sagueneens was Félix Potvin, who established himself as a premier NHL goaltender within just a couple of seasons with the Maple Leafs. The Greyhounds' professional hope was Adam Foote, who quietly developed into one of NHL's best defensive defencemen with the Colorado Avalanche, winning the Stanley Cup in 1996.

The **1992** Memorial Cup

The Kamloops Blazers' successful roots lie in Ernie "Punch" McLean's New Westminster Bruins. With the financial backing of Peter Pocklington and the Edmonton Oilers, the Bruins were purchased in 1981 and relocated to Kamloops. The Junior Oilers became the Blazers in 1984, when the team became community owned. Managed by Bob Brown and coached by Bill Laforge, the Kamloops Blazers quickly became a respectable contender. They were one of the most successful teams in junior hockey during the eighties, with one reservation: they never won the Memorial Cup. The Blazers were back in 1992, ready to do battle with the Sault Ste. Marie Greyhounds, Verdun College Français and their old rivals, the host Seattle Thunderbirds.

The Thunderbirds were born out of the old Kamloops Chiefs franchise that moved to Washington state in 1977. Originally known as the Seattle Breakers, the team was renamed by Earl Hale when he bought the organization in 1985, and it found a perennial playoff nemesis in the Kamloops Blazers. In 1992, the Thunderbirds were eliminated by the Blazers in six games in the WHL playoffs. Coached by Peter Anholt, the Thunderbirds included future NHLers Turner Stevenson, Mike Kennedy and goaltender Chris Osgood.

Kamloops' rookie coach Tom Renney inherited a strong team from Ken Hitchcock, who had moved on to the NHL. A number of Blazers had experience in the 1990 Memorial Cup, and Renney also had the good fortune of getting two key players back from the pro ranks. In mid-season, team captain Darryl Sydor and defenceman Scott Niedermayer were sent down from Los Angeles and New Jersey respectively. The Blazers' playoff roster also included Zac Boyer, David Wilkie and veteran goaltender Corey Hirsch. They began the playoffs by eliminating the Tacoma Rockets, Seattle Thunderbirds and Saskatoon Blades.

Claude Therien entered Memorial Cup competition at the helm of the Verdun College Français. Having already disposed of the St. Hyacinthe Lasers and Shawinigan Cataractes, Verdun emerged as QMJHL champions after a brutal seven-game series against the Trois-Rivieres Draveurs. Key players in the College Français lineup included Jean-Martin Morin, Yan Arsenault, Mario Nobili, Dominic Rheaume and goaltender Eric Raymond.

Sault Ste. Marie Greyhounds coach Ted Nolan also had Memorial Cup experience, having taken his team to the tournament the previous year. Like the other two league champions, his team had survived a seven-game series to reach the national championship. The Greyhounds began the playoffs with a seven-game scrap with the Kitchener Rangers before taking out the Niagara Falls Thunder in the division championship. They then defeated the North Bay Centennials in the OHL final. Sault Ste. Marie's key players included captain Rick Kowalsky, Chris Simon, Jarrett Reid, Colin Miller, Drew Bannister and netminder Kevin Hodson.

On May 9, the Memorial Cup tournament opened with a showdown between Seattle and Verdun. The Thunderbirds never trailed the game, scoring a 5–3 victory. George Zajankala fired a hat trick, while Blake Knox and Tyler Quiring scored singles. Replying for Verdun were Jean-Martin Morin, Yan Arsenault and Mario Nobili. In the other opening day matchup, the Greyhounds unleashed demons of Memorial Cups past upon Kamloops, sending the WHL champions down 6–3. By the first intermission, Tony Iob, Ralph Intranuovo and Jarrett Reid had paced Sault Ste. Marie to a 3–0 lead. The Greyhounds' Rick Kowalsky, Colin Miller and Shawn Imber also turned on the red light before the game was over. Kamloops received mediocre performances from many of its key players, getting offence only from goal scorers Todd Johnson, Jeff Watchorn and Shayne Green.

A recommitted Blazers team turned up for the next game at Seattle Centre Arena. With 3,587 fans on hand, they shut down Verdun by a score of 4–0. Corey Hirsch made 20 saves to earn the shutout, and Zac Boyer and Craig Lyons scored twice each. "Hirsch played great today and now we've got our confidence back," said rightwinger Boyer, perhaps sensing that his team was about to shed its Memorial Cup jinx.

On May 12, the Greyhounds scored 3 powerplay goals to dump the College Français 4–2, sending them out of the tournament with an 0–3 record. Sault Ste. Marie received goals from Iob, Reid, Kowalsky and defenceman Brian Goudie. Dominic Rheaume and Martin Tanguay scored in the Quebec champions' last stand. Sault Ste. Marie then clinched a spot in the final by defeating Seattle 4–3. The winner was a shorthanded goal by Rick Kowalsky, scored with two minutes remaining. Chris Simon, Drew Bannister and Reid scored the other Sault Ste. Marie goals, while the Thunderbirds got markers from Jeff Sebastian, Eric Bouchard and Kurt Seher. Having lost all three of their games in 1991, the Greyhounds held a 3–0 record after the current round robin.

The victory set up back-to-back games between Kamloops and Seattle, the last game of the round robin and the semi-final match. The Blazers won the first game 3–1, defenceman Niedermayer bagging a goal and 2 assists. Kamloops then bulldozed into the final by pounding the Thunderbirds 8–3. Mike Mathers tied a tournament record with a 6-point night, contributing 3 goals and 3 assists. Two focussed teams faced each other in the Memorial Cup final. Kamloops and Sault Ste. Marie played a stirring contest in front of 7,068 fans at Seattle Centre, with the Blazers prevailing in the dying seconds to win their first Memorial Cup.

Kamloops built a 3–0 lead fifteen minutes into the game, and then watched as the Greyhounds dismantled it. Colin Miller scored twice and Chris Simon once in the second, erasing first-period goals by Mathers, Todd Johnson and

David Wilkie, who led the Kamloops Blazers to victory with strong steady play, poses with the Memorial Cup. FEDORAK/BLAZERS

Boyer. Early in the third, Johnson scored again for the Blazers, who looked like they would hold the lead. But Simon banged in his second goal with only four minutes left on the clock. Deadlocked, the teams appeared headed for overtime. Less than a minute was left in the game when Blazer Ed Patterson, speared in a skirmish in the Sault Ste. Marie zone, struggled off the ice. Three Greyhounds, led by Kowalsky, headed up ice in a three-on-one attack. Scott Niedermayer, the lone man back for the Blazers, picked off Kowalsky's pass and spotted Zac Boyer coming on for Patterson.

Niedermayer coolly took one stride over the Blazers blueline and feathered a breakaway pass to an open Boyer, who had slipped behind the Greyhounds' defence as they moved to join the attack. Boyer deked to his backhand as goalie Hodson tried the poke check, and slid home the winner with 14.6 seconds remaining. "I guess I can thank Ed Patterson, because he came off the ice," Boyer said. "Niedermayer hit me at the right time. He could have iced it, but that's why he's such a great player." Niedermayer commented, "I didn't even know who it was until I saw number 11 go in with the puck."

The championship victory was especially gratifying for the Kamloops players who had been on the losing side at the 1990 Memorial Cup. Former Blazers coach Ken Hitchcock was on hand to see the 1992 team win the title that had eluded him in 1986 and 1990. Scott Niedermayer was named the tournament MVP, while Corey Hirsch was the top goaltender. Greyhounds centre Colin Miller was voted most sportsmanlike player. All three made the all-star team, as did Seattle rightwinger Turner Stevenson and Kamloops leftwinger Mike Mathers. Sault Ste. Marie's Drew Bannister joined Niedermayer on defence.

Scott Niedermayer became a valuable member of the New Jersey Devils' defensive corps, winning the Stanley Cup in 1995. Darryl Sydor developed into a solid blueliner with Ken Hitchcock's Dallas Stars after playing four seasons in Los Angeles.

Zac Boyer also played with Dallas, while David Wilkie started his NHL career with the Canadiens. Corey Hirsch was drafted by the Rangers before being traded to Vancouver, where he began to see regular action between the pipes in

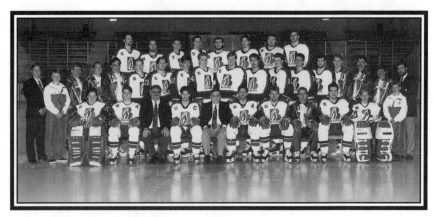

Kamloops Blazers. Fedorak Photo.

the mid-1990s. Eddie Patterson ground his way into the NHL with the Pittsburgh Penguins. Blazers coach Tom Renney also moved on to the NHL, taking over behind the bench of the Vancouver Canucks in 1996.

Seattle Thunderbirds goaltender Chris Osgood was named a second team NHL all-star in 1995–96 on the strength of his play with the Detroit Red Wings. In 1997 he lost his starter role to fellow Memorial Cup alumnus Mike Vernon, who led Osgood and the Wings to the Stanley Cup. Turner Stevenson brought his physical style to Montreal, and Mike Kennedy went on to the Dallas Stars and Toronto Maple Leafs. Big Chris Simon was important as a goal-scorer for the Greyhounds, but he established himself as an enforcer in the NHL with Quebec, Colorado and Washington. He won the Stanley Cup with the Avalanche in 1996. A number of other players from the 1992 Sault Ste. Marie Greyhounds would return to compete in the 1993 Memorial Cup.

The **1993** Memorial Cup

In 1991 the Sault Ste. Marie Greyhounds went winless at the Memorial Cup. A year later they went undefeated in the round robin, but lost the championship game. The Greyhounds would not be denied in 1993. Celebrating the seventy-fifth anniversary of the junior championship, Sault Ste. Marie played host to the Peterborough Petes, Swift Current Broncos and Laval Titan. The Greyhounds won the right to host the 1993 tournament with a four-game sweep of the Peterborough Petes in the Super Series played between OHL division champions. The OHL Super Series, which was also held in 1987, is played immediately after the regular season to determine the Ontario host of the Memorial Cup when one has not been previously named. The same teams met in the OHL championship series, where the Hounds prevailed again.

Peterborough was coached by Dick Todd, who joined the Petes organization in 1970 as a trainer. He had been coach and general manager of the team since the early 1980s. Captained by Geordie Kinnear and backstopped by goalie Chad Lang, the Petes featured some strong NHL prospects including Chris Pronger, Jason Dawe and Dave Roche. Sault Ste. Marie was still under the stewardship of Ted Nolan, and had six players back from the team that went to the 1992 final. In addition to returning players Ralph Intranuovo, Jarrett Reid, goaltender Kevin Hodson and captain Rick Kowalsky, the Greyhounds found new talent in Chad Penney, Aaron Gavey, Jeff Toms and Steve Sullivan. It was the team's fourth Memorial Cup appearance in nine years.

Still coached by Graham James, the Swift Current Broncos were probably the strongest team on paper. The Broncos had recorded their second best season in 1993 and defeated Medicine Hat, Regina and Portland in the playoffs. Swift Current was spearheaded by Jason Krywulak, the leading point scorer in the CHL and the WHL's Most Valuable Player. Captain Trent McCleary, Andy Schneider, Ashley Buckberger, Brent Bilodeau, Rick Girard, Todd Holt and netminder Milan Hnilicka were other key players on the roster.

The Laval Titan finished their QMJHL season with 88 points, giving them first place in the LeBel division. They captured the league championship in only thirteen playoff games, sweeping Verdun and Drummondville before defeating the Sherbrooke Faucons in five. Coached by Robert Hartley, the Titan lineup included captain Martin Lapointe, Jason Boudrias, Philippe Boucher, Yannick Dubé and goaltender Emmanuel Fernandez. The Titan were involved in the opening of the tournament on May 15 in Sault Ste. Marie Memorial Gardens. With 4,156 fans on hand, the Greyhounds edged Laval 3–2. Wade Gibson and Chad Penney each tallied 2 goals for Sault Ste. Marie, while Jason Boudrias and Philippe Boucher replied for the Titan.

Two games took place on the second day of the tournament. The matinee had Swift Current dumping the Greyhounds 5–3 on the strength of 2 goals by Jason Krywulak and 3 assists by over-age centre Andy Schneider. The Greyhounds outshot the Broncos 44–37 but lost the game in the second period. Swift Current fired 3 unanswered goals, subduing the crowd of 4,194 hometown fans. "I like facing a lot of shots because it gets me into the game," said netminder Milan Hnilicka, two gold chains dangling from his sweat-drenched neck. "I felt good."

The same evening, Jason Dawe notched 2 goals and an assist and centre Mike Harding added three helpers in the Peterborough Petes' 6–4 win over Laval. The Petes jumped to a 4–1 lead at the end of the first period and coasted to victory. Eric Veilleux scored twice to pace the Laval offence, but the real centre of attention was referee David Lynch. He handed out thirty-seven minors, thirteen majors and nine game misconducts for a total of 229 penalty minutes. The Memorial Cup disciplinary committee assessed fines totalling $1,500 to the Petes and Titans. "This is not the place for these things to happen," Peterborough centre Harding said.

"No one likes to see it," OHL Commissioner David Branch told Rob Vanstone of the *Regina Leader-Post*. "But I would suggest this is more of an aberration than the norm. The Quebec team, for whatever reason, decided to play that style. The referee made the calls and did what he could."

In the next outing, Peterborough whipped the Broncos 7–3 before 4,095 fans. All but 2 of the goals came in the first period. Things were tied at 2 midway through the opening frame when the Petes' Dave Roche and Dale McTavish scored one minute apart. Andy Schneider got 1 back for the Broncos, but Roche scored with twenty seconds left in the first to restore Sault Ste. Marie's 2-goal lead. "We always seem to do things the hard way," Swift Current defenceman Brent Bilodeau said. "The good thing is that we usually respond to pressure."

"The game was a lot closer than the score showed," Harding insisted. It was also tamer than the previous bout, with only thirty-nine penalty minutes.

Still looking for the victory to put them past the round robin, the Broncos expected to find it in their next game against Laval. However, the Titan ended a six-game QMJHL losing streak against WHL teams with a 4–3 win. In the third period, Yannick Dubé scored twice within twenty-four seconds to break a 2–2 tie. "We've got quite a battle ahead," Krywulak admitted, "but I've still got confidence in this team." Both 1–2 in games, Laval and Swift Current played a tie-breaker to decide the semi-finalist, but first the Petes and Greyhounds faced each other in the last game of the round robin. The winner would earn a place in the final.

Sault Ste. Marie was designated the visiting team, but a packed house of 4,433 hometown fans cheered them on to a 7–3 dusting of the Petes. Ralph Intranuovo had a goal and 3 assists to lead the Greyhounds, while Chad Penney scored twice. Peterborough gave up 4 powerplay goals and were fully outplayed in the game. The Greyhounds were now in the final, while the Petes awaited their semi-final opponent. Swift Current, with two consecutive defeats after their initial victory, had one last chance in the tie-breaker, played before 3,190 spectators. The Broncos rallied from 2–0 and 3–1 deficits to manage a 3–3 tie, but lost the game when Patrick Cassin scored with thirty-four seconds left in the third.

Swift Current Bronco Jason Krywulak was the leading point scorer in the CHL and the WHL's Most Valuable Player in 1993.

The Broncos, normally a high-flying offensive team, were outshot 14–0 in the first seventeen minutes. Laval held the lead through most of the game, on 2 goals from Dubé and one from Veilleux. Swift Current received offence from Bilodeau, Darren Perkins and Holt. Swift Current captain Trent McCleary was despondent after the defeat. "A way of life is sort of passing by," McCleary told the *Regina Leader-Post*. "I spent four years playing for the Broncos. We were building four years for this moment and we were so close. It's a terrible feeling."

Laval headed into the semi-final against the Petes. For a while, the Titan looked like they might push ahead to the final. But Peterborough prevailed, nailing down a 3–1 decision in front of 4,101 fans. Trailing 1–0 after two periods, the Petes scored 3 unanswered goals in the third. Laval appeared to have gone ahead by 2 in the second frame, when the puck got past goalie Chad Lang after a scramble in front. However, referee David Lynch had called the play dead, having lost sight of the puck in a maze of players. For Peterborough, Harding scored twice and Brent Tully added a single. "I feel we deserved to be in that final," Titan coach Hartley said. "But I refuse to discuss the negatives. I want to leave the Sault on a positive note. I feel we had excellent treatment here. I'd rather talk about the fans and the good times we had."

For the second time in three years, it was an all-Ontario Memorial Cup final. On May 23, a sold-out Memorial Arena crowd of 4,757 was in a rambunctious mood, blowing foghorns and ringing bells. The game was decided in the first period. Rick Kowalsky opened the scoring three minutes in, and then executed a give-and-go on a two-on-one break with Intranuovo, who gave the Greyhounds a 2–0 lead. Penney split the Petes' defence and scored on the powerplay late in the period, and Sullivan scored early in the second to give Sault Ste. Marie a 4-goal lead. As the middle frame progressed, the Petes came on stronger but couldn't beat Hodson. They had better success in the third, Ryan Black making it 4–1 and Weir scoring with seven minutes left. But that's as close as it got. The scoreboard showed Sault Ste. Marie 4, Peterborough 2 at the final buzzer.

Kevin Hodson, the game's first star, played a decisive role, turning aside 33 shots in the first two periods, 22 in the second when Peterborough stormed to the attack. The Greyhounds were outshot 47–32 by the Petes overall. Sault Ste. Marie captain Rick Kowalsky, a tenth-round pick of the Buffalo Sabres in the 1992 NHL draft, had been on a mission after losing in the final a year earlier. The rightwinger figured in the first two Greyhounds markers. "I couldn't get that out of my mind," Kowalsky said. "To see Kamloops carry the Memorial Cup around the Seattle ice in the 1992 tournament really hurt."

Head coach of the 1993 Memorial Cup-winning Sault Ste. Marie Greyhounds, Ted Nolan went to Buffalo to start a promising coaching career in the big league. He won the NHL's 1997 Jack Adams award as coach of the year.
DAN HAMILTON/VANTAGE POINT

For Greyhounds director of operations Sherry Bassin, the victory was especially gratifying. He had taken five previous runs at the Memorial Cup, three with the Greyhounds and two as general manager of the Oshawa Generals in 1983 and 1987. "I've been trying to get my hands on this sucker for a long time," said Bassin, who joined the Sault Ste. Marie organization in 1988 and played a large role in building it into a contender. "This is a credit to our people and our community," said Ted Nolan, who grew up in Sault Ste. Marie. "Four years ago we almost lost this team, but four years later we gave our people this."

Peterborough's Mike Harding walked away with the tournament scoring lead of 13 points. But like

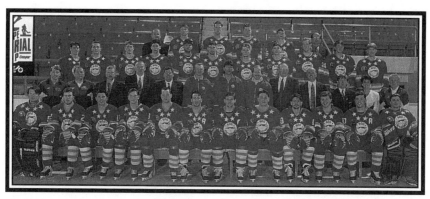

Sault Ste. Marie Greyhounds. Back row (l to r): George Shunock (president), Neal Martin, Joe Clarke, Joe Van Volsen, Steve Sullivan, Sherwood Bassin (general manager). Second row from back: Dan Cloutier, Oliver Pastinsky, Brad Baber, Gary Roach, Brian Thompson, Drew Bannister, Tom MacDonald, Aaron Gavey, Jeff Toms, Kiley Hill, Peter MacKellar. Third row from back: Maurice Sicard (therapist), John Mayne (equipment manager), Dave Mayville (director of player personnel), Ken Gregg (treasurer), Frank Sarlo (vice president), Mike Zuke (assistant coach), Ted Nolan (head coach), Danny Flynn (assistant coach and general manager), John Reynolds (secretary), Gino Cavallo (director of marketing and public relations), Dave Harris (public relations), Joanne Presgrave (executive secretary), Forrest Varcoe (trainer). Front row: Kevin Hodson, Mark Matier, David Matsos, Wade Gibson, Jodi Murphy, Jarret Reid, Rick Kowalsky, Sean Gagnon, Ralph Intranuovo, Chad Penney, Perry Pappas, Dan Tanevski.

the rest of the Petes' lineup, he was overlooked for the all-star team. The honours went to Sault Ste. Marie goalie Kevin Hodson, centre Ralph Intranuovo, leftwinger Chad Penney and defenceman Drew Bannister. Laval was represented by rightwinger Martin Lapointe and defenceman Michael Gaul. Hodson was voted the top goaltender, while Jason Dawe of Peterborough received recognition as the most sportsmanlike player. Ralph Intranuovo, who had spent the night before the final game in hospital passing a kidney stone, won the Stafford Smythe award as the tournament's MVP. "I was really scared," he said. "I was crying in the hospital, thinking I might not be able to play, the pain was so bad. I said, 'Please, make the pain go away.' If it was going to come back, I hoped it would be another day. I wanted to play in the Memorial Cup championship game."

Intranuovo would later see action in the NHL with Edmonton. Drew Bannister also played for the Oilers after a stint in Tampa Bay. Other Sault Ste. Marie Greyhounds who turned pro include Chad Penney with Ottawa, Aaron Gavey and Jeff Toms with Tampa Bay, and Steve Sullivan with New Jersey and Toronto. Playing for one of the NHL's top teams in the mid-1990s, Kevin Hodson managed to play in the occasional game in Detroit behind two other former Memorial Cup goalies, Mike Vernon and Chris Osgood. Detroit showed their confidence in Hodson in August of 1997 when they traded Vernon to the

San Jose Sharks after he had led Detroit to the 1997 Stanley Cup. Ted Nolan started a promising NHL coaching career in Buffalo, winning the Jack Adams Trophy as coach of the year for 1996–97.

From the Peterborough Petes, Chris Pronger was drafted second overall in the strong 1993 entry draft by Hartford, where he played for a couple of seasons before emerging as a force in St. Louis. Jason Dawe also became a dependable NHL regular in Buffalo. Dave Roche saw action with the Pittsburgh Penguins. Dale McTavish put in some shifts for the Calgary Flames.

Andy Schneider of the Swift Current Broncos went on to play with Ottawa, while Philippe Boucher skated with Buffalo and Los Angeles. Titan all-star Martin Lapointe became a regular on right wing with Detroit, winning the Stanley Cup in 1997. Other prospects on the Laval Titan had another chance to impress NHL scouts at the 1994 Memorial Cup.

The **1994** Memorial Cup

"When you put on a Blazers jersey, it's like putting on the Canadiens'," sixteen-year-old rookie Jarome Iginla explained to a Montreal *Gazette* reporter during the 1994 Memorial Cup. "You've got to perform." The Blazers were the youngest team in the tournament, but brought a tradition of twelve straight winning seasons into Laval, Quebec, where they faced the host Titan, the Chicoutimi Sagueneens and the top-ranked North Bay Centennials.

Michel Therrien's Laval Titan were bringing a solid tradition of their own to the series. They had appeared in four of the previous six Memorial Cups, but were still looking for their first title. Despite finishing first in the QMJHL during the regular season, they were swept in the league final by Chicoutimi, losing three games in overtime. Nonetheless, the Titan possessed key players with 1993 Memorial Cup experience, including Daniel Goneau and Marc Beaucage, who joined Alain Cote on the team's most potent forward line. Defencemen Sylvain Blouin and Michael Gaul, forward Yannick Dubé and goalie Emmanuel Fernandez were some of the other mainstays of the squad. The Chicoutimi Sagueneens were something of a dark horse, although their defeat of Laval in the Quebec championship served notice that the team should be taken seriously. Coached by Gaston Drapeau, Chicoutimi's lineup included two linchpins: CHL defenceman of the year Steve Gosselin and highly touted goaltender Eric Fichaud.

The North Bay Centennials entered the tournament as the highest-ranked junior team in the CHL. The Centennials' bench boss Bert Templeton was CHL coach of the year and had won a Memorial Cup with the Hamilton Fincups in 1976. In the 1994 OHL playoffs, the Centennials defeated the Detroit Junior Red Wings for the Ontario title. The gruelling series left North Bay's top gun Jeff Shevalier badly hampered by a shoulder injury. The team was counting on the hobbled Shevalier and CHL rookie of the year rightwinger Vitali Yachmenev to lead its offence, while defensive prospect Brad Brown anchored the Centennials' blueline.

The Kamloops Blazers needed six games to get past both Seattle and Portland, and were pushed to the limit by the Saskatoon Blades in the WHL final. Seven members had been on the Blazers roster that won the 1992 Memorial Cup, although only Jarrett Deuling, Rod Stevens and defenceman Scott Ferguson had seen regular action in that year's tournament. The Blazers' offence was spear-headed by Darcy Tucker, who finished second in the WHL scoring race. Aaron Keller and Nolan Baumgartner led the defensive corps. Tom Renney having moved on to become the Canadian Olympic and national team coach, Kamloops' coaching duties were taken over by longtime assistant coach Don Hay. He had taken a two-year leave of absence from firefighting to steer the team.

The city of Laval is situated in the Montreal metropolitan area. Titan man-agement passed up an offer to host the Cup in the Montreal Forum, choosing instead the familiar atmosphere of the 3,000-seat Laval Colisée, ominously dubbed "The House of Pain." They hoped that home ice would help to end the Quebec junior title drought, but only 1,836 paying customers showed up on May 14 for the opening game between Laval and North Bay.

Those on hand were not disappointed. The teams skated into overtime, where the Titan pulled out a gutsy 5–4 victory. David Haynes, who had scored just 4 goals in the regular season, struck at 6:45 of the extra period. Yannick Dubé figured in all five Laval goals, while the Centennials exhibited a nervous-ness that would haunt the team throughout the tournament.

Twenty-four hours later, Laval was back on the ice against Kamloops. This time, the Titan found themselves on the losing end of a 5–4 score. Kamloops was on fire, outshooting Laval 23–6 in the opening period, and 49–20 in the entire game. Only an equally hot Manny Fernandez in the Titan goal kept the score close. Hnat Domenichelli produced the game-winner. Kamloops also had a goal and 2 assists from Tucker. Laval's top unit of Goneau, Cote and Marc Beaucage did all the Titan scoring.

The Blazers showed no fear in the much-publicized House of Pain. "Laval Colisée was a lot like our old Memorial Arena," Hay said, "which fit right in with our tight forechecking game."

Things did get painful after the game, however, as referee Luc Lachapelle suffered face and head cuts when the window of the car he was riding in was smashed in the Colisée parking lot. According to Lachapelle, the damage was caused by Titan general manager Jean-Claude Morrissette's fist. The next day, Morrissette resigned, and a CHL disciplinary committee fined the Titan $10,000, barring Morrissette from the Colisée de Laval for the rest of the tournament. The QMJHL later suspended him from all league activities with any team for the 1994–95 season.

The Chicoutimi Sagueneens didn't take to the ice until game three. Like the Blazers, they had enjoyed an opportunity to scout their opponents. In their first match, Chicoutimi faced North Bay and scored a 3–1 victory on the strength of an impressive 39-save performance by Eric Fichaud.

Fichaud faced a more potent offence in the Sagueneens' next game. Kamloops blanked Chicoutimi 5–0, clinching a berth in the final. Darcy Tucker scored 3 second-period goals and goaltender Steve Passmore was unbeatable on

25 shots. "It was probably the easiest shutout I've ever had," Passmore observed. The Blazers fired 51 shots at Fichaud and pumped home 4 second-period goals. They forechecked with persistence and created constant traffic in front of the beleaguered Chicoutimi netminder.

In their next outing, the Blazers faced an anxious and battered North Bay team who needed a win to stay alive in the tournament. The young Blazers, however, were gaining more poise with every game and, despite already holding a berth in the final, gave no quarter. They thumped North Bay 5–1, eliminating them from the tournament. The Centennials were plagued by undisciplined penalties throughout the proceedings. For the Blazers, Darcy Tucker had a goal and 2 assists, which gave him the tournament scoring lead.

Chicoutimi and Laval next faced each other in back-to-back games: the final match of the round robin and the semi-final. The Sagueneens scored their fifth straight post-season victory over Laval in the first contest, getting second-period goals from Danny

Team captain Darcy Tucker played with the Kamloops Blazers for both their 1992 and 1994 Memorial Cup victories.
BRIAN SAMPSON/BLAZERS

Beauregard and Alexei Lojkin. An impeccable Fichaud made 33 saves in the 2–0 victory. But the Titan broke this lock in a timely fashion, defeating Chicoutimi in the semi-final by 4–2. Laval defenceman Michael Gaul scored twice and Alain Cote had three assists. Their team outshot Chicoutimi 39–23. The Titan headed into the final with Kamloops.

"The final is a one-shot deal, so anything can happen," coach Michel Therrien said. "We'll give it all we've got and I know my players will show up. We'll be tired, but that won't be an excuse. I want it to be a great day for the Quebec Major Junior Hockey League and for the Titan family."

But the Blazers held sway over much of the championship game, and were cruising with a 4–1 lead in the latter stages of the third period. Without warning, the Titan struck twice in fifty-four seconds. With six minutes left, the capacity crowd of 3,119 roared to life. Don Hay, whose Kamloops squad was feeling unaccustomed pressure, called a time out. "He just said that we were going good until we let a couple of checks get away and unfortunately the shots went in," Blazer Louis Dumont said afterwards. "He just said we had to screw our heads back on."

The Blazers returned to the ice and settled down. In the final seventy-five seconds, the Titan pulled Fernandez. But a fourth-line Blazers forward named Bob Maudie scored his only goal of the tournament to clinch a 5–3 victory. The Memorial Cup went to Kamloops.

Louis Dumont scored the Blazers' first goal and assisted on the second, both tallies coming as a result of the devastating Kamloops forechecking game. Mike Josephson, Ryan Huska and Darcy Tucker scored the other Kamloops goals. For the Titan, Daniel Goneau scored twice and Alain Cote once. "I believe in developing a player to be able to play in all situations," Don Hay philosophized. "I think being able to put four lines out there paid off, and my philosophy has always been to play the younger guys, as long as they are working hard."

Darcy Tucker, a draft pick of the Montreal Canadiens, won both the Memorial Cup scoring title and Most Valuable Player honours. "I was in the back yard of the team that drafted me," Tucker noted. "I knew how much pressure there would be from the media, and I knew the Canadiens would be watching. I put a lot of pressure on myself to do well." Defenceman Nolan Baumgartner also made the all-star team, as did teammate Aaron Keller. The forward line all-stars were centre Tucker, Blazers rightwinger Rod Stevens and Laval leftwinger Cote. The Titan's diminutive and classy forward Yannick Dubé was named most sportsmanlike player. Fichaud was voted the best goaltender.

Kamloops leftwinger Jarrett Deuling went on to play in the NHL for the New York Islanders. Darcy Tucker would see some action with the Montreal Canadiens, but first he returned to the 1995 Memorial Cup with the Kamloops Blazers. Nolan Baumgartner, Jarome Iginla, and Hnat Domenichelli would also return to the Memorial Cup in 1995. Brad Brown of North Bay entered the

Kamloops Blazers. BRIAN SAMPSON/BLAZERS

Montreal Canadiens lineup in 1996–97, while Vitali Yachmenev became a regular rightwinger for the Los Angeles Kings.

Eric Fichaud of the Chicoutimi Sagueneens was taken by Toronto in the first round of the 1994 NHL entry draft, although he later saw action with the Islanders.

Laval goalie Emmanuel Fernandez started his pro career in the minor leagues, also suiting up with Dallas for a handful of NHL games in the mid-1990s.

The **1995** Memorial Cup

"The Blazers don't rebuild, they reload."

As the 1995 Memorial Cup got under way, it was difficult to determine whether this was an exaggeration or an understatement. The team that had swept through the 1994 tournament was back almost intact. As hosts of the event, the Blazers had invited their alumni for a reunion. To onlookers, the Detroit Junior Red Wings, Brandon Wheat Kings and Hull Olympiques may have seemed more like props in a coronation than serious challengers to the junior throne.

Blazers forwards Tyson Nash, Ryan Huska and Darcy Tucker, veterans of the 1992 and 1994 championship teams, were seeking to become the first players in history to win three Memorial Cups with the same team. Rightwinger Ashley Buckberger had been acquired from Swift Current during the regular season, adding to the solid experience brought by captain Darcy Tucker, Hnat Domenichelli and defencemen Nolan Baumgartner and Aaron Keller. Younger players like Jarome Iginla and Shane Doan were one year older and better.

Although the Blazers were guaranteed a spot in the tournament as host team, they also went in as WHL champions, having defeated the Brandon Wheat Kings. The western final had them briefly on the ropes, when the Wheat Kings handed Kamloops their first back-to-back home losses of the year. But the Blazers came back to win the next four in a row, rookie goalie Randy Petruk proving himself to be up to playoff pressure.

Brandon had been without injured Calgary Flames draftee Chris Dingman for the western final, but they expected him back for the Memorial Cup. Dingman, a 6'4", 230-pound power forward with considerable skill around the net, was a key part of the Brandon offence, along with Darren Ritchie and WHL Most Valuable Player and captain Marty Murray. On defence, coach Bob Lowes's team was led by two highly touted prospects, Wade Redden and Bryan McCabe.

Like Brandon, Detroit started the tournament without one of its leaders. Over-age defenceman Shayne McCosh was nursing a fractured arm. Coach Paul Maurice was relying on forward Sean Haggerty, and defencemen Bryan Berard and Jamie Allison. Only twenty-eight years old, Maurice had seen Memorial Cup action in 1988 as a player with the OHL Windsor Spitfires. "We probably have less talent this year," said Maurice, comparing the two teams, "but better chemistry.

To get here, we had to beat three outstanding OHL teams in Windsor, Sudbury and Guelph."

Hull coach Robert Mongrain had also played in the Memorial Cup in 1979 with the Trois-Rivieres Draveurs. Experience was not something his team shared with him, however. Mongrain oversaw a group with eleven rookies, and his team was the decided underdog in a tough field. But the club had shown some giant-killer instinct earlier in the playoffs, when they upset the favoured Laval Titan in the QMJHL final. Unfortunately, the young team also had the weight of the Quebec Memorial Cup drought hanging around their necks, an albatross that was getting heavier by the year.

Hull captain and scoring leader Sebastien Bordeleau, son of former NHLer Paulin Bordeleau, carried some heavy expectations into the tournament. So did outstanding goaltending prospect Jose Theodore, who was Most Valuable Player during the Quebec league playoffs. The pair joined the Blazers' Tucker as a trio of Montreal Canadiens draft picks being watched closely in the tournament. Theodore was establishing himself as the latest member of a superb Quebec goal-tending fraternity that included NHLers Patrick Roy, Martin Brodeur, Félix Potvin and Jocelyn Thibault. "In the west and OHL, there's lots of hooking, backchecking and shots from bad angles," said Theodore, explaining the QMJHL's reliance on good netminders. "But in Quebec, we have a lot of break-aways and two-on-ones, and sometimes 40 or 50 quality shots."

Theodore got a rough reception from Brandon shooters in the opening game on May 13. The Olympiques were shelled by a score of 9–2. Rightwinger Darren Ritchie had a hat trick, and Theodore was pulled in the second period when the score reached 6–0. "We hadn't played a game that bad all season," coach Mongrain lamented. "Usually when we get a lead like that we don't bear down," Darren Ritchie admitted, "but we did today and got some good bounces, too." Like the other matches at the 1995 tournament, the game was a sellout, drawing 5,500 fans.

On day two of the tournament, the Jr. Red Wings achieved a narrow 4–3 win over Brandon. No goals were scored in the hard-hitting game until midway through the second period when defenceman Bryan Berard notched the first of three straight tallies by Detroit, giving them a 3–0 lead heading into the third. The teams exchanged goals early in the final frame, and then Brandon scored 2 late tallies in a comeback push that fell short.

Later the same day, Kamloops hosted Hull. The Blazers' power play had some early success, producing 3 goals with the man advantage to give Kamloops a 3–1 lead up to the first intermission. Shane Doan, who had missed the 1994 Memorial Cup with a knee injury, scored his first of the series for the Blazers. Kamloops outshot Hull 49–19 in the game, but put no more goals past Jose Theodore, who was regaining his composure after the opening day debacle. Iginla fired his second of the night into an empty net to seal the score at 4–1.

Doan scored another 2 and added an assist in the Blazers' next game, a tighter affair against the Jr. Red Wings. Kamloops nosed out a 5–4 win, Hnat Domenichelli opening the Kamloops scoring six minutes into the first period and Doan pulling the trigger twenty-four seconds later. The Blazers took a 3–2 lead into the third, firing 2 more goals in just over a minute to pad the margin. Detroit could not pull even.

Hull's offensive leader, Sebastien Bordeleau, opened the scoring in the fifth game with his first goal of the tournament. But the Detroit Jr. Red Wings came back with five in a row to post a 5–2 victory. Toronto Maple Leafs draft pick Sean Haggerty notched a hat trick. With an 0–3 record, Hull exited the tournament, prompting QMJHL president Gilles Corteau to pack his bags as well. He left the event a few days early. "I'm embarrassed," Corteau explained. "What can I say? There are no excuses. They played three of their worst games of the season."

"My team was very nervous for the three games," Mongrain suggested. "When you have young players, they start doubting."

Next Kamloops and Brandon faced each other, with a spot in the final riding on the outcome. Chris Dingman returned to the Wheat Kings' lineup but he could not make the difference as the Blazers skated to a 6–4 victory. Jarome Iginla scored twice, including the winner, while Doan had a goal and an assist. Mark Dutiame scored twice in the second period to bring the Wheat Kings back from a 4–1 deficit, but Kamloops put the game away in the final period. "We created some things with the forecheck," Brandon coach Lowes said. "At times we weren't on top of our game. There have just been too many times that we've shot ourselves in the foot."

He believed that his team, now headed into a semi-final with Detroit, would have another chance against the Blazers. "If we get on guys like Jamie Allison and Bryan Berard, I think we should be able to get in the final." But Brandon allowed a 1–0 third-period lead to slip away in the semi-final, and their hopes for the Memorial Cup disappeared with it. The Detroit Jr. Red Wings celebrated a 2–1 decision over the Wheat Kings. Although the shots on goal were almost equal, Brandon had numerous chances to improve on the 1–0 lead, but the Wheat Kings were stonewalled by red-hot Detroit goalie Jason Saal.

Early in the third, Detroit leftwinger Milan Kostolny finished off a two-on-one break to tie the score. The winner came with five minutes left, when Detroit's sterile power play finally connected on an odd goal. Matt Ball's shot from a difficult angle hit Brandon defenceman Sven Butenschon and deflected past startled Brandon goalie Byron Penstock. Detroit paid dearly for the win, though. Bryan Berard was put out of action with a charley horse, an injury that would hamper him in the final game.

It was not just a half-speed Berard that hampered Detroit in their title match against Kamloops. A full-speed Blazers power play also had something to do with it. Kamloops exploded for 5 goals on 8 chances against a Red Wings team boasting one of the best penalty-killing records in junior hockey. The Blazers cruised to an 8–2 win and claimed their second consecutive Memorial Cup. After one period, Kamloops had outshot Detroit 13–3. The entire second period, in which Kamloops fired another 28 shots, seemed to be in the Wings' end.

Seven Blazers goals came in the middle frame. All four forward lines had at least 1 goal, and two defencemen pitched in for good measure. Leading the way was the game's first star, Ryan Huska. The Chicago Blackhawk draftee had 2 goals and 2 assists, while Tyson Nash, Darcy Tucker, Aaron Keller, Brad Lukowich, Bob

Maudie and Jeff Antonovich also scored. Detroit received goals from Jeff Mitchell and Eric Manlow. Detroit captain Jamie Allison, a second-round draft pick of the Calgary Flames, reflected on the loss. "We kept killing penalties and killing penalties and I think that wore us down," he said. "The guys got demoralized and started worrying about the officials more than the game." Allison also praised Kamloops for their effort. "They're a great team all around, we didn't have much forecheck or defence against them."

With 3 goals and 6 assists, Shane Doan topped the tournament scoring race. He was also given Most Valuable Player honours and named the all-star rightwinger. Other all-stars included Darcy Tucker at centre and Detroit's Sean Haggerty on left wing. The defencemen were Blazer Nolan Baumgartner and Wheat King Bryan McCabe.

Detroit's Jason Saal was the top goalie and tournament all-star netminder. Jarome Iginla had 5 goals to top all Blazers scorers and was named most sportsman-like player. Ironically, he got into a scrap in the final minutes of the championship game, after the award had been finalized.

Iginla was taken in the first round of the 1995 entry draft by the Dallas Stars, although he would see his first NHL action with the Calgary Flames. Fellow Kamloops Blazer Shane Doan started his career in Winnipeg, then moved with the team to Phoenix. Hnat Domenichelli joined the NHL with the Calgary Flames in 1996–97. Darcy Tucker also stepped into the pros in 1996–97 by climbing his way up the Montreal Canadiens' depth chart. Nolan Baumgartner remained a minor-league prospect after his first couple of pro years but made his NHL debut with the Washington Capitals in 1995–96.

Sean Haggerty of the Jr. Red Wings also recorded his NHL debut in 1995–96, with the Toronto Maple Leafs. Jamie Allison joined Domenichelli in

In 1995 Jamie Allison led the Detroit Jr. Red Wings to the Memorial Cup finals, only to be defeated by the Kamloops Blazers.

Kamloops Blazers. BRIAN SAMPSON/BLAZERS

Calgary for part of the 1996–97 season. The season after taking Detroit to the Memorial Cup, Paul Maurice was named coach of the Hartford Whalers, becoming the youngest coach in the NHL. Don Hay also immediately joined the NHL as an assistant with the Calgary Flames. Only one year later, he joined the NHL's head coaching ranks with the Phoenix Coyotes.

Bryan Berard of the Detroit Jr. Red Wings and Wade Redden of the Brandon Wheat Kings made the best impression on the scouts for the upcoming 1995 entry draft. Berard went first overall to Ottawa, while Redden went second to the New York Islanders. After the Memorial Cup and the draft, their paths would cross yet another time when they were traded for each other in a swap involving three other players on January 23, 1996. While Redden continued to develop in Ottawa, Berard made an immediate impact on Long Island, winning the Calder Trophy for 1996–97.

From the Brandon Wheat Kings, Bryan McCabe jumped directly into the NHL with the New York Islanders. Marty Murray started his career in the minor leagues, but was occasionally called up to the NHL to play for the Calgary Flames.

The two stars of Hull, Sebastien Bordeleau and Jose Theodore, both saw duty with the Montreal Canadiens over the next couple of seasons.

The **1996** Memorial Cup

Michel Therrien, coach of the Granby Prédateurs since the beginning of the 1995–96 season, didn't harbour any false illusions about his team's playoff chances. "They haven't won and they don't know how to win," he said. "Even if they have the talent, we have a lot of work to do. They don't have a winning tradition here." The Prédateurs did have a lot of work to do if they wanted to win the Memorial Cup. None of the players had even been alive when Guy Lafleur led the Quebec Remparts to the 1971 title, Quebec's last hurrah. The 1996

Prédateurs met the Brandon Wheat Kings, Guelph Storm and host Peterborough Petes in the Memorial Cup championship. Peterborough had competed for the Memorial Cup many times, but had never played host to the event. Despite the Petes' many years of success, Peterborough was a controversial host for the tournament because of the poor condition of their home rink.

Michel Therrien was brought from Laval to Granby by the Morrissette brothers, who had formerly presided over the Titan. The new Granby hierarchy proceeded to gut and replace much of the team roster during 1995–96, making a number of deals involving Laval players. Captain Francis Bouillon and defenceman Jason Doig were among the players brought over from the Titan, as well as 100-point men Daniel Goneau and Benoit Gratton. Other Granby snipers included Xavier Delisle and Martin Chouinard, and goaltending was handled by Frédéric Deschênes. Strong on offence and defence, the once-humble Prédateurs became the winningest squad in the CHL. They roared through the playoffs, defeating the Beauport Harfangs for the league title.

The Dave MacQueen-coached Petes were led offensively by rightwinger Cameron Mann, who played on the team's most potent line with Jason MacMillan and Mike Williams. Their defensive leaders were Kevin Bolibruck and goalie Zac Bierk, a 6'4" walk-on addition and Tampa Bay Lightning draftee. Peterborough finished sixth in the OHL and eliminated Kingston, Sarnia and the highly touted Detroit Whalers en route to the league championship. The final series against Guelph was decided in overtime of the seventh game, when the Petes took an 8–7 win on a pot shot by defenceman Mike Martone.

Veteran NHL assistant coach E.J. McGuire had taken over coaching duties in Guelph for the 1995–96 season, replacing Craig Hartsburg who left to coach the Chicago Blackhawks. In the regular season, Guelph finished on top of the OHL. The Storm defeated Niagara Falls and Belleville in the playoffs before bowing to Peterborough. Highly ranked going into the Memorial Cup, the team was built around outstanding defence, solid goaltending and cohesive team play, all of which offset the lack of a big scorer. Jeff Williams emerged as the team's offensive leader in the playoffs, while Dan Cloutier emerged as the post-season netminder. Cloutier had previous Memorial Cup experience backing up Kevin Hodson in the Sault Ste. Marie Greyhounds' 1993 triumph.

Like Guelph, the Brandon Wheat Kings were a defensively sound team, but with a few more snipers in their lineup. Coached by Bob Lowes and captained by Chris Dingman, Brandon finished first in the WHL during the regular season before sidelining Saskatoon, Red Deer, Prince Albert and Spokane to claim the league championship. Veteran 1995 Memorial Cup defencemen Wade Redden, Justin Kurtz and Sven Butenschon led the deepest blue-line brigade in the tournament, while Mike Leclerc and Peter Schaefer were the Wheat Kings' offensive leaders.

On May 11, Granby opened the Memorial Cup by firing 8 holes through the touted Guelph defence, shutting out the Storm 8–0. Frédéric Deschênes gained the distinction of becoming the first goaltender for a Quebec-based team to record a shutout against an Ontario or western team since Bobby Bleau did the trick for the 1949 Montreal Royals. Granby opened the scoring a minute into the game, and had a 4–0 lead by the first intermission. Jason Doig scored twice, celebrating each of his goals by rolling on the ice. Daniel Goneau also bagged a pair, and Philippe Audet added a goal and 3 assists. A pleased Michel Therrien claimed the real indication his players were ready for business was that they took more stitches than scored goals during the game.

It took barely eleven minutes to settle the second game, as Brandon overcame an early deficit to take a 2–1 lead at 11:01 of the first period. From there, teams with comparable defensive styles squared off until the final whistle. Guelph, the top-ranked team in the tournament, was on the verge of elimination with the 2–1 loss. "You can't play a game without making mistakes," Brandon defenceman Wade Redden noted, "but we didn't give them a lot of chances."

Peterborough got into action on the same day. Zac Bierk turned in a strong performance, backstopping the Petes to a 6–3 win over Granby. The game was locked at 3 going into the final period, but Cameron Mann scored his second off a wild scramble to break the tie early in the third. The two goals gave Mann 29 in twenty-five playoff games, breaking a Peterborough franchise record held by Mike Ricci. "We just finished a tough seven games with Guelph and our guys might have wondered if this team [Granby] is 8 goals better than Guelph," coach MacQueen said, "but a video of the game showed them that Granby makes mistakes just like anybody else."

Game four saw Vancouver Canucks draft pick Peter Schaefer put Brandon temporarily in the driver's seat. He lifted a hard wrist shot under the crossbar at 3:58 of overtime to give the Wheat Kings a 3–2 victory over the Petes. "The plan was to go for the net in overtime and hopefully look for a cheesy one," Schaefer said, "but the way it worked out it was a pretty nice goal." In the first period, Brandon opened the scoring with a powerplay goal by Chris Dingman. But the Petes scored twice in the second to pull ahead. Wade Redden quickly evened things back up, then the teams played scoreless until overtime. "We're not a run and gun team," Brandon coach Bobby Lowes explained, "we have to work hard for our goals."

Goals were a problem for the Wheat Kings in their next game as well. Granby built a 3–1 lead in the first period and rode it to a spot in the final. The winning goal was scored by Xavier Delisle, who summed up his team's attitude after the game. "We came here with the big pressure because it's been twenty-five years since a Quebec team won the Memorial Cup," he said, "but we can win the Memorial Cup. We will win the Cup."

"My hat is off to Granby," said Lowes. "They deserve to be in the final. I think they outworked us and they were a lot more intense."

Game six brought the 0–2 Guelph Storm together with the 1–2 Petes. Guelph needed to defeat Peterborough by a sizeable goal differential to have any hope of advancing to the semi-final game. The Petes also needed a big spread to jump directly into the final. Neither team got what they wanted, but the Petes managed a 2–1 victory. The seesaw affair was viewed by a sellout crowd of 4,429 fans.

Goalie Zac Bierk seemed to gain inspiration from listening to his older brother Sebastian Bach of the rock band Skid Row howl a heavy metal rendition of "O

Philippe Audet of the Granby Prédateurs won the first Ed Chynoweth Trophy as Memorial Cup Tournament scoring champion with 4 goals and 4 assists.
DAN HAMILTON/VANTAGE POINT

Canada." Bierk withstood a first-period barrage, as Guelph outshot the Petes 17–7. "They had us on our heels in that first period and early in the second," MacQueen said. "We wouldn't be where we are today if it wasn't for Bierk's play all season." In the second period, Guelph took the lead on a goal by Jeff Williams but it lasted barely two minutes. Peterborough's Corey Crocker and Cameron Mann scored twenty-seven seconds apart to put their team ahead for good. "Our inability to score sometimes reared up and bit us during the year," Guelph coach Maguire summed up.

With Granby in the final, the Petes and Wheat Kings met in the semi-final. Having beaten Peterborough once already, the Wheat Kings were confident they could solve the goaltending of Zac Bierk. "You just have to shoot, shoot, shoot," said Wheat Kings' centre Bob Brown prior to the game. "There are rebounds to be had, he's down a lot, so we've got to get our shots up." Brown's strategy appeared to be working early on, as Brandon was ahead 2–0 just ten minutes into the game. Schaefer scored shorthanded and Brown on the powerplay. The Wheat Kings dominated the opening period before running into a rash of penalties. Their penalty killers were able to hold off the Petes' powerplay, but Brandon's momentum had stalled. The team's reliance on key players in the out-manned situations also took its toll in the sweltering conditions of the Peterborough Memorial Centre.

Peterborough climbed back into the game in the second period, and two goals later, had erased their opponents' lead. Eight minutes into the third, defenceman Matt Johnson scored his first-ever goal in major junior hockey, placing the Petes in front. Then Mann scored again. Although Mike Leclerc brought the Wheat Kings back to within 1, they could not get the equalizer, and the Petes rode a 4–3 victory to the final. "Our team was motivated by some of the press saying that we weren't good enough to host the Cup, let alone a good enough city," said MacQueen, referring to criticism of the old Peterborough Memorial Centre as the host facility. About the semi-final game he added, "It was a typical Peterborough Petes' game. This club never does anything easy, but we found a way to win."

The Petes couldn't find a way to beat Granby, however. The Prédateurs shut down the OHL champions 4–0 in the sweltering heat and foggy humidity of the championship game. The Petes dominated the first period, outshooting Granby 15–6. But the Prédateurs skated off their nervousness in the second to take control of the game. Philippe Audet scored on the powerplay six minutes into the middle frame, putting Granby ahead. The score remained 1–0 until Chouinard scored six minutes into the third. For a tired and emotionally drained Peterborough club, coming from behind must have seemed a monumental task, especially after David Brosseau and Daniel Goneau added 2 more goals for the Prédateurs.

Over the course of the match, the ice surface was increasingly affected by the building's Amazonian climate. The game took nearly four hours to complete, as playing conditions slowed everything to a crawl for almost the entire second period and part of the third. Maintenance crews made countless trips onto the ice to remove excess surface water resulting from the 27-degree Celsius temperature in the Memorial Centre.

The enervating conditions were an advantage for the Prédateurs, who were better rested and had a deeper roster. Peterborough relentlessly called upon their top line of Mann, MacMillan and Williams to try to get back in the game. "We didn't want to give them a lead," Therrien said, "so we were very happy after the first period that it was scoreless. Because they played [the previous day], we knew that the longer the game went on, the better it would be for us. The guys on both teams were dying out there."

"There was lots of water on the ice," said the Petes' Corey Crocker. "It was like skating on a pond after a big flood. With the fog too, you couldn't see a foot in front of you."

The Prédateurs, however, were euphoric with triumph. They skated proudly around the rink, draped in the fleur-de-lis. "Today we won respect for the QMJHL from all of Canada," Frédéric Deschênes said. "There is no better day in my life."

"We're back on the map," Daniel Goneau agreed. "When I scored the final goal, I cried. It was unbelievable. It's been a long time—twenty-five years. Lafleur had time to play in the NHL and he's retired now."

Detroit Red Wings draftee Philippe Audet won the newly instituted Ed Chynoweth Trophy as tournament scoring champion for his 4 goals and 4 assists. Boston pick Cameron Mann got the nod as Most Valuable Player. The Memorial Cup all-star team included Mann, Audet and Xavier Delisle, along with defencemen Jason Doig and Wade Redden and goalie Deschênes. Peterborough's Mike Williams was the most sportsmanlike player. In addition to being named the tournament's outstanding goalie, Deschênes became the first netminder ever to record two shutouts in a Memorial Cup championship. He was also the first

Granby Prédateurs. Back row (l to r): Richard Tremblay (assistant trainer), Jodi Van Rees (athletic therapist), Jean-François Brunelle, Benoit Gratton, Michel Massie, Todd Row, Philippe Grondin, Jonathan Desroches, Bard Sorlie, Stephane Dubé (conditioning coach), Patrick Léonard (trainer). Middle row: Samy Nasreddine, Philippe Audet, George Laraque, Christian Lefebvre, Yvan Charbonneau (assistant coach), Carole Morrissette, Jocelyn Morrissette, Pierre Morrissette and Regis Morrissette (owners), Joseph Devar (marketing director), Jason Doig, Kevin Bourque, David Brosseau, Jimmy Drolet. Front row: Frédéric Deschênes, Richard Lafreniere (scout), Martin Chouinard, George Morrissette (governor and general manager), Jean-François Tremblay, Daniel Bissonnette (assistant coach), Francis Bouillon, Michel Therrien (coach), Daniel Goneau, Jean-Claude Morrissette (special adviser), Xavier Delisle, Michel Trudel (president), Frederic Henry.

netminder since the round robin format had been introduced to record a shutout in the final game.

Brandon's Wade Redden started his NHL career the next season with the Ottawa Senators. Granby's Daniel Goneau quickly turned pro as well, playing half a year for the New York Rangers. But the first participant in the 1996 tournament to play pro was Jason Doig, who had already put in fifteen games for the Winnipeg Jets during the 1995–96 season.

The **1997** Memorial Cup

Having watched the Granby Prédateurs end Quebec's Memorial Cup drought in 1996, the Hull Olympiques felt they were in a good position to begin a new streak for Quebec teams. But despite their powerful roster and status as host of the tournament, the Olympiques were not an automatic pick against the Lethbridge Hurricanes, Oshawa Generals and Chicoutimi Sagueneens.

With eleven drafted players already on their team, the Olympiques found a centrepiece in Christian Dubé. They picked up the centre from Sherbrooke midway through the 1996–97 season in return for two draft picks and $50,000. Widely regarded as the best player in junior hockey, Dubé had spent the first part of the season in the NHL with the New York Rangers. In addition to Dubé, Hull had Pavel Rosa, the leading scorer in the QMJHL, sniper Martin Menard and goaltender Christian Bronsard. Coached by Claude Julien, the Olympiques defeated Drummondville, Val-d'Or and Chicoutimi for the President's Trophy, losing only twice.

The Oshawa Generals returned to Memorial Cup action by upsetting the Ottawa 67's. The classic series ended with Marc Savard scoring in overtime in the seventh game. Savard was the Generals' offensive leader and all-time leading scorer. Oshawa also relied on captain Ryan Lindsay, power forward John Tripp, defenceman Jan Snopek and goaltender David Arsenault, who had been let go by the Chicoutimi Sagueneens earlier in the year. The Generals defeated the Peterborough Petes and Kitchener Rangers prior to the OHL final versus Ottawa. Their coach was former NHL defenceman Bill Stewart.

The Chicoutimi Sagueneens defeated Rimouski, Victoriaville and Halifax to emerge as champions of the Dilio division of the QMJHL. Making the league final against Hull, the Memorial Cup's host team, guaranteed them a spot in the national tournament. But the championship of the Quebec league was still on the line and the Sagueneens lost it in four straight games. The Chicoutimi goalie factory that produced Félix Potvin and Eric Fichaud had another outstanding prospect in Marc Denis, voted the top CHL goaltender for 1996–97. Coached by Real Paiement, the Sagueneens also featured Frederic Bouchard, who had just set a record for the most points by a defenceman in the QMJHL playoffs.

The Lethbridge Hurricanes shored up a solid veteran lineup in a January trade with Prince Albert. High-scoring rightwinger Shane Willis, goaltender Blaine Russell and Chris Phillips, a defenceman drafted first overall by Ottawa in 1996, came to Lethbridge in the deal. The Hurricanes, a gritty squad that featured forwards Mike Josephson and Byron Ritchie, sidelined Prince Albert, Moose Jaw, Red Deer and Seattle in the WHL playoffs. Parry Shockey was behind the Hurricanes' bench, as two-time Memorial Cup-winning coach Bryan Maxwell was serving a one-year suspension, set to expire during the 1997 tournament, for assaulting a referee in the 1996 WHL playoffs.

On May 10, Oshawa and Chicoutimi opened the Memorial Cup series. The Generals claimed a dramatic 5–3 victory in the dying seconds of the game, Marty Wilford scoring the winner on a nicely executed set play from the faceoff. The lead went back and forth, and both clubs' special teams got plenty of work. Ryan Lindsay had 2 goals and an assist, while Marc Savard had 4 assists for the Generals. Frederic Bouchard continued his playoff point run with a Chicoutimi goal. Of the winning goal, Sagueneens coach Real Paiement commented, "It's unfortunate it comes off a technical play. We worked on faceoffs all year long." But the Generals felt they still had room for improvement. "Even though we got the win tonight, I don't think we played the best we could," Marc Savard said.

Less than twenty hours after their demoralizing loss, the Sagueneens were back on the ice against Lethbridge. Chris Phillips scored shorthanded less than two minutes in to get the Hurricanes off to a good start. Lethbridge was in control throughout the game, gradually building a 4–0 lead before coughing up 2 goals to Chicoutimi late in the third. Mike Josephson, the lone over-age Hurricane player, scored a goal and an assist for the Hurricanes in another penalty-filled affair.

The Olympiques made an impressive statement in their first outing, overpowering the Generals 8–0 before a partisan home crowd of 3,500. Christian Dubé accounted for over half of Hull's offence, scoring 4 times on the night and adding an assist. Pavel Rosa had 2 goals and 2 assists. Four of Hull's goals came on the powerplay in yet another referee-centred outing. Olympiques goalie Christian Bronsard stopped 20 shots to record the only shutout of the 1997 Memorial Cup. "I never thought I'd get a chance to play in the Memorial Cup," Dubé said, "so to score 4 goals in my first game, well, it's interesting."

"It won't be the last time I've been embarrassed in pro sports," Bill Stewart predicted. "We need to put this game aside as quickly as possible. It's a short week and things can change quickly."

The Lethbridge Hurricanes demonstrated how right Stewart was, stunning Hull in game four with one of the most incredible comebacks in Memorial Cup history. The game had been an exercise in boredom, with the Olympiques up 5–0 at the end of one and 6–1 heading into the third. But Lethbridge came out strong in the final frame, scoring twice in the opening minute to make the score 6–3. When Byron Ritchie scored his second of the game less than five minutes later, a comeback started to look like a real possibility. But there was no scoring for another ten minutes, and it appeared that Hull, although badly disorganized and outshot, might escape with the win. Then Mark Smith and Shane Willis of Lethbridge struck for a pair of

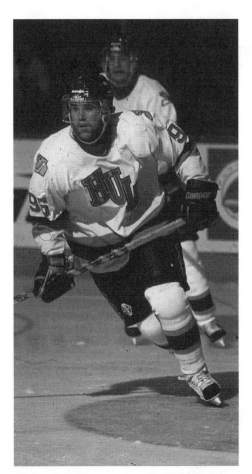

The first player from the 1997 Memorial Cup to see NHL action, Christian Dubé of the Hull Olympiques was touted as the greatest talent in junior hockey that year.
DAN HAMILTON/VANTAGE POINT

late goals to even the score.

The game went into overtime, where Hurricane Mike Josephson scored at 2:50 on a low wrist shot from the slot. He was mobbed joyfully by the Lethbridge players, while incredulous Hull fans watched in silence. "Everyone in the dressing room is trying to figure out what happened," said Claude Julien. "We'll see if it turns out to be a blessing in disguise."

"I don't know if we really thought we'd be able to come back and win it," Josephson said, "but we wanted to come back and show them that we could play with them, in case we met them in the final." Josephson had previously won a Memorial Cup with the 1994 Kamloops Blazers.

The amazing comeback sent a buzz around the tournament for days, but the Hurricanes were unable to carry their momentum into the next game. They were stopped 2–1 by the Generals in a much more tightly played affair. Chastened by their 8–0 drubbing and an animated chewing out at practice from coach Stewart, Oshawa took an early lead on goals by Kevin Colley and Jason Sweitzer. Bryce Salvador answered for Lethbridge early in the third, and the Hurricanes pressed for the tie, but were stopped with some key saves by David Arsenault. The parity of the teams was reflected in their shots on goal, even at 24. Only five penalties were called by referee Stephane Auger, marking a departure from the officiating seminars held in the earlier matches.

Hull went into the final game of the round robin in a good position to advance. But after their collapse against Lethbridge, the Olympiques were taking nothing for granted against the Sagueneens, and neither was anyone else. The Olympiques prevailed, but did not overwhelm, with an 8–5 win against a tenacious Chicoutimi team. This time, it was Martin Menard's turn to score four times, while Rosa and Dubé scored 1 apiece. Four times Hull took the lead, and four times the Sagueneens fought back. Then Menard's fourth goal, a powerplay marker early in the third, put the Olympiques ahead for good. Mario Larocque added insurance for Hull with 2 late tallies. The win put Hull into the title game, with Lethbridge and Oshawa set to face off again in the semi-final.

"They'll play Lethbridge Hurricanes hockey—in your face," Bill Stewart said. "Our courage will be challenged. Our level of skill will be challenged. We've faced challenges all year. That's why we're here." The two teams fought another close game, this one going to overtime. Byron Ritchie put the finishing touch on a hat trick at 4:42 of the extra period, giving Lethbridge a 5–4 victory. Ritchie had almost been suspended the previous day after making a derogatory remark about French Canadians in the game against Hull. The Lethbridge forward apologized and was allowed to play, but he was booed lustily by the crowd of 3,821 every time he touched the puck.

The teams went into the third period tied at 2. When the Hurricanes struck twice in the first minute, they appeared to have broken the game open. But the Generals fought back, evening the score in the final seconds. Ryan Lindsay sent a fluttering shot over Blaine Russell's shoulder with Arsenault halfway to the bench for an extra attacker. The overtime period began with great chances at both ends. It ended at 4:42 when Ritchie snapped at a puck lying in front of the net after Shane Willis had been stopped on a breakaway. The Hurricanes were on their way to the May 18 final, with the experienced Bryan Maxwell back at the helm.

This time, Hull was ready. As they had in their earlier meeting with Lethbridge, the Olympiques built a strong lead. But they built it more slowly and built it to last, taking the Memorial Cup with a 5–1 victory. The first period brought good chances on both sides, neither team gaining momentum. Hull took a 2–1 lead into the first intermission on goals by Menard and Donald MacLean, while Travis Brigley had scored shorthanded for Lethbridge. But as the game wore on, Christian Bronsard started to make the difference, foiling the Lethbridge shooters on a number of excellent opportunities.

A key moment came when Brigley walked in alone early in the second period only to be stoned by Bronsard. Seconds later, MacLean got his second of the game, putting Hull up 3–1. Menard scored another before the end of the second and Jonathan Delisle added a shorthanded marker to consolidate the Olympiques' advantage. The game wound down with the Hull crowd cheering every Olympiques hit, every cleared puck, and every Bronsard save. In the final minutes, 6'6" Hull enforcer Peter Worrell, who had assisted on Menard's goal, had tears in eyes as the crowd rose to its feet, eager to see their team crowned as champion.

"We started building a team three years ago," said Olympiques governor Charlie Henry, responding to suggestions that Hull management had purchased a winner. "We had our ups and downs, but we showed this week we can do it."

Christian Dubé was voted the tournament Most Valuable Player, and Bronsard was recognized as the best goaltender. The all-star team featured Dubé at centre, Martin Menard of Hull at right wing and Hurricane Byron Ritchie at left

Hull Olympiques.

wing. The defencemen were Chris Phillips of Lethbridge and Jan Snopek of Oshawa. Bronsard rounded out the all-star team in goal. The tournament's most sportsmanlike player was Chicoutimi's Radoslav Suchy.

Christian Dubé became the first player from the 1997 Memorial Cup to see NHL action. Immediately after the series he was called up by the New York Rangers, who were in the midst of a conference final battle with the Philadelphia Flyers. Despite the efforts of Dubé, Wayne Gretzky, Mark Messier and the other Rangers, the Flyers prevailed, led by another Memorial Cup graduate, Eric Lindros.

RECORDS & ROSTERS

Winners and Runners-Up

Year	Winning Team	Runner-up
1919	University of Toronto Schools	Regina Patricias
1920	Toronto Canoe Club Paddlers	Selkirk Juniors
1921	Winnipeg Falcons	Stratford Midgets
1922	Fort William War Veterans	Regina Patricias
1923	University of Manitoba Bisons	Kitchener Greenshirts
1924	Owen Sound Greys	Calgary Canadians
1925	Regina Patricias	Aura Lee
1926	Calgary Canadians	Queen's U. Queens
1927	Owen Sound Greys	Port Arthur West End Jrs.
1928	Regina Monarchs	Ottawa Gunners
1929	Toronto Marlboros	Elmwood Millionaires
1930	Regina Patricias	West Toronto
1931	Elmwood Millionaires	Ottawa Primroses
1932	Sudbury Cub Wolves	Winnipeg Monarchs
1933	Newmarket Redmen	Regina Patricias
1934	Toronto St. Michael's Majors	Edmonton Athletics
1935	Winnipeg Monarchs	Sudbury Cub Wolves
1936	West Toronto Nationals	Saskatoon Wesleys
1937	Winnipeg Monarchs	Copper Cliff Redmen
1938	St. Boniface Seals	Oshawa Generals
1939	Oshawa Generals	Edmonton Athletic Club
1940	Oshawa Generals	Kenora Thistles
1941	Winnipeg Rangers	Montreal Royals
1942	Portage la Prairie Terriers	Oshawa Generals
1943	Winnipeg Rangers	Oshawa Generals
1944	Oshawa Generals	Trail Smoke Eaters
1945	Toronto St. Michael's Majors	Moose Jaw Canucks
1946	Winnipeg Monarchs	Toronto St. Michael's Majors
1947	Toronto St. Michael's Majors	Moose Jaw Canucks
1948	Port Arthur West End Bruins	Barrie Flyers
1949	Montreal Royals	Brandon Wheat Kings
1950	Montreal Jr. Canadiens	Regina Patricias
1951	Barrie Flyers	Winnipeg Monarchs
1952	Guelph Biltmore Mad Hatters	Regina Patricias

1953	Barrie Flyers	St. Boniface Canadiens
1954	St. Catharines TeePees	Edmonton Oil Kings
1955	Toronto Marlboros	Regina Patricias
1956	Toronto Marlboros	Regina Patricias
1957	Flin Flon Bombers	Ottawa Canadiens
1958	Ottawa-Hull Canadiens	Regina Patricias
1959	Winnipeg Braves	Peterborough TPT Petes
1960	St. Catharines TeePees	Edmonton Oil Kings
1961	Toronto St. Micheal's Majors	Edmonton Oil Kings
1962	Hamilton Red Wings	Edmonton Oil Kings
1963	Edmonton Oil Kings	Niagara Falls Flyers
1964	Toronto Marlboros	Edmonton Oil Kings
1965	Niagara Falls Flyers	Edmonton Oil Kings
1966	Edmonton Oil Kings	Oshawa Generals
1967	Toronto Marlboros	Port Arthur Marrs
1968	Niagara Falls Flyers	Estevan Bruins
1969	Montreal Jr. Canadiens	Regina Patricias
1970	Montreal Jr. Canadiens	Weyburn Red Wings
1971	Quebec Remparts	Edmonton Oil Kings
1972	Cornwall Royals	Peterborough Petes
1973	Toronto Marlboros	Quebec Remparts
1974	Regina Patricias	Quebec Remparts
1975	Toronto Marlboros	New Westminster Bruins
1976	Hamilton Fincups	New Westminster Bruins
1977	New Westminster Bruins	Ottawa 67's
1978	New Westminster Bruins	Peterborough Petes
1979	Peterborough Petes	Brandon Wheat Kings
1980	Cornwall Royals	Peterborough Petes
1981	Cornwall Royals	Kitchener Rangers
1982	Kitchener Rangers	Sherbrooke Castors
1983	Portland Winter Hawks	Oshawa Generals
1984	Ottawa 67's	Kitchener Rangers
1985	Prince Albert Raiders	Shawinigan Cataractes
1986	Guelph Platers	Hull Olympiques
1987	Medicine Hat Tigers	Oshawa Generals
1988	Medicine Hat Tigers	Windsor Spitfires
1989	Swift Current Broncos	Saskatoon Blades
1990	Oshawa Generals	Kitchener Rangers
1991	Spokane Chiefs	Drummondville Voltigeurs
1992	Kamloops Blazers	Sault Ste. Marie Greyhounds
1993	Sault Ste. Marie Greyhounds	Peterborough Petes
1994	Kamloops Blazers	Laval Titan
1995	Kamloops Blazers	Detroit Jr. Red Wings
1996	Granby Prédateurs	Peterborough Petes
1997	Hull Olympiques	Lethbridge Hurricanes

Rosters of Winning Teams

1919
University of Toronto Schools: Jack Aggett, Steve Greey, Donald Gunn, Don Jeffrey, Richard Kearns, Duncan Munroe, Langton Rowell, Joe Sullivan, W. R. Baker (manager), Frank Carroll (coach).

1920
Toronto Canoe Club Paddlers: Harold Applegath, Billy Burch, Lionel Conacher, Sydney Hueston, Cyril J. Kelly, Francis McCurry, John A. Mollenhauer, Frank Moore, Wilfrid White, Roy Worters, Cyril Reid (manager), Dick Carroll (coach).

1921
Winnipeg Falcons: Freddie "Scotty" Comfort, Wally Fridfinnson, Sammy McCallum, Harold McMunn, Herb McMunn, Bill McPherson, Harry Neil, Dave Patrick, Art Somers, Frank Woodall, Connie Neil (coach).

1922
Fort William War Veterans: Walter Adams (captain), Johnny Bates, Jerry Bourke, Ted D'Arcy, John "Chic" Enwright, Alex Philips, Fred Thornes, Clark Whyte, Stan Bliss (manager, coach).

1923
University of Manitoba at Winnipeg: A. Chapman, C. S. Doupe, "Nip" Johnson, Jack Mitchell, Bob Moulden, Murray Murdoch, Art Puttee, F. Robertson, Blake Watson, Alston "Stony" Wise, Clare Williams, Hal Moulden (coach), R. Bruce (manager).

1924
Owen Sound Greys: James "Dutch" Cain, George Elliott, Bev Flarity, Ted Graham, Mel "Butch" Keeling, H. Silverthorne, Headley Smith, Ralph "Cooney" Weiland, E. "Shorty" Wright, Jim Jamieson (manager), E. T. Hicks (coach).

1925
Regina Patricias: Syl Acaster, Jack Cranstoun, Jack Crapper, Jack Cunning, Ken Doraty, Bert Dowie, Stan Fuller, Johnny Gottselig, Frank Ingram, Ike Morrison, Al Ritchie (manager, coach).

1926
Calgary Canadians: Charles "Chuck" Dunn, Irving Frew, Joe McGoldrich, Donnie McFadyen, George McTeer, Ronnie Martin, Tony Savage, Bert Taylor, Paul Thompson, Sam Timmins, Eddie Poulin (coach).

1927

Owen Sound Greys: Johnny "Red" Beattie, Benny Grant, John Grant, Martin Lauder, Harold "Shrimp" McDougall, Jack Markle, Alvin Moore, Hillis "Paddy" Paddon, H. Smith, A. Bennett (manager), Father J. Spratt and Bill Hancock (coach).

1928

Regina Monarchs: John Achtzner, Carl Bergl, Len Dowie, Charles "Chuck" Farrow, Jim Langford, Harold "Mush" March, G. Parron, Harold Shaw, K. "Swede" Williamson, Howie Milne (manager, coach).

1929

Toronto Marlboros: Clarence Christie, Charlie Conacher, Eddie Convey, Jim Darragh, Bob Gamble, Max Hackett, George "Red" Horner, Harvey "Busher" Jackson, Alex Levinsky, Harry Montgomery, Alf Moore, Laurie Moore, Ellis Pringle, Frank Selke (coach).

1930

Regina Patricias: Yates Acaster, Frank Boll, Art Dowie, Joe Dutkowski, Ken Campbell, Dave Gilhooley, Lon McPherson, Ken Moore, Gordon Pettinger, Len Rae, Ralph Redding, Eddie Wiseman, Al Ritchie (manager, coach).

1931

Elmwood Millionaires: George Brown, Archie Creighton, Albert "Spunk" Duncanson, Boyd Johnston, Don "Duke" McDonald, Bill MacKenzie (captain), Gordie MacKenzie, Kitson Massey, Art Rice-Jones, Cliff Workman, Norm Yellowlees, Jack Hughes (coach), Earl Adam (manager).

1932

Sudbury Cub Wolves: Max Bennett, Hector "Toe" Blake, Borden Caswell, Maurice Dabous, Peter Fenton, Ivan Fraser, Gordon Grant, Anthony Healey, Adelard LaFrance Jr., Larry LaFrance, Bob McInnes, Jack McInnes, Redmond "Red" Porter (captain), A. J. Powell, Don Price, Dalton "Nakina" Smith, Max Silverman (manager), Sam Rothschild (coach).

1933

Newmarket Redmen: Tod "Silver" Doran, Ran Forder, Frank "Chief" Huggins, Regis "Pep" Kelly, "Red" McArthur, Norm Mann, Aubrey Marshall, M. Ogilvie, Jimmy Parr, Howard Peterson, "Gar" Preston, Melville "Sparky" Vail (captain), Don Willson, Stan Smith (manager), Bill Hancock (coach).

1934

Toronto St. Michael's College: John Acheson, Bobby Bauer, Frank Bauer, J. J. Burke, Clarence "Mickey" Drouillard, John Hamilton, Reg Hamilton, Art Jackson, Regis "Pep" Kelly, Leo McLean, Nick Metz, Harvey Teno, Don Willson, J. J. Timmons (manager), Dr. W. J. LaFlamme (coach).

1935
Winnipeg Monarchs: Ken Barker, Pete Belanger (captain), Jack Boyd, Wilf Field, Paul Gauthier, Burr Keenan, Joe Krol, Romeo Martel, John "Ike" Prokaski, Paul Rheault, Fred White, Harry Neil (coach).

1936
West Toronto Nationals: Bert Conacher, Roy Conacher, Johnny "Bucky" Crawford, D. Fritz, Carl Gamble, Fred "Ginger" Hall, Robert "Red" Heron, Bill Jennings, Bob Laurent, F. Murray, Johnny "Peanuts" O'Flaherty, Ted Robertson, Gord Shill, Bill Thompson, Harold Ballard (manager), Clarence "Hap" Day (coach).

1937
Winnipeg Monarchs: Jack Atcheson, Ami Clement, Ted Dent, Zenon Ferley, Jack Fox, Dick Kowcinak, Pete Langelle, Johnny McCreedy, Lucien Martel, A. Peletier, Alf Pike (captain), Paul Rheault, Denny Robinson, Remi Vandaele, W. Webber (manager), Harry Neil (coach).

1938
St. Boniface Seals: Herb Burron, Pete "Patch" Couture, George Gordon, Herm Gruhn, Bert Janke (captain), Billy McGregor, Jack Messett, Frank Nickol, Billy Reay, Wally Stanowski, Jack Simpson, Doug Webb, Gil Paulley (manager), Mike Kryschuk (coach).

1939
Oshawa Generals: Les Colvin, Don Daniels, Joe Delmonte, Jim Drummond, Gerry Kinsella, Nick Knott, Jud McAtee, Norm McAtee, Dinny McManus, Gar Peters, George Ritchie, Roy Sawyer, Orville Smith, Billy Taylor (captain), Matt Leyden (manager), Tracy Shaw (coach).

1940
Oshawa Generals: Don Daniels, Frank Eddolls, Bud Hellyer, Jack Hewson, Nick Knott, Jud McAtee (captain), Norm McAtee, Dinny McManus, Gar Peters, George Ritchie, Roy Sawyer, Orville Smith, Doug Turner, Ron Wilson, Wally Wilson, Matt Leyden (manager), Tracy Shaw (coach).

1941
Winnipeg Rangers: Doug Baldwin, Bob Ballance, Bernie Bathgate, Tom Bredin, Sam Fabro, Earl Fast, Glen Harmon, Alan Hay, Bill Heindl, Les Hickey, Manning "Babe" Hobday, Hubert "Hub" Macey, Lou Medynski, Hugh Millar (captain), Bill Mortimer, Mike Peters, Bill Robinson, Hal Thompson, Lawrence "Baldy" Northcott (coach).

1942
Portage La Prairie Terriers: Gordon Bell, Jack Bell, Lin Bend, Don Campbell, Billy Gooden, Bill Heindl, Bobby Love, Jack McDonald (captain), Jack O'Reilly,

Bud Ritchie, Lloyd Smith, Wally Stefaniw, Jack Bend (manager), Addie Bell (coach).

1943

Winnipeg Rangers: Bill Boorman (captain), Tom Fowler, Cal Gardner, Jack Irvine, Doug Jackson, Ben Juzda, Eddie Kullman (Coleman), Ritchie McDonald, Frank Mathers, George Mundrick, Joe Peterson, Church Russell, Gus Schwartz, Jack Taggart, Bill Tindall, Bill Vickers, Stan Warecki, Bob Kinnear (coach).

1944

Oshawa Generals: Bill Barker, Don Batten, David Bauer, Harvey Bennett, Johnny Chenier, Floyd Curry, Bob Dawes, Bill Ezinicki, Ted Lindsay, Bobby Love, Murdie McMillan, Johnny Marois, Gus Mortson, Bob Porter, Bert Shewchuck, Ken Smith, Jack Taggart, Matt Leyden (manager), Charlie Conacher (coach).

1945

Toronto St. Michael's College: John Arundel, John Blute, Pat Boehmer, Les Costello, Leo Gravelle, Bob Gray, Johnny McCormack, Ted McLean, Jim Morrison, Gus Mortson, Bobby Paul, Joe Sadler, Phil Samis, Tod Sloan, Jimmy Thomson, Frank Turik, J. Frezell (manager), Joe Primeau (coach).

1946

Winnipeg Monarchs: Clint Allbright, Hy Beatty, Al Buchanan (captain), Ted Chitty, Dunc Daniels, Gord Fashoway, Jack Gibson, "Tank" Kummerfield, Don "Red" McRae, Eddie Marchant, Laurie May, Cam Millar, George Robertson, Tom Rockey, Gord Scott, Harry Taylor, Bill Tindall, P. Lyon (manager), Walter Monson (coach).

1947

Toronto St. Michael's College: Les Costello, Ray Hannigan, Ed Harrison, Howard Harvey, Leonard "Red" Kelly, Fleming Mackell, John McLellan, Clare Malone, Rudy Migay, Bobby Paul, Harry Psutka, Ed Sandford, John Williams, Warren Winslow, Benny Woit, Joe Primeau (coach).

1948

Port Arthur West End Bruins: Fred Baccari, Barton Bradley, Lorne Chabot, Alfie Childs, Dave Creighton, Pete Durham, Bobby Fero, Bert Fonso, Allan Forslund, Art Harris, Bill Johnson, Danny Lewicki, Rudy Migay, Norval Olsen, Benny Woit, Robbie Wrightsell, Jerry Zager, E. C. Whalen (manager), Ed Lauzon (coach).

1949

Montreal Royals: Eric Appleby, Gordon Armstrong, Matthew Benoit, Robert Bleau, Frederick Burchell, Mike Darling, Victor Fildes, Robert Frampton, John

Hirschfeld, Gordon Knutson, Neale Langill, Peter Larocque, Tommy Manastersky, Dickie Moore, William Rattray, Donald Rose, Roland Rousseau, Gus Ogilvie (general manager), J. T. Millar (coach).

1950

Montreal Junior Canadiens: Doug Binning, Kevin Conway, Bob Dawson, Herb English, Bill Goold, Reg Grigg, Charlie Hodge, Gordon Hollingworth, Dave McCready, Brian McKay, Don Marshall, Dickie Moore, Roger Morissette, Ernie Roche, Kevin Rochford, Art Rose, Bill Sinnett, Frank LeGrove (manager), Sam Pollock/Bill Reay (coach).

1951

Barrie Flyers: Lionel Barber, Marvin Brewer, Real Chevrefils, Don Emms, Paul Emms, Bill Hagan, Lorne Howes, Leo Labine, Jack McKnight, Doug Mohns, Jim Morrison, Daniel O'Connor, Lloyd Pearsall, George Stanutz, Jerry Toppazzini, Doug Towers, Jack White, Ralph Willis, Chuck Woods, Howard Norris (manager), Leighton "Hap" Emms (coach).

1952

Guelph Biltmore Mad Hatters: Doug Ashley, Andy Bathgate, Frank Bettiol, Louis "Louie the Leaper" Fontinato, Ken Graham, Aldo Guidolin, Terry Hagan, Chuck Henderson, Harry Howell, Ken Laufman, Doug Lessor, Bill McCreary, Ron Pirie, Dean Prentice, Ron Murphy, Ray Ross, Ron Stewart, Ken Uniac, Roy Mason (manager), Alf Pike (coach).

1953

Barrie Flyers: Orin Carver, Don Cherry, George Cuculick, Marv Edwards, Bill Harrington, Jack Higgins, Tim Hook, Don McKenny, John Martin, Doug Mohns, Fred Pletsch, Tony Poeta, Jim Robertson, Ken Robertson, Allen "Skip" Teal, Orval Tessier, Larry Thibault, Bob White, Ralph Willis, Howard Norris (manager), Leighton "Hap" Emms (coach).

1954

St. Catharines TeePees: Jack Armstrong, Hugh Barlow, Nelson Bulloch, Hank Ciesla, Barry Cullen, Brian Cullen, Ian Cushanen, Marv Edwards, Jack Higgins, Cecil Hoekstra, Pete Koval, Don McLean, Rob Maxwell, Wimpy Roberts, Reg Truax, Elmer Vasko, Chester Warchol, Rudy Pilous (coach).

1955

Toronto Marlboros: John Albani, Gary Aldcorn, Bob Baun, Ron Casey, Gary Collins, Glenn Cressman, Bob Dodds, Ken Girard, Billy Harris, Gerry James, Ron Kendall, Bill Kennedy, Al MacNeil, Mike Nykoluk, Gord Onotsky, Bob Pulford, Jake Smola, Ross Sneddon, Stafford Smythe (manager), Walter "Turk" Broda (coach).

1956
Toronto Marlboros: Bob Baun, Walt Boyer, Carl Brewer, Len Broderick, Stan Buda, Charlie Burns, Ron Casey, Gary Collins, Jim Crockett, Ron Farnfield, Ken Girard, Gord Haughton, Bill Kennedy, Al MacNeil, Jim Murchie, Harry Neale, Bob Nevin, Bob Pulford, Stafford Smythe (manager), Walter "Turk" Broda (coach).

1957
Flin Flon Bombers: Barry Beatty, Harvey Fleming, Carl Forster, Jean Gauthier, Pat Ginnell, Ted Hampson, Ron Hutchinson, Mike Kardash, George Konik, Orland Kurtenbach, Rod Lee, Cliff Lennartz, Mel Pearson, Duane Rupp, Ken Willey, George Wood, Bobby Kirk (coach).

1958
Ottawa-Hull Junior Canadiens: Jon Annable, Ralph Backstrom, Jacques Begin, Bob Boucher, Bill Carter, Claude Cyr, Dick Dawson, Claude Fournel, Bruce Gamble, Terry Gray, John Longarini, Nick Murray, Bob Olajos, Claude Richard, Bob Rousseau, Claude Ruel, André Tardif, Gilles Tremblay, Jean Claude Tremblay, Harold White, Sam Pollock (manager), Scotty Bowman (coach).

1959
Winnipeg Braves: Pat Angers, Don Atamanchuk, Al Baty, Gary Bergman, Ed Bradawski, René Brunel, Ted Green, Howie Hughes, Allan Ingimundson, Ken King, Ted Knight, Gerry Kruk, Laurie Langrell, Wayne Larkin (captain), Al LeBlanc, Bobby Leiter, Doug Monro, Zenon Moroz, Lew Mueller, John Rodgers, P. Sexsmith, John Sutherland, Ernie Wakely, Bob Wales, Wayne Winstone, Bill Addison (manager), Bill Allum (coach).

1960
St. Catharines TeePees: Pete Berge, John Brenneman, Larry Burns, Pete Creco, Roger Crozier, Ray Cullen, Don Grosso, Vic Hadfield, Murray Hall, Duke Harris, Bill Ives, Carlo Longarini, Terry McGuire, Chico Maki, Rich Predovich, Pete Riddle, Doug Robinson, Bill Speer, Rudy Pilous (manager), Max Kaminsky (coach).

1961
St. Michael's Majors: Arnold Brown, André Champagne, Gerry Cheevers, Terry Clancy, Jack Cole, Paul Conlin, Bruce Draper, Dave Draper, Dave Dryden, Roger Galipeau, Paul Jackson, Larry Keenan, Duncan MacDonald, Barry McKenzie, Bill MacMillan, Peter Noakes, Terry O'Malley, Sonny Osborne, Brian Walsh, Father David Bauer (manager, coach).

1962
Hamilton Red Wings: John "Bud" Blom, Joe Bujdoso, Bryan Campbell, Bob Dean, John Gofton, Bob Hamilton, Ron Harris, Larry Harrop, Earl Heiskala, Paul Henderson, Roger Lafreniere, Lowell MacDonald, Hubert "Pit" Martin, Jim

Peters, Wayne Rivers, Bob Wall, Jack Wildfong, Larry Ziliotto, Eddie Bush (coach).

1963

Edmonton Oil Kings: Ron Anderson, Butch Barber, Tom Bend, Roger Bourbonnais, Jim Brown, Rich Bulloch, Jim Chase, Vince Downey, Jim Eagle, Bob Falkenberg, Harold Fleming, Doug Fox, Russ Kirk, S. Knox, Bert Marshall, Max Mestinsek, Butch Paul, Greg Pilling, Pat Quinn, Dave Rochefort, Glen Sather, Reg Tashuk, Leo LeClerc (manager), Buster Brayshaw (coach).

1964

Toronto Marlboros: Wayne Carleton, André Champagne, Jack Chipchase, Gary Dineen, Ray Dupont, Ron Ellis, Nick Harbaruk, Bill Henderson, Paul Laurent, Jim McKenny, Grant Moore, Rod Seiling, Brit Selby, Gary Smith, Peter Stemkowski, Mike Walton, Barry Watson, Ray Winterstein, Buck Houle (manager), Jim Gregory (coach).

1965

Niagara Falls Flyers: Guy Allen, John Arbour, Steve Atkinson, Brian Bradley, Bud Debrody, Bill Goldsworthy, André Lajeunesse, Rick Ley, Jim Lorentz, Don Marcotte, Gilles Marotte, Rosaire Paiement, Bernard Parent, Jean Pronovost, Bobby Ring, Darek Sanderson, Mike Sherman, Ted Snell, Barry Wilkins, Dave Woodley, Leighton "Hap" Emms (manager), Bill Long (coach).

1966

Edmonton Oil Kings: Ron Anderson, Garnet Bailey, Doug Barrie, Brian Bennett, Don Caley, Craig Cameron, Bob Falkenberg, Brian Hague, Al Hamilton, Jim Harrison, Galen Head, Ted Hodgson, Kerry Ketter, Jim Knox, Ross Lonsberry, Don McLeod, Jim Mitchell, Harold Myers, Eugene Peacosh, Ross Perkins, Murray Pierce, Dave Rochefort, Ted Rogers, Jim Schraefel, Red Simpson, Ron Walters, Bill Hunter (manager), Ray Kinasewich (coach).

1967

Toronto Marlboros: Doug Acomb, Fred Barrett, Richie Bayes, Jim Blain, Mike Byers, Terry Caffery, Cam Crosby, Gord Davies, Gary Edwards, Chris Evans, Brian Glennie, Frank Hamill, Ken Kelly, Steve King, Tom Martin, Gerry Meehan, Cam Newton, Al Osborne, Brad Park, Mike Pelyk, Bob Whidden, John Wright, Jim Gregory (general manager), Gus Bodnar (coach).

1968

Niagara Falls Flyers: Steve Atkinson, Doug Brindley, Russ Frieson, Karl Haggarty, Doug Keeler, Mike Keeler, Rick Ley, Dan Makey, Phil Myre, Jim Notman, Phil Roberto, Ron Schwindt, Brad Selwood, Garry Swain, Don Tannahill, Dave Tataryn, Rick Thompson, Ross Webley, Tom Webster, Leighton "Hap" Emms (manager), Paul Emms (coach).

1969

Montreal Junior Canadiens: Jean-Pierre Bordeleau, Guy Charron, Gary Connelly, André Dupont, Normand Gratton, Jocelyn Guèvremont, Robert Guindon, Réjean Houle, Serge Lajeunesse, Robert Lalonde, Richard Lemieux, Richard Martin, Claude Moreau, Gilbert Perreault, Arthur Quoquochi, Jim Rutherford, Marc Tardif, Ted Tucker, Wayne Wood, Phil Wimmer (manager), Roger Bédard (coach).

1970

Montreal Junior Canadiens: Paulin Bordeleau, Pierre Brind'amour, Michel Dion, John Garrett, Allan Globensky, Norm Gratton, Jocelyn Guèvremont, Bobby Guindon, Serge Lajeunesse, Bobby Lalonde, Richard Lemieux, Richard Martin, Hartland Monahan, Claude Moreau, Gilbert Perreault, Ian Turnbull, Wayne Wood, Paul Wimmer (manager), Roger Bédard (coach).

1971

Quebec Remparts: Michel Brière, Charles Constantin, Pierre Deguay, Michel Deguise, Paul Dion, Raynald Fortier, Serge Gaudreault, Réjean Giroux, Richard Grenier, Yves Lacroix, Guy Lafleur, Jean Lamarre, René Lambert, Bill Landers, Jean Landry, Jacques Locas, Richard Perron, Jacques Richard, Pierre Roy, André Savard, Maurice Filion (general manager, coach).

1972

Cornwall Royals: Robbie Bingley, Yvon Blais, Brian Bowles, Richard Brodeur, Stuart Davison, Robert Geoffrion, Dave Johnson, Dan Lupenette, Tony McCarthy, Brian McCullough, Blair MacDonald, Bob Murray, John Nazar, Michel Renaud, Al Sims, Ron Smith, Gerry Teeple, Kevin Tracey, Pierre Viau, John Wensink, Tom Wynne, Jim Larin (general manager), Orval Tessier (coach).

1973

Toronto Marlboros: Paulin Bordeleau, Bruce Boudreau, Jim Clarke, Bob Dailey, Dick Decloe, Kevin Devine, Wayne Dillon, Tom Edur, Dan Glugosh, Glenn Goldup, Geoff Green, Mark Howe, Marty Howe, John Hughes, Peter Marrin, Keven Neville, Dennis Owchar, Mike Palmateer, Brad Winton, Jeff Woodyatt, Frank Bonello (general manager), George Armstrong (coach).

1974

Regina Patricias: Bill Bell, Glen Burdon, Drew Callander, Dave Faulkner, Clark Gillies, Jon Hammond, Mike Harazny, Greg Joly, Rob Laird, Bob Leslie, Kim McDougal, Jim Minor, Dennis Sobchuk, Ed Staniowski, Dave Thomas, Rob Tudor, Rich Uhrich, Mike Wanchuk, Mike Wirchowski, Del Wilson (general manager), Bob Turner (coach).

1975

Toronto Marlboros: John Anderson, Steve Bosco, Bruce Boudreau, Al

Cameron, Gary Carr, Craig Crawford, Brian Crichton, Steve Harrison, Trevor Johansen, Bernie Johnston, Lynn Jorgenson, Mike Kaszycki, Jim Kirkpatrick, Mike Kitchen, Mike McEwen, Mark Murphy, Mark Napier, Ed Saffrey, John Smrke, Bill Wells, Ron Wilson, Frank Bonello (general manager), George Armstrong (coach).

1976

Hamilton Fincups: Joe Contini, Mike Fedorko, Steve Hazlett, Cal Herd, Denis Houle, Willie Huber, Al Jensen, Mike Keating, Archie King, Joe Kowal, Mark Locken, Ted Long, Dale McCourt, Bob Mierkalns, Mark Perras, Bill Reilly, Ron Roscoe, Alan Secord, Ric Seiling, Danny Shearer, Ed Smith, Rob Street, Sean Sullivan, Dave Draper (general manager), Bert Templeton (coach).

1977

New Westminster Bruins: Bruce Andres, Barry Beck, Jerry Bell, Randy Betty, Ray Creasy, Larry Dean, Doug Derkson, Don Hobbins, John Paul Kelly, Mark Lofthouse, Brad Maxwell, Dave Orleski, Blaine Peterson, Randy Rudnyk, Stan Smyl, Carl Van Herrewyn, Carey Walker, Brian Young, Miles Zaharko, Bill Shinske (general manager), Ernie McLean (coach).

1978

New Westminster Bruins: Ken Berry, Doug Derkson, Jim Dobson, Boris Fistric, Bill Hobbins, Bruce Howes, Randy Irving, John Paul Kelly, Terry Kirkham, Larry Lozinsky, Scott McLeod, Richard Martens, Neil Meadmore, Larry Melnyk, John Ogrodnick, Kent Reardon, Rick Slawson, Stan Smyl, Carl Van Herrewyn, Brian Young, Bill Shinske (general manager), Ernie McLean (coach).

1979

Peterborough Petes: Bob Attwell, Dave Beckon, Terry Bovair, Carmine Cirella, Keith Crowder, Ken Ellacott, Dave Fenyves, Larry Floyd, Bill Gardner, Chris Halyk, Rick LaFerriere, Anssi Melametsa, Larry Murphy, Mark Reeds, Brad Ryder, Stuart Smith, Greg Theberge, Tim Trimper, Jim Wiemer, Gary Green (general manager, coach).

1980

Cornwall Royals: Scott Arniel, Fred Arthur, Fred Boimistruck, Dan Brown, Newell Brown, Mike Corrigan, Marc Crawford, Gilles Crépeau, Dan Daoust, Dave Ezard, Tom Graovac, Craig Halliday, Pat Haramis, Dale Hawerchuck, Bobby Hull Jr., Pat O'Kane, Robert Savard, Ron Scott, Ron Willard, Dan Zavarise, Doug Carpenter (coach).

1981

Cornwall Royals: Scott Arniel, Fred Arthur, Fred Boimistruck, Eric Calder, Marc Crawford, Gilles Crépeau, Jeff Eatough, Dan Frawley, Doug Gilmour, Tom Graovac, Craig Haliday, Dale Hawerchuk, John Kirk, Marc Lalonde, Joe

Mantione, Corrado Micalef, Sandy Mitchell, Stephen Molaski, Gérard Peltier, Roy Russell, Robert Savard, Bob Kilger (coach).

1982

Kitchener Rangers: Brian Bellows, Darryl Boudreau, Kevin Casey, Louis Crawford, Mike Eagles, Mike Hough, Jeff Larmer, Joel Levesque, Al MacInnis, Grant Martin, Mario Michieli, Mike Moher, Dave Nicholls, Jim Ralph, Robert Savard, Brad Schnurr, Dave Shaw, Scott Stevens, John Tucker, Wendell Young, Joe Crozier (general manager, coach).

1983

Portland Winter Hawks: Curt Brandolini, Bruno Campese, Brian Curran, Brad Duggan, Ray Ferraro, Randy Heath, Greg Holomay, Kelly Hubbard, Terry Jones, John Kordic, Rich Kromm, Derek Laxdal, Tim Lorenz, Cam Neely, Jim Playfair, Ray Podloski, Grant Sasser, Alfie Turcotte, Mike Vernon, Bryan Walker, Gord Walker, Ken Yaremchuk, Brian Shaw (general manager), Ken Hodge (coach).

1984

Ottawa 67's: Richard Adolfi, Bill Bennett, Bruce Cassidy, Todd Clarke, Greg Coram, Adam Creighton, Bob Giffin, Scott Hammond, John Hanna, Tim Helmer, Steve Hrynewich, Mike James, Don McLaren, Roy Myllari, Darren Pang, Mark Paterson, Phil Patterson, Gary Roberts, Darcy Roy, Brad Shaw, Steve Simoni, Brian Kilrea (general manager, coach).

1985

Prince Albert Raiders: Ken Baumgartner, Brad Bennett, Dean Braham, Rod Dallman, Neil Davey, Pat Elynuik, Collin Feser, Dave Goertz, Steve Gotaas, Tony Grenier, Roydon Gunn, Doug Hobson, Dan Hodgson, Curtis Hunt, Kim Issel, Wark Komonosky, Dale McFee, Dave Manson, Ken Morrison, Dave Pasin, Don Schmidt, Emanuel Viveiros, Kurt Woolf, Terry Simpson (general manager, coach).

1986

Guelph Platers: Rob Arabski, Paul Brydges, Steve Chiasson, Luciano Fagioli, Rob Graham, Steve Guenette, Brian Hayton, Andy Helmuth, Kerry Huffman, Paul Kelly, Lonnie Loach, Denis Larocque, Bill Loshaw, John McIntyre, Allan MacIsaac, Jamie McKinley, Keith Miller, Mike Murray, Tom Nickolau, Gary Roberts, Luc Sabourin, Marc Tournier, Robert Holody (general manager), Jacques Martin (coach).

1987

Medicine Hat Tigers: Ron Bonora, Neil Brady, Dean Chynoweth, Rob DiMaio, Rocky Dundas, Mark Fitzpatrick, Kelly Hitchins, Jamie Huscroft, Wayne Hynes, Kevin Knopp, Mark Kuntz, Dale Kushner, Kirby Lindal, Trevor Linden, Wayne McBean, Scott McCrady, Mike MacWilliam, Mark Pederson, Guy Phillips, Keith Van Rooyen, Jeff Wenaas, Rod Williams, Russ Farwell (general manager), Bryan Maxwell (coach).

1988
Medicine Hat Tigers: Mike Barlage, Vince Boe, Neil Brady, Dean Chynoweth, Rob DiMaio, Mark Fitzpatrick, Murray Garbutt, Wayne Hynes, Dan Kordic, Kirby Lindal, Trevor Linden, Wayne McBean, Scott McCrady, Ryan McGill, Jason Miller, Mark Pederson, Jason Prosofsky, Darren Taylor, Neil Wilkinson, Mark Woolf, Cal Zankowski, Russ Farwell (general manager), Barry Melrose (coach).

1989
Swift Current Broncos: Scott Albert, Kevin Barrett, Don Blishen, Kimbi Daniels, Peter Kasowski, Sheldon Kennedy, Jeff Knight, Kevin Knopp, Blake Knox, Darren Kruger, Trevor Kruger, Dan Lambert, Chris Larkin, Trent McCleary, Mark McFarlane, Evan Marble, Kyle Reeves, Matt Ripley, Brian Sakic, Geoff Sanderson, Trevor Sim, Wade Smith, Peter Soberlak, Tim Tisdale, Bob Wilkie, Graham James (general manager, coach).

1990
Oshawa Generals: Bill Armstrong, Cory Banika, Fred Brathwaite, Joe Busillo, Kevin Butt, Clair Cornish, David Craievich, Mike Craig, Dale Craigwell, Jean-Paul Davis, Mark Deazeley, Craig Donaldson, Iain Fraser, Brent Grieve, Brian Grieve, Matt Hoffman, Scott Hollis, Eric Lindros, Scott Luik, Trevor McIvor, Paul O'Hagan, Wade Simpson, Jarrod Skalde, Frank Jay (director of hockey operations), Rick Cornacchia (coach).

1991
Spokane Chiefs: Scott Bailey, Mike Chrun, Bart Cote, Cam Danyluk, Tommie Eriksen, Frank Evans, Danny Faasen, Pat Falloon, Murray Garbutt, Geoff Grandberg, Mike Jickling, Steve Junker, Trevor Kidd, Jon Klemm, Chris Lafrenière, Shane Maitland, Mark Szoke, Calvin Thudium, Brent Thurston, Kerry Toporowski, Trevor Tovell, Bram Vanderkracht, Ray Whitney, Mark Woolf, Tim Speltz (general manager), Bryan Maxwell (coach).

1992
Kamloops Blazers: Craig Bonner, Jarret Bousquet, Zac Boyer, Jarret Deuling, Scott Ferguson, Shayne Green, Corey Hirsch, Ryan Huska, Lance Johnson, Todd Johnson, Rob LeLacheur, Scott Loucks, Craig Lyons, Dale Masson, Mike Mathers, Chris Murray, Tyson Nash, Scott Niedermayer, Eddie Patterson, Rod Stevens, Darryl Sydor, Darcy Tucker, Jeff Watchorn, David Wilkie, Steve Yule, Bob Brown (general manager), Tom Renney (coach).

1993
Sault Ste. Marie Greyhounds: Brad Baber, Drew Bannister, Dan Cloutier, Sean Gagnon, Aaron Gavey, Wade Gibson, Kiley Hill, Kevin Hodson, Ralph Intranuovo, Rick Kowalsky, Tom MacDonald, Neal Martin, Mark Matier, David Matsos, Jodi Murphy, Perry Pappas, Oliver Pastinsky, Chad Penney, Jarret Reid, Gary Roach, Steve Sullivan, Dan Tanevski, Brian Thompson, Jeff Toms, Joe Van Volsen, Sherwood Bassin (director of hockey operations), Ted Nolan (coach).

1994

Kamloops Blazers: Nolan Baumgartner, Rod Branch, Jarrett Deuling, Hnat Domenichelli, Louis Dumont, Scott Ferguson, Dion Hagan, Greg Hart, Jason Holland, Ryan Huska, Jarome Iginla, Mike Josephson, Aaron Keller, Mike Krooshoop, Brad Lukowich, Sean Matile, Bob Maudie, Chris Murray, Tyson Nash, Steve Passmore, Rod Stevens, Jason Strudwick, Darcy Tucker, Bob Westerby, Bob Brown (general manager), Don Hay (coach).

1995

Kamloops Blazers: Jeff Ainsworth, Jeff Antonovich, Nolan Baumgartner, Rod Branch, Ashley Buckberger, Shane Doan, Hnat Domenichelli, Greg Hart, Jason Holland, Ryan Huska, Jarome Iginla, Aaron Keller, Donnie Kinney, Brad Lukowich, Keith McCambridge, Shawn McNeil, Bob Maudie, Tyson Nash, Jeff Oldenborger, Randy Petruk, Jason Strudwich, Darcy Tucker, Ivan Vologjaninov, Bob Westerby, Bob Brown (general manager), Don Hay (coach).

1996

Granby Prédateurs: Philippe Audet, Kevin Borque, Francis Bouillon, David Brosseau, Jean-François Brunelle, Martin Chouinard, Xavier Delisle, Frédéric Deschênes, Jason Doig, Jimmy Drolet, Daniel Goneau, Benoit Gratton, Philippe Grondin, Frederic Henry, Georges Laraque, Christian Lefebvre, Michel Massie, Samy Nasreddine, Todd Row, Bard Sorlie, Jean-François Tremblay, Georges Morrisette (general manager), Michel Therrien (coach).

1997

Hull Olympiques: Alexandre Audet, Francis Belanger, Martin Biron, Kevin Brochu, Christian Bronsard, Alexandre Couture, Jonathan Delisle, Mathieu Descoteaux, Christian Dubé, Martin Ethier, Eric Hunter, Marty Johnston, Mario Larocque, Ryan Lauzon, Steven Low, Donald MacLean, Martin Menard, Eric Naud, Francis Nault, Pavel Rosa, Jaret Sledz, Colin White, Peter Worrell, Claude Julien (general manager, coach).

Winning Teams by League

(since 1971, when the Memorial Cup was first awarded to the Major Junior national champion)

Western Hockey League teams	12
Ontario Hockey League teams	9
Quebec Major Junior Hockey League teams	6*

*The Cornwall Royals captured Memorial Cups in 1972, 1980, and 1981 when they played in the QMJHL before joining the OHL in the 1981–82 season.

Winning Teams by Province

Ontario-based teams	43
Manitoba-based teams	12
Saskatchewan-based teams	6
Quebec-based teams	6
Alberta-based teams	5
British Columbia-based teams	5
USA-based teams	2

Winners of Three or More Memorial Cups

Toronto Marlboros	7 (1929, 1955, 1956, 1964, 1967, 1973, 1975)
Toronto St. Michael's	4 (1934, 1945, 1947, 1961)
Oshawa Generals	4 (1939, 1940, 1944, 1990)
Winnipeg Monarchs	3 (1935, 1937, 1946)
Regina Pats	3 (1925, 1930, 1974)
Cornwall Royals	3 (1972, 1980, 1981)
Kamloops Blazers	3 (1992, 1994, 1995)

Winners of More Than Five Memorial Cups, by City

Toronto, 14: Marlboros (7), St. Michael's (4), West Toronto Redmen (in 1936), Toronto Canoe Club (in 1920), and University of Toronto Schools (in 1919). Winnipeg, 10: Monarchs (3), Braves (in 1958), Rangers (in 1941 and 1943), St. Boniface Seals (in 1938), Elmwoods (in 1931), University of Manitoba (in 1923), and Falcons (1921).

Winners of Back-to-Back Memorial Cups

Oshawa Generals	1939 and 1940
Toronto Marlboros	1955 and 1956
Montreal Junior Canadiens	1969 and 1970
New Westminster Bruins	1977 and 1978
Cornwall Royals	1980 and 1981
Medicine Hat Tigers	1987 and 1988
Kamloops Blazers	1994 and 1995

Attendance Records

(since first year of round robin format, 1972)

Highest total attendance, series

Year	Location	Games	Attendance	Average
1989	Saskatoon	9	77,296	8,588
1990	Hamilton	8	70,236	8,820
1977	Vancouver	7	58,995	8,428
1991	Quebec City	8	58,316	7,290
1983	Portland	8	54,090	6,761
1984	Kitchener	8	53,207	6,651

Highest average attendance, one series: 9,961 in 1973 at Montreal (4 games, 39,843 total).

Highest average percentage of capacity, complete tournament: 100% in 1984 at Kitchener (6,651); 1995 at Kamloops (5,500); 1996 at Peterborough (4,261).

Highest attendance, one game: 17,383 on May 13, 1990 at Hamilton (final game); 13,460 on May 14, 1977 at Vancouver (final game).

Highest attendance, round robin game: 12,699 on May 11, 1973 at Montreal; 11,134 on May 10, 1990 at Hamilton; 10,522 on May 11, 1977 at Vancouver.

Highest attendance, semi-final game: 10,188 on May 12, 1990 at Hamilton; 8,378 on May 12, 1989 at Saskatoon.

Highest attendance, final game: 17,383 on May 13, 1990 at Hamilton; 13,460 on May 14, 1977 at Vancouver.

Highest total attendance for a final series before the round robin format (1919 to 1971)

Year	Location	Games	Attendance	Average
1946	Toronto (MLG)	7	102,575	14,654
1943	Toronto (MLG)	6	73,867	12,311
1945	Toronto (MLG)	5	65,437	13,087

Team and Individual Records

(since first year of round robin format, 1972)

Team

Most Championships: 3, Cornwall Royals (1972, '80, '81); Kamloops Blazers (1992, '94, '95).

Most Championships (franchise): 5, New Westminster/Kamloops (1977, '78, '92, '94, '95).

Most Consecutive Championships: 2, New Westminster Bruins (1977, '78); Cornwall Royals (1980, '81); Medicine Hat Tigers (1987, '88); Kamloops Blazers (1994, '95).

Most Tournament Appearances: 7, Peterborough Petes (1972, '78, '79, '80, '89, '93, '96); 6, Kamloops (1984, '86, '90, '92, '94, '95); 4, New Westminster (1975, '76, '77, '78); 4, Kitchener (1981, '82, '84, '90); 4, Laval (1983, '89, '90, '93); 4, Sault Ste. Marie (1985, '91, '92, '93).

Most Appearances (franchise): 10, New Westminster/Kamloops (1975, '76, '77, '78, '84, '86, '90, '92, '94, '95).

Most Consecutive Appearances: 4, New Westminster Bruins (1975, '76, '77, '78); 3, Peterborough (1978, '79, '80); Sault Ste. Marie (1991, '92, '93).

Most Final Game Appearances: 6, Peterborough Petes (1972, '78, '79, '80, '93, '96); 4, New Westminster Bruins (1975, '76, '77, '78); Kitchener Rangers (1981, '82, '84, '90).

Most Tournament Wins: 19, Kamloops Blazers (7 appearances, 29 games); 19, Peterborough Petes (7 appearances, 33 games).

Longest Winning Streak: 12 games, Kamloops Blazers (1992, '94, '95); 5 games, Medicine Hat Tigers (1987–88).

Most Goals, One Series: 29, Prince Albert Raiders, 1985 (5 games).

Most Goals-Against, One Series: 28, Cornwall Royals, 1980 (5 games).

Most Goals Scored by All Teams, One Series: 86, 1983 at Portland (Portland, 28; Oshawa, 28; Verdun, 16; Lethbridge, 14), 8 games.

Most Shutouts (all teams), One Series: 2, 1994 at Laval (Steve Passmore, Kamloops 5–0 vs. Chicoutimi; Eric Fichaud, Chicoutimi 2–0 vs. Laval; 2, 1996 at Peterborough (Frédéric Deschênes, Granby 8–0 vs. Guelph, 4–0 vs. Peterborough).

Most Goals, One Game, One Team: 11, Quebec, May 10, 1974 vs. St. Catharines (Quebec 11, St. Catharines 3); Regina, May 8, 1980 vs. Cornwall (Regina 11, Cornwall 2).

Most Shots on Goal, One Game: 56, Hull, May 10, 1986 vs. Portland (Hull 7, Portland 5).

Fastest Three Goals: 38 seconds, New Westminster, May 11, 1978 vs. Trois-Rivières (New Westminster 6, Trois-Rivières 3). Scorers were Scott McLeod at 6:03, Ken Barry at 6:21 and Scott McLeod at 6:41, second period).

Longest Game: 84 minutes, 16 seconds, May 10, 1990, Oshawa 5 vs. Kitchener 4 (round robin game).

Individual

Most Memorial Cups Won (Player): 3, Ryan Huska, Kamloops (1992, '94, '95); Tyson Nash, Kamloops (1992, '94, '95); Darcy Tucker, Kamloops (1992, '94, '95); Robert Savard, Cornwall (1980, '81) and Kitchener (1982).

Most Memorial Cups Won (Coach): 2, Tracy Shaw, Oshawa (1939, '40); Joe Primeau (1945, '47); Leighton "Hap" Emms (1951, '53); Walter "Turk" Broda, Toronto Marlboros (1955, '56); Roger Bédard, Montreal (1969, '70); George Armstrong, Toronto Marlboros (1973, '75); Ernie McLean, New Westminster (1977, '78); Bryan Maxwell, Medicine Hat (1978) and Spokane (1991); Don Hay, Kamloops (1995, '96).

Most Memorial Cups Won (Manager): 3, Matt Leyden, Oshawa (1939, '40, '44); Bob Brown, Kamloops (1992, '94, '95).

Single Tournament

Most Goals: 8, Dale Hawerchuk, Cornwall, 1981; Luc Robitaille, Hull, 1986; Pat Falloon, Spokane, 1991.

Most Assists: 13, Dan Hodgson, Prince Albert, 1985.

Most Points: 16, Jeff Larmer, Kitchener, 1982; Guy Rouleau, Hull, 1986.

Most Penalty Minutes: 63, Kerry Toporowski, Spokane, 1991.

Most Game-Winning Goals: 3, Rick Kowalsky, Sault Ste. Marie, 1993; Zac Boyer, Kamloops, 1992; Cameron Mann, Peterborough, 1996.

Most Shutouts: 2, Frédéric Deschênes, Granby, May 11, 1996 vs. Guelph, 8–0; May 19, 1996 vs. Peterborough, 4–0.

Best Goals-Against Average: 1.67, Richard Brodeur, Cornwall, 1972; Trevor Kidd, Spokane, 1991.

Most Minutes Played, Goaltender: 354, Mike Torchia, Kitchener, 1990 (5 games).

Single Game

Most Goals: 5, Bruce Boudreau, Toronto, May 9, 1975 vs. Sherbrooke (Toronto 10, Sherbrooke 4).

Most Assists: 5, Dan Hodgson, Prince Albert, May 14, 1985 vs. Sault Ste. Marie (Prince Albert 8, Sault Ste. Marie 6).

Most Points: 6, Joe Contini, Hamilton, May 12, 1976 vs. New Westminster (3 goals, 3 assists; Hamilton 8, New Westminster 4); Guy Rouleau, Hull (twice) May 10, 1986 vs. Portland (3 goals, 3 assists; Hull 7, Portland 5) and May 16, 1986 vs. Kamloops (2 goals, 4 assists; Hull 9, Kamloops 3); Mike Mathers, Kamloops, May 16, 1992 vs. Seattle (3 goals, 3 assists; Kamloops 8, Seattle 3).

Fastest Opening Goal (first period): 11 seconds, Brian Bellows, Kitchener, May 9, 1982 vs. Portland (Kitchener 9, Portland 2).

Fastest Period Goal (other than first period): 6 seconds, Everett Sanipass, Verdun, May 12, 1985 vs. Sault Ste. Marie, third period (Sault Ste. Marie 6, Verdun 3).

Fastest Overtime Goal: 20 seconds, Keith Crowder, Peterborough, May 10, 1978 vs. New Westminster (Peterborough 4, New Westminster 3).

Fastest Two Goals (by one player): 8 seconds, Joe Contini, Hamilton, May 12, 1976 vs. New Westminster, at 8:57 and 9:05, first period (Hamilton 8, New Westminster 4).

Fastest Three Goals (by one player): 1 minute, 12 seconds, Joe Contini, Hamilton, May 12, 1976 vs. New Westminster, at 7:53, 8:57 and 9:05, first period.

Awards

Stafford Smythe Memorial Trophy (Most Valuable Player)

Year	Player, Team
1972	Richard Brodeur, Cornwall
1973	Mark Howe, Toronto
1974	Greg Joly, Regina
1975	Barry Smith, New Westminster
1976	Dale McCourt, Hamilton
1977	Barry Beck, New Westminster
1978	Stan Smyl, New Westminster
1979	Bart Hunter, Brandon
1980	Dave Ezard, Cornwall
1981	Dale Hawerchuk, Cornwall
1982	Sean McKenna, Sherbrooke
1983	Alfie Turcotte, Portland
1984	Adam Creighton, Ottawa
1985	Dan Hodgson, Prince Albert
1986	Steve Chiasson, Guelph
1987	Wayne McBean, Medicine Hat
1988	Rob DiMaio, Medicine Hat
1989	Dan Lambert, Swift Current
1990	Iain Fraser, Oshawa
1991	Pat Falloon, Spokane
1992	Scott Niedermayer, Kamloops
1993	Ralph Intranuovo, Sault Ste. Marie
1994	Darcy Tucker, Kamloops
1995	Shane Doan, Kamloops
1996	Cameron Mann, Peterborough
1997	Christian Dubé, Hull

Hap Emms Memorial Trophy (Outstanding Goaltender)

Year	Player, Team
1975	Gary Carr, Toronto
1976	Maurice Barrette, Quebec
1977	Pat Riggin, Ottawa
1978	Ken Ellacott, Peterborough
1979	Bart Hunter, Brandon
1980	Rick LaFerriere, Peterborough
1981	Corrado Micalef, Cornwall
1982	Michel Morrissette, Sherbrooke
1983	Mike Vernon, Portland
1984	Darren Pang, Ottawa
1985	Ward Komonosky, Prince Albert

1986	Steve Guenette, Guelph
1987	Mark Fitzpatrick, Medicine Hat
1988	Mark Fitzpatrick, Medicine Hat
1989	Mike Greenlay, Saskatoon
1990	Mike Torchia, Kitchener
1991	Félix Potvin, Chicoutimi
1992	Corey Hirsch, Kamloops
1993	Kevin Hodson, Sault Ste. Marie
1994	Eric Fichaud, Chicoutimi
1995	Jason Saal, Detroit
1996	Frédéric Deschênes, Granby
1997	Christian Bronsard, Hull

George Parsons Trophy (Most Sportsmanlike Player)

Year	Player, Team
1974	Guy Chouinard, Quebec
1975	John Smrke, Toronto
1976	Richard Shinske, New Westminster
1977	Bob Smith, Ottawa
1978	Mark Kirton, Peterborough
1979	Chris Halyk, Peterborough
1980	Dale Hawerchuk, Cornwall
1981	Mark Morrison, Victoria
1982	Brian Bellows, Kitchener
1983	David Gans, Oshawa
1984	Brian Wilks, Kitchener
1985	Tony Grenier, Prince Albert
1986	Kerry Huffman, Guelph
1987	Scott McCrory, Oshawa
1988	Martin Gelinas, Hull
1989	Jamie Hicks, Peterborough
1990	Jason Firth, Kitchener
1991	Ray Whitney, Spokane
1992	Colin Miller, Sault Ste. Marie
1993	Jason Dawe, Peterborough
1994	Yannick Dubé, Laval
1995	Jarome Iginla, Kamloops
1996	Mike Williams, Peterborough
1997	Radoslav Suchy, Chicoutimi

Ed Chynoweth Trophy (Leading Scorer)

Year	Player, Team
1996	Philippe Audet, Granby
1997	Christian Dubé, Hull

All-Star Teams

1975
Goal	Gary Carr, Toronto
Defence	Mike Kitchen, Toronto
	Brad Maxwell, New Westminster
Centre	Barry Smith, New Westminster
Left Wing	Claude Larose, Sherbrooke
Right Wing	John Anderson, Toronto

1976
Goal	Maurice Barrette, Quebec
Defence	Jean Gagnon, Quebec
	Barry Beck, New Westminster
Centre	Dale McCourt, Hamilton
Left Wing	Ric Seiling, Hamilton
Right Wing	Harold Phillipoff, New Westminster

1977
Goal	Pat Riggin, Ottawa
Defence	Barry Beck, New Westminster
	Brad Maxwell, New Westminster
Centre	Bob Smith, Ottawa
Left Wing	Jere Gillis, Sherbrooke
Right Wing	Mark Lofthouse, New Westminster

1978
Goal	Ken Ellacott, Peterborough
Defence	Paul MacKinnon, Peterborough
	Brian Young, New Westminster
Centre	Mark Kirton, Peterborough
Left Wing	Normand Lefebvre, Trois-Rivières
Right Wing	Stan Smyl, New Westminster

1979
Goal	Bart Hunter, Brandon
Defence	Norman Rochefort, Trois-Rivières
	Brad McCrimmon, Brandon
Centre	Laurie Boschman, Brandon
Left Wing	Ray Allison, Brandon
Right Wing	Tim Trimper, Peterborough

1980
Goal | Rick LaFerriere, Peterborough
Defence | Darren Veitch, Regina
 | Larry Murphy, Peterborough
Centre | Bill Gardner, Peterborough
Left Wing | Dale Hawerchuk, Cornwall
Right Wing | Mark Reeds, Peterborough

1981
Goal | Corrado Micalef, Cornwall
Defence | Fred Arthur, Cornwall
 | Joe McDonnell, Kitchener
Centre | Dale Hawerchuk, Cornwall
Left Wing | Marc Crawford, Cornwall
Right Wing | Brian Bellows, Kitchener

1982
Goal | Michel Morrissette, Sherbrooke
Defence | Paul Boutilier, Sherbrooke
 | Gary Nylund, Portland
 | Allan MacInnis, Kitchener (tie)
Centre | John Chabot, Sherbrooke
Left Wing | Jeff Larmer, Kitchener
Right Wing | Sean McKenna, Sherbrooke

1983
Goal | Peter Sidorkiewicz, Oshawa
Defence | Joe Cirella, Oshawa
 | Jerome Carrier, Verdun
Centre | Ken Yaremchuk, Portland
Left Wing | Randy Heath, Portland
Right Wing | John MacLean, Oshawa

1984
Goal | Darren Pang, Ottawa
Defence | Dave Shaw, Kitchener
 | Bruce Cassidy, Ottawa
Centre | Adam Creighton, Ottawa
Left Wing | Jim Camazzola, Kamloops
Right Wing | Don McLaren, Ottawa

1985

Goal	Robert Desjardins, Shawinigan
Defence	David Goertz, Prince Albert
	Yves Beaudoin, Shawinigan
Centre	Dan Hodgson, Prince Albert
Left Wing	Tony Grenier, Prince Albert
Right Wing	Patrice Lefebvre, Shawinigan

1986

Goal	Steve Guenette, Guelph
Defence	Steve Chiasson, Guelph
	Ron Shudra, Kamloops
Centre	Guy Rouleau, Hull
Left Wing	Luc Robitaille, Hull
Right Wing	Bob Foglietta, Portland

1987

Goal	Mark Fitzpatrick, Medicine Hat
Defence	Wayne McBean, Medicine Hat
	Gordon Murphy, Oshawa
Centre	Jeff Wenaas, Medicine Hat
Left Wing	Dale Kushner, Medicine Hat
Right Wing	Guy Phillips, Medicine Hat

1988

Goal	Mark Fitzpatrick, Medicine Hat
Defence	Dean Chynoweth, Medicine Hat
	Darryl Shannon, Windsor
Centre	Rob DiMaio, Medicine Hat
Left Wing	Darrin Shannon, Windsor
Right Wing	Trevor Linden, Medicine Hat

1989

Goal	Mike Greenlay, Saskatoon
Defence	Dan Lambert, Swift Current
	Ken Sutton, Saskatoon
Centre	Tim Tisdale, Swift Current
Left Wing	Neil Carnes, Laval
Right Wing	Sheldon Kennedy, Swift Current

1990
Goal   Mike Torchia, Kitchener
Defence   Cory Keenan, Kitchener
                Paul O'Hagan, Oshawa
Centre   Eric Lindros, Oshawa
Left Wing   Iain Fraser, Oshawa
Right Wing   Steven Rice, Kitchener

1991
Goal   Félix Potvin, Chicoutimi
Defence   Patrice Brisebois, Drummondville
                Brad Tiley, Sault Ste. Marie
Centre   Pat Falloon, Spokane
Left Wing   Ray Whitney, Spokane
Right Wing   Brent Thurston, Spokane

1992
Goal   Corey Hirsch, Kamloops
Defence   Scott Niedermayer, Kamloops
                Drew Bannister, Sault Ste. Marie
Centre   Colin Miller, Sault Ste. Marie
Left Wing   Mike Mathers, Kamloops
Right Wing   Turner Stevenson, Seattle

1993
Goal   Kevin Hodson, Sault Ste. Marie
Defence   Michael Gaul, Laval
                Drew Bannister, Sault Ste. Marie
Centre   Ralph Intranuovo, Sault Ste. Marie
Left Wing   Chad Penney, Sault Ste. Marie
Right Wing   Martin Lapointe, Laval

1994
Goal   Eric Fichaud, Chicoutimi
Defence   Aaron Keller, Kamloops
                Nolan Baumgartner, Kamloops
Centre   Darcy Tucker, Kamloops
Left Wing   Alain Côté, Laval
Right Wing   Rod Stevens, Kamloops

1995
Goal   Jason Saal, Detroit
Defence   Nolan Baumgartner, Kamloops
                Bryan McCabe, Brandon
Centre   Darcy Tucker, Kamloops
Left Wing   Sean Haggerty, Detroit
Right Wing   Shane Doan, Kamloops

1996
Goal   Frédéric Deschênes, Granby
Defence   Wade Redden, Brandon
                Jason Doig, Granby
Centre   Xavier Delisle, Granby
Left Wing   Philippe Audet, Granby
Right Wing   Cameron Mann, Peterborough

1997
Goal   Christian Bronsard, Hull
Defence   Chris Phillips, Lethbridge
                Jan Snopek, Oshawa
Centre   Christian Dubé, Hull
Left Wing   Byron Ritchie, Lethbridge
Right Wing   Martin Menard, Hull

INDEX